Advance Praise for *Poetry: A Pocket Anthology,* Fourth Edition

"I find the Introduction clear and concise and I think that it makes the book versatile enough for courses of many levels."

Margaret Noel Sipple
Northern Virginia Community College

"What makes this book truly exciting is that it has a great range of poems spanning the entire tradition of lyrical poetry in English, and yet it is infinitely more portable and a mere fraction of the cost of most poetry anthologies currently available."

Rick Hilles
University of Michigan, Ann Arbor

"Since this anthology contains such a fine survey of older and contemporary works, students always find it easy to select poems that speak to them."

Robin Woods
Ripon College

"Yes, I like the book. My students, in their course evaluations, were UNAMINOUS in their favorable comments. They were tired of huge anthologies that are difficult to use and just represent 'overkill' in the classroom."

Dan Sheridan
University of North Dakota

"This book is surprisingly inclusive for such a short book, and its apparatus is excellent."

Janet McCann
Texas A&M University

"The material on quoting and documentation is fabulous."

Terry Rasmussen
Casper College

R. S. Gwynn has edited several other books, including *Literature: A Pocket Anthology*; *Fiction: A Pocket Anthology*; *Drama: A Pocket Anthology*; *The Longman Anthology of Short Fiction* (with Dana Gioia); and *Contemporary American Poetry: A Pocket Anthology* (with April Lindner). He has also authored five collections of poetry, including *No Word of Farewell: Selected Poems, 1970–2000*. In 2004 he was awarded the Michael Braude Award for verse from the American Academy of Arts and Letters.

Gwynn is University Professor of English at Lamar University in Beaumont, Texas.

Poetry

A Pocket Anthology

FOURTH EDITION

Edited by

R. S. Gwynn
Lamar University

PENGUIN ACADEMICS

New York San Francisco Boston
London Toronto Sydney Tokyo Singapore Madrid
Mexico City Munich Paris Cape Town Hong Kong Montreal

Vice President and Editor in Chief: Joseph Terry
Managing Editor: Erika Berg
Development Editor: Kristen Mellitt
Executive Marketing Manager: Ann Stypuloski
Senior Supplements Editor: Donna Campion
Production Manager: Denise Phillip
Project Coordination, Text Design, and Electronic Page Makeup:
     Pre-Press Company, Inc.
Senior Designer/Manager: Nancy Danahy
Cover Photo: © Yiorgos Depollas
Senior Manufacturing Buyer: Dennis J. Para
Printer and Binder: Courier Westford, Inc.
Cover Printer: Phoenix Color Corporation

For permission to use copyrighted material, grateful acknowledgment is made
to the copyright holders on pp. 465–474, which are hereby made part of this
copyright page.

Library of Congress Cataloging-in-Publication Data

Poetry: a pocket anthology / edited by R.S. Gwynn.—4th ed.
     p. cm—(Penguin academics)
   Includes bibliographical references and index.
   ISBN 0-321-24496-6 (pbk.) —ISBN 0-321-27592-6 (exam)
     1. Poetry—Collections. I. Gwynn, R. S. II. Series.

PN6101.P52 2005
821.008—dc22

                                                             2004048693

Please visit us at http://www.ablongman.com

ISBN 0-321-24496-6

  3 4 5 6 7 8 9 10—DOH—07 06 05

Contents

Preface

When the *Pocket Anthology* series first appeared over a decade ago, our chief aim was to offer a clear alternative to the anthologies of fiction, poetry, and drama that were available at the time. *Poetry: A Pocket Anthology*, now in the Penguin Academics series (previously titled *Poetry: A Longman Pocket Anthology*), is here updated and revised for a fourth edition. *Poetry* is designed to be used in a wide range of courses. This brief anthology can be bundled with one or more of a rich selection of the most popular Penguin titles, which Longman offers at significantly reduced prices. Also, *Poetry* has been published concurrently with two companion volumes, *Fiction* and *Drama*, and in a combined edition, *Literature*. Your Longman representative can supply full details about these books and available Penguin titles.

Poetry addresses the four wishes and concerns most commonly expressed by both instructors and students. First, of course, is the variety of selections it contains. Admittedly, a pocket anthology has to be very selective in its contents, so we are especially proud that the over three hundred poems in this book include both a generous selection of works by poets from past centuries and a large number of contemporary poems that reflect the diversity of authorship, subject matter, and form that is essential to the study of contemporary poetry. Approximately one-third of the poems in *Poetry* are by women and minority writers, including such important contemporary voices as Julia Alvarez, Rita Dove, and Cathy Song. More important, the contents of *Poetry* have profited both from the advice of experienced instructors who have cited poems that possess appeal to students and from the editor's own long experience as a poet, critic, and teacher of literature and creative writing. A strong effort has been made to include a number of poems that reflect contemporary social questions and thus will easily stimulate classroom discussion; also, *Poetry* contains examples (many of them by contemporary poets) of virtually every traditional poetic form used in English-language poetry, ranging from the haiku and the cinquain to the rondeau redoublé and the sestina. These examples help to make *Poetry* invaluable for courses that emphasize analysis of poetic meter and form or composition of poems in formal patterns. Among the features in *Poetry* are two useful appendices, one grouping poems thematically and another grouping them by form, which provide students and instructors a quick way to locate poems of comparable types for discussion, analysis, and emulation.

Our second aim was flexibility. We wanted a book that could be used as both a primary and supplemental text in a wide range of courses, ranging from introduction to poetry courses to advanced classes in poetic analysis to creative writing workshops. When combined with one of its companion volumes, *Fiction* or *Drama,* or with novels, collections of short stories or poems by individual authors, or plays available from Penguin, *Poetry* may also be used in introductory literature courses. *Poetry* contains, in addition to its generous selection of poems, biographical headnotes for authors, an introduction that covers the techniques and terminology of the genre, and a concise section on writing about poetry and research procedures.

Third, we wanted an affordable book. Full-sized introductory literature books now cost upwards of sixty dollars, and many of the comprehensive anthologies of poetry are in the same price range. Longman is committed to keeping the price of the *Pocket Anthology* series reasonable without compromising on design or typeface. We believe that readers will find the attractive layout of *Poetry* preferable to the cramped margins and minuscule fonts found in many literature textbooks. Because of its low cost, *Poetry* may be easily supplemented in individual courses with works of criticism, handbooks of grammar and usage, or with manuals of style. The price of *Poetry* remains low, and we believe that earlier editions' claims that the book represents "a new standard of value" remain accurate.

Finally, we stressed portability. Many instructors expressed concern for students who must carry large literature books, many of which now approach 2000 pages, across large campuses in backpacks already laden with books and materials for other courses. A semester is a short time, and few courses can cover more than a fraction of the material that many full-sized collections contain. Because most instructors focus on a single genre at a time, *Poetry* and its companion volumes, *Fiction* and *Drama,* remain compact yet self-contained editions that, if a snug fit in most pockets, are still easy to handle and carry. We trust that sympathetic instructors and their students will be grateful for a book that does not add a physical burden to the already heavy intellectual one required by college courses.

In closing, we would like to express our gratitude to the instructors who reviewed the current edition and offered invaluable recommendations for improvements. They are Renée M. Brochu, University of Iowa; Logan Esdale, Chapman University; Jill A. Frederick, Minnesota State University–Moorhead; Rick Hilles, University of Michigan–Ann Arbor; Ann Neelon, Murray State University; and Kenneth Pobo, Widener University.

We also appreciate the suggestions of those who reviewed the third edition: Herman L. Asarnow, University of Portland; Francis Burch, St. Joseph's University; Kathleen Dale, University of Wisconsin, Milwaukee; Carol Ann Davis, College of Charleston; James Hirsh, Georgia State University; Edward H. Hoeppner, Oakland University; Jennifer Maier, Seattle Pacific University; Janet McCann, Texas A&M University, College Station; Terry Rasmussen, Casper College; Daniel Sheridan, University of North Dakota; Porter Shreve, University of Michigan, Ann Arbor; Margaret Sipple, Northern Virginia Community College; and Robin Woods, Ripon College.

These instructors reviewed the second edition: Shireen Carroll, Davidson College; Tracy Case, Yakima Valley Community College; Bill Clemente, Peru College; Michel de Benedictis, Miami-Dade Community College; Allen Kupser, Nassau Community College; Dwight McCawley, West Chester University of Pennsylvania; Robert L. McDonald, Virginia Military Institute; Jim Papworth, Ricks College; Frank Rooney, Wentworth Institute of Technology; John Ruszkiewicz, University of Texas; Charles Schuster, University of Wisconsin–Milwaukee; Deborah Sutton, Jefferson College; John Walsh, Saint Peter's College; and David Williams, San Francisco State University.

We are also grateful to the professors who commented on the first edition: Marsha Aldrich, Michigan State University; Herman L. Asarnow, University of Portland; Lea Baechler, Columbia University; Paul Bodmer, Bismark State College; Peggy F. Broder, Cleveland State University; William Covino, University of Chicago; Dwight Eddins, University of Alabama; Wil Gehne, State University of New York, Binghamton; Cheryl Glenn, Oregon State University; Julia Hamilton, Inver Hills Community College; Jennie Harrison, North Harris College; Mary Hojnacki, University of Massachusetts, Lowell; Jim Holte, East Carolina University; Aija Hoover, Odessa College; John Morris, Cameron University; Lee Patterson, Duke University; Marco Portales,

Texas A&M University; Lawrence Rainey, Yale University; Kim Roberts, University of Maryland; Danny Robinson, Bloomsburg University; Pam Schirmeister, New York University; James Schuttemeyer, Thomas More College; Shirely Simpson, Nicholls State University; Michael Steinman, Nassau Community College; Kathleen Thornton, State University of New York, Albany; and Clifford Dale Whitman, Southern Arkansas University.

Also, the editor wishes to acknowledge the invaluable assistance of Beverly Williams in preparing this book.

R. S. GWYNN
Lamar University

Introduction

An Anecdote: Where Poetry Starts

The room is not particularly grand—a large lecture hall in one of the old buildings on the college campus—and the small group of first-year students whose literature class has been dismissed so that they can attend the poetry reading have taken seats near the back of the room. They have been encouraged to come by their instructor, and when she enters she looks around the room and nods in their direction, smiling.

The seats gradually fill. The crowd is a mixed one—several men and women known by sight as senior faculty members; a scattering of other older visitors, many of them apparently from the community; a large contingent of instructors and graduate students from the English Department sitting in the front rows; and small clusters of undergraduates scattered throughout the room.

One of the students scans the crowd, wondering aloud which is the poet. On the walk to the reading, the class's consensus has been that the poet, a cadaverous gray-haired man wrapped in a black cloak, would recite his poems in a resonant monotone, preferably with a strong breeze tossing his hair. Speculation on how the wind effect might be managed inside a lecture hall makes them laugh.

Now the crowd grows quiet as the instructor steps to the podium and adjusts the microphone. She makes a few complimentary remarks about the strong turnout and thanks several benefactors for their financial support of poetry at the university. Then she introduces the guest. Her students know most of this information, for they have studied several of his poems in class that week, but they are still slightly surprised when he rises to polite applause and takes the lectern. The balding middle-aged man wearing a plaid shirt and loosely knotted tie could be taken for a professor in any campus department, and when he adjusts his glasses and clears his throat, blinking at the audience, there is little about him that would fit anyone's romantic stereotype of a poet.

Surprisingly, he does not begin with a poem. Instead, in a relaxed voice he tells an anecdote about his young daughter and an overdue science project. When he moves from the background story into the poem itself, there is little change in his volume level, and his tone remains conversational. The students find that the poem, which they had discussed in class only a couple of days before, takes on new meaning when its origins are explained by the poet himself. They find themselves listening attentively to his words, even laughing out loud several times. The hour goes by quickly, and at its end their applause, like that of the rest of the audience, is long and sincere.

At the next class meeting, the instructor asks for reactions to the reading. While some of the class members are slightly critical, faulting the speaker for his informal manner and his failure to maintain eye contact with the room, most of the remarks are positive. The comments that surface most often have to do with how much more meaningful the poems in the textbook become when the poet explains how he came to write them, how one poem is actually spoken in the voice of his dead father, how another is addressed to a friend who was paralyzed in an automobile accident. While these things could perhaps be inferred from the poems alone, the students are unanimous in their opinion that knowing the details beforehand adds a great deal to the first impression a poem makes. As one student puts it, "It's just that a poem makes a lot more sense when you know who's talking and when and where it's supposed to be taking place."

"It always helps to know where poetry starts," adds one of her classmates.

Speaker, Listener, and Context

The situation just described is hardly unique. Instructors have long encouraged, even begged, their students to attend events like this one, and the college poetry reading has become, for many Americans, the closest encounter they will have with this complex and often perplexing art form. But what students often find at such readings, sometimes to their amazement, is that poetry need not be intimidating or obscure, thus providing a gentle reminder that the roots of poetry, like those of all literature, were originally part of the **oral tradition**—stories and poems that were passed down from generation to generation in ancient societies and recited for audiences that included all members of the tribe, from the wizened elders to the youngest children. For most of its long history, poetry has been a popular art form aimed at *audiences* (remember that the word means "hearers"), and it is only recently, in the last four or five decades, that its most visible signs of life are to be found on college campuses. The reasons for this academic retreat are too complicated to go into here, but it is perhaps worth noting that we are daily exposed to a great deal of poetry in oral form, primarily through the medium of recorded song lyrics, and that the unique qualities of poetry throughout the ages—its ability to tell stories or summarize complicated emotions in a few well-chosen words— are demonstrated whenever we memorize the lines of a popular song and sing them to ourselves.

Of course, poetry written primarily for the page is usually more demanding than song lyrics. Writers of popular songs aim at a wide commercial audience, and this simple fact of economics, added to the fact that the lyrics are not intended primarily for publication but for being recorded with all the resources of studio technology, tends to make many song lyrics relatively uninteresting when they appear in print. A poem, on the other hand, will primarily exist as a printed text, although certainly its effect may be greatly enhanced through a skillful oral performance in which the poet can also explain the background of the poem, its setting and speaker, and the circumstances under which it was written. In general, these details, which are so crucial to understanding a poem yet are often only implied when the poem appears in print, are called the **dramatic situation** of a poem. Reduced to its simplest formulation, dramatic situation can be summed up in a question: *Who is speaking to whom under what circumstances?* If the poet fails to provide us with clues or if we are careless in picking up the information that is provided, then we may begin reading with no sense of reference and, thus, may go far astray. Even such words as "on," "upon," or "to" in titles can be crucial to our understanding of dramatic situation, telling us something about an event or object that provided the stimulus for the poem or about the identity of the "you" addressed in the poem.

An illustration may be helpful. Suppose we look at what is unquestionably the most widely known poem ever written by an American. It is a poem which virtually all Americans can recite in part and, in fact, do so by the millions every week. Yet if we were told that this poem is unusual in that its best-known section is a long, unanswered question addressed by the speaker to a companion about whether or not the object named in the title even exists, then it is likely that most of us would be confused. Before going further, let's look at the poem.

The Star-Spangled Banner

O say, can you see, by the dawn's early light,
    What so proudly we hailed at the twilight's last gleaming?
Whose broad stripes and bright stars thro' the perilous fight,
    O'er the ramparts we watched, were so gallantly streaming!
And the rockets' red glare, the bombs bursting in air,
    Gave proof through the night that our flag was still there:
O say, does that star-spangled banner yet wave
    O'er the land of the free and the home of the brave?

On the shore, dimly seen thro' the mists of the deep,
    Where the foe's haughty host in dread silence reposes,
What is that which the breeze, o'er the towering steep,
    As it fitfully blows, now conceals, now discloses?
Now it catches the gleam of the morning's first beam,
    In full glory reflected now shines on the stream:
'Tis the star-spangled banner! O long may it wave
    O'er the land of the free and the home of the brave!

And where is that band who so vauntingly swore
    That the havoc of war and the battle's confusion
A home and a country should leave us no more?
    Their blood has washed out their foul footsteps' pollution.
No refuge could save the hireling and slave
    From the terror of flight, or the gloom of the grave:
And the star-spangled banner in triumph doth wave
    O'er the land of the free and the home of the brave!

Oh! thus be it ever, when freemen shall stand
    Between their loved homes and the war's desolation!
Blest with victory and peace, may the heav'n-rescued land
    Praise the Pow'r that hath made and preserved us a nation.
Then conquer we must, when our cause it is just,
    And this be our motto: "In God is our trust."
And the star-spangled banner in triumph shall wave
    O'er the land of the free and the home of the brave!

"Now wait a minute!" you may be complaining. "'The Star-Spangled Banner' is a *song*, not a poem. And what's this *question* business? Don't we always sing it while facing the flag? Besides, it's just a patriotic song. Nobody really worries about what it *means*."

In answer to the first comment, "The Star-Spangled Banner" *was* in fact written as a poem and set to music only after its composition. Most of us probably will agree that the words are not particularly well-suited to the melody (which was taken, curiously, from a popular British barroom ballad) and the song remains notoriously difficult to sing, even for professional performers. Garth Brooks, the popular country singer, once remarked before attempting it at a Super Bowl game that it "is one of the hardest songs to sing," implying that the audience at such an event always seems ready to witness a failure. In its original form, "The Star-Spangled Banner" (or "The Defense of Fort McHenry," the title under which it was first published) is an example of **occasional verse**, a poem that is written about or for an important event (or *occasion*), sometimes private but usually of some public significance. While poems of this type are not printed on the front pages of newspapers as often they once were, they are still being written. Enough poems appeared after the assassination of President John F. Kennedy in 1963 to fill a book, *Of Poetry and Power,* and the Challenger disaster of 1986 stimulated a similar outpouring of occasional poems, one of them by Howard Nemerov, who served as poet laureate of the United States (1988–1990). In 1993, Maya Angelou recited "On the Pulse of Morning" at the first inauguration of President Bill Clinton, and Miller Williams read "Of History and Hope" at the second, in 1997. The author of "The Star-Spangled Banner," Francis Scott Key (1779–1843), wrote poetry as an avocation. Yet like many men and women who are not professional writers, Key was so deeply moved by an event that he witnessed that occasional poetry was the only medium through which he could express his feelings.

Now let's go back to our question about dramatic situation, taking it one part at a time: *Who is speaking?* A technical word that is often used to designate the speaker of a poem is **persona** (plural: **personae**), a word that meant "mask" in ancient Greek. Even though the persona of "The Star-Spangled Banner" never uses the word "I" in the poem, the speaker seems to be Key himself, a fact that can be verified by biographical research. Still, it is probably safer to look at poems carefully to see if they give any evidence that the speaker is someone other than the poet. Poems like "Ulysses" by Alfred, Lord Tennyson or "Porphyria's Lover" by Robert Browning have titles that identify personae who are, respectively, a character from ancient epic poetry and an unnamed man who is confessing the murder of his lover, Porphyria. In neither case should the persona be identified with the poet himself. Other poems may be somewhat more problematic. Edgar Allan Poe's "The Raven," like many of Poe's short stories, is spoken by a persona who should not be identified directly with the author, even though he shares many of the same morbid preoccupations of Poe's other characters; even Sylvia Plath, a poet usually associated with an extremely candid form of autobiographical poetry known as **confessional poetry,** identified the persona of her masterpiece "Daddy" as an invented character, "a girl with an Electra complex." Sometimes poems have more than one persona, which is the case with Thomas Hardy's "The Ruined Maid" and Robert Frost's "Home Burial," two poems which consist almost entirely of dialogue. In other poems, the voice may simply be a third-person **narrator** such as we might find in a short story or novel. While it is perhaps true that many poems (including the majority of those included in this text) are in fact spoken by the poet out of his or her most private feelings, it is not a good idea to leap too quickly to the assumption that the persona of a poem is identical to the poet and shares his or her views. Conclusions about the degree to which a poem is autobiographical can be verified only by research and familiarity with a poet's other works.

To return to our question: Who is speaking *to whom?* Another useful term is **auditor,** the person or persons being spoken to in a poem. Some poems identify no auditor; others clearly do specify an auditor or auditors, in most cases identified by name or by the second-person pronoun "you" (or "thee/thou" in older poetry). Again, the title may give clues: Poe's "To Helen" is addressed to the famous beauty of Homeric legend; Robert Herrick's "To the Virgins, to Make Much of Time" is addressed to a group of young women; William Cullen Bryant's "To the Fringed Gentian" is addressed to a common New England wildflower. (The figure of speech **apostrophe** is used when a nonhuman, inanimate, or abstract thing is directly addressed.) Relatively few poems are addressed directly to the reader, so when we read the opening of William Shakespeare's Sonnet 18 ("Shall I compare thee to a summer's day?") we should keep in mind that he is not addressing us but another individual, in this case a young male friend who is referred to in many of the sonnets. Claude McKay's sonnet "If We Must Die" begins in this manner:

If we must die, let it not be like hogs
Hunted and penned in an inglorious spot,

While round us bark the mad and hungry dogs,
Making their mock at our accursed lot.

Later in the poem McKay identifies his auditors as "Kinsmen." Without outside help, about all we can say with certainty at first glance is that the poet seems to be addressing a group of companions who share his desperate situation; when we learn, possibly through research, that McKay was an African-American poet writing about the Harlem race riots of 1919, the symbolic nature of his exhortation becomes clearer.

Now the final part of the question: Who is speaking to whom *under what circumstances?* First, we might ask if there is a relationship, either implied or stated, between persona and auditor. Obviously many love poems take the form of verbal transactions between two parties and, because relationships have their ups and downs, these shifts of mood are reflected in the poetry. One famous example is Michael Drayton's "Idea: Sonnet 61" ("Since there's no help, come let us kiss and part . . .") which begins with the persona threatening to end the relationship with the auditor but ends with an apparent reconciliation. Such "courtship ritual" poems as John Donne's "The Flea" or Andrew Marvell's "To His Coy Mistress" are witty arguments in favor of the couple's engaging in sexual relations, no more, no less. An example from poetry about marital love is Matthew Arnold's "Dover Beach," which ends with the plea "Ah, love, let us be true / To one another" as the only hope for stability the persona can find in a world filled with uncertainty and fear. Even an age disparity between persona and auditor can lend meaning to a poem, which is the case with the Herrick poem mentioned earlier and a dialogue poem like John Crowe Ransom's "Piazza Piece," a classic example of the debate between innocence and experience.

Other questions relating to circumstances of the dramatic situation might concern the poem's physical setting (if any), time (of day, year, historical era), or even such matters as weather. Thomas Hardy's "Neutral Tones" provides a good example of a poem in which the setting—a gray winter day in a barren, outdoor place—symbolically reinforces the persona's memory of the bitter end of a love affair. The shift in setting from the springtime idyll to the "cold hill side" in John Keats's "La Belle Dame sans Merci" cannot be overlooked in discussing the persona's disillusionment. Of course, many poems are explicitly occasional and may even contain an **epigraph** (a brief explanatory statement or quotation) or a **dedication,** which explains the setting. Sometimes footnotes or even outside research may be necessary. John Milton's "On the Late Massacre in Piedmont" will make little sense to readers if they do not know that the poet is reacting to the massacre of a group of Protestants by Roman Catholic soldiers and that Milton, an English Puritan, uses the occasion to attack the papacy as a "triple tyrant" and the "Babylonian woe."

To return, then, one final time to "The Star-Spangled Banner," let's apply our question to the poem. We have already determined that Key is the persona. Who is the "you" mentioned four words into the poem? It seems clear that Key is addressing an auditor standing close to him, either a single individual or a group, as he asks the auditor if he can see the flag that they both observed for the last time the previous day at sundown. Key tells us that it is now just at the moment of dawn, and that even though the flag could be glimpsed periodically in the "rockets' red glare" of the bombardment throughout the night, it cannot be clearly seen now. It is a crucial question, for if the flag is no longer flying "o'er the ramparts," it will mean that the fort has fallen to the enemy. The tension mounts and moves into the second stanza, where at last, "thro' the mists of the deep," the flag can be discerned, "dimly seen" at first, then clearly as it "catches the gleam" of the full sunlight.

The full story of how Key came to write the poem is fairly well known and supports this reading. The events that the poem describes took place on September 13 and 14, 1814, during the War of 1812. Key, a lawyer, came aboard a British warship anchored off Baltimore to argue for the release of a client and friend who had been taken hostage by the British. Key won his friend's release, but the British captain, fearing that Key might reveal information he had learned on board, kept Key overnight, releasing him and his client in the morning. It was during that night that Key witnessed the bombardment and, with it, the failure of the British to take Baltimore. The final half of the poem celebrates the American victory and offers a hopeful prayer that God will continue to smile on America "when our cause . . . is just." One might well argue that Key's phrase "conquer we must" contradicts the spirit of the earlier parts of the poem, but few people have argued that "The Star-Spangled Banner" is a consistently great poem. Still, it is an effective piece of patriotic verse that has a few moments of real drama, expressed in a vivid manner that lets its readers become eyewitnesses to an incident from American history.

Lyric, Narrative, Dramatic

The starting point for all literary criticism in Western civilization is Aristotle's *Poetics*, a work dating from the fourth century BC. While Aristotle's remarks on drama—tragedy, in particular—are more complete than his analysis of other types of literature, he does mention three main types of poetry: lyric, epic, and dithyrambic. In doing so, Aristotle outlines for the first time a theory of literature based on **genres**, or separate categories delineated by distinct style, form, and content. This three-fold division remains useful today, although in two cases different terminology is employed. The first genre, **lyric poetry,** originally comprised brief poems that were meant to be sung or chanted to the accompaniment of a lyre. Today we still use the word "lyrics" in a specialized sense when referring to the words of a song, but lyric poetry has become such a large category that it includes virtually all poems that are primarily *about* a subject and contain little narrative content. The subject of a lyric poem may be the poet's emotions, an abstract idea, a satirical insight, or a description of a person or place. The persona in a lyric is usually closely identified with the poet himself or herself; because we tend to identify the essence of poetry with personal, subjective expression of feelings or ideas, lyric poetry remains the largest genre, with a number of subtypes. Among them are the **epigram**, a short, satirical lyric usually aimed at a specific person; the **elegy**, a lyric on the occasion of a death; and the **ode**, a long lyric in elevated language on a serious theme.

Aristotle's second genre, the **epic,** has been expanded to include all types of **narrative poetry,** that is, poetry whose main function is to tell a story. Like prose fiction, a narrative poem has a plot, characters, a setting, and a point of view, and may be discussed in roughly the same terms as, say, a short story. The epic is a long narrative poem about the exploits of a hero. **Folk epics** like *The Iliad* or *Beowulf* were originally intended for public recitation and existed in oral form for a long period of time before they were transcribed. Little or nothing is known about the authors of folk epics. **Literary epics,** like Dante's *The Inferno* or Henry Wadsworth Longfellow's *The Song of Hiawatha,* differ in that they are the products of known authors who *wrote* their poems for publication. **Ballads** are generally shorter narratives with song-like qualities that often include rhyme and repeated refrains. **Folk ballads,** like folk epics, come from the oral tradition and are authored anonymously; "Bonny Barbara Allan" and "Sir Patrick Spens" are typical examples. **Art ballads** or **literary ballads,** on the other hand, are conscious imitations of the ballad style by later poets and are generally somewhat more sophisticated than folk ballads in their techniques. Examples of this popular genre include Keats's "La Belle Dame sans Merci," a recent specimen like Marilyn Nelson's "The Ballad of Aunt Geneva," and Samuel Taylor Coleridge's famous long art ballad, "The Rime of the Ancient Mariner." There are also other types of narrative poetry that have been popular through the centuries. **Metrical romances, verse tales** of the exploits of knights, were a popular genre of the Middle Ages and Renaissance; Edmund Spenser's *The Faerie Queene* is one of the most ambitious examples of the type. At the opposite extreme are **mock-heroic narratives** like John Dryden's *MacFlecknoe* or Lord Byron's *Don Juan,* which spoof the conventions of epic poetry for comic or satirical effect. **Realistic narratives** of medium length (under 1000 lines) like Robert Frost's "Home Burial" or, more recently, B. H. Fairchild's "Body and Soul" and Leon Stokesbury's "Evening End 1943–1970," have been popular since the early nineteenth century and are sometimes discussed as "poetic novellas" or "short stories in verse."

There is no exact contemporary analogue for Aristotle's third category, **dithyrambic** poetry. This type of poem was composed to be chanted at religious rituals by a chorus and was the forerunner of tragedy. Today the third category is called **dramatic poetry,** because it has perhaps as much in common with the separate genre of drama as with lyric and narrative poetry. In general, the persona in a dramatic poem is an invented character not to be identified with the poet. The poem is presented as a speech or dialogue that might be acted out like a soliloquy or a scene from a play. The **dramatic monologue** is a speech by a single character, usually delivered to a silent auditor; notable examples are Tennyson's "Ulysses" and Browning's "My Last Duchess." A dramatic monologue sometimes implies, in the words of its persona, a distinct setting and an interplay between persona and auditor. At the close of "Ulysses," the aged hero urges his "mariners" to listen closely and to observe the ship in the harbor waiting to take them off on a final voyage. Dramatic poetry can also take the form of **dialogue poetry,** in which two personae speak alternately. Examples are Christina Rossetti's "Up-Hill" and Hardy's "The Ruined Maid." In the past, a popular type of dialogue poem was the **débat,** or mock-debate, in which two characters, usually personified abstractions like the Soul and the Body, argued their respective merits.

While it is easy enough to find examples of "pure" lyrics, narratives, and dramatic monologues, sometimes the distinction between the three major types may become blurred, even in the same poem. "The Star-Spangled Banner," for example, contains elements of all three genres. The opening stanza, with its vivid recreation of a question asked at dawn, is closest to dramatic poetry. The second and third stanzas, which tell of the outcome of the battle, are primarily narrative. The final stanza, with its patriotic effusion and religious sentiment, is lyrical. Still, the three-fold division is useful in discussing a single author's various ways of dealing with subjects or in comparing examples of one type by separate authors. To cite three poems by the same poet in this collection, we might look at William Blake's "The Tyger," "A Poison Tree," and "The Chimney Sweeper." The first of these is a descriptive lyric, dwelling primarily on the symbolic meaning of the tiger's appearance; the second is a narrative that relates, in the allegorical manner of a parable, the events leading up to a murder; the third is a short dramatic monologue spoken by the persona identified in the title.

The Language of Poetry

One of the most persistent myths about poetry is that its language is artificial, "flowery," and essentially different from the language that people speak in going about their daily lives. While these beliefs may be true of some poetry, one can easily find numerous examples that reveal the opposite side of the coin. It is impossible to characterize poetic language narrowly, for poetry, which is after all the art of language, covers the widest range of linguistic possibilities. For example, here are several passages from different poets, all describing birds:

> Hail to thee, blithe Spirit!
>   Bird thou never wert—
> That from Heaven, or near it,
>   Pourest thy full heart
> In profuse strains of unpremeditated art.
>   Higher still and higher
> From the earth thou springest
>   Like a cloud of fire;
> The blue deep thou wingest,
>   And singing still dost soar, and soaring ever singest.
>
> *Percy Bysshe Shelley, "To a Skylark"*

> I caught this morning morning's minion, king-
>   dom of daylight's dauphin, dapple-dawn-drawn Falcon, in his
>   riding
> Of the rolling level underneath him steady air, and striding

High there, how he rung upon the rein of a wimpling wing
In his ecstacy!

Gerard Manley Hopkins, "The Windhover"

When the lilac-scent was in the air and Fifth-month grass was
    growing,
Up this seashore in some briers,
Two feather'd guests from Alabama, two together,
And their nest, and four light-green eggs spotted with brown,
And every day the he-bird to and fro near at hand,
And every day the she-bird crouch'd on her nest, silent, with bright
    eyes,
And every day I, a curious boy, never too close, never disturbing
    them,
Cautiously peering, absorbing, translating.

Walt Whitman, "Out of the Cradle Endlessly Rocking"

At once a voice arose among
    The bleak twigs overhead
In a full-hearted evensong
    Of joy illimited;
An aged thrush, frail, gaunt, and small,
    In blast-beruffled plume,
Had chosen thus to fling his soul
    Upon the growing gloom.

Thomas Hardy, "The Darkling Thrush"

There is a singer everyone has heard,
Loud, a mid-summer and a mid-wood bird,
Who makes the solid tree trunks sound again.
He says that leaves are old and that for flowers
Mid-summer is to spring as one to ten.

Robert Frost, "The Oven Bird"

The blue booby lives
on the bare rocks
of Galápagos
and fears nothing.
It is a simple life:
they live on fish,
and there are few predators.

James Tate, "The Blue Booby"

Of these quotes, only Shelley's, from the early nineteenth century, possesses the stereotypical characteristics of what we mean when we use the term "poetic" in a negative sense. Poetry, like any other art form, follows fashions that change over the years; by Shelley's day, the use of "thee" and "thou" and their related verb forms ("wert" and "wingest") had come full circle from their original use as a familiar form of the second person employed to address intimates and servants to an artificially heightened grammatical form reserved for prayers and poetry. Hopkins's language, from a poem of the 1870s, is artificial in an entirely different way: here the poet's **idiom**, the personal use of words that marks his poetry, is highly idiosyncratic; indeed, it would be hard to mistake a poem by Hopkins with one by any other poet. Whitman, on the other hand, should present few difficulties; the only oddities here are the spelling of "briers" and the use of "Fifth-month" instead of "May," a linguistic inheritance, perhaps, from Whitman's Quaker mother. Of course, one might argue that Whitman's "naturalness" results from his use of free verse, but both Hardy and Frost, who use rhymed, metrical verse, are hardly less natural. When we move to the contemporary period, we can find little difference between the language of many poems and conversational speech, as Tate's lines indicate.

Still, in reading a poem, particularly one from the past, we should be aware of certain problems that may impede our understanding. **Diction** refers to the individual words in a poem and may be classified in several ways. A poem's **level of diction** can range from slang at one extreme to formal usage at the other, although in an age in which most poems use a level of diction that stays in the middle of the scale, ranging between conversational and standard levels, these distinctions are useful only when a poet is being self-consciously formal (perhaps for ironic effect) or going to the opposite extreme to imitate the language of the streets. In past eras, the term **poetic diction** was used to indicate a level of speech somehow refined above ordinary usage and, thus, somehow superior to it; today the same term would most likely be used as a way of condemning a poet's language. Still, we should keep in mind that the slang of one era may become the standard usage of another.

A good dictionary is useful in many ways, particularly in dealing with **archaisms** (words that are no longer in common use) and other words that may not be familiar to the reader. Take, for example, the opening lines of Edgar Allan Poe's "To Helen":

Helen, thy beauty is to me
  Like those Nicean barks of yore,

That gently, o'er a perfumed sea,
  The weary, way-worn wanderer bore
  To his own native shore.

Several words here may give trouble to the average contemporary reader. First, "o'er," like "ne'er" or similar words such as "falt'ring" and "glimm'ring," is simply a contraction; this dropping of a letter, called **syncope,** is done for the sake of maintaining the poem's meter; in the fourth stanza of "The Star-Spangled Banner," the words "Pow'r" and "heav'n" are contracted for the same reason. "Barks of yore" will probably send most of us to the dictionary, for our sense of "bark" as either the outer surface of a tree or the noise that a dog makes does not fit here; likewise, "yore" is unfamiliar, possibly archaic. Looking up the literal sense of a word in a dictionary discloses its **denotation,** or literal meaning. Thus, we find that "barks" are small sailing ships and that "yore" refers to the distant past. Of course, Poe could have used "ships of the past" or a similar phrase, but his word choice was perhaps dictated by **connotation,** the implied meaning or feel that some words have acquired; it may be that even in Poe's day "barks of yore" had a remote quality that somehow evoked ancient Greece in a way that, say, "ancient ships" would not. But what are we to make of "Nicean," a proper adjective that sounds geographical but does not appear in either the dictionary or gazetteer? In this case we have encountered an example of a **coinage** or **neologism,** a word made up by the poet. Speculation on the source of "Nicean" has ranged from Nice, in the south of France, to Phoenician, but it is likely that Poe simply coined the word for its exotic sound. Similarly, we might note that the phrase "weary, way-worn wanderer" contains words that seem to have been chosen primarily for their alliterative sounds.

When we put a poem into our own words, we **paraphrase** it, a practice that is often useful when passages are hard to understand. Other than diction, **syntax** (the order of words in a sentence) may also give readers problems. Syntax in poetry, particularly in poems that use rhyme, is likely to be different from that of both speech and prose; if a poet decides to rhyme in a certain pattern, word order must be modified to fit the formal design, which may present difficulties to readers in understanding the grammar of a passage. Here is the opening of a familiar piece of American patriotic verse: "My country, 'tis of thee, / Sweet land of liberty, / Of thee I sing." What is the subject of this sentence? Would you be surprised to learn that the subject is "it" (contained in the contraction 'tis)? The passage from Poe presents few difficulties of this order

but does contain one example of **inversion,** words that fall out of their
expected order (a related syntactical problem lies in **ellipsis,** words that
are consciously omitted by the poet). If we do not allow for inverted syntax we are likely to be confused by "the weary, way-worn wanderer bore
/ To his own native shore." The wanderer bore *what?* A quick mental
sentence diagram shows that "wanderer" is the direct object of "bore,"
not its subject. A good paraphrase should simplify both diction and syntax: "Helen, to me your beauty is like those Nicean (?) ships of the ancient past that carried the weary, travel-worn wanderer gently over a
perfumed sea to his own native land." In paraphrasing, only the poten-
tially troublesome words and phrases should be substituted, leaving the
original language as intact as possible. Paraphrasing is a useful first step
toward unfolding a poem's literal sense, but it obviously takes few of a
poet's specific nuances of language into account. "Poetry," Robert Frost
famously remarked, "is what is lost in translation." He might have extended the complaint to include paraphrase as well.

Several other matters relevant to poetic language are worth mentioning. **Etymology,** the study of the sources of words, is a particularly
rewarding topic in English literature because our language has such an
unusually rich history—compare the size of an unabridged French dictionary to its English counterpart. Old English (or Anglo-Saxon), the
ancient language of the British Isles, was part of the Germanic family
of languages. When the Norman French successfully invaded Britain
in 1066 they brought with them their own language, part of the Romance language family (all originally derived from Latin). By the time
of Geoffrey Chaucer's death in 1400, these two linguistic traditions
had merged into a single language, Middle English, which can be read
today, despite its differences in spelling, pronunciation, and vocabulary. We can still, however, distinguish the words that show their Germanic heritage from those of Latinate origin. English is rich in synonyms, and the Germanic and Latinate words often have different
connotations. "Smart" is not quite the same as "intelligent," and a
"mapmaker" is subtly different from a "cartographer." A poet's pref-
erence for words of a certain origin is not always immediately clear,
but we can readily distinguish the wide gulf that separates a statement
like "I live in a house with my folks" from "I occupy a residence with
my parents."

A final tension exists in poems between their use of **concrete diction**
and **abstract diction.** Concrete words denote that which can be perceived by the senses, and the vividness of a poem's language resides primarily in the way it uses **imagery,** sensory details denoting specific

details of experience. Because sight is the most important of the five senses, **visual imagery** ("a dim light"; "a dirty rag"; "a golden daffodil") predominates in poems, but we should also be conscious of striking examples of the other types of imagery: **auditory** ("a pounding surf"), **tactile** ("a scratchy beard"), **olfactory** ("the scent of apple blossoms"), and **gustatory** ("the bitter tang of gin"). The use of specific imagery has always been crucial for poetry; think, for example, of the way Chaucer uses brilliantly chosen concrete details—a nun's coral jewelry, a monk's hood lined with fur, a festering sore on a cook's shin—to bring his pilgrims to life in the prologue to *The Canterbury Tales*. In the early twentieth century, a group of poets led by Americans Ezra Pound and H. D. (Hilda Doolittle) pioneered a poetic movement called **imagism,** in which concrete details predominate in short descriptive poems (see H. D.'s "Sea Rose"). "Go in fear of abstractions," commanded Pound, and his friend William Carlos Williams modified the remark to become a poetic credo: "No ideas but in things."

Still, for most poets abstract words remain important because they carry the burden of a poem's overall meaning or theme. William Butler Yeats's "Leda and the Swan" provides a good example of how concrete and abstract diction may coexist in a poem. In reading this account of the myth in which Zeus takes the form of a swan, impregnates a mortal woman, and thus sets in motion the chain of events that leads to the Trojan War (Leda was the mother of Helen of Troy), we will probably be struck at first by the way that tactile imagery ("a sudden blow"; fingers attempting to "push / The feathered glory" away; "A shudder in the loins") is used to describe an act of sexual violation. Even though some abstract words ("terrified"; "vague"; "glory"; "strange") appear in the first eight lines of the poem, they are all linked closely to concrete words like "fingers," "feathered," and "heart." In the last two lines of the poem, Yeats uses three large abstractions—"knowledge," "power," and "indifferent"—to state his theme (or at least ask the crucial rhetorical question about the meaning of the myth). More often than not, one can expect to encounter the largest number of abstract words near the conclusions of poems. Probably the most famous abstract statement in English poetry—John Keats's " 'Beauty is truth, truth beauty,' that is all / Ye know on earth, and all ye need to know."—appears in the last two lines of a fifty-line poem.

Two other poetic devices sometimes govern a poet's choice of words. **Onomatopoeia** refers to individual words like "splash" or "thud" whose meanings are closely related to their sounds. Auditory imagery in a poem can often be enhanced by the use of onomatopoeic words. In some cases, however, a whole line can be called ono-matopoeic, even if it contains no single word that illustrates the device. Hardy uses this line to describe the pounding of distant surf: "Where hill-hid tides throb, throe on throe." Here the repetition of similar sounds helps to imitate the sound of the ocean. A second device is the **pun**, the use of one word to imply the additional meaning of a similar-sounding word (the formal term is **paranomasia**). Thus, when Anne Bradstreet compares her first book to an illegitimate child, she addresses the book in this manner: "If for thy Father asked, say thou had'st none; / And for thy Mother, she alas is poor, / Which caused her thus to send thee out of door." The closeness of the interjection "alas" to the article and noun "a lass" is hardly coincidental. Poets in Bradstreet's day considered the pun a staple of their repertoire, even in serious poetry, but contemporary poets are more likely to use it primarily for comic effect:

> They have a dozen children; it's their diet,
> For they have bread too often. Please don't try it.
>
> *Anonymous*

More often than not, puns like these will elicit a groan from the audience, a response that may be exactly what the poet desires.

Figurative Language

We use figurative language in everyday speech without thinking of the poetic functions of the same devices. We can always relate experience in a purely literal fashion: "His table manners were deplorable. Mother scolded him severely, and Dad said some angry words to him. He left the table embarrassed and with his feelings hurt." But a more vivid way of saying the same thing might employ language used not in the literal but in the figurative sense. Thus, another version might run, "His table manners were swinish. Mother jumped on his back about them, and Dad scorched his ears. You should have seen him slink off like a scolded puppy." At least four comparisons are made here in an attempt to describe one character's table manners, his mother's scolding, his father's words, and the manner in which the character retreated from the table. In every case, the thing being described, what is called the **tenor** of the figure of speech, is linked with a concrete image or **vehicle**. All of the types of figurative language, what are called **figures of speech** or **tropes**, involve some kind of comparison, either explicit or implied. Thus, two of the figures of speech in the above example specifically compare aspects of the character's behavior to animal behavior. The other two imply parental words that were delivered with strong physical force or extreme anger. Some of the most common figures of speech are:

Metaphor: a direct comparison between two unlike things. Metaphors may take several forms.

> His words were sharp knives.
>
> The sharp knife of his words cut through the silence.
>
> He spoke sharp, cutting words with his knife-edged voice.
>
> His words knifed through the still air.
>
> "I will speak daggers to her. . . ." *(Shakespeare,* Hamlet)

Implied metaphor: a metaphor in which either the tenor or vehicle is implied, not stated.

> The running back gathered steam and chugged toward the end zone. (Compares the player to a steam locomotive without naming it explicitly.)
>
> "While smoke on its chin, that slithering gun
> Coiled back from its windowsill" *(X. J. Kennedy)*

Simile: a comparison using *like, as,* or *than* as a connective device.

> "My love is like a red, red rose . . ." *(Robert Burns)*
>
> My love smells as sweet as a rose.
>
> My love looks fresher than a newly budded rose.

Conceit: an extended or far-fetched metaphor, in most cases comparing things that apparently have almost nothing in common.

> "Make me, O Lord, thy spinning wheel complete. . . ."
> *(Edward Taylor)*
>
> (The poem, "Huswifery," draws an analogy between the process of salvation and the manufacture of cloth, ending with the persona attired in "holy robes.")

The **Petrarchan conceit,** named after the first great master of the sonnet, is a clichéd comparison usually relating to a woman's beauty (see Thomas Campion's "There Is a Garden in Her Face"; Shakespeare's

Sonnet 130 parodies this type of trope). The **metaphysical conceit** refers to the extended comparisons favored by such so-called metaphysical poets as John Donne, George Herbert, and Edward Taylor. The conceit in the final three stanzas of Donne's "A Valediction: Forbidding Mourning" compares the poet and his wife to a pair of drafting compasses, hardly an image that most people would choose to celebrate marital fidelity.

Hyperbole: overstatement, a comparison using conscious exaggeration.

He threw the ball so fast it caught the catcher's mitt on fire.

"And I will love thee still, my dear,
Till a' the seas gang dry." *(Robert Burns)*

Understatement: the opposite of hyperbole.

"I don't think we're in Kansas anymore, Toto."
(Dorothy, in *The Wizard of Oz*)

I had to spend a moment or two filling out my tax forms before I mailed them to the IRS.

"The space between [birth and death] is but an hour,
The frail duration of a flower." *(Philip Freneau)*

Allusion: metaphor making a direct comparison to a historical or literary event or character, a myth, a biblical reference, etc.

He is a Samson of strength but a Judas of duplicity.

"He dreamed of Thebes and Camelot,
And Priam's neighbors." *(Edwin Arlington Robinson)*

Metonymy: use of a related object to stand for the thing actually being talked about.

It's a white-collar street in a blue-collar town.

"And O ye high-flown quills [that is, literary critics] that soar the skies,
And ever with your prey still catch your praise." *(Anne Bradstreet)*

Synecdoche: use of a part for the whole, or vice versa.

The crowned heads of Europe were in attendance.

"Before the indifferent beak could let her drop."
(William Butler Yeats)

Personification: giving human characteristics to nonhuman things or to abstractions.

> Justice weighs the evidence in her golden scales.
>
> The ocean cursed and spat at us.
>
> "Of all her train, the hands of Spring
> First plant thee [a yellow violet] in the watery mould."
> *(William Cullen Bryant)*

Apostrophe: variety of personification in which a nonhuman thing, abstraction, or person not physically present is directly addressed as if it could respond.

> "Milton! Thou shouldst be living at this hour."
> *(William Wordsworth)*
>
> "Is it, O man, with such discordant noises,
>   With such accursed instruments as these,
> Thou drownest Nature's sweet and kindly voices,
>   And jarrest the celestial harmonies?"
> *(Henry Wadsworth Longfellow)*

Paradox: an apparent contradiction or illogical statement.

> I'll never forget old what's-his-name.
>
> "His [God's] hand hath made this noble work [the universe] which
>   Stands,
> His Glorious Handiwork not made by hands." *(Edward Taylor)*

Oxymoron: a short paradox, usually consisting of an adjective and noun with conflicting meanings.

> The touch of her lips was sweet agony.
>
> "Progress is a comfortable disease" *(e. e. cummings)*
>
> "A terrible beauty is born." *(William Butler Yeats)*

Synesthesia: a conscious mixing of two different types of sensory experience.

> A raw, red wind rushed from the north.
>
> "Leaves cast in casual potpourris
> Whisper their scents from pits and cellar-holes." *(Richard Wilbur)*

Transferred epithet: strictly speaking, not a trope; it occurs when an adjective is "transferred" from the word it actually modifies to a nearby word. In this example, the plowman is weary, not the path ("way") he walks upon.

"The plowman homeward plods his weary way." *(Thomas Gray)*

Allegory and Symbol

Related to the figurative devices are the various types of symbolism that may occur in poems. In many cases, a poem may seem so simple on the surface that we feel impelled to read deeper meanings into it; Robert Frost's "Stopping by Woods on a Snowy Evening" is a classic case in point. There is nothing wrong with searching for larger significance in a poem, but the reader should perhaps be wary of leaping to conclusions about symbolic meanings before fully exhausting the literal sense of a poem. Both allegory and symbolism require that the reader supply abstract or general meanings to the specific concrete details of the poem.

The simplest form taken by this substitution occurs in **allegory.** An allegory is usually a narrative that exists simultaneously on at least two levels, a literal level and a second level of abstract meaning. Throughout an allegory a consistent sequence of parallels exists between the literal and the abstract. Sometimes allegories may imply third or fourth levels of meaning as well, especially in long allegorical poems like Dante's *The Divine Comedy,* which has been interpreted in personal, political, ethical, and religious (Christian) terms. The characters and actions in an allegory explicitly signify the abstract level of meaning, and generally this second level of meaning is what the poet primarily intends to convey. For example, Robert Southwell's "The Burning Babe" is filled with fantastic incidents and paradoxical speech that are made clear in the poem's last line: "And straight I callèd unto mind that it was Christmas day." The literal burning babe of the title is revealed to be the Christ child, who predicts his own future to the amazed watcher. Thus, in interpreting the poem the reader must substitute theological terms like "redemption" or "original sin" for the literal details it contains.

Two types of prose allegories, the fable and the parable, have been universally popular. A fable is a short, nonrealistic narrative that is told to illustrate a universal moral concept. A parable is similar, but generally contains realistic characters and events. Thus, Aesop's fable of the tortoise and the hare, instead of telling us something about animal behavior, illustrates the virtue of persistence against seemingly unbeatable competition. Jesus' parable of the Good Samaritan tells the story of a man who is robbed and beaten and eventually rescued by a stranger of another race in order to define the concept of "neighbor" for a questioning lawyer. Poetic allegories like George Herbert's "Redemption" or Rossetti's "Up-Hill" can be read in Christian terms as symbolic accounts of the process of salvation. Robert Burns's witty ballad "John Barleycorn" tells on the literal surface the story of a violent murder, but the astute reader quickly discovers that the underlying meaning involves the poet's native Scotland's legendary taste for strong drink.

Many poems contain symbolic elements that are somewhat more elusive in meaning than the simple one-for-one equivalences presented by allegory. A **symbol**, then, is any concrete thing or any action in a poem that implies a meaning beyond its literal sense. Many of these things or actions are called **traditional symbols**, that is, symbols that hold roughly the same meanings for members of a given society. Certain flowers, colors, natural objects, and religious emblems possess meanings that we can generally agree upon. A white lily and a red rose suggest different occasions, mourning and passion. In Western societies, few would associate black with gaiety or red with innocence, and dawn and rainbows are traditional natural symbols of hope and new beginnings. It would be unlikely for a poet to mention a cross without expecting readers to think of its Christian associations.

Other types of symbols can be identified in poems that are otherwise not allegorical. A **private symbol** is one that has acquired certain meanings from a single poet's repeated use of it. Yeats's use of "gyres" is explained in some of his prose writings as a symbol for the turning of historical cycles, and his use of the word in his poems obviously goes beyond the literal level. Some visionary poets like Yeats and William Blake have devised complicated private symbolic systems, a sort of alternative mythology, and understanding the full import of these symbols becomes primarily the task of the specialist. Other poets may employ **incidental symbols**, things that are not usually considered symbolic but may be in a particular poem, or symbolic acts, a situation or response that seems of greater than literal import. As noted earlier, one of the most famous poems using these two devices is Frost's "Stopping by Woods on a Snowy Evening." In this poem, some readers see the "lovely, dark and deep" woods as inviting but threatening, and want to view the persona's rejection of their allure ("But I have promises to keep / And miles to go before I sleep") as some sort of life-affirming act. Frost himself was not particularly helpful in guiding his readers, often scoffing at those who had read too much metaphysical portent into such a simple lyric, although in other of his poems he presents objects—a fork in the road, an abandoned woodpile—that obviously possess some larger significance. There are many modern poems that remain so enigmatic that readers have consistently returned to them looking for new interpretations. Poems like these were to a degree influenced by the French symbolists, a group of poets of the late nineteenth century, who deliberately wrote poems filled with vague nuances subject to multiple interpretations. Such American attempts at symbolist experiments as Wallace Stevens's "Anecdote of the Jar" or "The Emperor of Ice-Cream" continue to perplex and fascinate readers, particularly those who are versed in recent schools of interpretation that focus on the indeterminacy of a poetic text.

Tone of Voice

Even the simplest statement is subject to multiple interpretations if it is delivered in several different tones of voice. Consider the shift in emphasis between saying "*I* gave you the money," "I *gave* you the money," and "I gave *you* the money." Even a seemingly innocent compliment like "You look lovely this morning" takes on a different meaning if it is delivered by a woman on New Year's Day to her hung-over husband. Still, these variations in **tone,** the speaker's implied attitude toward the words he or she says, depend primarily on vocal inflection. Because a poet only rarely gets the opportunity to elucidate his tone in a public performance, it is possible that readers may have difficulties in grasping the tone of a poem printed on the page. Still, many poems should present few tonal problems. The opening of Milton's sonnet "On the Late Massacre in Piedmont" ("Avenge, O Lord, thy slaughtered saints . . .") establishes a tone of righteous anger that is consistent throughout the poem. Keats's initial apostrophe in "Ode on a Grecian Urn" ("Thou still unravished bride of quietness, / Thou foster-child of silence and slow time . . .") strikes the reader as both passionate and reverent in the poet's response to an undamaged artifact of the ancient past. Thus, in many cases we can relate the tone of voice in poems to the emotions we employ in our own speech, and we would have to violate quite a few rules of common sense to argue that Milton is being flippant or that Keats is speaking sarcastically.

Irony is the element of tone by which a poet may imply an attitude that is in fact contrary to what his words appear to say. Of course, the simplest form of irony is **sarcasm,** the wounding tone of voice we use to imply exactly the opposite of what we say: "That's really a *great* excuse!" "What a *wonderful* performance!" One is almost tempted to add a firm "Not!" after such deliberately insincere bits of praise. **Verbal irony** is the conscious manipulation of tone by which the poet's actual attitude is the opposite of what he or she says. In a poem like Hardy's "The Ruined Maid," it is obvious that one speaker considers the meaning of "ruined" to be somewhat less severe than the other, and the whole poem hinges on this ironic counterpoint of definitions and the different moral and social attitudes they imply. Consider the opening lines of Oliver Wendell Holmes's "Old Ironsides," a piece of propaganda verse which succeeded in raising enough money to save the U.S.S. *Constitution* from the scrap yard: "Ay, tear her tattered ensign down! / Long has it waved on high, / And many an eye has danced to see / That banner in the sky. . . ." Because Holmes's poetic mission is to *save* the ship, it is obvious that he is speaking ironically in the opening line; he emphatically *does not* want the ship's flag stripped from her, an attitude that is made clear in the third and fourth lines. Verbal irony is also a conspicuous feature of **verse satire,** poetry that exists primarily to mock or ridicule, although often with serious intent. One famous example, in the form of a short satirical piece, or **epigram,** is Sarah N. Cleghorn's "The Golf Links," a poem written before the advent of child-labor laws:

> The golf links lie so near the mill
> That almost every day
> The laboring children can look out
> And see the men at play.

Here the weight of the verbal irony falls on two words, "laboring" and "play," and the way each is incongruously applied to the wrong group of people.

"The Golf Links," taken as a whole, also represents a second form of irony, **situational irony,** in which the setting of the poem (laboring children watching playing adults) contains a built-in incongruity. One master of ironic situation is Thomas Hardy, who used the title "Satires of Circumstances" in a series of short poems illustrating this sort of irony. Hardy's "Ah, Are You Digging on My Grave?" demonstrates a similar ironic situation, a ghostly persona asking questions of living speakers who can offer little comfort to the dead. **Dramatic irony,** the third type of irony, occurs when the persona of a poem is less aware of the full import of his or her words than is the reader. Blake's "The Chimney Sweeper" is spoken by a child who does not seem to fully realize how badly he is being exploited by his employer, who has apparently been using the promises of religion as a way of keeping his underage workers in line. A similar statement could be made of the persona of Walter Savage Landor's short dramatic monologue "Mother, I Cannot":

> Mother, I cannot mind my wheel;
>   My fingers ache, my lips are dry:
> Oh! if you felt the pain I feel!
>   But oh, who ever felt as I?
>
> No longer could I doubt him true;
>   All other men may use deceit:
> He always said my eyes were blue,
>   And often swore my lips were sweet.

The young woman speaking here apparently has not realized (or is deliberately unwilling to admit) that she has been sexually deceived and deserted by a scoundrel; "All other men may use deceit" gives the measure of her tragic naïvete. Dramatic irony, as the term implies, is most often found in dramatic monologues, where the gap between the speaker's perception of the situation and the reader's may be wide indeed.

Repetition: Sounds and Schemes

Because poetry uses language at its most intense level, we are aware of the weight of individual words and phrases to a degree that is usually lacking when we read prose. Poets have long known that the meanings that they attempt to convey often depend as much on the sound of the words as their meaning. We have already mentioned one sound device, onomatopoeia. Consider how much richer the experience of "the murmuring of innumerable bees" is than a synonymous phrase, "the faint sound of a lot of bees." It has often been said that all art aspires to the condition of music in the way that it affects an audience on some unconscious, visceral level. By carefully exploiting the repetition of sound devices, a poet may use some of the same effects that the musical composer does.

Of course, much of this sonic level of poetry is subjective; what strikes one listener as pleasant may overwhelm the ear of another. Still, it is useful to distinguish between a poet's use of **euphony,** a series of pleasant sounds, and **cacophony,** sounds that are deliberately unpleasant. Note the following passages from Alexander Pope's *An Essay on Criticism,* a didactic poem which attempts to illustrate many of the devices poets use:

> Soft is the strain when Zephyr gently blows,
> And the smooth stream in smoother numbers flows; . . .

The repetition of the initial consonant sounds is called **alliteration,** and here Pope concentrates on the *s* sound. The vowel sounds are generally long: str*ai*n, bl*ow*s, sm*oo*th, and so on. Here the description of the gentle west wind is assisted by the generally pleasing sense of euphony. But Pope, to illustrate the opposite quality, follows this couplet with a second:

> But when loud surges lash the sounding shore,
> The hoarse, rough verse should like the torrent roar.

Now the wind is anything but gentle, and the repetition of the *r* sounds in su*r*ges, sho*r*e, hoa*r*se, *r*ough, ve*r*se, to*r*rent, and *r*oar force the reader's voice into the back of the throat, making sounds that are anything but euphonious.

Repetition of sounds has no inherent meaning value (although some linguists might argue that certain sounds do stimulate particular emotions), but this repetition does call attention to itself and can be particularly effective when a poet wishes to emphasize a certain passage. We have already mentioned alliteration. Other sound patterns are **assonance,** the repetition of similar vowel sounds (st*ee*p, *e*v*e*n, rec*ei*ve, v*ea*l), and **consonance,** the repetition of similar consonant sounds (du*ck*, tor*que*, stri*ke*, tri*ck*le). It should go without saying that spelling has little to do with any sound pattern; an initial *f* will alliterate with an initial *ph*.

Rhyme is the most important sound device, and our delight in deftly executed rhymes (consider the possibilities of rhyming "neighbor" with "sabre," as Richard Wilbur does in one of his translations) goes beyond mere sound to include the pleasure we take when an unexpected word is magically made to fit with another. There are several types of rhyme. **Masculine rhyme** occurs between single stressed syllables: *fleece, release, surcease, Nice* (a city in France), and so on. **Feminine rhyme,** also called **double rhyme,** matches two syllables, one stressed and one usually unstressed: *stinging, upbringing, flinging.* **Triple rhyme** goes further:

slithering, withering. **Slant rhyme** (also called **near rhyme** and **off rhyme**) contains hints of sound repetition (sometimes related to assonance and consonance): *chill, dull, sale* are possibilities, although poets often grant themselves considerable leeway in counting as rhyming words pairs that often have only the slightest similarity. When rhymes fall in a pattern in a poem and are **end rhymes,** occurring at the end of lines, then it is convenient to assign letters to the matching sounds and speak of a **rhyme scheme.** Thus, a stanza of four lines ending with *heaven, hell, bell, eleven* is said to have a rhyme scheme of *abba.* Rhymes may also occasionally be found in the interior of lines, what is called **internal rhyme.**

More complicated patterns of repetition involve more than mere sounds but whole phrases and grammatical units. Ancient rhetoricians, in teaching the art of public speaking, identified several of these, and they are also found in poetry. **Parallel structure** is simply the repetition of grammatically similar phrases or clauses; for example, Tennyson's "To strive, to seek, to find, and not to yield." **Anaphora** and **epistrophe** are repeated words or phrases at, respectively, the beginnings and ends of lines. Whitman uses these schemes extensively, often in the same lines. This passage from *Song of Myself* illustrates both anaphora and epistrophe:

> If they are not yours as much as mine they are nothing, or next to
>   nothing,
> If they are not the riddle and the untying of the riddle they are
>   nothing,
> If they are not just as close as they are distant they are nothing.

Antithesis is the matching of parallel units which contain contrasting meanings, such as Whitman's "I am of old and young, of the foolish as much as the wise, / Regardless of others, ever regardful of others, / Maternal as well as paternal, a child as well as a man. . . ." While the rhetorical schemes are perhaps more native to the orator, the poet can still make occasional effective use of them. Whitman's poetry was influenced by many sources but perhaps by none so powerfully as the heavily schematic language of the King James Bible.

Meter and Rhythm

The subject of poetic meter and rhythm can be a difficult one, to say the least, and it is doubtless true that such phrases as *trochaic octameter* or *spondaic substitution* have an intimidating quality. Still, discussions of meter need not be limited to experts, and even beginning readers should be able to apply a few of the metrical principles that are commonly found in poetry written in English.

First, let's distinguish between two terms that are often used synonymously: **poetry** and **verse**. Poetry refers to a whole genre of literature and thus stands with fiction and drama as one of the three major types of writing. Verse, on the other hand, refers to a mode of writing in lines of a certain length; thus, many poets still retain the traditional practice of capitalizing the first word of each line to indicate its integrity as a unit of composition. Virtually any piece of writing can be versified (and sometimes rhymed as well). Especially useful are bits of **mnemonic verse,** in which information like the number of days in the months or simple spelling rules ("I before E / Except after C . . .") is cast in a form that is easy to remember. Although it is not strictly accurate to do so, many writers use verse to denote metrical writing that somehow does not quite measure up to the level of true poetry; phrases like **light verse** or **occasional verse** (lines written for a specific event, like a birthday or anniversary) are often used in this way.

If, on the other hand, a writer is unconcerned about the length of individual lines and is governed only by the width of the paper being used, then he or she is not writing verse but **prose.** All verse is metrical writing; prose is not. Surprisingly enough, there is a body of writing called **prose poetry,** which uses language in a poetic manner but avoids any type of meter; see Carolyn Forché's "The Colonel" for one example. Perhaps the simplest way to think of **meter** in verse is to think of its synonym, **measure** (think of the use of meter in words like odometer or kilometer). Thus, meter refers to the method by which a poet determines line length.

When we talk about meter in poetry, we ordinarily mean that the poet is employing some kind of consistent **prosody** or system of measurement. There are many possible prosodies, depending on what the poet decides to count as the unit of measurement in the line, but only three of these systems are common in English-language poetry. Perhaps the simplest is **syllabic verse.** In verse of this type, the length of the line is determined by counting the total number of syllables the line contains (see Sylvia Plath's "Metaphors" for one example). Much French poetry of the past was written in twelve-syllable lines, or **Alexandrines,** and a word like **octosyllabic** denotes a line of eight syllables. Because English is a language of strong stresses, most of our poets have favored other prosodic systems, but syllabic poetry has been attempted by many poets, among them Marianne Moore, Richard Wilbur, and Dylan Thomas. Moore, in particular, often wrote in **quantitative syllabics,** that is, in stanzas containing the same number of lines with identical numbers of syllables in the corresponding lines of different stanzas.

More natural to the English language is **accentual** verse, a prosodic system in which only accented or strongly stressed syllables are counted in a line, which can also contain a varying number of unaccented syllables. Much folk poetry, intended perhaps to be recited to the beat of a percussion instrument, retains this stress-based pattern, and the oldest verse in the British tradition, Anglo-Saxon poetry like *Beowulf*, is composed in four-stress lines which were recited to musical accompaniment. Many of the verses we recall from nursery rhymes, children's chanting games ("Red rover, red rover, / Send [any name from one to up to four syllables can be substituted here—*Bill, Susan, Latisha, Elizabeth*] right over") and sports cheers ("Two bits, four bits, six bits, a dollar! / All for the [*Owls, Cowboys, Cardinals, Thundering Herd*] stand up and holler!") retain the strong sense of rhythmical pulse that characterizes much accentual verse, a fact we recognize when we clap our hands and move rhythmically to the sound of the words. Indeed, the lyrics to most current rap music are actually composed in a four-stress accentual line, and the stresses or "beats" can be heard plainly when we listen or dance. Gerard Manley Hopkins, attempting to recapture some of the flavor of Anglo-Saxon verse, pioneered a type of accentual prosody that he called **sprung rhythm.** Accentual meters still supply possibilities for contemporary poets; indeed, what often appears to be free verse is revealed, on closer inspection, to be a poem written in accentual meter. Richard Wilbur's "The Writer," for example, is written in a stanza containing lines of three, five, and three strong stresses, respectively, but the stresses do not overwhelm the reader insistently. Wilbur's "Junk" employs Anglo-Saxon meter, and his strong alliteration helps the reader hear the four strong stresses in each line.

Accentual-syllabic verse is the most important prosodic system in English, dominating our poetry for the five centuries from Chaucer's time down to the early twentieth century. Even though in the last seventy years or so free verse has become the prevailing style in which poetry is written, accentual-syllabic verse still has many able practitioners. An accentual-syllabic prosody is somewhat more complicated than the two systems we have mentioned, for it requires that the poet count both the strongly stressed syllables and the total number of syllables in the line. Because stressed and unstressed syllables alternate fairly regularly in this system, four **metrical feet,** representing the most common patterns, designate the subdivisions of rhythm that make up the line (think of a yardstick divided into three feet). These feet are the **iamb** (or **iambic**

foot), one unstressed and one stressed syllable; the trochee (or trochaic foot), one stressed and one unstressed syllable; the anapest (or anapestic foot), two unstressed syllables and one stressed syllable; and the **dactyl** (or **dactylic foot**), one stressed and two unstressed syllables. The first two of these, iambic and trochaic, are called **double meters;** the second two, **triple meters.** Iambic and anapestic meters are sometimes called **rising meters** because they "rise" toward the stressed syllable; trochaic and dactylic meters are called **falling meters** for the opposite reason. Simple repetition of words or phrases can give us the sense of how these lines sound in a purely schematic sense. The **breve** (∪) and **ictus** (ʹ) are used to denote unstressed and stressed syllables, respectively.

Iambic:

∪ ʹ   ∪ ʹ   ∪ ʹ
release / release / release
∪ ʹ   ∪ ʹ   ∪ ʹ
to fall / into / despair
∪ ʹ   ∪ ʹ   ∪ ʹ ∪
Marie / discov / ers candy

Trochaic:

ʹ   ∪   ʹ   ∪   ʹ   ∪   ʹ   ∪
melting / melting / melting / melting
ʹ ∪   ʹ ∪   ʹ   ∪ ʹ ∪
Peter / disa / greed en / tirely
ʹ ∪   ʹ ∪   ʹ   ∪   ʹ
clever / writing / filled the / page

Anapestic:

∪ ∪   ʹ   ∪ ∪   ʹ
to the top / to the top
∪ ∪ ʹ   ∪ ∪ ʹ
a retriev / er appeared
∪ ∪ ʹ   ∪ ∪   ʹ ∪
and a ter / ri ble thunder

Dactylic:

ʹ ∪ ∪   ʹ ∪ ∪   ʹ ∪ ∪   ʹ ∪ ∪   ʹ ∪ ∪
shivering / shivering / shivering / shivering / shivering
ʹ ∪ ∪   ʹ   ∪ ∪   ʹ   ∪ ∪   ʹ ∪ ∪   ʹ ∪∪
terribly / ill with the / symptoms of / viral pneu / monia
ʹ   ∪ ∪   ʹ   ∪ ∪   ʹ   ∪ ∪   ʹ ∪∪   ʹ
note how the / minister / whispered at / Emily's / grave

Because each of these lines contains a certain number of feet, a second specialized term is used to denote how many times a pattern is repeated in a line:

one foot	**monometer**
two feet	**dimeter**
three feet	**trimeter**

four feet	tetrameter
five feet	pentameter
six feet	hexameter
seven feet	heptameter
eight feet	octameter

Thus, in the examples above, the first set of lines is iambic trimeter; the second, trochaic tetrameter; the third, anapestic dimeter; and the fourth, dactylic pentameter. The third lines in the iambic and anapestic examples are **hypermetrical**; that is, they contain an extra unstressed syllable or **feminine ending**. Conversely, the third lines in the trochaic and dactylic examples are missing one and two unstressed final syllables, respectively, a common practice called **catalexis**. Although over thirty combinations of foot type and number of feet per line are theoretically possible, relatively few are ordinarily encountered in poetry. The iambic foot is most common, followed by the anapest and the trochee; the dactylic foot is relatively rare. Line lengths tend to be from three to five feet, with anything shorter or longer used only sparingly. Still, there are famous exceptions like Poe's "The Raven," which is composed in trochaic octameters and tetrameters, or Southwell's "The Burning Babe," in iambic heptameter.

Meter denotes regularity, the "blueprint" for a line from which the poet works. Because iambic pentameter is the most common meter used in English, our subsequent discussion will focus on poems written in it. But most good poets quickly learn that a metronomic regularity, five iambic feet marching in lockstep line after line, is not a virtue and quickly becomes predictable. Thus, there are several ways by which poets can add variety to their lines so that the actual **rhythm** of the line, what is actually heard, plays a subtle counterpoint against the regularity of the meter. One way is to vary the placement of the **caesura** ‖ or pause within a line (usually indicated by a mark of punctuation). Another is by mixing **end-stopped lines,** which clearly pause at their conclusion, with **enjambed** lines, which run on into the next line with no pause. The following lines from Tennyson's "Ulysses" illustrate these techniques:

> This is my son, mine own Telemachus,
> To whom I leave the scepter and the isle,
> Well-loved of me, discerning to fulfill
> This labor, by slow prudence to make mild
> A rugged people, and through soft degrees
> Subdue them to the useful and the good.

Lines two and six have no caesurae; the others do, after either the third, fourth, or fifth syllable. Lines one, two, and six are end-stopped; the others are enjambed (or use **enjambment**).

Another technique of varying regularity is **metrical substitution,** where feet of a different type are substituted for what the meter calls for. In iambic meter, trochaic feet are often encountered at the beginnings of lines, or after a caesura. Two other feet, the **pyrrhic** (∪∪), consisting of two unstressed syllables, and the **spondee** (′′), consisting of two stressed syllables, are also commonly substituted. Here are Tennyson's lines with their scansion marked.

> This is / my son, ‖ / mine own / Telem / achus,
> To whom / I leave / the scep / ter and / the isle,
> Well-loved / of me, ‖ / discern / ing to / fulfill
> This la / bor, ‖ by / slow pru / dence to / make mild
> A rug / ged peo / ple, ‖ and / through soft / degrees
> Subdue / them to / the use / ful and / the good.

Even though these are fairly regular iambic pentameter lines, it should be observed that no single line is without some substitution. Still, the dominant pattern of five iambic feet per line should be apparent (out of thirty total feet, about twenty are iambs); there is even a strong tendency on the reader's part to "promote" the middle syllable of three unstressed syllables ("Subdue / them *to* / the use / ful *and* / the good") to keep the sense of the iambic rhythm.

How far can a poet depart from the pattern without losing contact with the original meter? That is a question that is impossible to answer in general terms. The following scansion will probably strike us at first as a far departure from regular iambic pentameter:

> ′ ‖ ′ / ∪ ‖ ′ / ∪ ∪ ‖ / ′ ∪ / ∪ ′

Yet it is actually the opening line of one of Shakespeare's most frequently quoted passages, Mark Antony's funeral oration from *Julius Caesar:*

> Friends, ‖ Ro / mans, ‖ coun / trymen, ‖ / lend me / your ears

Poets who have learned to use the full resources of meter do not consider it a restraint; instead, they are able to stretch the pattern to its limits without breaking it. A good analogy may be made between poetry and dance. Beginning dancers watch their feet and count the steps while making them; after considerable practice, the movements become second nature, and a skillful pair of partners can add dips and passes without losing the basic step of the dance.

Free Verse, Open Form, and Closed Form

Nothing has been so exhaustively debated in English-language poetry as the exact nature of free verse. The simplest definition may be the best: free verse is verse with no consistent metrical pattern. In free verse, line length is a subjective decision made by the poet, and length may be determined by grammatical phrases, the poet's own sense of individual "breath-units," or even by the visual arrangement of lines on the page. Clearly, it is easier to speak of what free verse is not than what it is, and free verse (a term, incidentally, that few poets, even its practitioners, seem very happy with) offers a wide variety of possibilities. Extensive use of free verse is a fairly recent phenomenon in the history of poetry. Even though there are many examples of free verse from the past (the Psalms, Ecclesiastes, and the Song of Solomon from the King James Bible), the modern history of free verse begins in 1855 with the publication of Walt Whitman's *Leaves of Grass*. Whitman, influenced by Ralph Waldo Emerson's statement that "it is not meters but meter-making argument that makes a poem," created a unique variety of long-line free verse based on grammatical units—phrases and clauses. Whitman's free verse is so distinctive that he has had few direct imitators (Robinson Jeffers is one from the twentieth century), and subsequent poets who have used free verse have written lines that vary widely in syllable count. Good free verse, as T. S. Eliot remarked, still contains some kind of "ghost of meter," and its rhythms can be as terse and clipped as those of Philip Levine or as lushly sensuous as those of Pattiann Rogers. The poet who claims that free verse is somehow easier to write than metrical verse would find many arguments to the contrary. As Eliot said, "No verse is free for the poet who wants to do a good job."

All poems have form, the arrangement of the poem on the page that differentiates it from prose. Sometimes this arrangement indicates that the poet is following a preconceived plan—a metrical pattern, a rhyme scheme, a purely visual design like that of concrete or spatial poetry, or a scheme like that of acrostic verse, in which the first letters of the lines spell a message. An analysis of poetic form notes how the lines are arranged, how long they are, and how they are grouped into blocks or

stanzas. Further analysis might reveal the existence of types of repetition, rhyme, or the use of a **refrain,** or a repeated line or groups of lines. A large number of the poems composed in the last 100 years have been written in **open form,** which simply means that there is no strict pattern of regularity in the elements mentioned previously; in other words, there is no consistent meter and no rhyme scheme. Still, even a famous poem in open form, such as William Carlos Williams's "The Red Wheelbarrow," can be described in formal terms:

> so much depends
> upon
>
> a red wheel
> barrow
>
> glazed with rain
> water
>
> beside the white
> chickens.

Here we observe that the eight-line poem is divided into **uniform stanzas** of two lines each (or couplets). Line length varies between four and two syllables per line. The odd-numbered lines each contain three words; the even, one. While there is no apparent use of rhyme or repetition here, many poems in open form contain some rhyme and metrical regularity at their conclusions. Alan Dugan's "Love Song: I and Thou" falls into regular iambic tetrameter in its final lines, and Naomi Shihab Nye's "The Traveling Onion," a typical contemporary example of an open form poem, concludes with a closing rhyme on "career" and "disappear."

Closed form, on the other hand, denotes the existence of some kind of regular pattern of meter, stanza, rhyme, or repetition. **Stanza forms** are consistent patterns in the individual units of the poem (*stanza* means "room" in Italian); **fixed forms** are patterns that encompass a complete poem, for example, a sonnet or a villanelle. **Traditional forms** are patterns that have been used for long periods of time and thus may be associated with certain subjects, themes, or types of poems. **Nonce forms** are patterns that originate in an individual poem and have not been widely used by other poets. Of course, it goes without saying that every traditional form was at first a nonce form; the Italian poet (now lost to memory) who first wrote a lyric consisting of fourteen rhymed eleven-syllable lines could not have foreseen that poets the world over in subsequent centuries would produce literally millions of sonnets that are all variations on the original model. Some of the most common stanza and fixed forms are briefly discussed herein.

Stanza Forms

Blank verse is not, strictly speaking, a stanza form because it consists of individual lines of iambic pentameter that do not rhyme. However, long poems written in blank verse may be arranged into **verse paragraphs** or stanzas with a varying number of lines. Blank verse originally appeared in English in the fifteenth century with the Earl of Surrey's translation of the *Aeneid;* such verse has been used extensively for narrative and dramatic purposes since, particularly in epics like Milton's *Paradise Lost* and in Shakespeare's plays. Also written in stanzas of varying lengths is the **irregular ode,** a poem which employs lines of varying lengths (although usually of a regular rhythm that is iambic or matches one of the other feet) and an irregular rhyme scheme.

Paired rhyming lines *(aabbcc . . .)* are called **couplets,** although they are only rarely printed as separate stanzas. **Short couplets** have a meter of iambic tetrameter (and are sometimes called **octosyllabic couplets**). If their rhymes are predominantly feminine and seem chosen for comic effect, they may be called **Hudibrastic couplets** after Samuel Butler's satirical poem *Hudibras* of the late 1600s. **Heroic couplets** have a meter of iambic pentameter and take their name from John Dryden's translation of the *Aeneid* (1697) and Alexander Pope's hugely successful translation of Homer's *Iliad* and *Odyssey* (1720–1726), all three of these being "heroic" or epic poems. Heroic couplets have also been used effectively in satirical poems like Pope's "mock epic" *The Dunciad* (1728–1743) and even in dramatic monologues like Browning's "My Last Duchess," where the rhymes are so effectively buried by enjambment that the poem approximates speech. Two other couplet forms, both rare, are **poulter's measure,** rhyming pairs of alternating lines of iambic hexameter and iambic heptameter, and **fourteeners,** pairs of iambic heptameter (fourteen-syllable) lines, which, because there is generally a caesura after the fourth foot, closely resemble common meter (see below).

A three-line stanza is called a **tercet.** If it rhymes in an *aaa bbb . . .* pattern, it is a **triplet;** sometimes triplets appear in poems written in heroic couplets, especially at the end of sections or where special emphasis is desired. Iambic pentameter tercets rhyming *aba bcb cdc* . . . are called **terza rima,** a pattern invented by Dante for *The Divine Comedy.*

A four-line stanza is known as a **quatrain.** Alternating lines of tetrameter and trimeter in any foot, rhyming *abcb* or *abab,* make up a **ballad stanza;** if the feet are strictly iambic, the quatrain is called **common meter,** the form of many popular hymns like "Amazing Grace." **Long meter,** also widely used in hymns, consists of iambic tetrameter lines rhyming *abcb* or *abab;* **short meter** has a similar rhyme scheme but contains first, second, and fourth lines of iambic trimeter and a third line of iambic tetrameter. The *In Memoriam* stanza, named after Tennyson's long poetic sequence, is iambic tetrameter rhyming *abba.* The *Rubaiyat* stanza, an import from Persia, consists of lines of either iambic tetrameter or pentameter, rhyming *aaba bbcb* . . . ; Edward FitzGerald's translation *The Rubaiyat of Omar Khayyam* employs this form. Four lines of iambic pentameter rhyming *abab* are known as an **English quatrain,** also known as the **elegiac stanza** (after Thomas Gray's "Elegy Written in a Country Churchyard"). Lines of the same meter rhyming *abba* make up an **Italian quatrain.** One other unusual quatrain stanza is an import from ancient Greece, the **Sapphic stanza,** named after the poet Sappho. The Sapphic stanza consists of three **hendecasyllabic** (eleven-syllable) lines of this pattern:

˘∪ / ˘∪ / ˘∪ ∪ / ˘∪ / ˘∪

and a fourth line called an **Adonic,** which is five syllables long and consists of one dactylic foot and one trochaic foot. The Sapphic stanza is usually unrhymed. The quatrain stanza is also used in another import, the **pantoum,** a poem in which the second and fourth lines of the first stanza become the first and third of the second, and the second and fourth of the second become the first and third of the fourth, and so on. Pantoums may be written in any meter and may or may not employ rhyme.

A five-line stanza is known as a **quintet** and is relatively rare in English poetry. The **sestet,** or six-line stanza, can be found with a number of different meters and rhyme schemes. A seven-line stanza is called a **septet;** one septet stanza form is **rime royal,** seven lines of iambic pentameter rhyming *ababbcc.* An eight-line stanza is called an **octave;** one widely used stanza of this length is **ottava rima,** iambic pentameter lines rhyming *abababcc.* Another octave form is the **Monk's Tale stanza,** named after one of Chaucer's tales; it is iambic pentameter and rhymes *ababbcbc*. The addition of a ninth line, rhyming *c* and having a meter of iambic hexameter, makes a **Spenserian stanza**, named after Edmund Spenser, the poet who invented it for *The Faerie Queene*, a long metrical romance.

Fixed Forms

Fixed forms are combinations of meter, rhyme scheme, and repetition that make up complete poems. One familiar three-line fixed form is the **haiku**, a Japanese import consisting of lines of five, seven, and five syllables, respectively. Related to the haiku is the **tanka**, which adds two additional seven-syllable lines.

The **clerihew**, named after its inventor, Edward Clerihew Bentley, is a humorous form in which the first line is a person's name; the clerihew has a rhyme scheme of *aabb*.

Two five-line fixed forms are the **limerick** and the **cinquain**. The limerick consists of anapestic trimeter in lines one, two, and five, and anapestic dimeter in three and four. The rhymes, *aabba*, are usually double rhymes used for comic effect. English poet Wendy Cope wittily reduced T. S. Eliot's complex modernist classic "The Waste Land," a long poem that contains phrases in foreign languages and the poet's own explanatory footnotes, to a set of five limericks. Here is the final one:

> No water. Dry rocks and dry throats,
> Then thunder, a shower of quotes
> From the Sanskrit and Dante.
> Da. Damyata. Shantih.
> I hope you'll make sense of the notes.

A cinquain, the invention of American poet Adelaide Crapsey, consists of five unrhymed lines of two, four, six, eight, and two syllables, respectively.

The most important of the fixed forms is the **sonnet**, which consists of fourteen lines of rhymed iambic pentameter. The original form of the sonnet is called the **Italian sonnet** or the **Petrarchan sonnet** after the fourteenth-century poet who popularized it. An Italian sonnet is usually cast in two stanzas, an octave rhyming *abbaabba* and a sestet with a variable rhyme scheme; *cdcdcd, cdecde, cddcee* are some of the possible patterns. A **volta** or "turn," usually a conjunction or conjunctive adverb like "but" or "then," may appear at the beginning of the sestet, signifying a slight change of direction in thought. Many Italian sonnets have a strong logical connection between octave and sestet—problem/solution, cause/effect, question/answer—and the volta helps to clarify the transition. The **English sonnet,** also known as the **Shakespearean sonnet** after its prime exemplar, was developed in the sixteenth century after the sonnet was imported to England and employs a different rhyme scheme that takes into consideration the relative scarcity of rhymes in English (compared with Italian). The English sonnet has a rhyme scheme of *ababcdcdefefgg* and is usually printed as a single stanza. The pattern of three English quatrains plus a heroic couplet often forces a slightly different organizational scheme on the poet, although many of Shakespeare's sonnets still employ a strong volta at the beginning of the ninth line. Other English sonnets may withhold the turn until the beginning of the closing couplet. A third sonnet type, relatively rare, is the **Spenserian sonnet,** named after Edmund Spenser, author of *Amoretti,* one of the earliest sonnet sequences in English. The Spenserian sonnet rhymes *ababbcbccdcdee.* There are many other sonnets written over the years which have other rhyme schemes, often hybrids of the Italian and English types. These are usually termed **nonce sonnets;** Shelley's "Ozymandias," with its unusual rhyme scheme of *ababacdcedefef,* is one notable example. In "Ode to the West Wind," Shelley also employs a fourteen-line stanza rhyming *aba bcb cdc ded ee,* which has been called a **terza rima sonnet.**

Several other fixed forms, all French imports, have appeared frequently in English poetry. The **rondeau** has fifteen lines of iambic tetrameter or pentameter arranged in three stanzas: *aabba aabR aabbaR;* the R here stands for the unrhymed refrain, which repeats the first few words of the poem's first line. A maddeningly complex variation is the thirty-one line **rondeau redoublé,** through which Wendy Cope wittily maneuvers in her poem of the same name. The **villanelle** is a nineteen-line poem, usually written in iambic pentameter, employing two refrain lines, A_1 and A_2, in a pattern of five tercets and a final quatrain: A_1bA_2 abA_1 abA_2 abA_1 abA_2 abA_1A_2. A related form, also nineteen lines long, is the **terzanelle,** which uses several more repeating lines (capitalized here): A_1BA_2 bCB cDC dED eFE f A_1FA_2. The **ballade** is twenty-eight lines of iambic tetrameter employing a refrain that appears at the end of its three octaves and final quatrain, or **envoy:** *ababbcbC ababbcbC ababbcbC bcbC.* Obviously the rhyming demands of the villanelle, the terzanelle, and the ballade pose serious challenges to English-language poets. A final fixed form is the thirty-nine-line **sestina,** which may be either metrical or in free verse and which uses a complicated sequence repeating, in different order, the six words that end the lines of the initial stanza. The sequence for the first six sestets is *123456 615243 364125 532614 451362 246531*. A final tercet uses three words in the interior of the lines and three at the ends in the pattern *(2)5(4)3(6)1*. Many sestinas hinge on the poet's choice of six end words that have multiple meanings and can serve as more than one part of speech.

Two contemporary poets, Billy Collins and Kim Addonizio, have recently created nonce forms. Collins's tongue-in-cheek description of the paradelle was taken seriously by many readers, and a whole anthology of poems in the form has been assembled. Addonizio's personalized variation on the sonnet, the sonnenizio, has also been imitated by other poets.

There are many other less familiar types of stanza forms and fixed forms; Lewis Turco's *The Book of Forms* and Miller Williams's *Patterns of Poetry* are two reference sources useful in identifying them.

Literary History and Poetic Conventions, and Theory

What a poet attempts to do in any given poem is always governed by the tension that exists between originality and convention, in other words, between the poet's desire, in Ezra Pound's famous phrase, to "make it new" and the various stylistic devices that other poets and readers are familiar with through their understanding of the poetic tradition. If we look at some of the most obscure passages of Pound's *Cantos* we may think that the poet has departed about as far from conventional modes of expression as possible, leaving his audience far behind him. Yet it is important to keep two facts in mind. First, this style was not arrived at overnight; Pound's early poetry is relatively traditional and should present little difficulty to most readers. He arrived at the style of the *Cantos* after a twenty-year apprenticeship to the styles of writers as different as Li-Po, Robert Browning, and William Butler Yeats. Second, by the time Pound was writing his mature poetry the modernist movement was in full flower, forcing the public not only to read poems but also to look at paintings and sculpture and to listen to music in ways that would have been unimaginable only a decade or two earlier. When we talk about the stylistic conventions of any given literary period, we should keep in mind that poets are rarely willing to go much beyond what they have educated their audiences to understand. This mutual sense of agreement is the essence of poetic convention.

One should be wary of making sweeping generalizations about "schools" of poetry or the shared conventions of literary periods. In any era, there is always a significant amount of diversity among individual poets. Further, an anthology of this limited scope, which by its very nature must exclude most long poems, is likely to contribute to a misleading view of literary history and the development of poetry in English. When we read Shakespeare's sonnets or Milton's shorter poems, we should not forget that their major reputations rest on poetry of a very different sort. The neoclassical era in English poetry, stretching from the late seventeenth century until almost the end of the eighteenth century, is poorly represented here because the satires of Dryden and Pope and long philosophical poems like Pope's *An Essay on Man* do not readily lend themselves to being excerpted. Poe once claimed that a long poem is "simply a contradiction in terms," but the continued high reputations of *The Faerie Queene, Paradise Lost, Don Juan,* and even a modern verse-novella like Robinson Jeffers's "The Roan Stallion" demonstrate that Poe's was far from the last word on the subject.

The earliest poems in this volume, all by anonymous poets, represent poetry's links to the oral folk tradition. The American folk songs that children learn to sing in elementary school represent our own inheritance of this rich legacy. The poets of the Tudor (1485–1558) and Elizabethan (1558–1603) eras excelled at lyric poetry; Sir Thomas Wyatt and Henry Howard, Earl of Surrey, had imported the sonnet form from Italy, and the form was perfected during this period. Much of the love poetry of this period is characterized by conventional imagery, so-called Petrarchan conceits, which even a later poet like Campion employs in "There Is a Garden in Her Face" and which Shakespeare satirizes brilliantly in his Sonnet 130 ("My mistress' eyes are nothing like the sun").

The poetry of the first half of the seventeenth century has several major schools: a smooth lyricism influenced by Ben Jonson that can be traced through the work of Herrick, Waller, and Lovelace; a serious body of devotional poetry by Donne, Herbert, and Milton; and the metaphysical style, which uses complex extended metaphors or metaphysical conceits—Donne and Herbert are its chief exemplars, followed by the early American poets Bradstreet and Taylor. Shortly after the English Restoration in 1660, a profound period of conservatism began in the arts, and the neoclassical era, lasting through most of the eighteenth century, drew heavily on Greek and Roman models. Poetry during this period—the age of Swift, Pope, and Gray—was dominated by one form, the heroic couplet; the genres of epic and satire; and an emphasis on human reason as the poet's chief guide. Never has the private voice been so subordinated to the public as in this period when, as Pope put it, a poet's highest aspiration should be to utter "What oft was thought, but ne'er so well expressed."

The first inklings of the romantic era coincide with the American and French revolutions, and poets of the latter half of the eighteenth century like Burns and Blake exhibit some of its characteristics. But it was not until the publication of *Lyrical Ballads* (1798), a book containing the best early work of Wordsworth and Coleridge, that the romantic era can be said to have truly flowered. Wordsworth's famous formulation of a poem as "the spontaneous overflow of powerful feeling recollected in tranquillity" remains one of romanticism's key definitions, with its emphasis on emotion, immediacy, and reflection; Wordsworth's own poetry, with its focus on the natural world, was tremendously influential. Most of the English and American poets of the first half of the nineteenth century have ties to romanticism in its various guises, and even a poet as late as Whitman (b. 1819) inherits many of its liberal, democratic attitudes. Poets of the Victorian era (1837–1901) continued to explore many of the same themes and genres as their romantic forebears, but certainly much of the optimism of the early years of the nineteenth century had dissipated by the time poets like Hardy, Housman, and Yeats, with their omnipresent irony and pessimism, came on the scene in the century's last decades.

The twentieth century and the beginning of the twenty-first century have been ruled by the upheavals that modernism caused in every art form. If anything characterized the first half of the twentieth century, it was its tireless experimentation with the forms of poetry. There is a continuum in English-language poetry from Chaucer through Frost and Robinson, but Pound, Williams, and Moore, to mention only three chief modernists, published poetry that would have totally mystified readers of their grandparents' day, just as Picasso and Matisse produced paintings that represented radical breaks with the forms of the past. Although many of the experiments of movements like imagism and surrealism seem quaint today, they parallel the general direction taken by most of the other arts during the same period.

For the sake of convenience more than anything else, it has been useful to refer to the era following the end of World War II as the postmodern era. Certainly many of the hard-won modernist gains—open form and increased candor in language and subject matter—have been taken for granted by poets writing in the contemporary period. The confessional poem, a frankly autobiographical genre that reveals what poets in earlier ages might have striven desperately to conceal, surfaced in the late 1950s in the works of Lowell, Snodgrass, Plath, and Sexton, and remains one of the chief post-modern genres. Still, as the selections here will attest, considerable variety exists in the contemporary scene, and it will perhaps be many years before critics have the necessary historical distance to assess the unique characteristics of the present period.

Writing About Poetry

Writing assignments vary widely and your teacher's instructions may range from general ("Discuss any two poems in your text which contain an effective use of imagery") to very specific ("Write an explication, in not less than 1000 words, of one of Edwin Arlington Robinson's sonnets, focusing on his use of form and his psychological insights into character"). Such processes as choosing, limiting, and developing a topic; "brainstorming" by taking notes on random ideas and refining those ideas further through group discussion or conferences with your instructor; using the library and the Internet to locate supporting secondary sources; and revising a first draft in light of critical remarks are undoubtedly techniques you have practiced in other composition classes. Basic types of organizational schemes learned in "theme-writing" courses can also be applied to writing about poetry. Formal assignments of these types should avoid contractions and jargon, and should be written in a clear, straightforward style. Most literary essays are not of the personal experience type, and you should follow common sense in avoiding the first person and slang. It goes without saying that you should carefully proofread your rough and final drafts to eliminate errors in spelling, punctuation, usage, and grammar.

Writing assignments on poetry usually fall into two categories: explication (or close reading) of single poems and analysis of poetic techniques in one or more poems. Because explication involves the careful "unfolding" of individual poems on a line-by-line basis, an assignment of this type will usually focus on a single short poem or a passage from a longer one. Some poems yield most of their meaning on a single reading; others, however, may contain complexities and nuances that deserve close inspection of how the poet utilizes the elements discussed in this introduction. A typical explication might examine both form and content. Because assignments in analysis usually involve many of the same techniques as explication, we will look at explication more closely. The following is a checklist of questions that you might ask yourself before explicating a poem; the sample passages of analysis apply to a poem from this book, Edwin Arlington Robinson's "Firelight."

Form

1. How many lines does the poem contain? How are they arranged into stanzas? Is either the whole poem or the stanza an example of a traditional poetic form?

> "Firelight" is an Italian sonnet. It is divided into two stanzas, an octave and sestet, and there is a tonal shift, or what is known in sonnets as a "turn" or <u>volta</u>, at the beginning of line nine, though here there is no single word that signals the shift.

2. Is there anything striking in the visual arrangement of the poem—indentation, spacing, etc.? Are capitalization and punctuation unusual?

> Capitalization and punctuation are standard in the poem, and Robinson follows the traditional practice of capitalizing the first word of each line.

3. In what meter, if any, is the poem written? Does the poet use any notable examples of substitution in the meter? Are the lines primarily end-stopped or enjambed?

> The meter is fairly regular iambic pentameter ("Hĕr thóughts / ă m̊o / mĕnt sińce / ŏf one / who shińes") with occasional substitution of trochees ("Wíseř / fŏr śi / leńce") and spondees ("thĕir jóy / recalls / Nó snáke, || / nó swórd").
>
> Enjambment occurs at the ends of lines two, five, six, seven, nine, ten, twelve, and thirteen; this has the effect of masking the regular meter and rhymes and enforcing a conversational tone, an effect

that is assisted by the caesurae in lines six, seven,
nine, and (most importantly) fourteen. The caesura in
this last line calls attention to "Apart," which
ironically contrasts with the poem's opening phrase:
"Ten years together."

4. What is the rhyme scheme, if any, of the poem? What types of
rhyme are used?

The rhyme scheme of this poem is abbaabba
cdecde. Robinson uses exact masculine rime; the only
possible exception is "intervals," where the meter
and rhyme scheme force a secondary stress on the
third syllable.

5. Are significant sound patterns evident? Is there any repetition of
whole lines, phrases, or words?

Alliteration is present in "firelight" and
"four" in line three and "wan" and "one" in line
eleven, and there are several instances of assonance
("Wiser for silence"; "endowed / And bowered") and
consonance ("Serenely and perennially endowed"; "the
wan face of one somewhere alone"). However, these
sound patterns do not call excessive attention to
themselves and depart from the poem's relaxed, conversational sound. "Firelight" contains no prominent
use of repetition, with the possible exception of the
pronoun "they" and its variant forms "their" and
"them" and the related use of the third-person singular pronouns "he" and "she" in the last five lines of
the poem. This pronoun usage, confusing at first
glance, indirectly carries the poem's theme of the
separateness of the lovers' thoughts. The only notable instance of parallel phrasing occurs in line
seven with "No snake, no sword."

Content

1. To what genre (lyric, narrative, dramatic) does the poem belong?
Does it contain elements of more than one genre?

"Firelight" is a narrative poem. Even though it has little plot in the conventional sense, it contains two characters in a specific setting who perform actions that give the reader insight into the true nature of their relationship. The sonnet form has traditionally been used for lyric poetry.

2. Who is the persona of the poem? Is there an auditor? If so, who? What is the relationship between persona and auditor? Does the poem have a specific setting? If so, where and when is it taking place? Is there any action that has taken place before the poem opens? What actions take place during the poem?

The persona here is a third-person omniscient narrator such as might be encountered in a short story; the narrator has the ability to read "Her thoughts a moment since" and directly comments that the couple is "Wiser for silence." The unnamed characters in the poem are a man and woman who have been married for ten years. The poem is set in their home, apparently in a comfortable room with a fireplace where they are spending a quiet evening together. Neither character speaks during the poem; the only action is their looking at "each other's eyes at intervals / Of gratefulness." Much of the poem's ironic meaning hinges on the couple's silence, "what neither says aloud."

3. Does the poem contain any difficulties with grammar or syntax? What individual words or phrases are striking because of their denotation or connotation?

The syntax of "Firelight" is straightforward and contains no inversions or ellipses. The poem's sentence structure is deceptively simple. The first four lines make up a single sentence with one main clause; the second four lines also make up a single sentence, this time with two main clauses; the final six lines also make up a single sentence, broken into two equal parts by the semicolon, and consisting of both main and dependent clauses. The poem's vocabulary is not

unusual, though "obliteration" (literally an erasure)
seems at first a curious choice to describe the effects of love. One should note the allusion implied
by "bowered," "snake," and "sword" in the octave and
the rather complicated use of the subjunctive "were"
in lines nine, ten, and twelve. Again, this slight
alteration in grammar bears indirectly on the theme
of the poem. "Yet" in the first line provides an in-
teresting touch since it injects a slight negative
note into the picture of marital bliss.

4. Does the poem use any figures of speech? If so, how do they add to
the overall meaning? Is the action of the poem to be taken literally,
symbolically, or both ways?

"Firelight" uses several figures of speech.
"Cloud" is a commonly employed metaphor for "forebod-
ing." "Firelight" and "four walls" are a metonymy and
synecdoche, respectively, for the couple's comfortable home. The allusion to the "snake" and "sword"
direct the reader to the Garden of Eden story. "Wiser
for silence" is a slight paradox. "The graven tale of
lines / On the wan face" is an implied metaphor which
compares the lines on a person's face to the written
("graven") story of her life. To say that a person
"shines" instead of "excels" is another familiar
metaphor. "Firelight" is to be understood primarily
on the literal level. The characters are symbolic
only in that the man and woman are perhaps representative of many married couples, who outwardly express
happiness yet inwardly carry regrets and fantasies
from past relationships.

5. Is the title of the poem appropriate? What are its subject, tone of
voice, and theme? Is the theme stated or implied?

"Firelight" is a good title since it carries
both the connotation of domestic tranquillity and a
hint of danger. "To bring to the light" means to reveal the truth, and the narrator in this poem does

this. Robinson's attitude toward the couple is
ironic. On the surface they seem to be the picture of
ideal happiness, but he reveals that this happiness
has been purchased, in the man's case, at the expense
of an earlier lover and, in the woman's, by settling
for someone who has achieved less than another man
for whom she apparently had unrequited love. Robinson's ironic view of marital stability is summed up
in the phrase "Wiser for silence." Several themes are
implied: the difference between surface appearance
and deeper insight; the cynical idea that in love ignorance of what one's partner is thinking may be the
key to bliss; the sense that individual happiness is
not without its costs. All of these are possible ways
to state Robinson's bittersweet theme.

Your instructor may ask you to employ specific strategies in your explication and may require a certain type of organization for the paper. In writing the body of the explication, you will probably proceed through the poem from beginning to end, summarizing and paraphrasing some lines and quoting others fully when you feel an explanation is required. It should be stressed that there are many ways, in theory, to approach a poem and that no two explications of the same poem will agree in every detail. Some instructors may favor an explication that links the poem to events in the author's life, to the sociohistorical context in which it was written, or to some other critical approach.

An assignment in analysis, which looks closely at the way a single element—dramatic situation, meter, form, imagery, one or more figures of speech, theme—functions in poetry, would probably require that you write on two or more poems; in such cases a comparison-contrast or definition-illustration paper may be called for. An assignment of this type might examine two related poems by the same poet, or it might inspect the way that several poets have used a poetic device or theme. Comparison-contrast essays look for both similarities and differences in two poems. Definition-illustration papers usually begin with a general discussion of the topic, say, a popular theme like the *carpe diem* motif, and then go on to illustrate how this motif may be found in several different poems. Assignments in analysis often lead to longer papers which may require the use of secondary sources. Appendix 1 lists some groups of poems that have elements in common.

You may be required to use secondary sources from the library or Internet in writing your paper. A subject search through your library's books is a good starting place, especially for material on older poets who have attracted extensive critical attention. Reference books like *Twentieth Century Authors, Contemporary Authors, Critical Survey of Poetry,* and the *Dictionary of Literary Biography* provide compact overviews of poets' careers. *Contemporary Literary Criticism* and *Poetry Criticism* contain excerpts from critical pieces on poets' works, and the *MLA Index* will direct you to articles on poets and poems in scholarly journals. There are several popular indexes of book reviews; one of these, the annual *Book Review Digest,* reprints brief passages from the most representative reviews. A useful index to poetry explications published in periodicals and books is *Poetry Explication: A Checklist of Interpretations Since 1925 of British and American Poems Past and Present;* many of the articles listed there first appeared in *The Explicator,* a periodical whose indexes are also worth inspecting. In recent years, the Internet has facilitated the chores of research, and many online databases, reference works, and periodicals may be quickly located using search engines like Yahoo (www.yahoo.com) and Google (www.google.com). The Internet also holds a wealth of information in the form of individual websites devoted to authors, most of which are run by universities or organizations. Navigating the Internet can be a forbidding task, and a book like Lester Faigley's *The Longman Guide to the Web* is an invaluable traveler's companion. Students should be aware, however, that websites vary widely in quality. Some are legitimate academic sources displaying sound scholarship; others are little more than "fan pages" that may contain erroneous or misleading information.

Careful documentation of your sources is essential; if you use any material other than what is termed "common knowledge," you must cite it in your paper. Common knowledge includes biographical information, an author's publications, prizes and awards received, and other information that can be found in more than one reference book. Anything else—direct quotes or material you have put in your own words by paraphrasing—requires both a parenthetical citation in the body of your paper and an entry on your works cited pages. Doing less than this is to commit an act of plagiarism, for which the penalties are usually severe. Internet materials, which are so easily cut and pasted into a manuscript, provide an easy temptation but are immediately noticeable. Nothing is easier to spot in a paper than an uncited "lift" from a source; in most cases, the vocabulary and sentence structure will be radically different from the rest of the paper.

The sixth edition of the *MLA Handbook for Writers of Research Papers*, which can be found in the reference section of almost any library and which, if you plan to write papers for other English courses, is a good addition to your personal library, contains formats for bibliographies and manuscripts that most instructors consider standard; indeed, most of the handbooks of grammar and usage commonly used in college courses follow MLA style and may be sufficient for your needs. If you have doubts, ask your instructor about what format is preferred. The type of parenthetical citation used today to indicate the source of quotations is simple to learn and dispenses with such time-consuming and repetitive chores as footnotes and endnotes. In using parenthetical citations remember that your goal is to direct your reader from the quoted passage in the paper to its source in your bibliography, and from there, if necessary, to the book or periodical from which the quote is taken. A good parenthetical citation gives only the *minimal* information needed to accomplish this. Following are a few examples from student papers on Edwin Arlington Robinson's poetry.

> Robinson's insights into character are never sharper than in "Miniver Cheevy," a portrait of a town drunk who loves "the days of old / When swords were bright and steeds were prancing" (5, 6) and dreams incongruously "of Thebes and Camelot, / And Priam's neighbors" (11-12).

Here you should note a couple of conventions about writing about poetry. One is that the present tense is used in discussing the poem; in general, use the present tense throughout your critical writing except when you are giving biographical or historical information. Second, note how only parts of lines are quoted here to support the sentence and how the parts fit smoothly into the author's sentence structure. In general, brackets and ellipses [. . .] are not necessary at the beginning or end of these quotes because it is clear that they are quoted fragmentarily; they should, however, be used if something is omitted from the middle of a quote ("the days of old / When [. . .] steeds were prancing"). The virgule or slash (/) is used to indicate line breaks; a double slash (//) indicates stanza breaks. Quotes of up to three lines should be treated in this manner. If a quote is longer than three lines, it should be indented ten spaces (with no quotation marks) and printed as it appears in the original poem:

> Robinson opens one of his most effective and piti-
> less character sketches with an unsparing portrait:
> > Miniver Cheevy, child of scorn,
> > Grew lean while he assailed the seasons;
> > He wept that he was ever born,
> > And he had reasons. (1-4)

The parenthetical citation here lists only line numbers because only one work by Robinson appears in the bibliography (note that the *MLA Handbook* suggests that you also give line numbers). If several works by the poet had been listed among the works cited, the parenthetical citation would clarify which one was being referred to by adding a shortened form of the poem's title: ("Miniver," 1-4). The reader finds the following entry among the sources:

> Robinson, Edwin Arlington. "Miniver Cheevy."
> > Collected Poems. New York: MacMillan, 1934. 347.

Similarly, quotes and paraphrases from secondary critical sources should follow the same rules of common sense.

> Louis O. Coxe observes that Robinson, even in
> using the most demanding forms, manages to avoid the
> artificial-sounding poetic diction of most son-
> neteers: "The best of Robinson's sonnets take an
> anti-rhetorical line though they often ride to elo-
> quence as they progress" (50-51).

In this case, the author of the quote is identified, so only the page numbers are included in the parenthetical citation. The reader knows where to look among the sources:

> Coxe, Louis O. Edwin Arlington Robinson: The Life of
> > Poetry. New York: Pegasus, 1969.

To simplify the whole matter of parenthetical citation, it is recommended that quotes from secondary sources be introduced, wherever possible, in a manner that identifies the author so that only the page number of the quote is needed inside of the parentheses.

Of course, different types of sources—reference book entries, poems in anthologies, articles in periodicals, and book reviews—require different bibliographical information, so be sure to check the *MLA Handbook* if you have questions. Here are a few more examples of the most commonly used bibliographical formats:

A BOOK WITH AUTHOR AND EDITOR

Robinson, Edwin Arlington. Edwin Arlington Robinson's
    Letters to Edith Brower. Ed. Richard Cary. Cam-
    bridge: Harvard UP, 1968.

A CASEBOOK OR COLLECTION OF CRITICAL ESSAYS

Barnard, Ellsworth, ed. Edwin Arlington Robinson:
    Centenary Essays. Athens: U of Georgia P, 1969.

A POEM REPRINTED IN AN ANTHOLOGY OR TEXTBOOK

Robinson, Edwin Arlington. "Richard Cory."
    Literature: An Introduction to Poetry, Fiction,
    and Drama. 9th ed. Ed. X. J. Kennedy and Dana
    Gioia. New York: Longman, 2005. 885.

AN ARTICLE IN A REFERENCE BOOK

Seymour-Smith, Martin. "Robinson, Edwin Arlington."
    Who's Who in Twentieth Century Literature. New
    York: McGraw, 1976.

AN ARTICLE IN A SCHOLARLY JOURNAL

Read, Arthur M., II. "Robinson's 'The Man Against the
    Sky.'" Explicator 26 (Feb. 1968): 49.

A BOOK REVIEW IN A PERIODICAL

Hutchison, Percy. "Robinson's Satire and Symbolism."
    Rev. of King Jasper, by Edwin Arlington Robin-
    son. New York Times Book Review 10 Nov. 1935: 8.

A WEBSITE

"A Page for Edwin." 5 Feb. 2001. 6 Mar. 2004.
    <http://www.du.edu/~dokonski/robin.html>.

An Online Reference Book

"Robinson, Edwin Arlington." <u>Encyclopedia Britannica</u>
   <u>Online</u>. 12 Dec. 2000. 25 Feb. 2004.
   <http://www.britannica.com/bcom/eb/article/
   8/0,5716,65558+1+63916,00.html?query=
   edwin%20arlington%20robinson>.

Poetry

Anonymous

Some of the popular ballads and lyrics of England and Scotland, composed for the most part between 1300 and 1500, were first collected in their current forms by Thomas Percy, whose Reliques of Ancient English Poetry *(1765) helped to revive interest in folk poetry. Francis James Child (1825–1896), an American, gathered over a thousand variant versions of the three hundred-odd core of poems. The Romantic poets of the early nineteenth century showed their debt to the folk tradition by writing imitative "art ballads" (see Keats's "La Belle Dame sans Merci" or Burns's "John Barleycorn"), which incorporate many of their stylistic devices.*

Western Wind

Western wind, when will thou blow,
   The small rain down can rain?
Christ, if my love were in my arms
   And I in my bed again!

—1450?

Bonny Barbara Allan

It was in and about the Martinmas° time,
   When the green leaves were a falling,
That Sir John Græme, in the West Country,
   Fell in love with Barbara Allan.

He sent his men down through the town,   5
   To the place where she was dwelling.
"O haste and come to my master dear,
   Gin° ye be Barbara Allan."

O hooly,° hooly rose she up,
   To the place where he was lying,   10
And when she drew the curtain by:
   "Young man, I think you're dying."

1 **Martinmas** November 11   8 **Gin** if   9 **hooly** slowly

"O it's I'm sick, and very, very sick,
    And 'tis a'° for Barbara Allan."
"O the better for me ye s'° never be,   15
    Though your heart's blood were a-spilling.

"O dinna° ye mind, young man," said she,
    "When ye was in the tavern a drinking,
That ye made the healths gae° round and round,
    And slighted Barbara Allan?"   20

He turned his face unto the wall,
    And death was with him dealing:
"Adieu, adieu, my dear friends all,
    And be kind to Barbara Allan."

And slowly, slowly raise she up,   25
    And slowly, slowly left him,
And sighing said she could not stay,
    Since death of life had reft him.

She had not gane° a mile but twa,°
    When she heard the dead-bell ringing,   30
And every jow° that the dead-bell geid,°
    It cried, "Woe to Barbara Allan!"

"O mother, mother, make my bed!
    O make it saft° and narrow!
Since my love died for me to-day,   35
    I'll die for him to-morrow."

                                                              —*1500?*

Sir Patrick Spens

The king sits in Dumferling town,
    Drinking the blude-reid° wine:
"O whar will I get guid sailor,
    To sail this ship of mine?"

14 a' all   **15 s'** shall   **17 dinna** do not   **19 gae** go   **29 gane** gone   **twa** two   **31 jow** stroke
geid gave   **34 saft** soft
2 blude-reid blood-red

Up and spak an eldern knicht,°   5
  Sat at the king's richt° knee:
"Sir Patrick Spens is the best sailor
  That sails upon the sea."

The king has written a braid° letter,
  And signed it wi' his hand,   10
And sent it to Sir Patrick Spens,
  Was walking on the sand.

The first line that Sir Patrick read,
  A loud lauch° lauched he;
The next line that Sir Patrick read,   15
  The tear blinded his ee.°

"O wha is this has done this deed,
  This ill deed done to me,
To send me out this time o' the year,
  To sail upon the sea?   20

"Mak haste, mak haste, my mirry men all,
  Our guid ship sails the morn."
"O say na sae,° my master dear,
  For I fear a deadly storm.

"Late, late yestre'en° I saw the new moon,   25
  Wi' the auld moon in hir arm,
And I fear, I fear, my dear master,
  That we will come to harm."

O our Scots nobles wer richt laith°
  To weet° their cork-heeled shoon,°   30
But lang or a'° the play were played,
  Their hats they swam aboon.°

O lang, lang may their ladies sit,
  Wi' their fans into their hand,
Or ere they see Sir Patrick Spens   35
  Come sailing to the land.

---

5 **eldern knicht** elderly knight   6 **richt** right   9 **braid** long   14 **lauch** laugh   16 **ee** eye   23 **na sae** not so   25 **yestre'en** last evening   29 **laith** loath   30 **weet** wet   **shoon** shoes   31 **lang or a'** long before   32 **Their hats they swam aboon** their hats swam above them

O lang, lang may the ladies stand,
   Wi' their gold kems° in their hair,
Waiting for their ain dear lords,
   For they'll see them na mair.   40

Half o'er, half o'er to Aberdour
   It's fifty fadom deep,
And there lies guid Sir Patrick Spens
   Wi' the Scots lords at his feet.

—1500?

Sir Thomas Wyatt (1503?–1542)

Sir Thomas Wyatt served Henry VIII as a diplomat in Italy. Wyatt read the love poetry of Petrarch (1304–1374) and is generally credited with having imported both the fashions of these lyrics—hyperbolic "conceits" or metaphorical descriptions of the woman's beauty and the lover's suffering—and their form, the sonnet, to England. "They Flee from Me," an example of one of his original lyrics, displays Wyatt's unique grasp of the rhythms of speech.

They Flee from Me

They flee from me, that sometime did me seek,
With naked foot stalking in my chamber.
I have seen them gentle, tame and meek,
That now are wild, and do not remember
That sometime they put themself in danger   5
To take bread at my hand; and now they range,
Busily seeking with a continual change.

Thanke'd be Fortune it hath been otherwise,
Twenty times better; but once in special,
In thin array, after a pleasant guise,°   10

---

38 kems combs
10 guise appearance

When her loose gown from her shoulders did fall,
And she me caught in her arms long and small,
And therewith all sweetly did me kiss
And softly said, "Dear heart, how like you this?"

It was no dream, I lay broad waking.   15
But all is turned, thorough° my gentleness,
Into a strange fashion of forsaking;
And I have leave to go, of her goodness,
And she also to use newfangleness.
But since that I so kindely° am served,   20
I fain° would know what she hath deserved.

—*1557*

Whoso List to Hunt

Whoso list° to hunt, I know where is an hind,°
But as for me, alas, I may no more:
The vain travail hath wearied me so sore.
I am of them that farthest cometh behind;
Yet may I by no means my wearied mind   5
Draw from the deer: but as she fleeth afore,
Fainting I follow. I leave off therefore,
Since in a net I seek to hold the wind.
Who list her to hunt, I put him out of doubt,
As well as I, may spend his time in vain: 10
And, graven with diamonds, in letters plain
There is written her fair neck round about:
Noli me tangere, for Caesar's I am,°
And wild for to hold, though I seem tame.

—*1557*

16 **thorough** through   20 **kindely** in this manner   21 **fain** gladly
1 **list** desire   **hind** doe   13 *Noli me tangere* Touch me not; the poem is said to refer to the second
wife of Henry VIII, Anne Boleyn.

Edmund Spenser (1552–1599)

Edmund Spenser was born in London, and spent most of his adult life in Ireland, where he held a variety of minor government posts. The Faerie Queene, *a long allegorical romance about Elizabethan England, was uncompleted at his death. The eighty-odd sonnets that make up the sequence called* Amoretti *are generally thought to detail his courtship of his second wife, Elizabeth Boyle, whom he married in 1594.*

Amoretti: Sonnet 75

One day I wrote her name upon the strand,
But came the waves and washèd it away:
Agayne I wrote it with a second hand,°
But came the tyde, and made my paynes his pray.
"Vayne man," sayd she, "that doest in vaine assay,°   5
A mortall thing so to immortalize,
For I my selve shall lyke° to this decay
And eek° my name bee wypèd out lykewize."
"Not so," quod° I, "let baser things devize
To dy in dust, but you shall live by fame: 10
My verse your vertues rare shall eternize,
And in the hevens wryte your glorious name.
Where whenas death shall all the world subdew
Our love shall live, and later life renew."

—*1595*

---

3 **second hand** second time   5 **assay** attempt   7 **lyke** be similar to   8 **eek** also   9 **quod** said

Sir Philip Sidney (1554–1586)

Sir Philip Sidney embodied many of the aspects of the ideal man of the Renaissance; he was a courtier, scholar, patron of the arts, and soldier who died of wounds received at the battle of Zutphen. His sonnet sequence Astrophel and Stella *appeared in 1591, several years before Spenser's Amoretti, and helped to precipitate the fashion for sonnets that lasted in England well into the next century.*

Astrophel and Stella: Sonnet 1

1

Loving in truth, and fain° in verse my love to show,
That she dear she might take some pleasure of my pain,
Pleasure might cause her read, reading might make her know,
Knowledge might pity win, and pity grace obtain,
I sought fit words to paint the blackest face of woe: 5
Studying inventions fine, her wits to entertain,
Oft turning others' leaves,° to see if thence would flow
Some fresh and fruitful showers upon my sunburned brain.
But words came halting forth, wanting Invention's stay;
Invention, Nature's child, fled stepdame Study's blows;   10
And others' feet° still seemed but strangers in my way.
Thus, great with child to speak, and helpless in my throes,
Biting my truant pen, beating myself for spite:
"Fool," said my Muse to me, "look in thy heart, and write."

—*1582*

---

1 **fain** glad   7 **leaves** pages   11 **feet** metrical feet in poetry

Robert Southwell (1561?–1595)

Robert Southwell was a Roman Catholic priest in Elizabeth's Protestant England, who was executed for his religious beliefs. His devotional poems, most of them on the subject of spiritual love, were largely written during his three years in prison. Southwell was declared a saint in the Roman Catholic Church in 1970.

The Burning Babe

As I in hoary winter's night stood shivering in the snow,
Surprised I was with sudden heat which made my heart to glow;
And lifting up a fearful eye to view what fire was near,
A pretty babe all burning bright did in the air appear;
Who, scorchèd with excessive heat, such floods of tears did shed   5
As though his floods should quench his flames which with his tears
    were fed.
"Alas," quoth he, "but newly born in fiery heats I fry,
Yet none approach to warm their hearts or feel my fire but I!
My faultless breast the furnace is, the fuel wounding thorns,
Love is the fire, and sighs the smoke, the ashes shame and scorns;   10
The fuel justice layeth on, and mercy blows the coals,
The metal in this furnace wrought are men's defilèd souls,
For which, as now on fire I am to work them to their good,
So will I melt into a bath to wash them in my blood."
With this he vanished out of sight and swiftly shrunk away,   15
And straight I callèd unto mind that it was Christmas day.

—1602

Michael Drayton (1563–1631)

*Michael Drayton, like his contemporary, Shakespeare, excelled in several
literary genres. He collaborated on plays with Thomas Dekker and wrote
long poems on English history, biography, and topography. Drayton labored almost three decades on the sixty-three sonnets in* Idea, *publishing
them in their present form in 1619.*

Idea: Sonnet 61

Since there's no help, come let us kiss and part;
Nay, I have done, you get no more of me,
And I am glad, yea glad with all my heart
That thus so cleanly I myself can free;
Shake hands forever, cancel all our vows,   5
And when we meet at any time again,
Be it not seen in either of our brows
That we one jot of former love retain.
Now at the last gasp of love's latest breath,
When, his pulse failing, passion speechless lies,   10
When faith is kneeling by his bed of death,
And innocence is closing up his eyes,
    Now if thou wouldst, when all have given him over,
    From death to life thou mightst him yet recover.

—1619

William Shakespeare (1564–1616)

William Shakespeare first printed his sonnets in 1609, during the last years of his active career as a playwright, but they had circulated privately a dozen years before. Given the lack of concrete details about Shakespeare's life outside the theatre, critics have found the sonnets fertile ground for biographical speculation, and the sequence of 154 poems does contain distinct characters—a handsome youth to whom most of the first 126 sonnets are addressed, a "Dark Lady" who figures strongly in the remaining poems, and the poet himself, whose name is the source of many puns in the poems. There is probably no definitive "key" to the sonnets, but there is also little doubt that their place is secure among the monuments of English lyric verse. Shakespeare's other nondramatic poems include narratives, allegories, and songs, of which "When Daisies Pied," the companion pieces from his early comedy Love's Labour's Lost, *are perhaps the best examples.*

Sonnet 18

Shall I compare thee to a summer's day?
Thou art more lovely and more temperate:
Rough winds do shake the darling buds of May,
And summer's lease hath all too short a date:
Sometimes too hot the eye of heaven shines,   5
And often is his gold complexion dimmed;
And every fair from fair° sometimes declines,
By chance or nature's changing course untrimmed;°
But thy eternal summer shall not fade,
Nor lose possession of that fair thou ow'st;°   10
Nor shall death brag thou wander'st in his shade,
When in eternal lines to time thou grow'st:
So long as men can breathe, or eyes can see,
So long lives this, and this gives life to thee.

—*1609*

---

7 **fair from fair** every fair thing from its fairness   8 **untrimmed** stripped   10 **ow'st** ownest

Sonnet 20

A woman's face, with nature's own hand painted,
Hast thou, the master mistress of my passion—
A woman's gentle heart, but not acquainted
With shifting change, as is false women's fashion;
An eye more bright than theirs, less false in rolling,°   5
Gilding the object whereupon it gazeth;
A man in hue all hues in his controlling,
Which steals men's eyes and women's souls amazeth.
And for a woman wert thou first created,
Till nature as she wrought thee fell a-doting,   10
And by addition me of thee defeated,
By adding one thing to my purpose nothing.
But since she pricked thee out for women's pleasure,
    Mine be thy love and thy love's use their treasure.

—*1609*

Sonnet 29

When, in disgrace with fortune and men's eyes,
I all alone beweep my outcast state,
And trouble deaf heaven with my bootless° cries,
And look upon myself, and curse my fate,
Wishing me like to one more rich in hope,   5
Featured like him, like him with friends possessed,
Desiring this man's art and that man's scope,
With what I most enjoy contented least;
Yet in these thoughts myself almost despising,
Haply° I think on thee—and then my state,   10
Like to the lark at break of day arising
From sullen earth, sings hymns at heaven's gate;
For thy sweet love remembered such wealth brings
That then I scorn to change my state with kings.

—*1609*

5 rolling wandering
3 bootless useless   10 Haply fortunately

Sonnet 73

That time of year thou mayst in me behold
When yellow leaves, or none, or few, do hang
Upon those boughs which shake against the cold,
Bare ruined choirs, where late the sweet birds sang.
In me thou see'st the twilight of such day   5
As after sunset fadeth in the west;
Which by and by black night doth take away,
Death's second self, that seals up all in rest.
In me thou see'st the glowing of such fire,
That on the ashes of his youth doth lie,   10
As the deathbed whereon it must expire,
Consumed with that which it was nourished by.
This thou perceiv'st, which makes thy love more strong,
To love that well which thou must leave ere long.

—*1609*

Sonnet 116

Let me not to the marriage of true minds
Admit impediments. Love is not love
Which alters when it alteration finds,
Or bends with the remover to remove:
Oh, no! it is an ever-fixèd mark,   5
That looks on tempests and is never shaken:
It is the star to every wandering bark°,
Whose worth's unknown, although his height be taken.°
Love's not Time's fool, though rosy lips and cheeks
Within his bending sickle's compass° come;   10
Love alters not with his brief hours and weeks,
But bears it out even to the edge of doom.
If this be error and upon me proved,
I never writ, nor no man ever loved.

—*1609*

7 **bark** boat   8 **height be taken** elevation be measured   **10 compass** range

Sonnet 129

Th' expense of spirit in a waste° of shame
Is lust in action; and, till action, lust
Is perjured, murd'rous, bloody, full of blame,
Savage, extreme, rude, cruel, not to trust;
Enjoyed no sooner but despiséd straight;   5
Past reason hunted, and no sooner had,
Past reason hated, as a swallowed bait
On purpose laid to make the taker mad;
Mad in pursuit, and in possession so;
Had, having, and in quest to have, extreme;   10
A bliss in proof—and proved, a very woe;
Before, a joy proposed; behind, a dream.
All this the world well knows; yet none knows well
    To shun the heaven that leads men to this hell.

—*1609*

Sonnet 130

My mistress' eyes are nothing like the sun;
Coral is far more red than her lips' red;
If snow be white, why then her breasts are dun;
If hairs be wires, black wires grow on her head.
I have seen roses damasked,° red and white,   5
But no such roses see I in her cheeks;
And in some perfumes is there more delight
Than in the breath that from my mistress reeks.
I love to hear her speak, yet well I know
That music hath a far more pleasing sound;   10
I grant I never saw a goddess go;
My mistress, when she walks, treads on the ground.
And yet, by heaven, I think my love as rare
As any she belied° with false compare.°

—*1609*

1 **waste** desert
5 **damasked** multi-colored   14 **belied** lied about   **compare** comparisons

When Daisies Pied°

SPRING

When daisies pied and violets blue
    And ladysmocks all silver-white
And cuckoobuds of yellow hue
    Do paint the meadows with delight,
The cuckoo then, on every tree,   5
Mocks married men;° for thus sings he,
        Cuckoo;
Cuckoo, cuckoo: Oh word of fear,
Unpleasing to a married ear!
When shepherds pipe on oaten straws,   10
    And merry larks are plowmen's clocks,
When turtles tread,° and rooks, and daws,
And maidens bleach their summer smocks,
The cuckoo then, on every tree,
Mocks married men; for thus sings he,   15
        Cuckoo;
Cuckoo, cuckoo: Oh word of fear,
Unpleasing to a married ear!

    WINTER

When icicles hang by the wall
And Dick the shepherd blows his nail°   20
And Tom bears logs into the hall,
    And milk comes frozen home in pail,
When blood is nipped and ways be foul,
Then nightly sings the staring owl,
        Tu-who;   25
Tu-whit, tu-who: a merry note,
While greasy Joan doth keel° the pot.

When all aloud the wind doth blow,
    And coughing drowns the parson's saw,°
And birds sit brooding in the snow,   30
    And Marian's nose looks red and raw,

Pied multi-colored   6 Mocks married men The pun is on the similarity between "cuckoo" and
"cuckold."   12 turtles tread turtledoves mate   20 nail fingernails   27 keel stir   29 saw saying

When roasted crabs° hiss in the bowl,
Then nightly sings the staring owl,
    Tu-who;
Tu-whit, tu-who: a merry note   35
While greasy Joan doth keel the pot.

—1598

Thomas Campion (1567–1620)

Thomas Campion was a poet and physician who wrote music and lyrics in a manner that was "chiefly aimed to couple my words and notes lovingly together." The imagery in "There Is a Garden in Her Face" represents a late flowering of the conceits of Petrarchan love poetry, so wittily mocked by Shakespeare in "Sonnet 130."

There Is a Garden in Her Face

There is a garden in her face,
Where roses and white lilies grow,
A heavenly paradise is that place,
Wherein all pleasant fruits do flow.
There cherries grow which none may buy   5
Till "Cherry-ripe!" themselves do cry.

Those cherries fairly do enclose
Of orient pearl a double row,
Which when her lovely laughter shows,
They look like rosebuds filled with snow.   10
Yet them nor peer nor prince can buy,
Till "Cherry-ripe!" themselves do cry.

Her eyes like angels watch them still;
Her brows like bended bows do stand,

32 crabs crabapples

Threatening with piercing frowns to kill   15
All that attempt with eye or hand
Those sacred cherries to come nigh,
Till "Cherry-ripe!" themselves do cry.

—*1617*

John Donne (1572–1631)

*John Donne was trained in the law for a career in government service,
but Donne became the greatest preacher of his day, ending his life as
dean of St. Paul's Cathedral in London. Only two of Donne's poems
and a handful of his sermons were printed during his life, but both circulated widely in manuscript and his literary reputation among his contemporaries was considerable. His poetry falls into two distinct periods:
the witty love poetry of his youth and the sober religious meditations of
his maturity. In both, however, Donne shows remarkable originality in
rhythm, diction, and the use of metaphor and conceit, which marks him
as the chief poet of what has become commonly known as the metaphysical style.*

The Canonization

For God's sake hold your tongue, and let me love,
   Or chide my palsy, or my gout,
My five gray hairs, or ruined fortune, flout,
     With wealth your state, your mind with arts improve,
       Take you a course, get you a place,   5
       Observe His Honor, or His Grace,
Or the king's real,° or his stampèd face
   Contèmplate; what you will, approve,°
   So you will let me love.

Alas, alas, who's injured by my love?   10
   What merchant's ships have my sighs drowned?
Who says my tears have overflowed his ground?
   When did my colds a forward° spring remove?

---

7 **real** coinage   8 **approve** attempt   13 **forward** early

When did the heats which my veins fill
  Add one more to the plaguy bill?°   15
Soldiers find wars, and lawyers find out still
  Litigious men, which quarrels move,
  Though she and I do love.

Call us what you will, we're made such by love;
  Call her one, me another fly,   20
We're tapers too, and at our own cost die,°
And we in us find th' eagle and the dove.
The phoenix° riddle hath more wit
By us: we two being one, are it.
So, to one neutral thing both sexes fit,   25
  We die and rise the same, and prove
  Mysterious by this love.

We can die by it, if not live by love,
  And if unfit for tomb and hearse
Our legend be, it will be fit for verse;   30
  And if no piece of chronicle° we prove,
    We'll build in sonnets pretty rooms;
    As well a well-wrought urn becomes
The greatest ashes, as half-acre tombs;
  And by these hymns, all shall approve   35
  Us canonized for love:

And thus invoke us, "You whom reverend love
  Made one another's hermitage;
You, to whom love was peace, that now is rage;
  Who did the whole world's soul contract, and drove   40
    Into the glasses of your eyes
    (So made such mirrors, and such spies,°
That they did all to you epitomize)
  Countries, towns, courts: Beg from above
  A pattern of your love!"   45

—*1633*

---

15 **plaguy bill** list of dead by plague   21 **die** i.e., to have sexual intercourse   23 **phoenix** legendary bird that is reborn from its own ashes   31 **chronicle** history   42 **spies** telescopes

The Flea

Mark but this flea, and mark in this,
How little that which thou deniest me is;
Me it sucked first, and now sucks thee,
And in this flea our two bloods mingled be;
Thou know'st that this cannot be said   5
A sin, or shame, or loss of maidenhead,
   Yet this enjoys before it woo,
    And pampered swells with one blood made of two,
    And this, alas, is more than we would do.

Oh stay, three lives in one flea spare,   10
Where we almost, nay more than married are.
This flea is you and I, and this
Our marriage bed and marriage temple is;
Though parents grudge, and you, we are met,
And cloistered in these living walls of jet.°   15
   Though use° make you apt to kill me
    Let not to that, self-murder added be,
    And sacrilege, three sins in killing three.

Cruel and sudden, hast thou since
Purpled thy nail° in blood of innocence?   20
Wherein could this flea guilty be,
Except in that drop which it sucked from thee?
Yet thou triumph'st, and say'st that thou
Find'st not thy self nor me the weaker now;
   'Tis true; then learn how false fears be: 25
    Just so much honor, when thou yield'st to me,
    Will waste, as this flea's death took life from thee.

—*1633*

---

15 jet black   **16 use** familiarity, especially in the sexual sense   **20 Purpled thy nail** bloodied your fingernail

Holy Sonnet 10

Death, be not proud, though some have callèd thee
Mighty and dreadful, for thou art not so;
For those whom thou think'st thou dost overthrow
Die not, poor Death, nor yet canst thou kill me.
From rest and sleep, which but thy pictures be,   5
Much pleasure; then from thee much more must flow,
And soonest our best men with thee do go,
Rest of their bones, and soul's delivery.
Thou'art slave to fate, chance, kings, and desperate men,
And dost with poison, war, and sickness dwell,   10
And poppy° or charms can make us sleep as well
And better than thy stroke; why swell'st thou then?
One short sleep past, we wake eternally,
And death shall be no more; Death, thou shalt die.

—*1633*

Holy Sonnet 14

Batter my heart, three-personed God; for You
As yet but knock, breathe, shine, and seek to mend;
That I may rise, and stand, o'erthrow me, and bend
Your force to break, blow, burn, and make me new.
I, like an usurped town, to another due,   5
Labor to admit You, but O, to no end;
Reason, Your viceroy in me, me should defend,
But is captived, and proves weak or untrue.
Yet dearly I love You, and would be lovèd fain,°
But am betrothed unto Your enemy.   10
Divorce me, untie or break that knot again;
Take me to You, imprison me, for I,
Except You enthrall me, never shall be free,
Nor ever chaste, except You ravish me.

—*1633*

11 **poppy** opium
9 **fain** gladly

A Valediction:°
Forbidding Mourning

As virtuous men pass mildly away,
   And whisper to their souls to go,
Whilst some of their sad friends do say
   The breath goes now, and some say, No;

So let us melt, and make no noise,   5
   No tear-floods, nor sigh-tempests move,
'Twere profanation of our joys
   To tell the laity our love.

Moving of th' earth brings harms and fears,
   Men reckon what it did and meant;   10
But trepidation of the spheres,°
   Though greater far, is innocent.

Dull sublunary° lovers' love,
   (Whose soul is sense) cannot admit
Absence, because it doth remove   15
   Those things which elemented it.

But we by a love so much refined
   That our selves know not what it is,
Inter-assurèd of the mind,
   Care less, eyes, lips, and hands to miss.   20

Our two souls therefore, which are one,
   Though I must go, endure not yet
A breach, but an expansion,
   Like gold to airy thinness beat.

If they be two, they are two so   25
   As stiff twin compasses° are two;
Thy soul, the fixed foot, makes no show
   To move, but doth, if th' other do.

Valediction farewell speech; Donne is addressing his wife before leaving on a diplomatic mission.
11 trepidation of the spheres natural trembling of the heavenly spheres, a concept of Ptolemaic
astronomy   **13 sublunary** under the moon, hence, changeable (a Ptolemaic concept)   **26 stiff twin
compasses** drafting compasses

And though it in the center sit,
    Yet when the other far doth roam,   30
It leans and hearkens after it,
    And grows erect, as that comes home.

Such wilt thou be to me, who must
    Like th' other foot, obliquely run;
Thy firmness makes my circle just,°   35
    And makes me end where I begun.

—1633

Ben Jonson (1573–1637)

Ben Jonson was Shakespeare's chief rival on the stage, and their contentious friendship has been the subject of much speculation. Jonson became England's first unofficial poet laureate, receiving a royal stipend from James I, and was a great influence of a group of younger poets who became known as the "Tribe of Ben." His tragedies are little regarded today, and his comedies, while still performed occasionally, have nevertheless failed to hold the stage as brilliantly as Shakespeare's. Still, he was a poet of considerable talents, particularly in short forms. His elegy on Shakespeare contains a famous assessment: "He was not of an age, but for all time!"

On My First Son

Farewell, thou child of my right hand,° and joy;
My sin was too much hope of thee, loved boy:
Seven years thou'wert lent to me, and I thee pay,
Exacted by thy fate, on the just day.°
Oh, could I lose all father now! for why   5
Will man lament the state he should envy,
To have so soon 'scaped world's and flesh's rage,
And, if no other misery, yet age?

35 just complete
1 child of my right hand Benjamin, the child's name, means this in Hebrew.   4 the just day Jonson's
son died on his seventh birthday.

Rest in soft peace, and asked, say, "Here doth lie
Ben Jonson his best piece of poetry."   10
For whose sake henceforth all his vows be such
As what he loves may never like too much.

—*1616*

Slow, Slow, Fresh Fount

From Cynthia's Revels°

Slow, slow, fresh fount, keep time with my salt tears;
Yet slower, yet, O faintly, gentle springs!
List to the heavy part the music bears,
Woe weeps out her division,° when she sings.
    Droop herbs and flowers;   5
    Fall grief in showers;
Our beauties are not ours. O, I could still,
Like melting snow upon some craggy hill,
    Drop, drop, drop, drop,
Since nature's pride is now a withered daffodil.   10

—*1600*

Slow, Slow, Fresh Fount: From Cynthia's Revels spoken in this masque by the nymph Echo to the dead Narcissus   **4 division** part of a song

Mary Wroth (1587?–1651)

Mary Wroth was the niece of Sir Philip Sidney and the cousin of Sir Walter Raleigh, both distinguished poets and courtiers. A friend of poet Ben Jonson, who dedicated The Alchemist *to her, she was prominent in the court of King James I. Her prose romance,* Urania (1621), *stirred controversy because of its similarities to actual people and events. Wroth may have fallen into disfavor at court after the publication of* Urania, *and few facts are known about her later life.*

In This Strange Labyrinth How Shall I Turn

In this strange labyrinth how shall I turn,
Ways° are on all sides, while the way I miss:
If to the right hand, there in love I burn,
Let me go forward, therein danger is.
If to the left, suspicion hinders bliss: 5
Let me turn back, shame cries I ought return:
Nor faint, though crosses° with my fortunes kiss.
Stand still is harder, although sure to mourn.
Thus let me take the right, or left hand way,
Go forward, or stand still, or back retire: 10
I must these doubts endure without allay°
Or help, but travail find for my best hire
Yet that which most my troubled sense doth move,
Is to leave all and take the thread of Love°

—*1621*

2 **Ways** paths   7 **crosses** troubles   11 **allay** alleviation   14 **Love** an allusion to the myth of Theseus, who, with the help of Ariadne, unrolled a thread behind him as he entered the labyrinth of Crete.

Robert Herrick (1591–1674)

*Robert Herrick was the most distinguished member of the "Tribe of Ben."
Herrick is grouped with the Cavalier poets, whose graceful lyrics are
marked by wit and gentle irony. Surprisingly, Herrick was a minister; his
Royalist sympathies during the English Civil War caused him hardship
during the Puritan era, but his position in the church was returned to him
by Charles II after the Restoration.*

To the Virgins, to Make Much of Time

Gather ye rosebuds while ye may,
   Old time is still a-flying;
And this same flower that smiles today
   Tomorrow will be dying.

The glorious lamp of heaven, the sun,   5
   The higher he's a-getting,
The sooner will his race be run,
   And nearer he's to setting.

That age is best which is the first,
   When youth and blood are warmer;   10
But being spent, the worse, and worst
   Times still succeed the former.

Then be not coy, but use your time,
   And, while ye may, go marry;
For, having lost but once your prime,   15
   You may forever tarry.

—1648

George Herbert (1593–1633)

George Herbert was the great master of the English devotional lyric. Herbert was born into a distinguished family which included his mother, the formidable literary patroness Lady Magdalen Herbert, and his brother, the poet and statesman Edward, Lord Herbert of Cherbury. Like John Donne, with whom he shares the metaphysical label, Herbert early aimed at a political career but turned to the clergy, spending several happy years as rector of Bemerton before his death at age 40. The Temple, which contains most of his poems, was published posthumously in 1633.

Easter Wings

Lord, who createdst man in wealth and store,°
   Though foolishly he lost the same,
      Decaying more and more
         Till he became
           Most poor: 5
           With Thee
           O let me rise
         As larks, harmoniously,
   And sing this day Thy victories:
Then shall the fall further the flight in me.   10

   My tender age in sorrow did begin;
   And still with sicknesses and shame
      Thou didst so punish sin,
         That I became
           Most thin.   15
           With Thee
           Let me combine,
         And feel this day thy victory;
   For, if I imp my wing on thine,°
Affliction shall advance the flight in me.   20

—1633

---

1 store abundance   **19 imp my wing on thine** to graft feathers from a strong wing onto a weak one, a term from falconry

Love (III)

Love bade me welcome: yet my soul drew back,
  Guilty of dust and sin.
But quick-eyed Love, observing me grow slack
  From my first entrance in,
Drew nearer to me, sweetly questioning   5
  If I lacked anything.

"A guest," I answered, "worthy to be here":
  Love said, "You shall be he."
"I, the unkind, ungrateful? Ah, my dear,
  I cannot look on thee."   10
Love took my hand, and smiling did reply,
  "Who made the eyes but I?"

"Truth, Lord, but I have marred them; let my shame
  Go where it doth deserve."
"And know you not," says Love, "who bore the blame?"   15
  "My dear, then I will serve."
"You must sit down," says Love, "and taste my meat."
  So I did sit and eat.

—*1633*

The Pulley

  When God at first made man,
Having a glass of blessings standing by,
  "Let us," said he, "pour on him all we can.
Let the world's riches, which dispersèd lie,
  Contract into a span."°   5

  So strength first made a way;
Then beauty flowed, then wisdom, honor, pleasure.
  When almost all was out, God made a stay,
Perceiving that, alone of all his treasure,
  Rest in the bottom lay.   10

5 **span** the distance between thumb tip and the tip of the little finger

"For if I should," said he,
"Bestow this jewel also on my creature,
    He would adore my gifts instead of me,
And rest in Nature, not the God of Nature;
    So both should losers be.   15

"Yet let him keep the rest,
    But keep them with repining restlessness.
Let him be rich and weary, that at least,
    If goodness lead him not, yet weariness
May toss him to my breast."   20

                                                        —*1633*

Redemption

Having been tenant long to a rich lord,
    Not thriving, I resolvèd to be bold,
    And make a suit° unto him, to afford°
A new small-rented lease, and cancel the old.
In heaven at his manor I him sought;   5
    They told me there that he was lately gone
    About some land, which he had dearly bought
Long since on earth, to take possession.

I straight returned, and knowing his great birth,
    Sought him accordingly in great resorts;   10
    In cities, theaters, gardens, parks, and courts;
At length I heard a ragged noise and mirth
    Of thieves and murderers; there I him espied,°
    Who straight, *Your suit is granted,* said, and died.

                                                        —*1633*

---

3 **make a suit** formally request   **afford** grant (me)   13 **him espied** saw him

Edmund Waller (1606–1687)

Edmund Waller was another Royalist sympathizer who suffered after the English Civil War, during Oliver Cromwell's protectorate. Waller is noted for having pioneered the use of the heroic couplet as a popular verse form. He has been often praised for the smoothness of his rhythms and sound patterns.

Song

Go, lovely rose!
Tell her that wastes her time and me
   That now she knows,
When I resemble° her to thee,
How sweet and fair she seems to be.   5

   Tell her that's young,
And shuns to have her graces spied,
   That hadst thou sprung
In deserts, where no men abide,
Thou must have uncommended died.   10

   Small is the worth
Of beauty from the light retired;
   Bid her come forth,
Suffer herself to be desired,
And not blush so to be admired.   15

   Then die! that she
The common fate of all things rare
   May read in thee;
How small a part of time they share
That are so wondrous sweet and fair!   20

—1645

---

4 resemble compare

John Milton (1608–1674)

John Milton is best known as the author of Paradise Lost, *the greatest English epic poem. His life included service in the Puritan government of Cromwell, pamphleteering for liberal political causes, and brief imprisonment after the Restoration. Milton suffered from blindness in his later years. He excelled in the sonnet, a form to which he returned throughout his long literary life.*

How Soon Hath Time

How soon hath Time, the subtle thief of youth,
   Stol'n on his wing my three and twentieth year!
   My hasting days fly on with full career,
   But my late spring no bud or blossom shew'th.°
Perhaps my semblance might deceive the truth,   5
   That I to manhood am arrived so near,
   And inward ripeness doth much less appear,
   That some more timely-happy spirits endu'th.°
Yet be it less or more, or soon or slow,
   It shall be still in strictest measure even°   10
   To that same lot, however mean or high,
Toward which Time leads me, and the will of Heaven;
   All is, if I have grace to use it so,
   As ever in my great Taskmaster's eye.

—1645

On the Late Massacre in Piedmont°

Avenge, O Lord, thy slaughtered saints, whose bones
   Lie scattered on the Alpine mountains cold,
   Even them who kept thy truth so pure of old
   When all our fathers worshiped stocks and stones,°

4 **shew'th** shows   8 **endu'th** endows   10 **even** equal
Massacre in Piedmont 1700 Protestants from this North Italian state were massacred by Papal forces on Easter Day, 1655.   4 **stocks and stones** idols

Forget not: in thy book record their groans 5
    Who were thy sheep and in their ancient fold
    Slain by the bloody Piedmontese that rolled
    Mother with infant down the rocks. Their moans
The vales redoubled to the hills, and they
    To Heaven. Their martyred blood and ashes sow 10
    O'er all th'Italian fields where still doth sway
The triple tyrant:° that from these may grow
    A hundredfold, who having learnt thy way
    Early may fly the Babylonian woe.°

—*1655*

When I Consider How My Light Is Spent

When I consider how my light is spent
    Ere half my days, in this dark world and wide,
    And that one talent which is death to hide°
    Lodged with me useless, though my soul more bent
To serve therewith my Maker, and present 5
    My true account, lest he returning chide;
    "Doth God exact day-labor, light denied?"
    I fondly° ask; but Patience to prevent
That murmur, soon replies, "God doth not need
    Either man's work or his own gifts; who best 10
    Bear his mild yoke, they serve him best. His state
Is kingly. Thousands at his bidding speed
    And post o'er land and ocean without rest:
    They also serve who only stand and wait."

—*1673*

12 **triple tyrant** the Pope   14 **Babylonian woe** Early Protestants often linked ancient Babylon to modern Rome as centers of vice.
3 **talent which is death to hide** See the Parable of the Talents, Matthew 25:14–30.   8 **fondly** foolishly

Anne Bradstreet (1612–1672)

*Anne Bradstreet was an American Puritan who was one of the first settlers
of the Massachusetts Bay Colony, along with her husband Simon, later
governor of the colony. The Tenth Muse Lately Sprung Up in America,
published abroad by a relative without her knowledge, was the first American book of poetry published in England, and the circumstances of its appearance lie behind the witty tone of "The Author to Her Book."*

The Author to Her Book

Thou ill-formed offspring of my feeble brain,
Who after birth didst by my side remain,
Till snatched from thence by friends, less wise than true,
Who thee abroad, exposed to public view,
Made thee in rags, halting to th' press° to trudge,   5
Where errors were not lessened (all may judge).
At thy return my blushing was not small,
My rambling brat (in print) should mother call,
I cast thee by as one unfit for light,
Thy visage was so irksome in my sight;   10
Yet being mine own, at length affection would
Thy blemishes amend, if so I could:
I washed thy face, but more defects I saw,
And rubbing off a spot still made a flaw.
I stretched thy joints to make thee even feet,°   15
Yet still thou run'st more hobbling than is meet;
In better dress to trim thee was my mind,
But nought save homespun cloth i' th' house I find.
In this array 'mongst vulgars° may'st thou roam.
In critic's hands beware thou dost not come,   20
And take thy way where yet thou art not known;
If for thy Father asked, say thou had'st none;
And for thy Mother, she alas is poor,
Which caused her thus to send thee out of door.

—1678

5 press printing press; also a clothes closet or chest   **15 even feet** a pun on metrical feet   **19 vulgars**
common people, i.e., average readers

Richard Lovelace (1618–1658)

Richard Lovelace was another Cavalier lyricist who was a staunch supporter of Charles I, serving as a soldier in Scotland and France. He composed many of his poems in prison following the English Civil War.

To Lucasta, Going to the Wars

Tell me not, sweet, I am unkind
That from the nunnery
Of thy chaste breast and quiet mind,
To war and arms I fly.

True, a new mistress now I chase,   5
The first foe in the field;
And with a stronger faith embrace
A sword, a horse, a shield.

Yet this inconstancy is such
As you too shall adore;   10
I could not love thee, dear, so much,
Loved I not honor more.

—1649

Andrew Marvell (1621–1678)

Andrew Marvell was widely known for the playful sexual wit of this most famous example of the carpé diem *poem in English. Marvell was a learned Latin scholar who moved in high circles of government under both the Puritans and Charles II, serving as a member of parliament for two decades. Oddly, Marvell was almost completely forgotten as a lyric poet for almost two hundred years after his death, although today he is considered the last of the great exemplars of the metaphysical style.*

To His Coy Mistress

Had we but world enough, and time,
This coyness,° lady, were no crime.
We would sit down, and think which way
To walk, and pass our long love's day.
Thou by the Indian Ganges' side   5
Shouldst rubies find; I by the tide
Of Humber° would complain. I would
Love you ten years before the flood,
And you should, if you please, refuse
Till the conversion of the Jews.°   10
My vegetable° love should grow
Vaster than empires, and more slow;
An hundred years should go to praise
Thine eyes, and on thy forehead gaze;
Two hundred to adore each breast,   15
But thirty thousand to the rest;
An age at least to every part,
And the last age should show your heart.
For, lady, you deserve this state,°
Nor would I love at lower rate.   20
    But at my back I always hear
Time's wingèd chariot hurrying near;
And yonder all before us lie

---

2 **coyness** here, artificial sexual reluctance   7 **Humber** an English river near Marvell's home
10 **conversion of the Jews** at the end of time   11 **vegetable** flourishing   19 **state** estate

Deserts of vast eternity.
Thy beauty shall no more be found;   25
Nor, in thy marble vault, shall sound
My echoing song; then worms shall try°
That long-preserved virginity,
And your quaint° honor turn to dust,
And into ashes all my lust: 30
The grave's a fine and private place,
But none, I think, do there embrace.
       Now therefore, while the youthful hue
Sits on thy skin like morning glow,
And while thy willing soul transpires   35
At every pore with instant fires,
Now let us sport us while we may,
And now, like amorous birds of prey,
Rather at once our time devour
Than languish in his slow-chapped° power.   40
Let us roll all our strength and all
Our sweetness up into one ball,
And tear our pleasures with rough strife
Thorough the iron gates of life:
Thus, though we cannot make our sun   45
Stand still, yet we will make him run.

                                                           —*1681*

---

27 **try** test   29 **quaint** too subtle   40 **chapped** jawed

John Dryden (1631–1700)

John Dryden excelled at long forms—verse dramas like All for Love, *his version of Shakespeare's* Antony and Cleopatra, *his translation of Virgil's* Aeneid, *political allegories like* Absalom and Achitophel, *and* MacFlecknoe, *the first great English literary satire. Dryden's balance and formal conservatism introduced the neoclassical style to English poetry, a manner that prevailed for a century after his death. He became poet laureate of England in 1668.*

To the Memory of Mr. Oldham°

Farewell, too little, and too lately known,
Whom I began to think and call my own:
For sure our souls were near allied, and thine
Cast in the same poetic mold with mine.
One common note on either lyre did strike,   5
And knaves and fools we both abhorred alike.
To the same goal did both our studies drive;
The last set out the soonest did arrive.
Thus Nisus° fell upon the slippery place,
While his young friend performed and won the race.   10
O early ripe! to thy abundant store
What could advancing age have added more?
It might (what nature never gives the young)
Have taught the numbers° of thy native tongue.
But satire needs not those, and wit will shine   15
Through the harsh cadence of a rugged line:
A noble error, and but seldom made,
When poets are by too much force betrayed.
Thy generous fruits, though gathered ere their prime,
Still showed a quickness, and maturing time   20
But mellows what we write to the dull sweets of rhyme.
Once more, hail and farewell; farewell, thou young,
But ah too short, Marcellus° of our tongue;

John Oldham (1653–1683) was a poet and a satirist.   **9 Nisus** In Virgil's *Aeneid* he is defeated in a footrace by Euryalus, his friend.   **14 numbers** poetic meters   **23 Marcellus** Roman military leader who died at age twenty

Thy brows with ivy, and with laurels bound
But fate and gloomy night encompass thee around.   25

                                                        —1684

Edward Taylor (1642–1729)

*Edward Taylor was a Calvinist minister in a village outside of Boston,
Massachusetts, whose eccentric religious poems (obviously influenced by
Donne and Herbert) remained in manuscript for over two centuries after
his death, when they were discovered in the Yale University Library. Taylor was a true amateur, writing in isolation and apparently intending his
poems as meditative exercises to assist him in his clerical duties. Taylor's
poems were not published until the twentieth century.*

Huswifery

Make me, O Lord, thy spinning wheel complete.
    Thy holy word my distaff° make for me.
Make mine affections thy swift flyers° neat,
    And make my soul thy holy spool° to be.
    My conversation make to be thy reel,°   5
    And reel the yarn thereon spun of thy wheel.

Make me thy loom then, knit therein this twine;
    And make thy holy spirit, Lord, wind quills.°
Then weave the web thyself. The yarn is fine.
    Thine ordinances make my fulling mills.°   10
    Then dye the same in heavenly colors choice,
    All pinked° with varnished° flowers of paradise.

Then clothe therewith mine understanding, will,
    Affections, judgment, conscience, memory,
My words, and actions, that their shine may fill   15
    My ways with glory and thee glorify.
    Then mine apparel shall display before ye
    That I am clothed in holy robes for glory.

                                                        —1685?

2 **distaff** part of a spinning wheel that holds raw material   3 **flyers** impart twist to yarn   4 **spool**
collects spun yarn   5 **reel** receives finished thread   8 **quills** spools   10 **fulling mills** where cloth is
cleaned after weaving   12 **pinked** decorated   **varnished** shiny

Jonathan Swift (1667–1745)

Jonathan Swift, the author of Gulliver's Travels, *stands unchallenged as the greatest English prose satirist, but his poetry too is remarkable in the unsparing realism of its best passages. Like many poets of the neoclassical era, Swift adds tension to his poetry by ironically emphasizing parallels between the heroic past and the familiar characters and scenes of contemporary London. A native of Dublin, Swift returned to Ireland in his maturity as dean of St. Patrick's Cathedral.*

A Description of a City Shower

Careful observers may foretell the hour
(By sure prognostics)° when to dread a shower:
While rain depends,° the pensive cat gives o'er
Her frolics, and pursues her tail no more.
Returning home at night, you'll find the sink°   5
Strike your offended sense with double stink.
If you be wise, then go not far to dine;
You'll spend in coach hire more than save in wine.
A coming shower your shooting corns presage,
Old achès throb, your hollow tooth will rage.   10
Sauntering in coffeehouse is Dulman° seen;
He damns the climate and complains of spleen.°
    Meanwhile the South, rising with dabbled wings,
A sable cloud athwart the welkin° flings,
That swilled more liquor than it could contain,   15
And, like a drunkard, gives it up again.
Brisk Susan whips her linen from the rope,
While the first drizzling shower is borne aslope:
Such is that sprinkling which some careless quean°
Flirts on you from her mop, but not so clean: 20
You fly, invoke the gods; then turning, stop
To rail; she singing, still whirls on her mop.
Not yet the dust had shunned the unequal strife,

2 **prognostics** forecasts   3 **depends** is imminent   5 **sink** sewer   11 **Dulman** i.e., dull man
12 **spleen** mental depression   14 **welkin** sky   19 **quean** ill-mannered woman

But, aided by the wind, fought still for life,
And wafted with its foe by violent gust,   25
'Twas doubtful which was rain and which was dust.
Ah! where must needy poet seek for aid,
When dust and rain at once his coat invade?
Sole coat, where dust cemented by the rain
Erects the nap, and leaves a mingled stain.   30
  Now in contiguous drops the flood comes down,
Threatening with deluge this devoted° town.
To shops in crowds the daggled° females fly,
Pretend to cheapen° goods, but nothing buy.
The Templar° spruce, while every spout's abroach,°   35
Stays till 'tis fair, yet seems to call a coach.
The tucked-up sempstress walks with hasty strides,
While streams run down her oiled umbrella's sides.
Here various kinds, by various fortunes led,
Commence acquaintance underneath a shed.   40
Triumphant Tories and desponding Whigs°
Forget their feuds, and join to save their wigs.
Boxed in a chair° the beau impatient sits,
While spouts run clattering o'er the roof by fits,
And ever and anon with frightful din   45
The leather sounds; he trembles from within.
So when Troy chairmen bore the wooden steed,
Pregnant with Greeks impatient to be freed
(Those bully Greeks, who, as the moderns do,
Instead of paying chairmen, run them through),   50
Laocoön° struck the outside with his spear,
And each imprisoned hero quaked for fear.
  Now from all parts the swelling kennels° flow,
And bear their trophies with them as they go:
Filth of all hues and odors seem to tell   55
What street they sailed from, by their sight and smell.
They, as each torrent drives with rapid force,
From Smithfield° or St. Pulchre's shape their course,
And in huge confluence joined at Snow Hill ridge,
Fall from the conduit prone to Holborn Bridge.   60

---

32 **devoted** doomed   33 **daggled** spattered   34 **cheapen** inspect prices of   35 **Templar** law student
abroach pouring   41 **Tories . . . Whigs** rival political factions   43 **chair** sedan chair   51 **Laocoön**
For his attempt to warn the Trojans, he was crushed by sea serpents sent by Poseidon.   53 **kennels**
storm drains   58 **Smithfield** site of London cattle exchange

Sweepings from butchers' stalls, dung, guts, and blood,
Drowned puppies, stinking sprats,° all drenched in mud,
Dead cats, and turnip tops, come tumbling down the flood.

—1710

Alexander Pope (1688–1744)

Alexander Pope was a tiny man who was afflicted in childhood by a crippling disease. Pope was the dominant poet of eighteenth-century England, particularly excelling as a master of mock-epic satire in "The Rape of the Lock" and "The Dunciad." His translations of the Iliad *and the* Odyssey *made him famous and financially independent and remained the standard versions of Homer for almost two hundred years. "An Essay on Criticism," a long didactic poem modeled on Horace's* Ars Poetica, *remains the most complete statement of the neoclassical aesthetic.*

from An Essay on Criticism

But most by numbers judge a poet's song,
And smooth or rough with them is right or wrong.
In the bright Muse though thousand charms conspire,
Her voice is all these tuneful fools admire,
Who haunt Parnassus° but to please their ear,   5
Not mend their minds; as some to church repair,
Not for the doctrine, but the music there.
These equal syllables alone require,
Though oft the ear the open vowels tire,
While expletives° their feeble aid do join,   10
And ten low words oft creep in one dull line:
While they ring round the same unvaried chimes,
With sure returns of still expected rhymes;
Where'er you find "the cooling western breeze,"
In the next line, it "whispers through the trees";   15

62 **sprats** small fish
5 **Parnassus** mountain of the Muses   10 **expletives** unnecessary filler words

If crystal streams "with pleasing murmurs creep,"
The reader's threatened (not in vain) with "sleep";
Then, at the last and only couplet fraught
With some unmeaning thing they call a thought,
A needless Alexandrine° ends the song   20
That, like a wounded snake, drags its slow length along.
Leave such to tune their own dull rhymes, and know
What's roundly smooth or languishingly slow;
And praise the easy vigor of a line
Where Denham's strength and Waller's° sweetness join.   25
True ease in writing comes from art, not chance,
As those move easiest who have learned to dance.
'Tis not enough no harshness gives offense,
The sound must seem an echo to the sense.
Soft is the strain when Zephyr° gently blows,   30
And the smooth stream in smoother numbers flows;
But when loud surges lash the sounding shore,
The hoarse, rough verse should like the torrent roar.
When Ajax° strives some rock's vast weight to throw,
The line too labors, and the words move slow;   35
Not so when swift Camilla° scours the plain,
Flies o'er the unbending corn, and skims along the main.
Hear how Timotheus'° varied lays surprise,
And bid alternate passions fall and rise!
While at each change the son of Libyan Jove°   40
Now burns with glory, and then melts with love;
Now his fierce eyes with sparkling fury glow,
Now sighs steal out, and tears begin to flow:
Persians and Greeks like turns of nature found
And the world's victor stood subdued by sound!   45
The power of music all our hearts allow,
And what Timotheus was is Dryden now.
     Avoid extremes; and shun the fault of such
Who still are pleased too little or too much.
At every trifle scorn to take offense: 50
That always shows great pride, or little sense.
Those heads, as stomachs, are not sure the best,

---

20 **Alexandrine** line of six iambic feet (as in the next line)   25 **Denham's** . . . **Waller's** earlier English
poets praised by Pope   30 **Zephyr** the west wind   34 **Ajax** legendary strong man of the *Iliad*
36 **Camilla** messenger of the goddess Diana   38 **Timotheus** a legendary musician   40 **son of Libyan
Jove** Alexander the Great

Which nauseate all, and nothing can digest.
Yet let not each gay turn thy rapture move;
For fools admire, but men of sense approve: 55
As things seem large which we through mists descry,
Dullness is ever apt to magnify.

—1711

Ode on Solitude

Happy the man whose wish and care
　　A few paternal acres bound,
Content to breathe his native air,
　　　In his own ground.

Whose herds with milk, whose fields with bread,   5
　　Whose flocks supply him with attire,
Whose trees in summer yield him shade,
　　　In winter fire.

Blest, who can unconcernedly find
　　Hours, days, and years slide soft away,   10
In health of body, peace of mind,
　　　Quiet by day,

Sound sleep by night; study and ease,
　　Together mixed; sweet recreation;
And innocence, which most does please   15
　　With meditation.

Thus let me live, unseen, unknown;
　　Thus unlamented let me die;
Steal from the world, and not a stone
　　　Tell where I lie.   20

—1736

Thomas Gray (1716–1771)

Thomas Gray possesses a contemporary reputation that rests primarily on a single poem, but it remains one of the most often quoted in the whole English canon, and the quatrain stanza is often called "elegiac" in its honor. Gray lived almost all of his adult life at Cambridge University, where he was a professor of history and languages. He declined the poet laureateship of England in 1757.

Elegy Written in a Country Churchyard

The curfew tolls the knell of parting day,
    The lowing herd wind slowly o'er the lea,
The plowman homeward plods his weary way,
    And leaves the world to darkness and to me.

Now fades the glimmering landscape on the sight,   5
    And all the air a solemn stillness holds,
Save where the beetle wheels his droning flight,
    And drowsy tinklings lull the distant folds;

Save that from yonder ivy-mantled tower
    The moping owl does to the moon complain   10
Of such, as wandering near her secret bower,
    Molest her ancient solitary reign.

Beneath those rugged elms, that yew tree's shade,
    Where heaves the turf in many a moldering heap,
Each in his narrow cell forever laid,   15
    The rude° forefathers of the hamlet sleep.

The breezy call of incense-breathing morn,
    The swallow twittering from the straw-built shed,
The cock's shrill clarion, or the echoing horn,
    No more shall rouse them from their lowly bed.   20

For them no more the blazing hearth shall burn,
    Or busy housewife ply her evening care;

---

16 rude unlearned

No children run to lisp their sire's return,
  Or climb his knees the envied kiss to share.

Oft did the harvest to their sickle yield,   25
  Their furrow oft the stubborn glebe° has broke;
How jocund did they drive their team afield!
  How bowed the woods beneath their sturdy stroke!

Let not Ambition mock their useful toil,
  Their homely joys, and destiny obscure;   30
Nor Grandeur hear with a disdainful smile
  The short and simple annals of the poor.

The boast of heraldry, the pomp of power,
  And all that beauty, all that wealth e'er gave,
Awaits alike the inevitable hour.   35
  The paths of glory lead but to the grave.

Nor you, ye proud, impute to these the fault,
  If Memory o'er their tomb no trophies raise,
Where through the long-drawn aisle and fretted° vault
  The pealing anthem swells the note of praise.   40

Can storied urn or animated bust
  Back to its mansion call the fleeting breath?
Can Honor's voice provoke the silent dust,
  Or Flattery soothe the dull cold ear of Death?

Perhaps in this neglected spot is laid   45
  Some heart once pregnant with celestial fire;
Hands that the rod of empire might have swayed,
  Or waked to ecstasy the living lyre.

But Knowledge to their eyes her ample page
  Rich with the spoils of time did ne'er unroll;   50
Chill Penury repressed their noble rage,
  And froze the genial current of the soul.

Full many a gem of purest ray serene,
  The dark unfathomed caves of ocean bear:
Full many a flower is born to blush unseen,   55
  And waste its sweetness on the desert air.

26 glebe plot of farmland   **39 fretted** carved

Some village Hampden,° that with dauntless breast
  The little tyrant of his field withstood;
Some mute inglorious Milton here may rest,
  Some Cromwell° guiltless of his country's blood.   60

The applause of listening senates to command,
  The threats of pain and ruin to despise,
To scatter plenty o'er a smiling land,
  And read their history in a nation's eyes,

Their lot forbade: nor circumscribed alone   65
  Their growing virtues, but their crimes confined;
Forbade to wade through slaughter to a throne,
  And shut the gates of mercy on mankind,

The struggling pangs of conscious truth to hide,
  To quench the blushes of ingenuous shame,   70
Or heap the shrine of Luxury and Pride
  With incense kindled at the Muse's flame.

Far from the madding° crowd's ignoble strife,
  Their sober wishes never learned to stray;
Along the cool sequestered vale of life   75
  They kept the noiseless tenor of their way.

Yet even these bones from insult to protect
  Some frail memorial still erected nigh,
With uncouth rhymes and shapeless sculpture decked,
  Implores the passing tribute of a sigh.   80

Their name, their years, spelt by the unlettered Muse,
  The place of fame and elegy supply:
And many a holy text around she strews,
  That teach the rustic moralist to die.

For who to dumb Forgetfulness a prey,   85
  This pleasing anxious being e'er resigned,
Left the warm precincts of the cheerful day,
  Nor cast one longing lingering look behind?

On some fond breast the parting soul relies,
  Some pious drops the closing eye requires;   90

57 **Hampden** hero of the English Civil War   60 **Cromwell** Lord Protector of England from 1653 to 1658   73 **madding** frenzied

Even from the tomb the voice of Nature cries,
  Even in our ashes live their wonted fires.

For thee, who mindful of the unhonored dead
  Dost in these lines their artless tale relate;
If chance, by lonely contemplation led,   95
  Some kindred spirit shall inquire thy fate,

Haply some hoary°-headed swain° may say,
  "Oft have we seen him at the peep of dawn
Brushing with hasty steps the dews away
  To meet the sun upon the upland lawn.   100

"There at the foot of yonder nodding beech
  That wreathes its old fantastic roots so high,
His listless length at noontide would he stretch,
  And pore upon the brook that babbles by.

"Hard by yon wood, now smiling as in scorn,   105
  Muttering his wayward fancies he would rove,
Now drooping, woeful wan, like one forlorn,
  Or crazed with care, or crossed in hopeless love.

"One morn I missed him on the customed hill,
  Along the heath and near his favorite tree;   110
Another came; nor yet beside the rill,
  Nor up the lawn, nor at the wood was he;

"The next with dirges due in sad array
  Slow through the churchway path we saw him borne.
Approach and read (for thou canst read) the lay,   115
  Graved on the stone beneath yon aged thorn."

THE EPITAPH

Here rests his head upon the lap of Earth
  A youth to Fortune and to Fame unknown.
Fair Science frowned not on his humble birth,
  And Melancholy marked him for her own.   120

Large was his bounty, and his soul sincere,
  Heaven did a recompense as largely send:

---

97 **hoary** frosty, white   **swain** peasant

He gave to Misery all he had, a tear,
    He gained from Heaven ('twas all he wished) a friend.

No farther seek his merits to disclose,   125
    Or draw his frailties from their dread abode
(There they alike in trembling hope repose),
    The bosom of his Father and his God.

                            —1751

Christopher Smart (1722–1771)

Christopher Smart was educated, like Thomas Gray, at Cambridge, but fell victim to religious mania and insanity yet continued to write throughout his life. Jubilate Agno ("Rejoice in the Lamb") is a long meditation on the immanence of God, even in such insignificant forms as Smart's cat Jeoffry. The poem is one of the earliest examples of free verse in English.

from Jubilate Agno

For I will consider my Cat Jeoffry.
For he is the servant of the Living God, duly and daily serving him.
For at the first glance of the glory of God in the East he worships in
    his way.
For is this done by wreathing his body seven times round with elegant
    quickness.
For then he leaps up to catch the musk,° which is the blessing of   5
    God upon his prayer.
For he rolls upon prank to work it in.
For having done duty and received blessing he begins to
    consider himself.
For this he performs in ten degrees.
For first he looks upon his forepaws to see if they are clean.
For secondly he kicks up behind to clear away there.   10
For thirdly he works it upon stretch with the forepaws extended.
For fourthly he sharpens his paws by wood.
For fifthly he washes himself.
For sixthly he rolls upon wash.

---

5 musk scented object or toy

For seventhly he fleas himself, that he may not be   15
    interrupted upon the beat.°
For eighthly he rubs himself against a post.
For ninthly he looks up for his instructions.
For tenthly he goes in quest of food.
For having considered God and himself he will consider
    his neighbor.
For if he meets another cat he will kiss her in kindness.   20
For when he takes his prey he plays with it to give it a chance.
For one mouse in seven escapes by his dallying.
For when his day's work is done his business more properly begins.
For he keeps the Lord's watch in the night against the adversary.°
For he counteracts the powers of darkness by his electrical skin and   25
    glaring eyes.
For he counteracts the Devil, who is death, by brisking about the life.
For in his morning orisons he loves the sun and the sun loves him.
For he is of the tribe of Tiger.
For the Cherub Cat is a term° of the Angel Tiger.
For he has the subtlety and hissing of a serpent, which in   30
    goodness he suppresses.
For he will not do destruction if he is well-fed, neither will he spit
    without provocation.
For he purrs in thankfulness when God tells him he's a good Cat.
For he is an instrument for the children to learn benevolence upon.
For every house is incomplete without him, and a blessing is lacking in
    the spirit.
For the Lord commanded Moses concerning the cats at the   35
    departure of the Children of Israel from Egypt.
For every family had one cat at least in the bag.
For the English Cats are the best in Europe.
For he is the cleanest in the use of his forepaws of any quadruped.
For the dexterity of his defense is an instance of the love of God to him
    exceedingly.
For he is the quickest to his mark of any creature.   40
For he is tenacious of his point.
For he is a mixture of gravity and waggery.
For he knows that God is his Saviour.
For there is nothing sweeter than his peace when at rest.
For there is nothing brisker than his life when in motion.   45

15 beat accustomed path   **24 adversary** i.e., Satan   **29 term** immature version

For he is of the Lord's poor, and so indeed is he called by benevolence
    perpetually—Poor Jeoffry! poor Jeoffry! the rat has bit thy throat.
For I bless the name of the Lord Jesus that Jeoffry is better.
For the divine spirit comes about his body to sustain it in complete cat.
For his tongue is exceeding pure so that it has in purity what it wants
    in music.
For he is docile and can learn certain things.   50
For he can sit up with gravity, which is patience upon approbation.
For he can fetch and carry, which is patience in employment.
For he can jump over a stick, which is patience upon proof positive.
For he can spraggle upon waggle at the word of command.
For he can jump from an eminence into his master's bosom.   55
For he can catch the cork and toss it again.
For he is hated by the hypocrite and miser.
For the former is afraid of detection.
For the latter refuses the charge.
For he camels his back to bear the first notion of business.   60
For he is good to think on, if a man would express himself neatly.
For he made a great figure in Egypt for his signal services.
For he killed the Icneumon° rat, very pernicious by land.
For his ears are so acute that they sting again.
For from this proceeds the passing quickness of his attention.   65
For by stroking of him I have found out electricity.
For I perceived God's light about him both wax and fire.
For the electrical fire is the spiritual substance which God sends from
    heaven to sustain the bodies both of man and beast.
For God has blessed him in the variety of his movements.
For, though he cannot fly, he is an excellent clamberer.   70
For his motions upon the face of the earth are more than any other
    quadruped.
For he can tread to all the measures upon the music.
For he can swim for life.
For he can creep.

—*ca. 1760*

---

63 **Icneumon** resembling the mongoose *(Herpestes ichneumon)*

William Blake (1757–1827)

William Blake was a poet, painter, engraver, and visionary. Blake does not fit easily into any single category, although his political sympathies link him to the later romantic poets. His first book, Poetical Sketches, *attracted little attention, but his mature works, starting with* Songs of Innocence *and* Songs of Experience, *combine poetry with his own remarkable illustrations and are unique in English literature. Thought mad by many in his own day, Blake anticipated many future directions of both literature and modern psychology.*

The Chimney Sweeper

When my mother died I was very young,
And my father sold me while yet my tongue
Could scarcely cry "'weep! 'weep! 'weep! 'weep!"
So your chimneys I sweep & in soot I sleep.

There's little Tom Dacre, who cried when his head   5
That curl'd like a lamb's back, was shav'd, so I said,
"Hush, Tom! never mind it, for when your head's bare,
You know that the soot cannot spoil your white hair."

And so he was quiet, & that very night,
As Tom was a-sleeping, he had such a sight!   10
That thousands of sweepers, Dick, Joe, Ned, & Jack,
Were all of them lock'd up in coffins of black;

And by came an Angel who had a bright key,
And he open'd the coffins & set them all free;
Then down a green plain, leaping, laughing, they run,   15
And wash in a river and shine in the Sun.

Then naked & white, all their bags left behind,
They rise upon clouds, and sport in the wind.
And the Angel told Tom, if he'd be a good boy,
He'd have God for his father, & never want joy.   20

And so Tom awoke; and we rose in the dark,
And got with our bags & our brushes to work.
Tho' the morning was cold, Tom was happy & warm;
So if all do their duty, they need not fear harm.

—1789

The Little Black° Boy

My mother bore me in the southern wild,
And I am black, but O! my soul is white;
White as an angel is the English child:
But I am black as if bereav'd of light.

My mother taught me underneath a tree,   5
And sitting down before the heat of day,
She took me on her lap and kissèd me,
And pointing to the east, began to say:

"Look on the rising sun: there God does live,
And gives his light, and gives his heat away;   10
And flowers and trees and beasts and men receive
Comfort in morning, joy in the noon day.

"And we are put on earth a little space,
That we may learn to bear the beams of love,
And these black bodies and this sun-burnt face   15
Is but a cloud, and like a shady grove.

"For when our souls have learn'd the heat to bear,
The cloud will vanish; we shall hear his voice,
Saying: 'Come out from the grove, my love & care,
And round my golden tent like lambs rejoice.'"   20

Thus did my mother say, and kissèd me;
And thus I say to little English boy:
When I from black and he from white cloud free,
And round the tent of God like lambs we joy,

I'll shade him from the heat till he can bear   25
To lean in joy upon our father's knee:
And then I'll stand and stroke his silver hair,
And be like him, and he will then love me.

—*1789*

Black probably Indian rather than African

A Poison Tree

I was angry with my friend:
I told my wrath, my wrath did end.
I was angry with my foe:
I told it not, my wrath did grow.

And I water'd it in fears,   5
Night & morning with my tears;
And I sunnèd it with smiles,
And with soft deceitful wiles.

And it grew both day and night,
Till it bore an apple bright;   10
And my foe beheld it shine,
And he knew that it was mine,

And into my garden stole
When the night had veil'd the pole;
In the morning glad I see   15
My foe outstretch'd beneath the tree.

                                                    —1794

The Tyger

Tyger! Tyger! burning bright
In the forests of the night,
What immortal hand or eye
Could frame thy fearful symmetry?

In what distant deeps or skies   5
Burnt the fire of thine eyes?
On what wings dare he aspire?
What the hand, dare seize the fire?

And what shoulder, & what art,
Could twist the sinews of thy heart?   10
And when thy heart began to beat,
What dread hand? & what dread feet?

What the hammer? what the chain?
In what furnace was thy brain?

What the anvil? what dread grasp   15
Dare its deadly terrors clasp?

When the stars threw down their spears,
And water'd heaven with their tears,
Did he smile his work to see?
Did he who made the Lamb make thee?   20

Tyger! Tyger! burning bright
In the forests of the night,
What immortal hand or eye,
Dare frame thy fearful symmetry?

—1794

Robert Burns (1759–1796)

*Robert Burns was a Scot known in his day as the "Ploughman Poet" and
was one of the first English poets to put dialect to serious literary purpose.
Chiefly known for his realistic depictions of peasant life, he was also an
important lyric poet who prefigured many of the later concerns of the romantic era.*

A Red, Red Rose

O my luve's like a red, red rose,
    That's newly sprung in June;
O my luve's like the melodie
    That's sweetly played in tune.

As fair art thou, my bonnie lass,   5
    So deep in luve am I;
And I will luve thee still, my dear,
    Till a' the seas gang° dry.

Till a' the seas gang dry, my dear,
    And the rocks melt wi' the sun;   10
O I will luve thee still, my dear,
    While the sands o' life shall run.

8 gang go

And fare thee weel, my only luve,
    And fare thee weel awhile!
And I will come again, my luve   15
    Though it were ten thousand mile.

—1791

John Barleycorn

There were three kings into the east,
Three kings both great and high;
And they has sworn a solemn oath
John Barleycorn should die.

They took a plough and plough'd him down,   5
Put clods upon his head;
And they hae sworn a solemn oath
John Barleycorn was dead.

But the cheerful spring came kindly on,
And showers began to fall;   10
John Barleycorn got up again,
And sore surprised them all.

The sultry suns of summer came,
And he grew thick and strong;
His head well armed wi' point'd spears,   15
That no one should him wrong.

The sober autumn enter'd mild,
When he grew wan and pale;
His bending joints and drooping head
Show'd he began to fail.   20

His colour sicken'd more and more
He faded into age;
And then his enemies began
To show their deadly rage.

They've ta'en a weapon long and sharp,   25
And cut him by the knee;
Then tied him fast upon a cart,
Like a rogue for forgery.

They laid him down upon his back,
And cudgell'd him full sore;   30
They hung him up before the storm,
And turn'd him o'er and o'er.

They fill'd up a darksome pit
With water to the brim;
They heaved in John Barleycorn,   35
There let him sink or swim.

They laid him out upon the floor,
To work him further woe;
And still as signs of life appear'd,
They toss'd him to and fro.   40

They wasted o'er a scorching flame
The marrow of his bones;
But a miller used him worst of all
He crushed him 'tween two stones.

And they has ta'en his very heart's blood,   45
And drank it round and round,
And still the more and more they drank,
Their joy did more abound.

John Barleycorn was a hero bold,
Of noble enterprise;   50
For if you do but taste his blood,
'Twill make your courage rise.

'Twill make a man forget his woe;
'Twill heighten all his joy;
'Twill make the widow's heart to sing,   55
Though the tear were in her eye.

Then let us toast John Barleycorn,
Each man a glass in hand;
And may his great posterity
Ne'er fail in old Scotland!   60

—*1786*

William Wordsworth (1770–1850)

William Wordsworth is generally considered the first of the English ro-
mantics. Lyrical Ballads, the 1798 volume that introduced both his poetry
and Samuel Taylor Coleridge's to a wide readership, remains one of the
most influential collections of poetry ever published. Wordsworth's preface
to the revised edition of 1800 contains the famous Romantic formulation
of poetry as the "spontaneous overflow of powerful feelings," a theory ex-
emplified in short lyrics like "I Wandered Lonely as a Cloud" and in
longer meditative pieces like "Tintern Abbey" (the title by which "Lines"
is commonly known). Wordsworth served as poet laureate from 1843 to
his death.

I Wandered Lonely as a Cloud

I wandered lonely as a cloud
That floats on high o'er vales and hills,
When all at once I saw a crowd,
A host, of golden daffodils;
Beside the lake, beneath the trees,   5
Fluttering and dancing in the breeze.

Continuous as the stars that shine
And twinkle on the milky way,
They stretched in never-ending line
Along the margin of a bay: 10
Ten thousand saw I at a glance,
Tossing their heads in sprightly dance.

The waves beside them danced, but they
Outdid the sparkling waves in glee;
A poet could not but be gay,   15
In such a jocund company;
I gazed—and gazed—but little thought
What wealth the show to me had brought:

For oft, when on my couch I lie
In vacant or in pensive mood,   20
They flash upon that inward eye

Which is the bliss of solitude;
And then my heart with pleasure fills,
And dances with the daffodils.

—1807

It Is a Beauteous Evening

It is a beauteous evening, calm and free,
The holy time is quiet as a Nun
Breathless with adoration; the broad sun
Is sinking down in its tranquillity;
The gentleness of heaven broods o'er the Sea: 5
Listen! the mighty Being is awake,
And doth with his eternal motion make
A sound like thunder—everlastingly.
Dear Child! dear Girl!° that walkest with me here,
If thou appear untouched by solemn thought,   10
Thy nature is not therefore less divine:
Thou liest in Abraham's bosom° all the year,
And worship'st at the Temple's inner shrine,
God being with thee when we know it not.

—1807

Nuns Fret Not at Their Convent's Narrow Room

Nuns fret not at their convent's narrow room;
And hermits are contented with their cells;
And students with their pensive citadels;
Maids at the wheel, the weaver at his loom,
Sit blithe and happy; bees that soar for bloom,   5
High as the highest Peak of Furness-fells,°

---

9 **Dear Child! dear Girl!** the poet's daughter   12 **Abraham's bosom** where souls rest in Heaven
6 **Furness-fells** mountains located in the English Lake District

Will murmur by the hour in foxglove bells:
In truth the prison, into which we doom
Ourselves, no prison is: and hence for me,
In sundry moods, 'twas pastime to be bound   10
Within the Sonnet's scanty plot of ground;
Pleased if some Souls (for such there needs must be)
Who have felt the weight of too much liberty,
Should find brief solace there, as I have found.

—1807

Ode

Intimations of Immortality
from Recollections of Early Childhood

The Child is Father of the Man;
And I could wish my days to be
Bound each to each by natural piety.°

1

There was a time when meadow, grove, and stream,
The earth, and every common sight,
        To me did seem
        Appareled in celestial light,
The glory and the freshness of a dream.   5
It is not now as it hath been of yore;—
        Turn wheresoe'er I may,
        By night or day,
The things which I have seen I now can see no more.

2

        The Rainbow comes and goes,   10
        And lovely is the Rose,
        The Moon doth with delight
Look round her when the heavens are bare,
        Waters on a starry night
        Are beautiful and fair;   15

The Child . . . natural piety last three lines of the poet's "My Heart Leaps Up"

The sunshine is a glorious birth;
But yet I know, where'er I go,
That there hath past away a glory from the earth.

3

Now, while the birds thus sing a joyous song,
    And while the young lambs bound   20
        As to the tabor's° sound,
To me alone there came a thought of grief:
A timely utterance gave that thought relief,
        And I again am strong:
The cataracts blow their trumpets from the steep;   25
No more shall grief of mine the season wrong;
I hear the Echoes through the mountains throng,
The Winds come to me from the fields of sleep,
        And all the earth is gay;
            Land and sea   30
        Give themselves up to jollity,
        And with the heart of May
        Doth every Beast keep holiday;—
            Thou Child of Joy,
Shout round me, let me hear thy shouts, thou happy
    Shepherd-boy!   35

4

Ye blessèd Creatures, I have heard the call
    Ye to each other make; I see
The heavens laugh with you in your jubilee;
    My heart is at your festival,   40
    My head hath its coronal,°
The fulness of your bliss, I feel—I feel it all.
        Oh evil day! if I were sullen
        While Earth herself is adorning,
            This sweet May-morning,   45
        And the Children are culling
            On every side,
        In a thousand valleys far and wide,
        Fresh flowers; while the sun shines warm,

21 tabor's small drum's   **41 coronal** floral crown

And the Babe leaps up on his Mother's arm: - 50
    I hear, I hear, with joy I hear!
—But there's a Tree, of many, one,
A single Field which I have looked upon,
Both of them speak of something that is gone:
    The Pansy at my feet 55
    Doth the same tale repeat:
Whither is fled the visionary gleam?
Where is it now, the glory and the dream?

    5

Our birth is but a sleep and a forgetting:
The Soul that rises with us, our life's Star, 60
    Hath had elsewhere its setting,
        And cometh from afar:
    Not in entire forgetfulness,
    And not in utter nakedness,
But trailing clouds of glory do we come 65
    From God, who is our home:
Heaven lies about us in our infancy!
Shades of the prison-house begin to close
    Upon the growing Boy,
But he beholds the light, and whence it flows, 70
    He sees it in his joy;
The Youth, who daily farther from the east
    Must travel, still is Nature's Priest,
    And by the vision splendid
    Is on his way attended; 75
At length the Man perceives it die away,
And fade into the light of common day.

    6

Earth fills her lap with pleasures of her own;
Yearnings she hath in her own natural kind,
And, even with something of a Mother's mind, 80
    And no unworthy aim,
    The homely Nurse doth all she can
To make her Foster-child, her Inmate Man,
    Forget the glories he hath known,
And that imperial palace whence he came. 85

7

Behold the Child among his new-born blisses,
A six years' Darling of a pigmy size!
See where 'mid work of his own hand he lies,
Fretted° by sallies of his mother's kisses,
With light upon him from his father's eyes!   90
See, at his feet, some little plan or chart,
Some fragment from his dream of human life,
Shaped by himself with newly-learnèd art;
    A wedding or a festival,
    A mourning or a funeral;   95
      And this hath now his heart,
    And unto this he frames his song:
    Then will he fit his tongue
To dialogues of business, love, or strife;
    But it will not be long   100
    Ere this be thrown aside,
    And with new joy and pride
The little Actor cons another part;
Filling from time to time his "humorous stage"°
With all the Persons, down to palsied Age,   105
That Life brings with her in her equipage;
    As if his whole vocation
    Were endless imitation.

    8

Thou whose exterior semblance doth belie
    Thy Soul's immensity;   110
Thou best Philosopher, who yet dost keep
Thy heritage, thou Eye among the blind,
That, deaf and silent, read'st the eternal deep,
Haunted for ever by the eternal mind,—
    Mighty Prophet! Seer blest!   115
    On whom those truths do rest,
Which we are toiling all our lives to find,
In darkness lost, the darkness of the grave;
Thou, over whom thy Immortality

89 **fretted** annoyed or marked 104 **"humorous stage"** phrase from poet Samuel Daniel
(1563–1619)

Broods like the Day, a Master o'er a Slave, 120
A Presence which is not to be put by;
Thou little Child, yet glorious in the might
Of heaven-born freedom on thy being's height,
Why with such earnest pains dost thou provoke
The years to bring the inevitable yoke, 125
Thus blindly with thy blessedness at strife?
Full soon thy Soul shall have her earthly freight,
And custom lie upon thee with a weight,
Heavy as frost, and deep almost as life!

9

      O joy! that in our embers 130
      Is something that doth live,
      That nature yet remembers
      What was so fugitive!
The thought of our past years in me doth breed
Perpetual benediction: not indeed 135
For that which is most worthy to be blest;
Delight and liberty, the simple creed
Of Childhood, whether busy or at rest,
With new-fledged hope still fluttering in his breast:—
      Not for these I raise 140
      The song of thanks and praise;
    But for those obstinate questionings
    Of sense and outward things,
    Fallings from us, vanishings;
    Blank misgivings of a Creature 145
Moving about in worlds not realized,
High instincts before which our mortal Nature
Did tremble like a guilty Thing surprised:
      But for those first affections,
      Those shadowy recollections, 150
    Which, be they what they may,
Are yet the fountain light of all our day,
Are yet a master light of all our seeing;
    Uphold us, cherish, and have power to make
Our noisy years seem moments in the being 155
Of the eternal Silence: truths that wake,
      To perish never;

Which neither listlessness, nor mad endeavour,
   Nor Man nor Boy,
Nor all that is at enmity with joy,   160
Can utterly abolish or destroy!
  Hence in a season of calm weather
    Though inland far we be,
Our Souls have sight of that immortal sea
    Which brought us hither,   165
   Can in a moment travel thither,
And see the Children sport upon the shore,
And hear the mighty waters rolling evermore.

   10

Then sing, ye Birds, sing, sing a joyous song!
    And let the young Lambs bound   170
    As to the tabor's sound!
We in thought will join your throng,
   Ye that pipe and ye that play,
   Ye that through your hearts to-day
   Feel the gladness of the May!   175
What though the radiance which was once so bright
Be now for ever taken from my sight,
   Though nothing can bring back the hour
Of splendour in the grass, of glory in the flower;
   We will grieve not, rather find   180
   Strength in what remains behind;
   In the primal sympathy
   Which having been must ever be;
   In the soothing thoughts that spring
   Out of human suffering;   185
   In the faith that looks through death,
In years that bring the philosophic mind.

   11

And O, ye Fountains, Meadows, Hills, and Groves,
Forbode not any severing of our loves!
Yet in my heart of hearts I feel your might;   190
I only have relinquished one delight
To live beneath your more habitual sway.
I love the Brooks which down their channels fret,

Even more than when I tripped lightly as they;
The innocent brightness of a new-born Day   195
      Is lovely yet;
The Clouds that gather round the setting sun
Do take a sober colouring from an eye
That hath kept watch o'er man's mortality;
Another race hath been, and other palms are won.   200
Thanks to the human heart by which we live,
Thanks to its tenderness, its joys, and fears,
To me the meanest° flower that blows can give
Thoughts that do often lie too deep for tears.

                                              —*1807*

Samuel Taylor Coleridge (1772–1834)

Samuel Taylor Coleridge, inspired but erratic, did his best work, like Wordsworth, during the great first decade of their friendship, the period that produced Lyrical Ballads. *Coleridge's later life is a tragic tale of financial and marital problems, unfinished projects, and a ruinous addiction to opium. A brilliant critic, Coleridge lectured on Shakespeare and other writers and wrote the* Biographia Literaria, *perhaps the greatest literary autobiography ever written.*

Frost at Midnight

    The Frost performs its secret ministry,
Unhelped by any wind. The owlet's cry
Came loud—and hark, again! loud as before.
The inmates of my cottage, all at rest,
Have left me to that solitude, which suits   5
Abstruser musings: save that at my side
My cradled infant° slumbers peacefully.
'Tis calm indeed! so calm, that it disturbs
And vexes meditation, with its strange
And extreme silentness. Sea, hill, and wood,   10
This populous village! Sea, and hill, and wood,
With all the numberless goings-on of life,

203 **meanest** least significant
7 **My cradled infant** the poet's son Hartley (1796–1849)

Inaudible as dreams! the thin blue flame
Lies on my low-burnt fire, and quivers not;
Only that film,° which fluttered on the grate,   15
Still flutters there, the sole unquiet thing.
Methinks its motion in this hush of nature
Gives it dim sympathies with me who live,
Making it a companionable form,
Whose puny flaps and freaks the idling Spirit   20
By its own moods interprets, everywhere
Echo or mirror seeking of itself,
And makes a toy of Thought.
       But O! how oft,
How oft, at school, with most believing mind,
Presageful,° have I gazed upon the bars,   25
To watch that fluttering *stranger!* and as oft
With unclosed lids, already had I dreamt
Of my sweet birthplace, and the old church tower,
Whose bells, the poor man's only music, rang
From morn to evening, all the hot Fair-day,   30
So sweetly, that they stirred and haunted me
With a wild pleasure, falling on mine ear
Most like articulate sounds of things to come!
So gazed I, till the soothing things, I dreamt,
Lulled me to sleep, and sleep prolonged my dreams!   35
And so I brooded all the following morn,
Awed by the stern preceptor's° face, mine eye
Fixed with mock study on my swimming book:
Save if the door half opened, and I snatched
A hasty glance, and still my heart leaped up,   40
For still I hoped to see the *stranger's* face,
Townsman, or aunt, or sister more beloved,
My playmate when we both were clothed alike!

 Dear Babe, that sleepest cradled by my side,
Whose gentle breathings, heard in this deep calm,   45
Fill up the interspersèd vacancies
And momentary pauses of the thought!
My babe so beautiful! it thrills my heart
With tender gladness, thus to look at thee,
And think that thou shalt learn far other lore,   50

15 **film** a piece of ash 25 **Presageful** with hints of the future 37 **preceptor** teacher

And in far other scenes! For I was reared
In the great city, pent 'mid cloisters dim,
And saw nought lovely but the sky and stars.
But *thou,* my babe! shalt wander like a breeze
By lakes and sandy shores, beneath the crags   55
Of ancient mountain, and beneath the clouds,
Which image in their bulk both lakes and shores
And mountain crags: so shalt thou see and hear
The lovely shapes and sounds intelligible
Of that eternal language, which thy God   60
Utters, who from eternity doth teach
Himself in all, and all things in himself.
Great universal Teacher! he shall mold
Thy spirit, and by giving make it ask.

Therefore all seasons shall be sweet to thee,   65
Whether the summer clothe the general earth
With greenness, or the redbreast sit and sing
Betwixt the tufts of snow on the bare branch
Of mossy apple tree, while the nigh thatch
Smokes in the sun-thaw; whether the eave-drops fall   70
Heard only in the trances of the blast,
Or if the secret ministry of frost
Shall hang them up in silent icicles,
Quietly shining to the quiet Moon.

                                                       —*1798*

Kubla Khan°

OR A VISION IN A DREAM,° A FRAGMENT

In Xanadu did Kubla Khan
A stately pleasure-dome decree:
Where Alph, the sacred river, ran

Kubla Khan ruler of China (1216–1294)   **vision in a dream** Coleridge's own account tells how he took opium for an illness and slept for three hours, during which time he envisioned a complete poem of some 300 lines. When he awoke, he began to write down the details of his dream. "At this moment he was unfortunately called out by a person on business from Porlock, and detained by him above an hour, and on his return to the room found, to his no small surprise and mortification, that though he still retained some vague and dim recollection of the general purport of the vision, yet, with the exception of some eight or ten scattered lines and images on the surface of a stream into which a stone has been cast . . " [Coleridge's note].

Through caverns measureless to man
   Down to a sunless sea.   5
So twice five miles of fertile ground
With walls and towers were girdled round:
And there were gardens bright with sinuous rills,
Where blossomed many an incense-bearing tree;
And here were forests ancient as the hills,   10
Enfolding sunny spots of greenery.

But oh! that deep romantic chasm which slanted
Down the green hill athwart a cedarn cover!
A savage place! as holy and enchanted
As e'er beneath a waning moon was haunted   15
By woman wailing for her demon lover!
And from this chasm, with ceaseless turmoil seething,
As if this earth in fast thick pants were breathing,
A mighty fountain momently was forced:
Amid whose swift half-intermitted burst   20
Huge fragments vaulted like rebounding hail,
Or chaffy grain beneath the thresher's flail:
And 'mid these dancing rocks at once and ever
It flung up momently the sacred river.
Five miles meandering with a mazy motion   25
Through wood and dale the sacred river ran,
Then reached the caverns measureless to man,
And sank in tumult to a lifeless ocean:
And 'mid this tumult Kubla heard from far
Ancestral voices prophesying war!   30

   The shadow of the dome of pleasure
   Floated midway on the waves;
   Where was heard the mingled measure
   From the fountain and the caves.
It was a miracle of rare device,   35
A sunny pleasure-dome with caves of ice!

   A damsel with a dulcimer
   In a vision once I saw:
   It was an Abyssinian maid,
   And on her dulcimer she played,   40
   Singing of Mount Abora.
   Could I revive within me

Her symphony and song,
   To such a deep delight 'twould win me,
That with music loud and long,   45
I would build that dome in air,
   That sunny dome! those caves of ice!
And all who heard should see them there,
And all should cry, Beware! Beware!
His flashing eyes, his floating hair!   50
Weave a circle round him thrice,
And close your eyes with holy dread,
For he on honey-dew hath fed,
And drunk the milk of Paradise.

—1797–98

Work Without Hope

Lines Composed 21st February 1825

All Nature seems at work. Slugs leave their lair—
The bees are stirring—birds are on the wing—
And Winter slumbering in the open air
Wears on his smiling face a dream of Spring!
And I the while, the sole unbusy thing,   5
Nor honey make, nor pair, nor build, nor sing.

   Yet well I ken° the banks where amaranths° blow,
Have traced the fount whence streams of nectar flow.
Bloom, O ye amaranths! bloom for whom ye may,
For me ye bloom not! Glide, rich streams, away!   10
With lips unbrightened, wreathless brow, I stroll:
And would you learn the spells that drowse my soul?
Work without Hope draws° nectar in a sieve,
And Hope without an object cannot live.

—1828

---

7 **ken** know   **amaranths** legendary flowers that never fade   13 **draws** dips

George Gordon, Lord Byron (1788–1824)

*George Gordon, Lord Byron attained flamboyant celebrity status, leading
an unconventional lifestyle that contributed to his notoriety. Byron was
the most widely read of all the English romantic poets, but his verse romances and mock-epic poems like* Don Juan *have not proved as popular
in our era. An English aristocrat who was committed to revolutionary
ideals, Byron died while lending military assistance to the cause of Greek
freedom.*

She Walks in Beauty

She walks in beauty, like the night
   Of cloudless climes and starry skies;
And all that's best of dark and bright
   Meet in her aspect and her eyes:
Thus mellowed to that tender light   5
   Which heaven to gaudy day denies.

One shade the more, one ray the less,
   Had half impaired the nameless grace
Which waves in every raven tress,
   Or softly lightens o'er her face;   10
Where thoughts serenely sweet express
   How pure, how dear their dwelling-place.

And on that cheek, and o'er that brow,
   So soft, so calm, yet eloquent,
The smiles that win, the tints that glow,   15
   But tell of days in goodness spent,
A mind at peace with all below,
   A heart whose love is innocent!

—1815

Stanzas

When A Man Hath No Freedom To Fight For At Home

When a man hath no freedom to fight for at home,
    Let him combat for that of his neighbors;
Let him think of the glories of Greece and of Rome,
    And get knocked on his head for his labors.

To do good to mankind is the chivalrous plan,   5
    And is always as nobly requited:
Then battle for freedom wherever you can,
    And, if not shot or hanged, you'll get knighted.

                    —1824

When We Two Parted

When we two parted
    In silence and tears,
Half broken hearted
    To sever for years,
Pale grew thy cheek and cold,   5
    Colder thy kiss;
Truly that hour foretold
    Sorrow to this.

The dew of the morning
    Sunk chill on my brow—   10
It felt like the warning
    Of what I feel now.
Thy vows are all broken,
    And light is thy fame;
I hear thy name spoken,   15
    And share in its shame.

They name thee before me,
    A knell to mine ear;
A shudder comes o'er me—
    Why wert thou so dear?   20

They know not I knew thee,
  Who knew thee too well:—
Long, long shall I rue thee,
  Too deeply to tell.

In secret we met—   25
  In silence I grieve
That thy heart could forget,
  Thy spirit deceive.
If I should meet thee
  After long years,   30
How should I greet thee?—
  With silence and tears.

—1813

Percy Bysshe Shelley (1792–1822)

Percy Bysshe Shelley, like his friend Byron, has not found as much favor in recent eras as the other English romantics, although his political liberalism anticipates many currents of our own day. Perhaps his unbridled emotionalism is sometimes too intense for modern readers. His wife, Mary Wollstonecraft Shelley, will be remembered as the author of the classic horror novel Frankenstein.

Ode to the West Wind

1

O wild West Wind, thou breath of Autumn's being,
Thou, from whose unseen presence the leaves dead
Are driven, like ghosts from an enchanter fleeing,

Yellow, and black, and pale, and hectic red,
Pestilence-stricken multitudes: O thou,   5
Who chariotest to their dark wintry bed

The wingèd seeds, where they lie cold and low,
Each like a corpse within its grave, until
Thine azure sister of the Spring° shall blow

9 azure sister of the Spring i.e., the South Wind

Her clarion o'er the dreaming earth, and fill   10
(Driving sweet buds like flocks to feed in air)
With living hues and odors plain and hill:

Wild Spirit, which art moving everywhere;
Destroyer and preserver; hear, oh, hear!

2

Thou on whose stream, mid the steep sky's commotion,   15
Loose clouds like earth's decaying leaves are shed,
Shook from the tangled boughs of Heaven and Ocean,

Angels of rain and lightning: there are spread
On the blue surface of thine aëry surge,
Like the bright hair uplifted from the head   20

Of some fierce Mænad,° even from the dim verge
Of the horizon to the zenith's height,
The locks of the approaching storm. Thou dirge

Of the dying year, to which this closing night
Will be the dome of a vast sepulcher,   25
Vaulted with all thy congregated might

Of vapors, from whose solid atmosphere
Black rain, and fire, and hail will burst: oh, hear!

3

Thou who didst waken from his summer dreams
The blue Mediterranean, where he lay,   30
Lulled by the coil of his crystàlline streams,

Beside a pumice isle in Baiae's bay,°
And saw in sleep old palaces and towers
Quivering within the wave's intenser day,

All overgrown with azure moss and flowers   35
So sweet, the sense faints picturing them! Thou
For whose path the Atlantic's level powers

---

21 **Mænad** female worshipper of Bacchus, god of wine   32 **Baiae's bay** near Naples

Cleave themselves into chasms, while far below
The sea-blooms and the oozy woods which wear
The sapless foliage of the ocean, know   40

Thy voice, and suddenly grow gray with fear,
And tremble and despoil themselves: oh, hear!

4

If I were a dead leaf thou mightest bear;
If I were a swift cloud to fly with thee;
A wave to pant beneath thy power, and share   45

The impulse of thy strength, only less free
Than thou, O uncontrollable! If even
I were as in my boyhood, and could be

The comrade of thy wanderings over Heaven,
As then, when to outstrip thy skyey speed   50
Scarce seemed a vision; I would ne'er have striven

As thus with thee in prayer in my sore need.
Oh, lift me as a wave, a leaf, a cloud!
I fall upon the thorns of life! I bleed!

A heavy weight of hours has chained and bowed   55
One too like thee: tameless, and swift, and proud.

5

Make me thy lyre, even as the forest is:
What if my leaves are falling like its own!
The tumult of thy mighty harmonies

Will take from both a deep, autumnal tone,   60
Sweet though in sadness. Be thou, Spirit fierce,
My spirit! Be thou me, impetuous one!

Drive my dead thoughts over the universe
Like withered leaves to quicken a new birth!
And, by the incantation of this verse,   65

Scatter, as from an unextinguished hearth
Ashes and sparks, my words among mankind!
Be through my lips to unawakened earth

The trumpet of a prophecy! O Wind,
If Winter comes, can Spring be far behind?   70

—*1820*

Ozymandias°

I met a traveler from an antique land
Who said: Two vast and trunkless legs of stone
Stand in the desert. . . . Near them, on the sand,
Half sunk, a shattered visage lies, whose frown,
And wrinkled lip, and sneer of cold command,   5
Tell that its sculptor well those passions read
Which yet survive, stamped on these lifeless things,
The hand that mocked them, and the heart that fed:
And on the pedestal these words appear:
"My name is Ozymandias, king of kings: 10
Look on my works, ye Mighty, and despair!"
Nothing beside remains. Round the decay
Of that colossal wreck, boundless and bare
The lone and level sands stretch far away.

—*1818*

William Cullen Bryant (1794–1878)

*William Cullen Bryant was often called "the American Wordsworth" for
his adaptation of the techniques of English romanticism to the American
landscape. Bryant's observations of nature have rarely been equaled.*

To the Fringed Gentian

Thou blossom bright with autumn dew,
And colored with the heaven's own blue,
That openest when the quiet light
Succeeds the keen and frosty night—

Ozymandias Ramses II of Egypt (c. 1250 BC)

Thou comest not when violets lean   5
O'er wandering brooks and springs unseen,
Or columbines, in purple dressed,
Nod o'er the ground-bird's hidden nest.

Thou waitest late and com'st alone,
When woods are bare and birds are flown,   10
And frosts and shortening days portend
The aged year is near his end.

Then doth thy sweet and quiet eye
Look through its fringes to the sky,
Blue—blue—as if that sky let fall   15
A flower from its cerulean° wall.

I would that thus, when I shall see
The hour of death draw near to me,
Hope, blossoming within my heart,
May look to heaven as I depart.   20

—*1829*

John Keats (1795–1821)

*John Keats is now perhaps the most admired of all the major romantics.
Certainly his tragic death from tuberculosis in his twenties gives poignancy
to thoughts of the doomed young poet writing feverishly in a futile race
against time; "Here lies one whose name was writ in water" are the words
he chose for his own epitaph. Many of Keats's poems are concerned with
glimpses of the eternal, whether a translation of an ancient epic poem or a
pristine artifact of a vanished civilization.*

La Belle Dame sans Merci°

O what can ail thee, Knight at arms,
    Alone and palely loitering?
The sedge has withered from the Lake
    And no birds sing!

16 cerulean heavenly blue
La Belle Dame sans Merci "the beautiful lady without pity"

O what can ail thee, Knight at arms,   5
    So haggard, and so woebegone?
The squirrel's granary is full
    And the harvest's done.

I see a lily on thy brow
    With anguish moist and fever dew,   10
And on thy cheeks a fading rose
    Fast withereth too.

"I met a Lady in the Meads,
    Full beautiful, a faery's child,
Her hair was long, her foot was light,   15
    And her eyes were wild.

"I made a Garland for her head,
    And bracelets too, and fragrant Zone;°
She looked at me as she did love
    And made sweet moan.   20

"I set her on my pacing steed
    And nothing else saw all day long,
For sidelong would she bend and sing
    A faery's song.

"She found me roots of relish sweet,   25
    And honey wild, and manna dew,
And sure in language strange she said
    'I love thee true.'

"She took me to her elfin grot°
    And there she wept and sighed full sore,   30
And there I shut her wild wild eyes
    With kisses four.

"And there she lullèd me asleep,
    And there I dreamed, Ah Woe betide!
The latest dream I ever dreamt   35
    On the cold hill side.

"I saw pale Kings, and Princes too,
    Pale warriors, death-pale were they all;
They cried, 'La belle Dame sans merci
    Hath thee in thrall!'   40

18 Zone belt   **29 grot** cave

"I saw their starved lips in the gloam
   With horrid warning gapèd wide,
And I awoke, and found me here
   On the cold hill's side.

"And this is why I sojourn here   45
   Alone and palely loitering;
Though the sedge is withered from the Lake,
   And no birds sing."

—1819

Ode on a Grecian Urn

1

Thou still unravished bride of quietness,
   Thou foster-child of silence and slow time,
Sylvan historian, who canst thus express
   A flowery tale more sweetly than our rhyme:
What leaf-fringed legend haunts about thy shape   5
   Of deities or mortals, or of both,
      In Tempe or the dales of Arcady?°
   What men or gods are these? What maidens loath?°
What mad pursuit? What struggle to escape?
      What pipes and timbrels?° What wild ecstasy?   10

2

Heard melodies are sweet, but those unheard
   Are sweeter; therefore, ye soft pipes, play on;
Not to the sensual ear, but, more endeared,
   Pipe to the spirit ditties of no tone:
Fair youth, beneath the trees, thou canst not leave   15
   Thy song, nor ever can those trees be bare;
      Bold Lover, never, never canst thou kiss,
Though winning near the goal—yet, do not grieve;
      She cannot fade, though thou hast not thy bliss,
   Forever wilt thou love, and she be fair!   20

---

7 Tempe or the dales of Arcady idealized Greek settings   **8 loath** reluctant   **10 timbrels**
tambourines

3

Ah, happy, happy boughs! that cannot shed
  Your leaves, nor ever bid the Spring adieu;
And, happy melodist, unwearièd,
  Forever piping songs forever new;
More happy love! more happy, happy love!   25
  Forever warm and still to be enjoyed,
    Forever panting, and forever young;
All breathing human passion far above,
  That leaves a heart high-sorrowful and cloyed,
    A burning forehead, and a parching tongue.   30

4

Who are these coming to the sacrifice?
  To what green altar, O mysterious priest,
Lead'st thou that heifer lowing at the skies,
  And all her silken flanks with garlands dressed?
What little town by river or sea shore,   35
  Or mountain-built with peaceful citadel,
    Is emptied of this folk, this pious morn?
And, little town, thy streets forevermore
  Will silent be; and not a soul to tell
    Why thou art desolate, can e'er return.   40

5

O Attic° shape! Fair attitude! with brede°
  Of marble men and maidens overwrought,
With forest branches and the trodden weed;
  Thou, silent form, dost tease us out of thought
As doth eternity: Cold Pastoral!   45
  When old age shall this generation waste,
    Thou shalt remain, in midst of other woe
Than ours, a friend to man, to whom thou say'st,
  "Beauty is truth, truth beauty,"—that is all
    Ye know on earth, and all ye need to know.   50

—1819

41 Attic Greek   brede ornamental pattern

Ode to a Nightingale

1

My heart aches, and a drowsy numbness pains
    My sense, as though of hemlock° I had drunk,
Or emptied some dull opiate to the drains
    One minute past, and Lethe-wards° had sunk.
'Tis not through envy of thy happy lot,   5
    But being too happy in thine happiness—
        That thou, light-wingèd Dryad° of the trees,
            In some melodious plot
Of beechen green, and shadows numberless,
        Singest of summer in full-throated ease.   10

2

O, for a draught of vintage! that hath been
    Cooled a long age in the deep-delvèd earth,
Tasting of Flora° and the country green,
    Dance, and Provençal° song, and sunburnt mirth!
O for a beaker full of the warm South,   15
    Full of the true, the blushful Hippocrene,°
        With beaded bubbles winking at the brim,
            And purple-stainèd mouth;
That I might drink, and leave the world unseen,
        And with thee fade away into the forest dim: 20

3

Fade far away, dissolve, and quite forget
    What thou among the leaves hast never known,
The weariness, the fever, and the fret
    Here, where men sit and hear each other groan;
Where palsy shakes a few, sad, last gray hairs,   25
    Where youth grows pale, and specter-thin, and dies;
        Where but to think is to be full of sorrow
            And leaden-eyed despairs,
    Where Beauty cannot keep her lustrous eyes,

2 hemlock a deadly poison   **4 Lethe-wards** toward the waters of forgetfulness   **7 Dryad** tree nymph
13 Flora Roman goddess of spring   **14 Provençal** of Provence, in South of France   **16 Hippocrene**
fountain of the Muses

Or new Love pine at them beyond tomorrow.   30

4

Away! away! for I will fly to thee,
   Not charioted by Bacchus° and his pards,°
But on the viewless wings of Poesy,°
   Though the dull brain perplexes and retards:
Already with thee! tender is the night,   35
     And haply the Queen-Moon is on her throne,
        Clustered around by all her starry Fays;°
          But here there is no light,
Save what from heaven is with the breezes blown
     Through verdurous glooms and winding mossy ways.   40

5

I cannot see what flowers are at my feet,
   Nor what soft incense hangs upon the boughs,
But, in embalmèd darkness, guess each sweet
   Wherewith the seasonable month endows
The grass, the thicket, and the fruit-tree wild;   45
     White hawthorn, and the pastoral eglantine;
        Fast fading violets covered up in leaves;
          And mid-May's eldest child,
     The coming musk-rose, full of dewy wine,
        The murmurous haunt of flies on summer eves.   50

6

Darkling° I listen; and for many a time
   I have been half in love with easeful Death,
Called him soft names in many a musèd rhyme,
   To take into the air my quiet breath;
Now more than ever seems it rich to die,   55
     To cease upon the midnight with no pain,
        While thou art pouring forth thy soul abroad
          In such an ecstasy!
     Still wouldst thou sing, and I have ears in vain—
        To thy high requiem become a sod.   60

---

32 Bacchus Roman god of wine   **pards** leopards   **33 Poesy** poetry   **37 Fays** fairies   **51 Darkling** in the dark

7

Thou wast not born for death, immortal Bird!
   No hungry generations tread thee down;
The voice I hear this passing night was heard
   In ancient days by emperor and clown;
Perhaps the selfsame song that found a path   65
     Through the sad heart of Ruth, when, sick for home,
       She stood in tears amid the alien corn;°
          The same that ofttimes hath
     Charmed magic casements, opening on the foam
       Of perilous seas, in faery lands forlorn.   70

8

Forlorn! the very word is like a bell
   To toll me back from thee to my sole self!
Adieu! the fancy cannot cheat so well
   As she is famed to do, deceiving elf.
Adieu! adieu! thy plaintive anthem fades   75
     Past the near meadows, over the still stream,
       Up the hill side; and now 'tis buried deep
          In the next valley-glades:
     Was it a vision, or a waking dream?
       Fled is that music:—Do I wake or sleep?   80

—*1819*

On First Looking into Chapman's Homer°

Much have I traveled in the realms of gold,
   And many goodly states and kingdoms seen;
   Round many western islands have I been
Which bards in fealty to Apollo° hold.

66–67 Ruth . . . alien corn in the Old Testament she is a Moabite working in the grain fields of Boaz in Judah
Chapman's Homer translation of the *Iliad* and *Odyssey* by George Chapman (1559–1634)
4 Apollo here, the god of poetry

Oft of one wide expanse had I been told   5
   That deep-browed Homer ruled as his demesne;
   Yet did I never breathe its pure serene
Till I heard Chapman speak out loud and bold:
Then felt I like some watcher of the skies
   When a new planet swims into his ken;   10
Or like stout Cortez° when with eagle eyes
   He stared at the Pacific—and all his men
Looked at each other with a wild surmise—
   Silent, upon a peak in Darien.°

—1816

When I Have Fears

When I have fears that I may cease to be
   Before my pen has gleaned my teeming brain,
Before high-pilèd books, in charact'ry,°
   Hold like rich garners the full-ripened grain;
When I behold, upon the night's starred face,   5
   Huge cloudy symbols of a high romance,
And think that I may never live to trace
   Their shadows, with the magic hand of chance;
And when I feel, fair creature of an hour,
   That I shall never look upon thee more,   10
Never have relish in the faery power
   Of unreflecting love!—then on the shore
Of the wide world I stand alone, and think
Till Love and Fame to nothingness do sink.

—1818

---

11 **Cortez** Balboa was actually the first European to see the Pacific   14 **Darien** in modern-day
Panama
3 **charact'ry** writing

Elizabeth Barrett Browning (1806–1861)

Elizabeth Barrett Browning was already a famous poet when she met her husband-to-be, Robert Browning, who had been corresponding with her on literary matters. She originally published her famous sonnet sequence, written in the first years of her marriage, in the guise of a translation of Portuguese poems, perhaps to mask their personal revelations.

Sonnets from the Portuguese, 18

I never gave a lock of hair away
To a man, dearest, except this to thee,
Which now upon my fingers thoughtfully,
I ring out to the full brown length and say
"Take it." My day of youth went yesterday;   5
My hair no longer bounds to my foot's glee,
Nor plant I it from rose or myrtle-tree,
As girls do, any more: it only may
Now shade on two pale cheeks the mark of tears,
Taught drooping from the head that hangs aside   10
Through sorrow's trick. I thought the funeral-shears
Would take this first, but Love is justified,—
Take it thou,—finding pure, from all those years,
The kiss my mother left here when she died.

—1845–46

Sonnets from the Portuguese, 43

How do I love thee? Let me count the ways.
I love thee to the depth and breadth and height
My soul can reach, when feeling out of sight
For the ends of Being and ideal Grace.
I love thee to the level of everyday's   5
Most quiet need, by sun and candle-light.

I love thee freely, as men strive for Right;
I love thee purely, as they turn from Praise.
I love thee with the passion put to use
In my old griefs, and with my childhood's faith.   10
I love thee with a love I seemed to lose
With my lost saints—I love thee with the breath,
Smiles, tears, of all my life!—and, if God choose,
I shall but love thee better after death.

—*1845–46*

Henry Wadsworth Longfellow (1807–1882)

Henry Wadsworth Longfellow was by far the most prominent nineteenth-century American poet, and his international fame led to his bust being placed in Westminster Abbey after his death. The long epic poems like Evangeline *and* Hiawatha *that were immensely popular among contemporary readers are seldom read today, but his shorter poems reveal a level of craftsmanship that few poets have equaled.*

The Arsenal at Springfield

This is the Arsenal. From floor to ceiling,
    Like a huge organ, rise the burnished arms;
But from their silent pipes no anthem pealing
    Startles the villages with strange alarms.

Ah! what a sound will rise, how wild and dreary,   5
    When the death-angel touches those swift keys!
What loud lament and dismal Miserere°
    Will mingle with their awful symphonies!

I hear even now the infinite fierce chorus,
    The cries of agony, the endless groan,   10
Which, through the ages that have gone before us,
    In long reverberations reach our own.

On helm and harness rings the Saxon hammer,
    Through Cimbric° forest roars the Norseman's song,

7 **Miserere** Latin hymn from Psalm 1: "Have mercy on me, Lord."   14 **Cimbric** in Denmark

And loud, amid the universal clamor, 15
    O'er distant deserts sounds the Tartar gong.

I hear the Florentine, who from his palace
    Wheels out his battle-bell with dreadful din,
And Aztec priests upon their teocallis°
    Beat the wild war-drums made of serpent's skin; 20

The tumult of each sacked and burning village;
    The shout that every prayer for mercy drowns;
The soldiers' revels in the midst of pillage;
    The wail of famine in beleaguered towns;

The bursting shell, the gateway wrenched asunder, 25
    The rattling musketry, the clashing blade;
And ever and anon, in tones of thunder
    The diapason° of the cannonade.

Is it, O man, with such discordant noises,
    With such accursed instruments as these, 30
Thou drownest Nature's sweet and kindly voices,
    And jarrest the celestial harmonies?

Were half the power, that fills the world with terror,
    Were half the wealth bestowed on camps and courts,
Given to redeem the human mind from error, 35
    There were no need of arsenals or forts:

The warrior's name would be a name abhorred!
    And every nation, that should lift again
Its hand against a brother, on its forehead
    Would wear forevermore the curse of Cain! 40

Down the dark future, through long generations,
    The echoing sounds grow fainter and then cease;
And like a bell, with solemn, sweet vibrations,
    I hear once more the voice of Christ say, "Peace!"

Peace! and no longer from its brazen portals 45
    The blast of War's great organ shakes the skies!
But beautiful as songs of the immortals,
    The holy melodies of love arise.

—1846

---

19 teocallis temples atop pyramids   **28 diapason** full range of pipe organ

The Cross of Snow

In the long, sleepless watches of the night,
    A gentle face—the face of one long dead—
    Looks at me from the wall, where round its head
    The night-lamp casts a halo of pale light.
Here in this room she died; and soul more white   5
    Never through martyrdom of fire° was led
    To its repose; nor can in books be read
    The legend of a life more benedight.°
There is a mountain in the distant West
    That, sun-defying, in its deep ravines   10
    Displays a cross of snow upon its side.
Such is the cross I wear upon my breast
    These eighteen years, through all the changing scenes
    And seasons, changeless since the day she died.

                                      —1886

Edgar Allan Poe (1809–1849)

Edgar Allan Poe has survived his own myth as a deranged, drug-crazed genius, despite the wealth of evidence to the contrary that can be gleaned from his brilliant, though erratic, career as a poet, short-story writer, critic, and editor. Poe's brand of romanticism seems at odds with that of other American poets of his day, and is perhaps more in keeping with the spirit of Coleridge than that of Wordsworth. "The Raven" has been parodied perhaps more than any other American poem, yet it still retains a powerful hold on its audience.

The Haunted Palace

In the greenest of our valleys,
    By good angels tenanted,
Once a fair and stately palace—
    Radiant palace—reared its head.

---

6 **martyrdom of fire** Longfellow's second wife, Frances, died as the result of a household fire in 1861.
8 **benedight** blessed

In the monarch Thought's dominion—   5
    It stood there!
Never seraph spread a pinion
    Over fabric half so fair!

Banners yellow, glorious, golden,
    On its roof did float and flow,   10
(This—all this—was in the olden
    Time long ago,)
And every gentle air that dallied,
    In that sweet day,
Along the ramparts plumed and pallid,   15
    A wingéd odor went away.

Wanderers in that happy valley,
    Through two luminous windows, saw
Spirits moving musically
    To a lute's well-tunéd law,   20
Round about a throne where, sitting,
    Porphyrogene!°
In state his glory well befitting,
    The ruler of the realm was seen.

And all with pearl and ruby glowing   25
    Was the fair palace door,
Through which came flowing, flowing, flowing,
    And sparkling evermore,
A troop of Echoes, whose sweet duty
    Was but to sing,   30
In voices of surpassing beauty,
    The wit and wisdom of their king.

But evil things, in robes of sorrow,
    Assailed the monarch's high estate.
(Ah, let us mourn!—for never morrow   35
    Shall dawn upon him, desolate!)
And round about his home the glory
    That blushed and bloomed,
Is but a dim-remembered story
    Of the old time entombed.   40

---

22 Porphyrogene born to the purple, i.e., royal

and travellers, now, within that valley,
    Through the red-litten windows see
Vast forms that move fantastically
    To a discordant melody,
While, like a ghastly rapid river,   45
    Through the pale door
A hideous throng rush out forever,
    And laugh—but smile no more.

                          —*1845*

Israfel

In Heaven a spirit doth dwell
    "Whose heart-strings are a lute;"
None sing so wildly well
As the angel Israfel,°
And the giddy stars (so legends tell)   5
Ceasing their hymns, attend the spell
    Of his voice, all mute.

Tottering above
    In her highest noon,
    The enamoured moon   10
Blushes with love,
    While, to listen, the red levin
    (With the rapid Pleiads,° even,
    Which were seven,)
    Pauses in Heaven.   15

And they say (the starry choir
    And the other listening things)
That Israfeli's fire
Is owing to that lyre
    By which he sits and sings—   20
The trembling living wire
    Of those unusual strings.

But the skies that angel trod,
    Where deep thoughts are a duty—

4 Israfel an angel found in the Koran   **13 Pleiads** a constellation

Where Love's a grown-up God— 25
   Where the Houri° glances are
   Imbued with all the beauty
   Which we worship in a star.

Therefore, thou art not wrong,
   Israfeli, who despisest 30
An unimpassioned song;
To thee the laurels belong,
   Best bard, because the wisest!
Merrily live, and long!

The ecstasies above 35
   With thy burning measures suit—
Thy grief, thy joy, thy hate, thy love,
With the fervour of thy lute—
   Well may the stars be mute!

Yes, Heaven is thine; but this
   Is a world of sweets and sours;
   Our flowers are merely—flowers, 40
And the shadow of thy perfect bliss
   Is the sunshine of ours.

If I could dwell 45
Where Israfel
   Hath dwelt, and he where I,
He might not sing so wildly well
   A mortal melody,
While a bolder note than this might swell 50
   From my lyre within the sky.

—1831

The Raven

Once upon a midnight dreary, while I pondered, weak and weary,
Over many a quaint and curious volume of forgotten lore—
While I nodded, nearly napping, suddenly there came a tapping,
As of some one gently rapping, rapping at my chamber door.

26 **Houri** nymphs

"'Tis some visitor," I muttered, "tapping at my chamber door—   5
               Only this and nothing more."

Ah, distinctly I remember it was in the bleak December;
And each separate dying ember wrought its ghost upon the floor.
Eagerly I wished the morrow;—vainly I had sought to borrow
From my books surcease of sorrow—sorrow for the lost Lenore—   10
For the rare and radiant maiden whom the angels name Lenore—
               Nameless *here* for evermore.

And the silken, sad, uncertain rustling of each purple curtain
Thrilled me—filled me with fantastic terrors never felt before;
So that now, to still the beating of my heart, I stood repeating   15
"'Tis some visitor entreating entrance at my chamber door;—
Some late visitor entreating entrance at my chamber door;—
               This it is and nothing more."

Presently my soul grew stronger; hesitating then no longer,
"Sir," said I, "or Madam, truly your forgiveness I implore;   20
But the fact is I was napping, and so gently you came rapping,
And so faintly you came tapping, tapping at my chamber door,
That I scarce was sure I heard you"—here I opened wide the door;—
               Darkness there and nothing more.

Deep into that darkness peering, long I stood there wondering,   25
   fearing,
Doubting, dreaming dreams no mortal ever dared to dream before;
But the silence was unbroken, and the stillness gave no token,
And the only word there spoken was the whispered word, "Lenore?"
This I whispered, and an echo murmured back the word, "Lenore!"
               Merely this and nothing more.   30

Back into the chamber turning, all my soul within me burning,
Soon again I heard a tapping somewhat louder than before.
"Surely," said I, "surely that is something at my window lattice;
Let me see, then, what thereat is, and this mystery explore—
Let my heart be still a moment and this mystery explore;—   35
               'Tis the wind and nothing more!"

Open here I flung the shutter, when, with many a flirt and flutter,
In there stepped a stately Raven of the saintly days of yore;
Not the least obeisance made he; not a minute stopped or stayed he;
But, with mien of lord or lady, perched above my chamber door—   40

Perched upon a bust of Pallas° just above my chamber door—
Perched, and sat, and nothing more.

Then this ebony bird beguiling my sad fancy into smiling,
By the grave and stern decorum of the countenance it wore,
"Though thy crest be shorn and shaven, thou," I said, "art sure no   45
craven,
Ghastly grim and ancient Raven wandering from the Nightly shore—
Tell me what thy lordly name is on the Night's Plutonian° shore!"
Quoth the Raven, "Nevermore."

Much I marvelled this ungainly fowl to hear discourse so plainly,
Though its answer little meaning—little relevancy bore;   50
For we cannot help agreeing that no living human being
Ever yet was blessed with seeing bird above his chamber door—
Bird or beast upon the sculptured bust above his chamber door,
With such name as "Nevermore."

But the Raven, sitting lonely on the placid bust, spoke only   55
That one word, as if his soul in that one word he did outpour.
Nothing farther then he uttered—not a feather then he fluttered—
Till I scarcely more than muttered, "Other friends have flown before—
On the morrow *he* will leave me, as my Hopes have flown before."
Then the bird said, "Nevermore."   60

Startled at the stillness broken by reply so aptly spoken,
"Doubtless," said I, "what it utters is its only stock and store
Caught from some unhappy master whom unmerciful Disaster
Followed fast and followed faster till his songs one burden bore—
Till the dirges of his Hope that melancholy burden bore   65
Of 'Never—nevermore.'"

But the Raven still beguiling all my sad fancy into smiling,
Straight I wheeled a cushioned seat in front of bird and bust and door;
Then, upon the velvet sinking, I betook myself to linking
Fancy unto fancy, thinking what this ominous bird of yore—   70
What this grim, ungainly, ghastly, gaunt, and ominous bird of yore
Meant in croaking "Nevermore."

This I sat engaged in guessing, but no syllable expressing
To the fowl whose fiery eyes now burned into my bosom's core;
This and more I sat divining, with my head at ease reclining   75
On the cushion's velvet lining that the lamp-light gloated o'er,

---

41 Pallas Athena, goddess of wisdom   **47 Plutonian** after Pluto, Roman god of the underworld

But whose velvet-violet lining with the lamp-light gloating o'er,
    She shall press, ah, nevermore!

Then, methought, the air grew denser, perfumed from an unseen
    censer
Swung by seraphim whose foot-falls tinkled on the tufted floor.   80
"Wretch," I cried, "thy God hath lent thee—by these angels he
    hath sent thee.
Respite—respite and nepenthe° from thy memories of Lenore;
Quaff, oh quaff this kind nepenthe and forget this lost Lenore!"
    Quoth the Raven, "Nevermore."

"Prophet!" said I, "thing of evil!—prophet still, if bird or devil!—   85
Whether Tempter sent, or whether tempest tossed thee here ashore,
Desolate yet all undaunted, on this desert land enchanted—
On this home by Horror haunted—tell me truly, I implore—
Is there— *is* there balm in Gilead?—tell me—tell me, I implore!"
    Quoth the Raven, "Nevermore."   90

"Prophet!" said I, "thing of evil!—prophet still, if bird or devil!
By that Heaven that bends above us—by that God we both adore—
Tell this soul with sorrow laden if, within the distant Aidenn,°
It shall clasp a sainted maiden whom the angels name Lenore—
Clasp a rare and radiant maiden whom the angels name Lenore."   95
    Quoth the Raven, "Nevermore."

"Be that word our sign of parting, bird or fiend!" I shrieked,
    upstarting—
"Get thee back into the tempest and the Night's Plutonian shore!
Leave no black plume as a token of that lie thy soul hath spoken!
Leave my loneliness unbroken!—quit the bust above my door!   100
Take thy beak from out my heart, and take thy form from off my
    door!"
    Quoth the Raven, "Nevermore."

And the Raven, never flitting, still is sitting, *still* is sitting
On the pallid bust of Pallas just above my chamber door;
And his eyes have all the seeming of a demon's that is dreaming,   105
And the lamp-light o'er him streaming throws his shadow on the floor;
And my soul from out that shadow that lies floating on the floor
    Shall be lifted—nevermore!

                                                    —1845

82 nepenthe drug causing forgetfulness   93 Aidenn Eden

To Helen

Helen, thy beauty is to me
    Like those Nicean° barks of yore,
That gently, o'er a perfumed sea,
    The weary, way-worn wanderer bore
    To his own native shore.   5

On desperate seas long wont to roam,
    Thy hyacinth° hair, thy classic face
Thy Naiad° airs have brought me home
    To the glory that was Greece
And the grandeur that was Rome.   10

Lo! in yon brilliant window-niche
    How statue-like I see thee stand!
    The agate lamp within thy hand,
Ah! Psyche,° from the regions which
    Are Holy Land!   15

                                      —1831

---

2 **Nicean** possibly of Nice (in the South of France); or Phoenician   7 **hyacinth** reddish, like the flower of Greek myth   8 **Naiad** water nymph   14 **Psyche** the soul

Alfred, Lord Tennyson (1809–1892)

Alfred, Lord Tennyson became the most famous English poet with the 1850 publication of In Memoriam, *a sequence of poems on the death of his friend A. H. Hallam. In the same year he became poet laureate. Modern critical opinion has focused more favorably on Tennyson's lyrical gifts than on his talents for narrative or drama. T. S. Eliot and W. H. Auden, among other critics, praised Tennyson's rhythms and sound patterns but had reservations about his depth of intellect, especially when he took on the role of official apologist for Victorian England.*

The Eagle

FRAGMENT

He clasps the crag with crooked hands;
Close to the sun in lonely lands,
Ringed with the azure world, he stands.

The wrinkled sea beneath him crawls;
He watches from his mountain walls,   5
And like a thunderbolt he falls.

—*1851*

The Lady of Shalott

PART 1

On either side the river lie
Long fields of barley and of rye,
That clothe the wold° and meet the sky;
And through the field the road runs by
        To many-towered Camelot;   5
And up and down the people go,
Gazing where the lilies blow
Round an island there below,
        The island of Shalott.

3 **wold** plain

Willows whiten, aspens quiver,   10
Little breezes dusk and shiver
Through the wave that runs forever
By the island in the river
      Flowing down to Camelot.
Four gray walls, and four gray towers,   15
Overlook a space of flowers,
And the silent isle embowers
      The Lady of Shalott.

By the margin, willow-veiled,
Slide the heavy barges trailed
By slow horses; and unhailed   20
The shallop° flitteth silken-sailed
      Skimming down to Camelot:
But who hath seen her wave her hand?
Or at the casement seen her stand?
Or is she known in all the land,   25
      The Lady of Shalott?

Only reapers, reaping early
In among the bearded barley,
Hear a song that echoes cheerly
From the river winding clearly,   30
      Down to towered Camelot;
And by the moon the reaper weary,
Piling sheaves in uplands airy,
Listening, whispers, "'Tis the fairy   35
      Lady of Shalott."

    PART 2

There she weaves by night and day
A magic web with colors gay.
She has heard a whisper say,
A curse is on her if she stay   40
      To look down to Camelot.
She knows not what the curse may be,
And so she weaveth steadily,
And little other care hath she,
      The Lady of Shalott.   45

22 **shallop** open boat

And moving through a mirror clear
That hangs before her all the year,
Shadows of the world appear.
There she sees the highway near
    Winding down to Camelot;   50
There the river eddy whirls,
And there the surly village-churls,
And the red cloaks of market girls,
    Pass onward from Shalott.

Sometimes a troop of damsels glad,   55
An abbot on an ambling pad,°
Sometimes a curly shepherd-lad,
Or long-haired page in crimson clad,
    Goes by to towered Camelot;
And sometimes through the mirror blue   60
The knights come riding two and two;
She hath no loyal knight and true,
    The Lady of Shalott.

But in her web she still delights
To weave the mirror's magic sights,   65
For often through the silent nights
A funeral, with plumes and lights
    And music, went to Camelot;
Or when the moon was overhead,
Came two young lovers lately wed;   70
"I am half sick of shadows," said
    The Lady of Shalott.

PART 3

A bow-shot from her bower eaves,
He rode between the barley sheaves;
The sun came dazzling through the leaves,   75
And flamed upon the brazen greaves°
    Of bold Sir Lancelot.
A red-cross knight forever kneeled
To a lady in his shield.
That sparkled on the yellow field,   80
    Beside remote Shalott.

56 pad horse   **76 greaves** armor for legs

The gemmy bridle glittered free,
Like to some branch of stars we see
Hung in the golden Galaxy.
The bridle bells rang merrily   85
     As he rode down to Camelot;
And from his blazoned baldric° slung
A mighty silver bugle hung,
And as he rode his armor rung,
     Beside remote Shalott.   90

All in the blue unclouded weather
Thick-jeweled shone the saddle-leather,
The helmet and the helmet-feather
Burned like one burning flame together
     As he rode down to Camelot;   95
As often through the purple night,
Below the starry clusters bright,
Some bearded meteor, trailing light,
     Moves over still Shalott.

His broad clear brow in sunlight glowed;   100
On burnished hooves his war horse trode;
From underneath his helmet flowed
His coal-black curls as on he rode,
     As he rode down to Camelot.
From the bank and from the river   105
He flashed into the crystal mirror,
"Tirra lirra," by the river
     Sang Sir Lancelot.

She left the web, she left the loom,
She made three paces through the room,   110
She saw the water lily bloom,
She saw the helmet and the plume,
     She looked down to Camelot.
Out flew the web and floated wide;
The mirror cracked from side to side;   115
"The curse is come upon me," cried
     The Lady of Shalott.

87 baldric belt to support a sword

PART 4

In the stormy east wind straining,
The pale yellow woods were waning,
The broad stream in his banks complaining.   120
Heavily the low sky raining
    Over towered Camelot;
Down she came and found a boat
Beneath a willow left afloat,
And round about the prow she wrote   125
    The Lady of Shalott.

And down the river's dim expanse
Like some bold seer in a trance,
Seeing all his own mischance—
With a glassy countenance   130
    Did she look to Camelot.
And at the closing of the day
She loosed the chain, and down she lay;
The broad stream bore her far away,
    The Lady of Shalott.   135

Lying, robed in snowy white
That loosely flew to left and right—
The leaves upon her falling light—
Through the noises of the night
    She floated down to Camelot;   140
And as the boat-head wound along
The willowy hills and fields among,
They heard her singing her last song,
    The Lady of Shalott.

Heard a carol, mournful, holy,   145
Chanted loudly, chanted lowly,
Till her blood was frozen slowly,
And her eyes were darkened wholly,
    Turned to towered Camelot.
For ere she reached upon the tide   150
The first house by the waterside,
Singing in her song she died,
    The Lady of Shalott.

Under tower and balcony,
By garden wall and gallery,   155

A gleaming shape she floated by,
Dead-pale between the houses high,
    Silent into Camelot.
Out upon the wharfs they came,
Knight and burgher, lord and dame,   160
And round the prow they read her name,
    The Lady of Shalott.

Who is this? And what is here?
And in the lighted palace near
Died the sound of royal cheer;   165
And they crossed themselves for fear,
    All the knights at Camelot.
But Lancelot mused a little space;
He said, "She has a lovely face;
God in his mercy lend her grace,   170
    The Lady of Shalott."

                          —*1842*

Tears, Idle Tears

FROM THE PRINCESS

    Tears, idle tears, I know not what they mean,
Tears from the depth of some divine despair
Rise in the heart, and gather to the eyes,
In looking on the happy autumn-fields,
And thinking of the days that are no more.   5

    Fresh as the first beam glittering on a sail,
That brings our friends up from the underworld,
Sad as the last which reddens over one
That sinks with all we love below the verge;
So sad, so fresh, the days that are no more.   10

    Ah, sad and strange as in dark summer dawns
The earliest pipe of half-awakened birds
To dying ears, when unto dying eyes
The casement slowly grows a glimmering square;
So sad, so strange, the days that are no more.   15

Dear as remembered kisses after death,
And sweet as those by hopeless fancy feigned
On lips that are for others; deep as love,
Deep as first love, and wild with all regret;
O Death in Life, the days that are no more!   20

—1847

Ulysses°

It little profits that an idle king,
By this still hearth, among these barren crags,
Matched with an aged wife, I mete and dole
Unequal laws unto a savage race,
That hoard, and sleep, and feed, and know not me.   5
I cannot rest from travel; I will drink
Life to the lees. All times I have enjoyed
Greatly, have suffered greatly, both with those
That loved me, and alone; on shore, and when
Through scudding drifts the rainy Hyades°   10
Vexed the dim sea. I am become a name;
For always roaming with a hungry heart
Much have I seen and known—cities of men
And manners, climates, councils, governments,
Myself not least, but honored of them all—   15
And drunk delight of battle with my peers,
Far on the ringing plains of windy Troy.
I am a part of all that I have met;
Yet all experience is an arch wherethrough
Gleams that untraveled world whose margin fades   20
For ever and for ever when I move.
How dull it is to pause, to make an end,
To rust unburnished, not to shine in use!
As though to breathe were life! Life piled on life
Were all too little, and of one to me   25
Little remains; but every hour is saved
From that eternal silence, something more,

Ulysses Homer's *Odyssey* ends with the return of Odysseus (Ulysses) to his island kingdom, Ithaca.
Tennyson's poem takes place some years later.   **10 Hyades** a constellation thought to predict rain

A bringer of new things; and vile it were
For some three suns to store and hoard myself,
And this gray spirit yearning in desire   30
To follow knowledge like a sinking star,
Beyond the utmost bound of human thought.
     This is my son, mine own Telemachus,
To whom I leave the scepter and the isle,
Well-loved of me, discerning to fulfill   35
This labor, by slow prudence to make mild
A rugged people, and through soft degrees
Subdue them to the useful and the good.
Most blameless is he, centered in the sphere
Of common duties, decent not to fail   40
In offices of tenderness, and pay
Meet adoration to my household gods,
When I am gone. He works his work, I mine.
     There lies the port; the vessel puffs her sail;
There gloom the dark, broad seas. My mariners,   45
Souls that have toiled, and wrought, and thought with me,
That ever with a frolic welcome took
The thunder and the sunshine, and opposed
Free hearts, free foreheads—you and I are old;
Old age hath yet his honor and his toil.   50
Death closes all; but something ere the end,
Some work of noble note, may yet be done,
Not unbecoming men that strove with gods.
The lights begin to twinkle from the rocks;
The long day wanes; the low moon climbs; the deep   55
Moans round with many voices. Come, my friends,
'Tis not too late to seek a newer world.
Push off, and sitting well in order smite
The sounding furrows; for my purpose holds
To sail beyond the sunset, and the baths   60
Of all the western stars, until I die.
It may be that the gulfs will wash us down;
It may be we shall touch the Happy Isles,°
And see the great Achilles, whom we knew.
Though much is taken, much abides; and though   65
We are not now that strength which in old days

63 **Happy Isles** Elysium, the resting place of dead heroes

Moved earth and heaven, that which we are, we are,
One equal temper of heroic hearts,
Made weak by time and fate, but strong in will
To strive, to seek, to find, and not to yield. 70

—*1833*

Robert Browning (1812–1889)

Robert Browning wrote many successful dramatic monologues that are his lasting legacy, for he brings the genre to a level of achievement rarely equaled. Less regarded during his lifetime than his contemporary Tennyson, he has consistently risen in the esteem of modern readers. Often overlooked in his gallery of often grotesque characters are his considerable metrical skills and ability to simulate speech while working in demanding poetic forms.

My Last Duchess

FERRARA°

That's my last duchess painted on the wall,
Looking as if she were alive. I call
That piece a wonder, now: Frà Pandolf's° hands
Worked busily a day, and there she stands.
Will't please you sit and look at her? I said 5
"Frà Pandolf" by design, for never read
Strangers like you that pictured countenance,
The depth and passion of its earnest glance,
But to myself they turned (since none puts by
The curtain I have drawn for you, but I) 10
And seemed as they would ask me, if they durst,
How such a glance came there; so, not the first
Are you to turn and ask thus. Sir, 'twas not
Her husband's presence only, called that spot

Ferrara The speaker is probably Alfonso II d'Este, Duke of Ferrara (1533–158?)   **3 Frà Pandolf** an imaginary painter

Of joy into the Duchess' cheek: perhaps   15
Frà Pandolf chanced to say "Her mantle laps
Over my lady's wrist too much," or "Paint
Must never hope to reproduce the faint
Half-flush that dies along her throat": such stuff
Was courtesy, she thought, and cause enough   20
For calling up that spot of joy. She had
A heart—how shall I say?—too soon made glad,
Too easily impressed; she liked whate'er
She looked on, and her looks went everywhere.
Sir, 'twas all one! My favor at her breast,   25
The dropping of the daylight in the West,
The bough of cherries some officious fool
Broke in the orchard for her, the white mule
She rode with round the terrace—all and each
Would draw from her alike the approving speech,   30
Or blush, at least. She thanked men—good! but thanked
Somehow—I know not how—as if she ranked
My gift of a nine-hundred-years-old name
With anybody's gift. Who'd stoop to blame
This sort of trifling? Even had you skill   35
In speech—which I have not—to make your will
Quite clear to such an one, and say, "Just this
Or that in you disgusts me; here you miss,
Or there exceed the mark"—and if she let
Herself be lessoned so, nor plainly set   40
Her wits to yours, forsooth, and made excuse,
—E'en then would be some stooping; and I choose
Never to stoop. Oh sir, she smiled, no doubt,
Whene'er I passed her; but who passed without
Much the same smile? This grew; I gave commands;   45
Then all smiles stopped together. There she stands
As if alive. Will't please you rise? We'll meet
The company below, then. I repeat,
The Count your master's° known munificence
Is ample warrant that no just pretense   50
Of mine for dowry will be disallowed;
Though his fair daughter's self, as I avowed

---

49 Count your master's The auditor is apparently an envoy sent to arrange a marriage between the Duke of Ferrara and a count's daughter

At starting, is my object. Nay, we'll go
Together down, sir. Notice Neptune, though,
Taming a sea horse, thought a rarity,   55
Which Claus of Innsbruck cast in bronze for me!

—1842

Porphyria's° Lover

The rain set early in tonight,
    The sullen wind was soon awake,
It tore the elm-tops down for spite,
    And did its worst to vex the lake:
    I listened with heart fit to break.   5
When glided in Porphyria; straight
    She shut the cold out and the storm,
And kneeled and made the cheerless grate
    Blaze up, and all the cottage warm;
    Which done, she rose, and from her form   10
Withdrew the dripping cloak and shawl,
    And laid her soiled gloves by, untied
Her hat and let the damp hair fall,
    And, last, she sat down by my side
    And called me. When no voice replied,   15
She put my arm about her waist,
    And made her smooth white shoulder bare,
And all her yellow hair displaced,
    And, stooping, made my cheek lie there,
    And spread, o'er all, her yellow hair,   20
Murmuring how she loved me—she
    Too weak, for all her heart's endeavor,
To set its struggling passion free
    From pride, and vainer ties dissever,
    And give herself to me forever.   25
But passion sometimes would prevail,
    Nor could tonight's gay feast restrain
A sudden thought of one so pale

Porphyria name suggesting purple, the color of nobility and royalty

For love of her, and all in vain:
    So, she was come through wind and rain.   30
Be sure I looked up at her eyes
    Happy and proud; at last I knew
Porphyria worshipped me; surprise
    Made my heart swell, and still it grew
    While I debated what to do.   35
That moment she was mine, mine, fair,
    Perfectly pure and good: I found
A thing to do, and all her hair
    In one long yellow string I wound
    Three times her little throat around,   40
And strangled her. No pain felt she;
    I am quite sure she felt no pain.
As a shut bud that holds a bee,
    I warily oped her lids: again
    Laughed the blue eyes without a stain.   45
And I untightened next the tress
    About her neck; her cheek once more
Blushed bright beneath my burning kiss:
    I propped her head up as before,
    Only, this time my shoulder bore   50
Her head, which droops upon it still:
    The smiling rosy little head
So glad it has its utmost will,
    That all it scorned at once is fled,
    And I, its love, am gained instead!   55
Porphyria's love: she guessed not how
    Her darling one wish would be heard.
And thus we sit together now,
    And all night long we have not stirred,
    And yet God has not said a word!   60

—*1842*

Walt Whitman (1819–1892)

Walt Whitman pioneered the use of free verse, which established him as one of the forebears of modern poetry, but his subject matter, often dealing with sexual topics, and his unsparing realism were equally controversial in his day. An admirer of Emerson, he adapted many of the ideas of transcendentalism in Song of Myself, *his first major sequence, and also incorporated many of Emerson's calls for poets to use American subjects and patterns of speech.* Leaves of Grass, *which he revised from 1855 until his death, expanded to include virtually all of his poems, including the graphic poems he wrote while serving as a volunteer in Civil War army hospitals.*

Crossing Brooklyn Ferry

1

Flood-tide below me! I see you face to face!
Clouds of the west—sun there half an hour high—I see you also face
    to face.

Crowds of men and women attired in the usual costumes, how
    curious you are to me!
On the ferry-boats the hundreds and hundreds that cross,
    returning home, are more curious to me than you suppose,
And you that shall cross from shore to shore years hence are
    more to me, and more in my meditations, than you might
    suppose.   5

2

The impalpable sustenance of me from all things at all hours of
    the day,
The simple, compact, well-join'd scheme, myself disintegrated,
    every one disintegrated yet part of the scheme,
The similitudes of the past and those of the future,
The glories strung like beads on my smallest sights and hearings,
    on the walk in the street and the passage over the river,
The current rushing so swiftly and swimming with me far away,   10
The others that are to follow me, the ties between me and them,
The certainty of others, the life, love, sight, hearing of others.

Others will enter the gates of the ferry and cross from shore to shore,
Others will watch the run of the flood-tide,
Others will see the shipping of Manhattan north and west, and
    the heights of Brooklyn to the south and east,   15
Others will see the islands large and small;
Fifty years hence, others will see them as they cross, the sun
    half an hour high,
A hundred years hence, or ever so many hundred years hence,
    others will see them,
Will enjoy the sunset, the pouring-in of the flood-tide, the
    falling-back to the sea of the ebb-tide.

3

It avails not, time nor place—distance avails not,   20
I am with you, you men and women of a generation, or ever so
    many generations hence,
Just as you feel when you look on the river and sky, so I felt,
Just as any of you is one of a living crowd, I was one of a crowd,
Just as you are refresh'd by the gladness of the river and the
    bright flow, I was refresh'd,
Just as you stand and lean on the rail, yet hurry with the swift
    current, I stood yet was hurried,   25
Just as you look on the numberless masts of ships and the
    thick-stemm'd pipes of steamboats, I look'd.

I too many and many a time cross'd the river of old,
Watched the Twelfth-month° sea-gulls, saw them high in the
    air floating with motionless wings, oscillating their bodies,
Saw how the glistening yellow lit up parts of their bodies and
    left the rest in strong shadow,
Saw the slow-wheeling circles and the gradual edging toward
    the south,   30
Saw the reflection of the summer sky in the water,
Had my eyes dazzled by the shimmering track of beams,
Look'd at the fine centrifugal spokes of light round the shape
    of my head in the sunlit water,
Look'd on the haze on the hills southward and south-westward,
Look'd on the vapor as it flew in fleeces tinged with violet,   35
Look'd toward the lower bay to notice the vessels arriving,

---

28 Twelfth-month Whitman's mother was a Quaker, hence this phrase for December.

Saw their approach, saw aboard those that were near me,
Saw the white sails of schooners and sloops, saw the ships at
    anchor,
The sailors at work in the rigging or out astride the spars,
The round masts, the swinging motion of the hulls, the slender
    serpentine pennants,   40
The large and small steamers in motion, the pilots in their
    pilothouses,
The white wake left by the passage, the quick tremulous whirl
    of the wheels,
The flags of all nations, the falling of them at sunset,
The scallop-edged waves in the twilight, the ladled cups, the
    frolicsome crests and glistening,
The stretch afar growing dimmer and dimmer, the gray walls
    of the granite storehouses by the docks,   45
On the river the shadowy group, the big steam-tug closely
    flank'd on each side by the barges, the hay-boat, the belated
    lighter,
On the neighboring shore the fires from the foundry chimneys
    burning high and glaringly into the night,
Casting their flicker of black contrasted with wild red and yellow
    light over the tops of houses, and down into the clefts of streets.

    4

These and all else were to me the same as they are to you,
I loved well those cities, loved well the stately and rapid river,   50
The men and women I saw were all near to me,
Others the same—others who look back on me because I look'd
    forward to them,
(The time will come, though I stop here to-day and to-night.)

    5

What is it then between us?
What is the count of the scores or hundreds of years between us?   55

Whatever it is, it avails not—distance avails not, and place avails not,
I too lived, Brooklyn of ample hills was mine,
I too walk'd the streets of Manhattan island, and bathed in the
    waters around it,
I too felt the curious abrupt questionings stir within me,

In the day among crowds of people sometimes they came
    upon me,   60
In my walks home late at night or as I lay in my bed they came
    upon me,
I too had been struck from the float forever held in solution,
I too had receiv'd identity by my body,
That I was I knew was of my body, and what I should be
    I knew I should be of my body.

6

It is not upon you alone the dark patches fall,   65
The dark threw its patches down upon me also,
The best I had done seem'd to me blank and suspicious,
My great thoughts as I supposed them, were they not in reality
    meagre?
Nor is it you alone who know what it is to be evil,
I am he who knew what it was to be evil,   70
I too knitted the old knot of contrariety,
Blabb'd, blush'd, resented, lied, stole, grudg'd,
Had guile, anger, lust, hot wishes I dared not speak,
Was wayward, vain, greedy, shallow, sly, cowardly, malignant,
The wolf, the snake, the hog, not wanting in me,   75
The cheating look, the frivolous word, the adulterous wish,
    not wanting,
Refusals, hates, postponements, meanness, laziness, none of
    these wanting,
Was one with the rest, the days and haps of the rest,
Was call'd by my nighest name by clear loud voices of young
    men as they saw me approaching or passing,
Felt their arms on my neck as I stood, or the negligent leaning
    of their flesh against me as I sat,   80
Saw many I loved in the street or ferry-boat or public
    assembly, yet never told them a word,
Lived the same life with the rest, the same old laughing,
    gnawing, sleeping,
Play'd the part that still looks back on the actor or actress,
The same old role, the role that is what we make it, as great as
    we like,
Or as small as we like, or both great and small.   85

7

Closer yet I approach you,
What thought you have of me now, I had as much of you—I laid
in my stores in advance,
I consider'd long and seriously of you before you were born.
Who was to know what should come home to me?
Who knows but I am enjoying this? 90
Who knows, for all the distance, but I am as good as looking
at you now, for all you cannot see me?

8

Ah, what can ever be more stately and admirable to me than
mast-hemm'd Manhattan?
River and sunset and scallop-edg'd waves of flood-tide?
The sea-gulls oscillating their bodies, the hay-boat in the twilight,
and the belated lighter?
What gods can exceed these that clasp me by the hand, and
with voices I love call me promptly and loudly by my
nighest name as I approach? 95
What is more subtle than this which ties me to the woman or
man that looks in my face?
Which fuses me into you now, and pours my meaning into you?

We understand then do we not?
What I promis'd without mentioning it, have you not accepted?
What the study could not teach—what the preaching could not
accomplish is accomplish'd, is it not? 100

9

Flow on, river! flow with the flood-tide, and ebb with the ebbtide!
Frolic on, crested and scallop-edg'd waves!
Gorgeous clouds of the sunset! drench with your splendor me, or
the men and women generations after me!
Cross from shore to shore, countless crowds of passengers!
Stand up, tall masts of Mannahatta! stand up, beautiful hills
of Brooklyn! 105
Throb, baffled and curious brain! throw out questions and
answers!
Suspend here and everywhere, eternal float of solution!

Gaze, loving and thirsting eyes, in the house or street or public
    assembly!
Sound out, voices of young men! loudly and musically call me
    by my nighest name!
Live, old life! play the part that looks back on the actor or
    actress! 110
Play the old role, the role that is great or small according as one
    makes it!
Consider, you who peruse me, whether I may not in unknown
    ways be looking upon you;
Be firm, rail over the river, to support those who lean idly, yet
    haste with the hasting current;
Fly on, sea-birds! fly sideways, or wheel in large circles high in
    the air;
Receive the summer sky, you water, and faithfully hold it till all
    downcast eyes have time to take it from you! 115
Diverge, fine spokes of light, from the shape of my head, or
    any one's head, in the sunlit water!
Come on, ships from the lower bay! pass up or down, white-sail'd
    schooners, sloops, lighters!
Flaunt away, flags of all nations! be duly lower'd at sunset!
Burn high your fires, foundry chimneys! cast black shadows at
    nightfall! cast red and yellow light over the tops of the
    houses!
Appearances, now or henceforth, indicate what you are, 120
You necessary film, continue to envelop the soul,
About my body for me, and your body for you, be hung our
    divinest aromas,
Thrive, cities—bring your freight, bring your shows, ample and
    sufficient rivers,
Expand, being than which none else is perhaps more
    spiritual,
Keep your places, objects than which none else is more
    lasting. 125

You have waited, you always wait, you dumb, beautiful ministers,
We receive you with free sense at last, and are insatiate hence-
    forward,
Not you any more shall be able to foil us, or withhold yourselves
    from us,

We use you, and do not cast you aside—we plant you
    permanently within us,
We fathom you not—we love you—there is perfection in you
    also,   130
You furnish your parts toward eternity,
Great or small, you furnish your parts toward the soul.

                                    —1881–82

A Noiseless Patient Spider

A noiseless patient spider,
I mark'd where on a little promontory it stood isolated,
Mark'd how to explore the vacant vast surrounding,
It launch'd forth filament, filament, filament, out of itself,
Ever unreeling them, ever tirelessly speeding them.   5

And you O my soul where you stand,
Surrounded, detached, in measureless oceans of space,
Ceaselessly musing, venturing, throwing, seeking the spheres to
    connect them,
Till the bridge you will need be form'd, till the ductile anchor
    hold,
Till the gossamer thread you fling catch somewhere, O my
    soul.   10

                                      —1876

O Captain! My Captain!°

    1

O Captain! my Captain! our fearful trip is done;
The ship has weather'd every rack, the prize we sought is won;
The port is near, the bells I hear, the people all exulting,

O Captain! My Captain! This atypical ballad was written after the assassination of Abraham Lincoln and ironically became Whitman's most popular poem during his lifetime.

While follow eyes the steady keel, the vessel grim and daring:
　　But O heart! heart! heart! 　　　　　　　　　　　　　　5
　　　　O the bleeding drops of red,
　　　　　　Where on the deck my Captain lies,
　　　　　　　Fallen cold and dead.

　　2

O Captain! my Captain! rise up and hear the bells;
Rise up—for you the flag is flung—for you the bugle trills; 　　10
For you bouquets and ribbon'd wreaths—for you the shores a-crowding;
For you they call, the swaying mass, their eager faces turning;
　　Here Captain! dear father!
　　　　This arm beneath your head;
　　　　　It is some dream that on the deck, 　　　　　　15
　　　　　　You've fallen cold and dead.

　　3

My Captain does not answer, his lips are pale and still;
My father does not feel my arm, he has no pulse nor will;
The ship is anchor'd safe and sound, its voyage closed and done;
From fearful trip, the victor ship, comes in with object won; 　　20
　　Exult, O shores, and ring, O bells!
　　　　But I, with mournful tread,
　　　　　Walk the deck my Captain lies,
　　　　　　Fallen cold and dead.

　　　　　　　　　　　　　　　　　　—1865

Out of the Cradle Endlessly Rocking

Out of the cradle endlessly rocking,
Out of the mocking-bird's throat, the musical shuttle,
Out of the Ninth-month° midnight,
Over the sterile sands and the fields beyond, where the child
　　leaving his bed wander'd alone, bareheaded, barefoot,

---

3 **Ninth-month** Quaker term for September

Down from the shower'd halo,   5
Up from the mystic play of shadows twining and twisting as if
    they were alive,
Out from the patches of briers and blackberries,
From the memories of the bird that chanted to me,
From your memories sad brother, from the fitful risings and
    fallings I heard,
From under that yellow half-moon late-risen and swollen as if
    with tears,   10
From those beginning notes of yearning and love there in the mist,
From the thousand responses of my heart never to cease,
From the myriad thence-arous'd words,
From the word stronger and more delicious than any,
From such as now they start the scene revisiting,   15
As a flock, twittering, rising, or overhead passing,
Borne hither, ere all eludes me, hurriedly,
A man, yet by these tears a little boy again,
Throwing myself on the sand, confronting the waves,
I, chanter of pains and joys, uniter of here and hereafter,   20
Taking all hints to use them, but swiftly leaping beyond them,
A reminiscence sing.

Once Paumanok,°
When the lilac-scent was in the air and Fifth-month° grass was
    growing,
Up this seashore in some briers,   25
Two feather'd guests from Alabama, two together,
And their nest, and four light-green eggs spotted with brown,
And every day the he-bird to and fro near at hand,
And every day the she-bird crouch'd on her nest, silent, with
    bright eyes,
And every day I, a curious boy, never too close, never
    disturbing them,   30
Cautiously peering, absorbing, translating.

Shine! shine! shine!
Pour down your warmth, great sun!
While we bask, we two together.

Two together!   35
Winds blow south, or winds blow north,

23 **Paumanok** Indian name for Long Island   24 **Fifth-month** May (Quaker)

Day come white, or night come black,
Home, or rivers and mountains from home,
Singing all time, minding no time,
While we two keep together.   40

Till of a sudden,
May-be kill'd, unknown to her mate,
One forenoon the she-bird crouch'd not on the nest,
Nor return'd that afternoon, nor the next,
Nor ever appear'd again.   45

And thenceforward all summer in the sound of the sea,
And at night under the full of the moon in calmer weather,
Over the hoarse surging of the sea,
Or flitting from brier to brier by day,
I saw, I heard at intervals the remaining one, the he-bird,   50
The solitary guest from Alabama.

Blow! blow! blow!
Blow up sea-winds along Paumanok's shore;
I wait and I wait till you blow my mate to me.

Yes, when the stars glisten'd,   55
All night long on the prong of a moss-scallop'd stake,
Down almost amid the slapping waves,
Sat the lone singer wonderful causing tears.
He call'd on his mate,
He pour'd forth the meaning which I of all men know.   60
Yes my brother I know,
The rest might not, but I have treasur'd every note,
For more than once dimly down to the beach gliding,
Silent, avoiding the moonbeams, blending myself with the
    shadows,
Recalling now the obscure shapes, the echoes, the sounds and
    sights after their sorts,   65
The white arms out in the breakers tirelessly tossing,
I, with bare feet, a child, the wind wafting my hair,
Listen'd long and long.

Listen'd to keep, to sing, now translating the notes,
Following you my brother.   70

Soothe! soothe! soothe!
Close on its wave soothes the wave behind,

And again another behind embracing and lapping, every one close,
But my love soothes not me, not me.

Low hangs the moon, it rose late,   75
It is lagging—O I think it is heavy with love, with love.

O madly the sea pushes upon the land,
With love, with love.

O night! do I not see my love fluttering out among the breakers?
What is that little black thing I see there in the white?   80

Loud! loud! loud!
Loud I call to you, my love!

High and clear I shoot my voice over the waves,
Surely you must know who is here, is here,
You must know who I am, my love.   85

Low-hanging moon!
What is that dusky spot in your brown yellow?
O it is the shape, the shape of my mate!
O moon do not keep her from me any longer.

Land! land! O land!   90
Whichever way I turn, O I think you could give me my mate
*   back again if you only would,*
For I am almost sure I see her dimly whichever way I look.

O rising stars!
Perhaps the one I want so much will rise, will rise with some
*   of you.*

O throat! O trembling throat!   95
Sound clearer through the atmosphere!
Pierce the woods, the earth,
Somewhere listening to catch you must be the one I want.

Shake out carols!
Solitary here, the night's carols!   100
Carols of lonesome love! death's carols!
Carols under that lagging, yellow, waning moon!
O under that moon where she droops almost down into the sea!
O reckless despairing carols.

But soft! sink low!   105
Soft! let me just murmur,

And do you wait a moment you husky-nois'd sea,
For somewhere I believe I heard my mate responding to me,
So faint, I must be still, be still to listen,
But not altogether still, for then she might not come
    immediately to me.   110

Hither my love!
Here I am! here!
With this just-sustain'd note I announce myself to you,
This gentle call is for you my love, for you.

Do not be decoy'd elsewhere,   115
That is the whistle of the wind, it is not my voice,
That is the fluttering, the fluttering of the spray,
Those are the shadows of leaves.

O darkness! O in vain!
O I am very sick and sorrowful.   120

O brown halo in the sky near the moon, drooping upon the sea!
O troubled reflection in the sea!
O throat! O throbbing heart!
And I singing uselessly, uselessly all the night.

O past! O happy life! O songs of joy!   125
In the air, in the woods, over fields,
Loved! loved! loved! loved! loved!
But my mate no more, no more with me!
We two together no more.

The aria sinking,   130
All else continuing, the stars shining,
The winds blowing, the notes of the bird continuous echoing,
With angry moans the fierce old mother incessantly moaning,
On the sands of Paumanok's shore gray and rustling,
The yellow half-moon enlarged, sagging down, drooping, the
    face of the sea almost touching,   135
The boy ecstatic, with his bare feet the waves, with his hair
    the atmosphere dallying,
The love in the heart long pent, now loose, now at last
    tumultuously bursting,
The aria's meaning, the ears, the soul, swiftly depositing,
The strange tears down the cheeks coursing,

The colloquy there, the trio, each uttering,   140
The undertone, the savage old mother incessantly crying,
To the boy's soul's questions sullenly timing, some drown'd
    secret hissing,
To the outsetting bard.

Demon or bird! (said the boy's soul,)
Is it indeed toward your mate you sing? or is it really to me?   145
For I, that was a child, my tongue's use sleeping, now I have
    heard you,
Now in a moment I know what I am for, I awake,
And already a thousand singers, a thousand songs, clearer,
    louder and more sorrowful than yours,
A thousand warbling echoes have started to life within me,
    never to die.

O you singer solitary, singing by yourself, projecting me,   150
O solitary me listening, never more shall I cease perpetuating you,
Never more shall I escape, never more the reverberations,
Never more the cries of unsatisfied love be absent from me,
Never again leave me to be the peaceful child I was before
    what there in the night,
By the sea under the yellow and sagging moon,   155
The messenger there arous'd, the fire, the sweet hell within,
The unknown want, the destiny of me.

O give me the clew!° (it lurks in the night here somewhere,)
O if I am to have so much, let me have more!

A word then, (for I will conquer it,)   160
The word final, superior to all,
Subtle, sent up—what is it?—I listen;
Are you whispering it, and have been all the time, you sea waves?
Is that it from your liquid rims and wet sands?

Whereto answering, the sea,   165
Delaying not, hurrying not,
Whisper'd me through the night, and very plainly before
    daybreak,
Lisp'd to me the low and delicious word death,
And again death, death, death, death,

158 clew clue

Hissing melodious, neither like the bird nor like my arous'd
    child's heart, 170
But edging near as privately for me rustling at my feet,
Creeping thence steadily up to my ears and laving me softly
    all over,
Death, death, death, death, death.

Which I do not forget,
But fuse the song of my dusky demon and brother, 175
That he sang to me in the moonlight on Paumanok's gray
    beach,
With the thousand responsive songs at random,
My own songs awaked from that hour,
And with them the key, the word up from the waves,
The word of the sweetest song and all songs, 180
That strong and delicious word which, creeping to my feet,
(Or like some old crone rocking the cradle, swathed in sweet
    garments, bending aside,)
The sea whisper'd me.

                                    —*1881–82*

Song of Myself, 6

A child said *What is the grass?* fetching it to me with full hands;
How could I answer the child? I do not know what it is any more
    than he.

I guess it must be the flag of my disposition, out of hopeful green
    stuff woven.

Or I guess it is the handkerchief of the Lord,
A scented gift and remembrancer designedly dropped, 5
Bearing the owner's name someway in the corners, that we may see
    and remark, and say *Whose?*

Or I guess the grass is itself a child, the produced babe of the
    vegetation.

Or I guess it is a uniform hieroglyphic,
And it means, Sprouting alike in broad zones and narrow
    zones,

Growing among black folks as among white,   10
Kanuck,° Tuckahoe,° Congressman, Cuff,° I give them the same,
    I receive them the same.

And now it seems to me the beautiful uncut hair of graves.

Tenderly will I use you curling grass,
It may be you transpire from the breasts of young men,
It may be if I had known them I would have loved them,   15
It may be you are from old people, or from offspring taken
    soon out of their mothers' laps,
And here you are the mothers' laps.

This grass is very dark to be from the white heads of old mothers.
Darker than the colorless beards of old men.
Dark to come from under the faint red roofs of mouths.   20

O I perceive after all so many uttering tongues,
And I perceive they do not come from the roofs of mouths for
    nothing.

I wish I could translate the hints about the dead young men
    and women,
And the hints about old men and mothers, and the offspring
    taken soon out of their laps.

What do you think has become of the young and old men?   25
And what do you think has become of the women and children?

They are alive and well somewhere,
The smallest sprout shows there is really no death,
And if ever there was it led forward life, and does not wait at
    the end to arrest it.
And ceased the moment life appeared.   30

All goes onward and outward, nothing collapses.
And to die is different from what anyone supposed, and luckier.

                                                            —*1855*

---

11 **Kanuck** French-Canadian   **Tuckahoe** coastal Virginian   **Cuff** a black slave

Song of myself, 11

Twenty-eight young men bathe by the shore,
Twenty-eight young men and all so friendly;
Twenty-eight years of womanly life and all so lonesome.

She owns the fine house by the rise of the bank,
She hides handsome and richly drest aft the blinds of the window.   5

Which of the young men does she like the best?
Ah the homeliest of them is beautiful to her.

Where are you off to, lady? for I see you,
You splash in the water there, yet stay stock still in your room.

Dancing and laughing along the beach came the twenty-ninth
    bather,   10
The rest did not see her, but she saw them and loved them.

The beards of the young men glisten'd with wet, it ran from their
    long hair,
Little streams pass'd all over their bodies.

An unseen hand also pass'd over their bodies,
It descended trembling from their temples and ribs.   15

The young men float on their backs, their white bellies bulge to the
    sun, they do not ask who seizes fast to them,
They do not know who puffs and declines with pendant and
    bending arch,
They do not think whom they souse with spray.

—1855

When I Heard the Learn'd Astronomer

When I heard the learn'd astronomer,
When the proofs, the figures, were ranged in columns before me,
When I was shown the charts and diagrams, to add, divide, and
    measure them,
When I sitting heard the astronomer where he lectured with much
    applause in the lecture-room,
How soon unaccountable I became tired and sick, 5
Till rising and gliding out I wander'd off by myself,
In the mystical moist night-air, and from time to time,
Look'd up in perfect silence at the stars.

                        —1865

Matthew Arnold (1822–1888)

Matthew Arnold was the son of the headmaster of Rugby School and himself served as an inspector of schools during much of his adult life. An influential essayist as well as a poet, Arnold was unsparing in his criticism of middle-class "Philistinism." At least part of "Dover Beach" is thought to date from his honeymoon in 1851.

Dover Beach

The sea is calm tonight.
The tide is full, the moon lies fair
Upon the straits; on the French coast the light
Gleams and is gone; the cliffs of England stand,
Glimmering and vast, out in the tranquil bay. 5
Come to the window, sweet is the night-air!
Only, from the long line of spray
Where the sea meets the moon-blanched land,
Listen! you hear the grating roar

Of pebbles which the waves draw back, and fling,   10
At their return, up the high strand,
Begin, and cease, and then again begin,
With tremulous cadence slow, and bring
The eternal note of sadness in.

Sophocles° long ago   15
Heard it on the Aegean, and it brought
Into his mind the turbid ebb and flow
Of human misery; we
Find also in the sound a thought,
Hearing it by this distant northern sea.   20

The Sea of Faith
Was once, too, at the full, and round earth's shore
Lay like the folds of a bright girdle° furled.
But now I only hear
Its melancholy, long, withdrawing roar,   25
Retreating, to the breath
Of the night-wind, down the vast edges drear
And naked shingles° of the world.

Ah, love, let us be true
To one another! for the world, which seems   30
To lie before us like a land of dreams,
So various, so beautiful, so new,
Hath really neither joy, nor love, nor light,
Nor certitude, nor peace, nor help for pain;
And we are here as on a darkling plain   35
Swept with confused alarms of struggle and flight,
Where ignorant armies clash by night.

—1867

---

15 **Sophocles** Athenian tragic poet (496–406 BC)   **23 girdle** sash   **28 shingles** beach pebbles

Emily Dickinson (1830–1886)

Emily Dickinson has been reinvented with each generation, and readers' views of her have ranged between two extremes—one perceiving her as the abnormally shy "Belle of Amherst" making poetry out of her own neuroses and another seeing her as a proto-feminist carving out a world of her own in self-willed isolation. What remains is her brilliant poetry—unique, original, and marked with the stamp of individual talent. Dickinson published only seven poems during her lifetime, but left behind hundreds of poems in manuscript at her death. Published by her relatives, they were immediately popular, but it was not until the edition of Thomas Johnson in 1955 that they were read with Dickinson's unusual punctuation and capitalization intact.

After Great Pain, a Formal Feeling Comes

After great pain, a formal feeling comes—
The Nerves sit ceremonious, like Tombs—
The stiff Heart questions was it He, that bore,
And Yesterday, or Centuries before?

The Feet, mechanical, go round—   5
Of Ground, or Air, or Ought—
A Wooden way
Regardless grown,
A Quartz contentment, like a stone—

This is the Hour of Lead—   10
Remembered, if outlived,
As Freezing persons, recollect the Snow—
First—Chill—then Stupor—then the letting go—

—1929

Because I Could Not Stop for Death

Because I could not stop for Death—
He kindly stopped for me—
The Carriage held but just Ourselves—
And Immortality.

We slowly drove—He knew no haste   5
And I had put away
My labor and my leisure too,
For His Civility—

We passed the School, where Children strove
At Recess—in the Ring—   10
We passed the Fields of Gazing Grain—
We passed the Setting Sun—

Or rather—He passed Us—
The Dews drew quivering and chill—
For only Gossamer, my Gown—   15
My Tippet°—only Tulle°—

We paused before a House that seemed
A Swelling of the Ground—
The Roof was scarcely visible—
The Cornice—in the Ground—   20

Since then—'tis Centuries—and yet
Feels shorter than the Day
I first surmised the Horses' Heads
Were toward Eternity—

—*1890*

16 **Tippet** shawl   **Tulle** net-like fabric

I Felt a Funeral, in My Brain

I felt a Funeral, in my Brain,
And Mourners to and fro
Kept treading—treading—till it seemed
That Sense was breaking through—

And when they all were scated,   5
A Service, like a Drum—
Kept beating—beating—till I thought
My Mind was going numb—

And then I heard them lift a Box
And creak across my Soul   10
With those same Boots of Lead, again,
Then Space—began to toll,

As all the Heavens were a Bell,
And Being, but an Ear,
And I, and Silence, some strange Race   15
Wrecked, solitary, here—

And then a Plank in Reason, broke,
And I dropped down, and down—
And hit a World, at every plunge,
And Finished knowing—then—   20

—1896

Much Madness Is Divinest Sense

Much Madness is divinest Sense—
To a discerning Eye—
Much Sense—the starkest Madness—
'Tis the Majority
In this, as All, prevail—   5

Assent—and you are sane—
Demur—you're straightway dangerous—
And handled with a Chain—

—1890

A Narrow Fellow in the Grass

A narrow Fellow in the Grass
Occasionally rides—
You may have met Him—did you not
His notice sudden is—

The Grass divides as with a Comb—   5
A spotted shaft is seen—
And then it closes at your feet
And opens further on—

He likes a Boggy Acre
A Floor to cool for Corn—   10
Yet when a Boy, and Barefoot—
I more than once at Noon
Have passed, I thought, a Whip lash
Unbraiding in the Sun
When stooping to secure it   15
It wrinkled, and was gone—

Several of Nature's People
I know, and they know me—
I feel for them a transport
Of cordiality—   20

But never met this Fellow
Attended, or alone
Without a tighter breathing
And Zero at the Bone—

—1866

Some Keep the Sabbath Going to Church

Some keep the Sabbath going to Church—
I keep it, staying at Home—
With a Bobolink for a Chorister—
And an Orchard, for a Dome—

Some keep the Sabbath in Surplice—   5
I just wear my Wings—
And instead of tolling the Bell, for Church,
Our little Sexton—sings.

God preaches, a noted Clergyman—
And the sermon is never long,   10
So instead of getting to Heaven, at least—
I'm going, all along.

                                                        —1864

The Soul Selects Her Own Society—

The Soul selects her own Society—
Then—shuts the Door—
To her divine Majority—
Present no more—

Unmoved—she notes the Chariots—pausing—   5
At her low Gate—
Unmoved—an Emperor be kneeling
Upon her Mat—

I've known her—from an ample nation—
Choose One—   10
Then—close the Valves° of her attention—
Like Stone—

                                                        —1890

11 **Valves** sliding doors

There's a Certain Slant of Light

There's a certain Slant of light,
Winter Afternoons—
That oppresses, like the Heft
Of Cathedral Tunes—

Heavenly Hurt, it gives us—   5
We can find no scar,
But internal difference,
Where the Meanings, are—

None may teach it—Any—
'Tis the Seal Despair—   10
An imperial affliction
Sent us of the Air—

When it comes, the Landscape listens—
Shadows—hold their breath—
When it goes, 'tis like the Distance   15
On the look of Death—

—1890

Wild Nights— Wild Nights!

Wild Nights—Wild Nights!
Were I with thee
Wild Nights should be
Our luxury!

Futile—the Winds—   5
To a Heart in port—
Done with the Compass—
Done with the Chart!

Rowing in Eden—
Ah, the Sea!   10
Might I but moor—Tonight—
In Thee!

—1891

Christina Rossetti (1830–1894)

*Christina Rossetti was the younger sister of Dante Gabriel and William,
also distinguished writers, and was the author of numerous devotional poems and prose works. Her collected poems, edited by her brother William,
appeared posthumously in 1904.*

Up-Hill

Does the road wind up-hill all the way?
    Yes, to the very end.
Will the day's journey take the whole long day?
    From morn to night, my friend.

But is there for the night a resting-place?   5
    A roof for when the slow dark hours begin.
May not the darkness hide it from my face?
    You cannot miss that inn.

Shall I meet other wayfarers at night?
    Those who have gone before.   10
Then must I knock, or call when just in sight?
    They will not keep you waiting at that door.

Shall I find comfort, travel-sore and weak?
    Of labor you shall find the sum.
Will there be beds for me and all who seek?   15
    Yea, beds for all who come.

—1858

Thomas Hardy (1840–1928)

Thomas Hardy, after the disappointing response to his novel Jude the Obscure *in 1895, returned to his first love, writing poetry for the last thirty years of his long life. The language and life of Hardy's native Wessex inform both his novels and poems. His subject matter is very much of the nineteenth century, but his ironic, disillusioned point of view marks him as one of the chief predecessors of modernism.*

Ah, Are You Digging on My Grave?

"Ah, are you digging on my grave
     My loved one?—planting rue?"°
—"No: yesterday he went to wed
One of the brightest wealth has bred.
'It cannot hurt her now,' he said,   5
     'That I should not be true.'"

"Then who is digging on my grave?
     My nearest dearest kin?"
—"Ah, no; they sit and think, 'What use!
What good will planting flowers produce?   10
No tendance of her mound can loose
     Her spirit from Death's gin.'"°

"But some one digs upon my grave?
     My enemy?—prodding sly?"
—"Nay: when she heard you had passed the Gate   15
That shuts on all flesh soon or late.
She thought you no more worth her hate,
     And cares not where you lie."

"Then who is digging on my grave?
     Say—since I have not guessed!"   20
—"O it is I, my mistress dear,

2 rue yellow flower traditionally associated with sadness   **12 gin** grip

Your little dog, who still lives near,
And much I hope my movements here
     Have not disturbed your rest?"

"Ah, yes! *You* dig upon my grave . . .   25
     Why flashed it not on me
That one true heart was left behind!
What feeling do we ever find
To equal among human kind
     A dog's fidelity!"   30

"Mistress, I dug upon your grave
     To bury a bone, in case
I should be hungry near this spot
When passing on my daily trot.
I am sorry, but I quite forgot   35
     It was your resting-place."

                     —1914

The Convergence of the Twain

Lines on the Loss of the Titanic

1

     In a solitude of the sea
     Deep from human vanity,
And the Pride of Life that planned her, stilly couches she.

2

     Steel chambers, late the pyres
     Of her salamadrine fires,°   5
Cold currents thrid,° and turn to rhythmic tidal lyres.

---

5 **salamandrine fires** The salamander, according to legend, could live in fire   **6 thrid** thread

3

    Over the mirrors meant
    To glass the opulent
The sea-worm crawls—grotesque, slimed, dumb, indifferent.

4

    Jewels in joy designed   10
    To ravish the sensuous mind
Lie lightless, all their sparkles bleared and black and blind.

5

    Dim moon-eyed fishes near
    Gaze at the gilded gear
And query: "What does this vaingloriousness down here?"   15

6

    Well: while was fashioning
    This creature of cleaving wing,
The Immanent Will° that stirs and urges everything

7

    Prepared a sinister mate
    For her—so gaily great—   20
A Shape of Ice, for the time far and dissociate.

8

    And as the smart ship grew
    In stature, grace, and hue,
In shadowy silent distance grew the Iceberg too.

9

    Alien they seemed to be: 25
    No mortal eye could see
The intimate welding of their later history,

18 Immanent Will term used by Hardy for fate

10

    Or sign that they were bent
    By paths coincident
On being anon twin halves of one august event,   30

11

    Till the Spinner of the Years
    Said "Now!" And each one hears,
And consummation comes, and jars two hemispheres.

                    —1912

Neutral Tones

We stood by a pond that winter day,
And the sun was white, as though chidden of God,
And a few leaves lay on the starving sod;
    —They had fallen from an ash, and were gray.

Your eyes on me were as eyes that rove   5
Over tedious riddles of years ago;
And some words played between us to and fro
    On which lost the more by our love.

The smile on your mouth was the deadest thing
Alive enough to have strength to die;   10
And a grin of bitterness swept thereby
    Like an ominous bird a-wing . . .

Since then, keen lessons that love deceives,
And wrings with wrong, have shaped to me
Your face, and the God-curst sun, and a tree,   15
    And a pond edged with grayish leaves.

                    —1898

The Ruined Maid

"O 'Melia, my dear, this does everything crown!
Who could have supposed I should meet you in Town?
And whence such fair garments, such prosperi-ty?"
"O didn't you know I'd been ruined?" said she.

"You left us in tatters, without shoes or socks,   5
Tired of digging potatoes, and spudding up docks;°
And now you've gay bracelets and bright feathers three!"
"Yes: that's how we dress when we're ruined," said she.

"At home in the barton° you said 'thee' and 'thou,'
And 'thik oon,' and 'theäs oon,'° and 't'other'; but now   10
Your talking quite fits 'ee for high compa-ny!"
"Some polish is gained with one's ruin," said she.

"Your hands were like paws then, your face blue and bleak
But now I'm bewitched by your delicate cheek,
And your little gloves fit as on any la-dy!"   15
"We never do work when we're ruined," said she.

"You used to call home-life a hag-ridden dream,
And you'd sigh, and you'd sock; but at present you seem
To know not of megrims° or melancho-ly!"
"True. One's pretty lively when ruined," said she.   20

"I wish I had feathers, a fine sweeping gown,
And a delicate face, and could strut about Town!"
"My dear—a raw country girl, such as you be,
Cannot quite expect that. You ain't ruined," said she.

—*1866*

---

6 docks weeds   **9 barton** barnyard   **10 thik oon and theäs oon** dialect: "that one and this one"
19 megrims migraines

Gerard Manley Hopkins (1844–1889)

Gerard Manley Hopkins was an English Jesuit priest who developed elaborate theories of poetic meter (what he called "sprung rhythm") and language to express his own spiritual ardor. Most of his work was posthumously printed through the efforts of his Oxford friend and later correspondent Robert Bridges, who was poet laureate.

God's Grandeur

The world is charged with the grandeur of God.
   It will flame out, like shining from shook foil;°
   It gathers to a greatness, like the ooze of oil
Crushed.° Why do men then now not reck his rod?
Generations have trod, have trod, have trod;   5
   And all is seared with trade; bleared, smeared with toil;
   And wears man's smudge and shares man's smell: the soil
Is bare now, nor can foot feel, being shod.

And for all this, nature is never spent;
   There lives the dearest freshness deep down things;   10
And though the last lights off the black West went
   Oh, morning, at the brown brink eastward, springs—
Because the Holy Ghost over the bent
   World broods with warm breast and with ah! bright wings.

                                  —*1877*

Pied Beauty

Glory be to God for dappled things—
   For skies of couple-color as a brinded° cow;
      For rose-moles all in stipple upon trout that swim;
Fresh-firecoal chestnut-falls;° finches' wings;
   Landscape plotted and pieced—fold, fallow, and plough;   5
      And all trades, their gear and tackle and trim.

2 **foil** gold leaf   4 **Crushed** Hopkins is referring to olive oil
2 **brinded** streaked   4 **Fresh-firecoal chestnut-falls** according to the poet, chestnuts have a red color

All things counter, original, spare, strange;
    Whatever is fickle, freckled (who knows how?)
        With swift, slow; sweet, sour; adazzle, dim;
He fathers-forth whose beauty is past change: 10
        Praise him.

                        —1877

Spring and Fall

to a young child

Márgarét, are you gríeving?
Over Goldengrove unleaving?
Leáves, líke the things of man, you
With your fresh thoughts care for, can you?
Ah! ás the heart grows older   5
It will come to such sights colder
By and by, nor spare a sigh
Though worlds of wanwood leafmeal lie;
And yet you wíll weep and know why.
Now no matter, child, the name: 10
Sórrow's spríngs áre the same.
Nor mouth had, no nor mind, expressed
What heart heard of, ghost guessed:
It ís the blight man was born for,
It is Margaret you mourn for.   15

                        —1880

The Windhover°

To Christ Our Lord

I caught this morning morning's minion,° kingdom
    of daylight's dauphin, dapple-dawn-drawn Falcon, in his riding
    Of the rolling level underneath him steady air, and striding

---

Windhover small hawk   **1 minion** favorite, echoed in *dauphin* (prince) and *chevalier* (knight)

High there, how he rung upon the rein of a wimpling° wing
In his ecstasy! then off, off forth on a swing,
As a skate's heel sweeps smooth on a bow-bend—the hurl and
gliding   5
Rebuffed the big wind. My heart in hiding
Stirred for a bird—the achieve of, the mastery of the thing!

Brute beauty and valor and act, oh, air, pride, plume, here
Buckle! AND the fire that breaks from thee then, a billion
Times told lovelier, more dangerous, O my chevalier!   10
No wonder of it: shéer plód makes plow down sillion
Shine,° and blue-bleak embers, ah, my dear,
Fall, gall° themselves, and gash gold-vermilion.

—1877

Emma Lazarus (1849–1887)

*Emma Lazarus was born in New York City, one of seven children of a
wealthy Jewish-American sugar refiner. Her famous sonnet "The New
Colossus" was written in 1883 for an art auction raising money to build a
pedestal for the Statue of Liberty, which had been given to the United
States by France. During Lazarus's short life she became a powerful
spokesperson for the rights of immigrants and called on Jews to claim a
homeland in Palestine. Sixteen years after her death, "The New Colossus"
was engraved on a plaque for the statue's base.*

The New Colossus

Not like the brazen giant of Greek fame,
With conquering limbs astride from land to land;
Here at our sea-washed, sunset gates shall stand
A mighty woman with a torch, whose flame
Is the imprisoned lightning, and her name   5
Mother of Exiles. From her beacon-hand
Glows world-wide welcome; her mild eyes command

---

3 **wimpling** beating   11–12 **sheer plod . . . sillion/Shine** that is, hard labor makes a plow shine as it
cuts a furrow and raises up a ridge (sillion)   13 **gall** break open

The air-bridged harbor that twin cities frame.
"Keep, ancient lands, your storied pomp!" cries she
With silent lips. "Give me your tired, your poor,   10
Your huddled masses yearning to breathe free,
The wretched refuse of your teeming shore.
Send these, the homeless, tempest-tost to me,
I lift my lamp beside the golden door!"

—1883

A. E. Housman (1859–1936)

A. E. Housman was educated in the classics at Oxford and was almost forty before he began to write verse seriously. His ballad-like poems of Shropshire (an area in which he never actually lived) have proved some of the most popular lyrics in English, despite their pervasive mood of bittersweet pessimism.

Eight O'Clock

He stood, and heard the steeple
    Sprinkle the quarters° on the morning town.
One, two, three, four, to market-place and people
    It tossed them down.

Strapped, noosed, nighing his hour,   5
    He stood and counted them and cursed his luck;
And then the clock collected in the tower
    Its strength, and struck.

—1922

2 quarters quarter hours

Loveliest of Trees, the Cherry Now

Loveliest of trees, the cherry now
Is hung with bloom along the bough,
And stands about the woodland ride
Wearing white for Eastertide.

Now, of my threescore years and ten,   5
Twenty will not come again,
And take from seventy springs a score,
It only leaves me fifty more.

And since to look at things in bloom
Fifty springs are little room,   10
About the woodlands I will go
To see the cherry hung with snow.

—1896

Stars, I Have Seen Them Fall

Stars, I have seen them fall,
    But when they drop and die
No star is lost at all
    From all the star-sown sky.
The toil of all that be   5
    Helps not the primal fault;
It rains into the sea
    And still the sea is salt.

—1936

"Terence, This Is Stupid Stuff . . ."

"Terence, this is stupid stuff:
You eat your victuals fast enough;
There can't be much amiss, 'tis clear,
To see the rate you drink your beer.
But oh, good Lord, the verse you make,   5
It gives a chap the belly-ache.
The cow, the old cow, she is dead;
It sleeps well, the hornèd head:
We poor lads, 'tis our turn now
To hear such tunes as killed the cow.   10
Pretty friendship 'tis to rhyme
Your friends to death before their time
Moping melancholy mad:
Come, pipe a tune to dance to, lad."

Why, if 'tis dancing you would be,   15
There's brisker pipes than poetry.
Say, for what were hop-yards meant,
Or why was Burton built on Trent?°
Oh many a peer of England brews
Livelier liquor than the Muse,   20
And malt does more than Milton can
To justify God's ways to man.
Ale, man, ale's the stuff to drink
For fellows whom it hurts to think:
Look into the pewter pot   25
To see the world as the world's not.
And faith, 'tis pleasant till 'tis past:
The mischief is that 'twill not last.
Oh I have been to Ludlow fair
And left my necktie God knows where,   30
And carried halfway home, or near,
Pints and quarts of Ludlow beer:
Then the world seemed none so bad,

18 **Burton built on Trent** site of breweries

And I myself a sterling lad;
And down in lovely muck I've lain,   35
Happy till I woke again.
Then I saw the morning sky:
Heigho, the tale was all a lie;
The world, it was the old world yet,
I was I, my things were wet,   40
And nothing now remained to do
But begin the game anew.

    Therefore, since the world has still
Much good, but much less good than ill,
And while the sun and moon endure   45
Luck's a chance, but trouble's sure,
I'd face it as a wise man would,
And train for ill and not for good.
'Tis true, the stuff I bring for sale
Is not so brisk a brew as ale: 50
Out of a stem that scored the hand
I wrung it in a weary land.
But take it: if the smack is sour,
The better for the embittered hour;
It should do good to heart and head   55
When your soul is in my soul's stead;
And I will friend you, if I may,
In the dark and cloudy day.

    There was a king reigned in the East:
There, when kings will sit to feast,   60
They get their fill before they think
With poisoned meat and poisoned drink.
He gathered all that springs to birth
From the many-venomed earth;
First a little, thence to more,   65
He sampled all her killing store;
And easy, smiling, seasoned sound,
Sate the king when healths went round.
They put arsenic in his meat
And stared aghast to watch him eat;   70
They poured strychnine in his cup
And shook to see him drink it up:

They shook, they stared as white's their shirt:
Them it was their poison hurt.
—I tell the tale that I heard told.   75
Mithridates,° he died old.

—*1896*

William Butler Yeats (1865–1939)

*William Butler Yeats is considered the greatest Irish poet and provides an
important link between the late romantic era and early modernism. His
early poetry, focusing on Irish legend and landscape, is regional in the best
sense of the term, but his later work, with its prophetic tone and symbolist
texture, moves on a larger stage. Yeats lived in London for many years and
was at the center of British literary life. He was awarded the Nobel Prize
in 1923.*

The Lake Isle of Innisfree

I will arise and go now, and go to Innisfree,
And a small cabin build there, of clay and wattles° made:
Nine bean-rows will I have there, a hive for the honey-bee,
And live alone in the bee-loud glade.

And I shall have some peace there, for peace comes dropping slow,   5
Dropping from the veils of the morning to where the cricket sings;
There midnight's all a glimmer, and noon a purple glow,
And evening full of the linnet's wings.

I will arise and go now, for always night and day
I hear lake water lapping with low sounds by the shore;   10
While I stand on the roadway, or on the pavements gray,
I hear it in the deep heart's core.

—*1892*

---

76 **Mithridates** legendary King of Pontus, he protected himself from poisons by taking small doses
regularly
2 **wattles** woven poles and reeds

Leda° and the Swan

A sudden blow: the great wings beating still
Above the staggering girl, her thighs caressed
By the dark webs, her nape caught in his bill,
He holds her helpless breast upon his breast.

How can those terrified vague fingers push   5
The feathered glory from her loosening thighs?
And how can body, laid in that white rush,
But feel the strange heart beating where it lies?

A shudder in the loins engenders there
The broken wall, the burning roof and tower   10
And Agamemnon dead.°
       Being so Being so caught up,
So mastered by the brute blood of the air,
Did she put on his knowledge with his power
Before the indifferent beak could let her drop?

—*1923*

Sailing to Byzantium°

1

That is no country for old men. The young
In one another's arms, birds in the trees
—Those dying generations—at their song,
The salmon-falls, the mackerel-crowded seas,
Fish, flesh, or fowl, commend all summer long   5
Whatever is begotten, born, and dies.
Caught in that sensual music all neglect
Monuments of unaging intellect.

Leda mortal mother of Helen of Troy and Clytemnestra, wife and assassin of Agamemnon
10–11 The broken wall . . . Agamemnon dead events that occurred during and after the Trojan War
Byzantium Constantinople or Istanbul, capital of the Eastern Roman Empire

2

An aged man is but a paltry thing,
A tattered coat upon a stick, unless   10
Soul clap its hands and sing, and louder sing
For every tatter in its mortal dress,
Nor is there singing school but studying
Monuments of its own magnificence;
And therefore I have sailed the seas and come   15
To the holy city of Byzantium.

3

O sages standing in God's holy fire
As in the gold mosaic of a wall,
Come from the holy fire, perne in a gyre,°
And be the singing-masters of my soul.   20
Consume my heart away; sick with desire
And fastened to a dying animal
It knows not what it is; and gather me
Into the artifice of eternity.

4

Once out of nature I shall never take   25
My bodily form from any natural thing,
But such a form as Grecian goldsmiths make
Of hammered gold and gold enamelling
To keep a drowsy Emperor awake;
Or set upon a golden bough to sing   30
To lords and ladies of Byzantium
Of what is past, or passing, or to come.

—*1927*

The Second Coming

Turning and turning in the widening gyre°
The falcon cannot hear the falconer;
Things fall apart; the center cannot hold;

19 **perne in a gyre** descend in a spiral; the gyre for Yeats was a private symbol of historical cycles
1 **gyre** see note to "Sailing to Byzantium"

Mere anarchy is loosed upon the world,
The blood-dimmed tide is loosed, and everywhere   5
The ceremony of innocence is drowned;
The best lack all conviction, while the worst
Are full of passionate intensity.

Surely some revelation is at hand;
Surely the Second Coming is at hand.   10
The Second Coming! Hardly are those words out
When a vast image out of *Spiritus Mundi*°
Troubles my sight: somewhere in the sands of the desert
A shape with lion body and the head of a man,
A gaze blank and pitiless as the sun,   15
Is moving its slow thighs, while all about it
Reel shadows of the indignant desert birds.
The darkness drops again; but now I know
That twenty centuries of stony sleep
Were vexed to nightmare by a rocking cradle,   20
And what rough beast, its hour come round at last,
Slouches towards Bethlehem to be born?

                                              —*1921*

The Song of
Wandering Aengus°

I went out to the hazel wood,
Because a fire was in my head,
And cut and peeled a hazel wand,
And hooked a berry to a thread;
And when white moths were on the wing,   5
And moth-like stars were flickering out,
I dropped the berry in a stream
And caught a little silver trout.

When I had laid it on the floor
I went to blow the fire aflame,   10

12 *Spiritus Mundi* World-Spirit
Aengus Among the Sidhe (native Irish deities), the god of youth, love, beauty, and poetry. Yeats once also called him the "Master of Love." Here, however, he seems mortal.

But something rustled on the floor,
And some one called me by my name:
It had become a glimmering girl
With apple blossom in her hair
Who called me by my name and ran   15
And faded through the brightening air.

Though I am old with wandering
Through hollow lands and hilly lands,
I will find out where she has gone,
And kiss her lips and take her hands;   20
And walk among long dappled grass,
And pluck till time and times are done
The silver apples of the moon,
The golden apples of the sun.

—1899

Edwin Arlington Robinson (1869–1935)

Edwin Arlington Robinson wrote many poems set in "Tilbury," a recreation of his hometown of Gardiner, Maine. These poems continue to present readers with a memorable cast of eccentric characters who somehow manifest universal human desires. Robinson languished in poverty and obscurity for many years before his reputation began to flourish as a result of the interest taken in his work by President Theodore Roosevelt, who obtained a government job for Robinson and wrote a favorable review of one of his books.

Firelight

Ten years together without yet a cloud,
They seek each other's eyes at intervals
Of gratefulness to firelight and four walls
For love's obliteration of the crowd.
Serenely and perennially endowed   5
And bowered as few may be, their joy recalls
No snake, no sword; and over them there falls
The blessing of what neither says aloud.

Wiser for silence, they were not so glad
Were she to read the graven° tale of lines   10
On the wan face of one somewhere alone;
Nor were they more content could he have had
Her thoughts a moment since of one who shines
Apart, and would be hers if he had known.

                                                —1920

Eros Turannos°

She fears him, and will always ask
    What fated her to choose him;
She meets in his engaging mask
    All reasons to refuse him
But what she meets and what she fears   5
Are less than are the downward years,
Drawn slowly to the foamless weirs
    Of age, were she to lose him.

Between a blurred sagacity
    That once had power to sound him,   10
And Love, that will not let him be
    The Judas that she found him,
Her pride assuages her almost,
As if it were alone the cost.—
He sees that he will not be lost,   15
    And waits and looks around him.

A sense of ocean and old trees
    Envelops and allures him;
Tradition, touching all he sees,
    Beguiles and reassures him;   20
And all her doubts of what he says
Are dimmed with what she knows of days—
Till even prejudice delays
    And fades, and she secures him.

10 graven engraved
Eros Turannos "Love, the Tyrant"

The falling leaf inaugurates   25
    The reign of her confusion;
The pounding wave reverberates
    The dirge of her illusion;
And home, where passion lived and died
Becomes a place where she can hide,   30
While all the town and harbor side
    Vibrate with her seclusion.

We tell you, tapping on our brows,
    The story as it should be,—
As if the story of a house   35
    Were told, or ever could be;
We'll have no kindly veil between
Her visions and those we have seen,—
As if we guessed what hers have been,
    Or what they are or would be.   40

Meanwhile we do no harm; for they
    That with a god have striven,
Not hearing much of what we say
    Take what the god has given;
Though like waves breaking it may be   45
Or like a changed familiar tree,
Or like a stairway to the sea
    Where down the blind are driven.

                                                         —1916

The Mill

The miller's wife had waited long,
    The tea was cold, the fire was dead;
And there might yet be nothing wrong
    In how he went and what he said:
"There are no millers any more,"   5
    Was all that she had heard him say;
And he had lingered at the door
    So long that it seemed yesterday.

Sick with a fear that had no form
    She knew that she was there at last;   10

And in the mill there was a warm
    And mealy fragrance of the past.
What else there was would only seem
    To say again what he had meant;
And what was hanging from a beam   15
    Would not have heeded where she went.

And if she thought it followed her,
    She may have reasoned in the dark
That one way of the few there were
    Would hide her and would leave no mark: 20
Black water, smooth above the weir
    Like starry velvet in the night,
Though ruffled once, would soon appear
    The same as ever to the sight.

—1920

Richard Cory

Whenever Richard Cory went down town,
We people on the pavement looked at him:
He was a gentleman from sole to crown,
Clean favored, and imperially slim.

And he was always quietly arrayed,   5
And he was always human when he talked;
But still he fluttered pulses when he said,
"Good-morning," and he glittered when he walked.

And he was rich—yes, richer than a king—
And admirably schooled in every grace: 10
In fine, we thought that he was everything
To make us wish that we were in his place.

So on we worked, and waited for the light,
And went without the meat, and cursed the bread;
And Richard Cory, one calm summer night,   15
Went home and put a bullet through his head.

—1896

Stephen Crane (1871–1900)

Stephen Crane was the brilliant young journalist who wrote The Red
Badge of Courage *and was also an unconventional poet whose skeptical
epigrams and fables today seem far ahead of their time. In many ways he
mirrors the cosmic pessimism of contemporaries like Hardy, Housman,
and Robinson, all of whom were influenced by the currents of determinism
that ran so strongly at the end of the nineteenth century.*

The Trees in the Garden Rained Flowers

The trees in the garden rained flowers.
Children ran there joyously.
They gathered the flowers
Each to himself.
Now there were some   5
Who gathered great heaps—
Having opportunity and skill—
Until, behold, only chance blossoms
Remained for the feeble.
Then a little spindling tutor   10
Ran importantly to the father, crying:
"Pray, come hither!
See this unjust thing in your garden!"
But when the father had surveyed,
He admonished the tutor: 15
"Not so, small sage!
This thing is just.
For, look you,
Are not they who possess the flowers
Stronger, bolder, shrewder   20
Than they who have none?
Why should the strong—
The beautiful strong—
Why should they not have the flowers?"
Upon reflection, the tutor bowed to the ground,   25

"My lord," he said,
"The stars are displaced
By this towering wisdom."

—1899

The Wayfarer

The wayfarer.
Perceiving the pathway to truth,
Was struck with astonishment.
It was thickly grown with weeds.
"Ha," he said,   5
"I see that none has passed here
In a long time."
Later he saw that each weed
Was a singular knife.
"Well," he mumbled at last,   10
"Doubtless there are other roads."

—1899

Paul Laurence Dunbar   (1872–1906)

Paul Laurence Dunbar, a native of Dayton, Ohio, was one of the first black poets to make a mark in American literature. Many of his dialect poems reflect a sentimentalized view of life in the South, which he did not know directly. However, he was also capable of powerful expressions of racial protest.

We Wear the Mask

We wear the mask that grins and lies,
It hides our cheeks and shades our eyes,—
This debt we pay to human guile;
With torn and bleeding hearts we smile,
And mouth with myriad subtleties.   5

Why should the world be over-wise,
In counting all our tears and sighs?
Nay, let them only see us, while
    We wear the mask.

We smile, but, O great Christ, our cries   10
To thee from tortured souls arise.
We sing, but oh the clay is vile
Beneath our feet, and long the mile;
But let the world dream otherwise,
    We wear the mask!   15

—*1896*

Robert Frost (1874–1963)

Robert Frost, during the second half of his long life, was a public figure who attained a popularity unmatched by any American poet of the last century. His reading at the inauguration of John F. Kennedy in 1961 capped an impressive career that included four Pulitzer Prizes. Unattracted by the more exotic aspects of modernism, Frost nevertheless remains a poet who speaks eloquently to contemporary uncertainties about humanity's place in a universe that does not seem to care much for its existence. While Frost is rarely directly an autobiographical poet ("Home Burial" may reflect the death of Frost's son Elliot at age three), his work always bears the stamp of his powerful personality and identification with the New England landscape.

Acquainted with the Night

I have been one acquainted with the night.
I have walked out in rain—and back in rain.
I have outwalked the furthest city light.

I have looked down the saddest city lane.
I have passed by the watchman on his beat   5
And dropped my eyes, unwilling to explain.

I have stood still and stopped the sound of feet
When far away an interrupted cry
Came over houses from another street,

But not to call me back or say good-bye;   10
And further still at an unearthly height
One luminary clock against the sky

Proclaimed the time was neither wrong nor right.
I have been one acquainted with the night.

—1928

After Apple-Picking

My long two-pointed ladder's sticking through a tree
Toward heaven still,
And there's a barrel that I didn't fill
Beside it, and there may be two or three
Apples I didn't pick upon some bough.   5
But I am done with apple-picking now.
Essence of winter sleep is on the night,
The scent of apples: I am drowsing off.
I cannot rub the strangeness from my sight
I got from looking through a pane of glass   10
I skimmed this morning from the drinking trough
And held against the world of hoary grass.
It melted, and I let it fall and break.
But I was well
Upon my way to sleep before it fell,   15
And I could tell
What form my dreaming was about to take.
Magnified apples appear and disappear,
Stem end and blossom end,
And every fleck of russet showing clear.   20
My instep arch not only keeps the ache,
It keeps the pressure of a ladder-round.
I feel the ladder sway as the boughs bend.
And I keep hearing from the cellar bin
The rumbling sound   25
Of load on load of apples coming in.
For I have had too much
Of apple-picking: I am overtired
Of the great harvest I myself desired.

There were ten thousand thousand fruit to touch,   30
Cherish in hand, lift down, and not let fall.
For all
That struck the earth,
No matter if not bruised or spiked with stubble,
Went surely to the cider-apple heap   35
As of no worth.
One can see what will trouble
This sleep of mine, whatever sleep it is.
Were he not gone,
The woodchuck could say whether it's like his   40
Long sleep, as I describe its coming on,
Or just some human sleep.

                                                        —*1914*

Design

I found a dimpled spider, fat and white,
On a white heal-all,° holding up a moth
Like a white piece of rigid satin cloth—
Assorted characters of death and blight
Mixed ready to begin the morning right,   5
Like the ingredients of a witches' broth—
A snow-drop spider, a flower like a froth,
And dead wings carried like a paper kite.

What had that flower to do with being white,
The wayside blue and innocent heal-all?   10
What brought the kindred spider to that height,
Then steered the white moth thither in the night?
What but design of darkness to appall?—
If design govern in a thing so small.

                                                        —*1936*

2 **heal-all** a wildflower, usually blue

Home Burial

He saw her from the bottom of the stairs
Before she saw him. She was starting down,
Looking back over her shoulder at some fear.
She took a doubtful step and then undid it
To raise herself and look again. He spoke   5
Advancing toward her: "What is it you see
From up there always?—for I want to know."
She turned and sank upon her skirts at that,
And her face changed from terrified to dull.
He said to gain time: "What is it you see?"   10
Mounting until she cowered under him.
"I will find out now—you must tell me, dear."
She, in her place, refused him any help,
With the least stiffening of her neck and silence.
She let him look, sure that he wouldn't see,   15
Blind creature; and awhile he didn't see.
But at last he murmured, "Oh," and again, "Oh."

"What is it—what?" she said.

                          "Just that I see."

"You don't," she challenged. "Tell me what it is."

"The wonder is I didn't see at once.   20
I never noticed it from here before.
I must be wonted to it—that's the reason.
The little graveyard where my people are!
So small the window frames the whole of it.
Not so much larger than a bedroom, is it?   25
There are three stones of slate and one of marble,
Broad-shouldered little slabs there in the sunlight
On the sidehill. We haven't to mind *those*.
But I understand: it is not the stones,
But the child's mound—"

                          "Don't, don't, don't, don't," she cried.   30

She withdrew, shrinking from beneath his arm
That rested on the banister, and slid downstairs;
And turned on him with such a daunting look,

He said twice over before he knew himself:
"Can't a man speak of his own child he's lost?"   35

"Not you!—Oh, where's my hat? Oh, I don't need it!
I must get out of here. I must get air.—
I don't know rightly whether any man can."

"Amy! Don't go to someone else this time.
Listen to me. I won't come down the stairs."   40
He sat and fixed his chin between his fists.
"There's something I should like to ask you, dear."

"You don't know how to ask it."

                              "Help me, then."

Her fingers moved the latch for all reply.

"My words are nearly always an offense.   45
I don't know how to speak of anything
So as to please you. But I might be taught,
I should suppose. I can't say I see how.
A man must partly give up being a man
With womenfolk. We could have some arrangement   50
By which I'd bind myself to keep hands off
Anything special you're a-mind to name.
Though I don't like such things 'twixt those that love.
Two that don't love can't live together without them.
But two that do can't live together with them."   55
She moved the latch a little. "Don't—don't go.
Don't carry it to someone else this time.
Tell me about it if it's something human.
Let me into your grief. I'm not so much
Unlike other folks as your standing there   60
Apart would make me out. Give me my chance.
I do think, though, you overdo it a little.
What was it brought you up to think it the thing
To take your mother-loss of a first child
So inconsolably—in the face of love.   65
You'd think his memory might be satisfied—"

"There you go sneering now!"

                              "I'm not, I'm not!

You make me angry. I'll come down to you.
God, what a woman! And it's come to this,
A man can't speak of his own child that's dead."   70

"You can't because you don't know how to speak.
If you had any feelings, you that dug
With your own hand—how could you?—his little grave;
I saw you from that very window there,
Making the gravel leap and leap in air,   75
Leap up, like that, like that, and land so lightly
And roll back down the mound beside the hole.
I thought, Who is that man? I didn't know you.
And I crept down the stairs and up the stairs
To look again, and still your spade kept lifting.   80
Then you came in. I heard your rumbling voice
Out in the kitchen, and I don't know why,
But I went near to see with my own eyes.
You could sit there with the stains on your shoes
Of the fresh earth from your own baby's grave   85
And talk about your everyday concerns.
You had stood the spade up against the wall
Outside there in the entry, for I saw it."

"I shall laugh the worst laugh I ever laughed.
I'm cursed. God, if I don't believe I'm cursed."   90

"I can repeat the very words you were saying:
'Three foggy mornings and one rainy day
Will rot the best birch fence a man can build.'
Think of it, talk like that at such a time!
What had how long it takes a birch to rot   95
To do with what was in the darkened parlor?
You *couldn't* care! The nearest friends can go
With anyone to death, comes so far short
They might as well not try to go at all.
No, from the time when one is sick to death,   100
One is alone, and he dies more alone.
Friends make pretense of following to the grave,
But before one is in it, their minds are turned
And making the best of their way back to life
And living people, and things they understand.   105

But the world's evil. I won't have grief so
If I can change it. Oh, I won't, I won't!"

"There, you have said it all and you feel better.
You won't go now. You're crying. Close the door.
The heart's gone out of it: why keep it up?   110
Amy! There's someone coming down the road!"

"You—oh, you think the talk is all. I must go—
Somewhere out of this house. How can I make you—"

"If—you—do!" She was opening the door wider.
"Where do you mean to go? First tell me that.   115
I'll follow and bring you back by force. I *will!*—"

—1914

The Need of Being Versed in Country Things

The house had gone to bring again
To the midnight sky a sunset glow.
Now the chimney was all of the house that stood,
Like a pistil after the petals go.

The barn opposed across the way,   5
That would have joined the house in flame
Had it been the will of the wind, was left
To bear forsaken the place's name.

No more it opened with all one end
For teams that came by the stony road   10
To drum on the floor with scurrying hoofs
And brush the mow with the summer load.

The birds that came to it through the air
At broken windows flew out and in,
Their murmur more like the sigh we sigh   15
From too much dwelling on what has been.

Yet for them the lilac renewed its leaf,
And the aged elm, though touched with fire;

And the dry pump flung up an awkward arm;
And the fence post carried a strand of wire.   20

For them there was really nothing sad.
But though they rejoiced in the nest they kept,
One had to be versed in country things
Not to believe the phoebes wept.

—1923

The Road Not Taken

Two roads diverged in a yellow wood,
And sorry I could not travel both
And be one traveler, long I stood
And looked down one as far as I could
To where it bent in the undergrowth;   5

Then took the other, as just as fair,
And having perhaps the better claim,
Because it was grassy and wanted wear;
Though as for that, the passing there
Had worn them really about the same,   10

And both that morning equally lay
In leaves no step had trodden black.
Oh, I kept the first for another day!
Yet knowing how way leads on to way,
I doubted if I should ever come back.   15

I shall be telling this with a sigh
Somewhere ages and ages hence:
Two roads diverged in a wood, and I,
I took the one less traveled by,
And that has made all the difference.   20

—1916

Stopping by Woods on a Snowy Evening

Whose woods these are I think I know.
His house is in the village though;
He will not see me stopping here
To watch his woods fill up with snow.

My little horse must think it queer   5
To stop without a farmhouse near
Between the woods and frozen lake
The darkest evening of the year.

He gives his harness bells a shake
To ask if there is some mistake.   10
The only other sound's the sweep
Of easy wind and downy flake.

The woods are lovely, dark and deep,
But I have promises to keep,
And miles to go before I sleep,   15
And miles to go before I sleep.

—1923

Adelaide Crapsey (1878–1914)

Adelaide Crapsey was born in Brooklyn, New York, the daughter of an Episcopalian minister. After graduation from college and travel abroad, she became an instructor of poetics at Smith College, but her declining health forced her to resign after only one year of teaching, and she died three years later from tuberculosis. Chiefly remembered as the inventor of the cinquain form, Crapsey was influenced by Asian poetry and anticipated many of the practices of imagists, who were coming to prominence in her final years. Her poetry and criticism were published posthumously.

Amaze

I know
Not these my hands
And yet I think there was

A woman like me once had hands
Like these.   5

—*1915*

Languor After Pain

Pain ebbs,
And like cool balm,
An opiate weariness
Settles on eye-lids, on relaxed
Pale wrists.   5

—*1915*

Trapped

Well and
If day on day
Follows, and weary year
On year . . . and ever days and years . . .
Well?   5

—*1915*

Wallace Stevens (1879–1955)

Wallace Stevens was a lawyer specializing in surety bonds and rose to be a vice-president of the Hartford Accident and Indemnity Company. His poetry was collected for the first time in Harmonium *when he was forty-five, and while he published widely during his lifetime, his poetry was only slowly recognized as the work of a major modernist whose originality has not been surpassed. Stevens's idea of poetry as a force taking the place of religion has had a profound influence on poets and critics of this century.*

Anecdote of the Jar

I placed a jar in Tennessee,
And round it was, upon a hill.
It made the slovenly wilderness
Surround that hill.

The wilderness rose up to it,   5
And sprawled around, no longer wild.
The jar was round upon the ground
And tall and of a port in air.

It took dominion everywhere.
The jar was gray and bare.   10
It did not give of bird or bush,
Like nothing else in Tennessee.

—*1923*

Disillusionment of Ten O'Clock

The houses are haunted
By white night-gowns.
None are green,
Or purple with green rings,
Or green with yellow rings,   5
Or yellow with blue rings.
None of them are strange,
With socks of lace
And beaded ceintures.°
People are not going   10
To dream of baboons and periwinkles.°
Only, here and there, an old sailor,
Drunk and asleep in his boots,
Catches tigers
In red weather.   15

—*1923*

---

9 ceintures sashes   **11 periwinkles** either wildflowers or small mollusks

The Emperor of Ice-Cream

Call the roller of big cigars,
The muscular one, and bid him whip
In kitchen cups concupiscent° curds.
Let the wenches dawdle in such dress
As they are used to wear, and let the boys   5
Bring flowers in last month's newspapers.
Let be be finale of seem.
The only emperor is the emperor of ice-cream.

Take from the dresser of deal,°
Lacking the three glass knobs, that sheet   10
On which she embroidered fantails° once
And spread it so as to cover her face.
If her horny feet protrude, they come
To show how cold she is, and dumb.
Let the lamp affix its beam.   15
The only emperor is the emperor of ice-cream.

—*1923*

The Snow Man

One must have a mind of winter
To regard the frost and the boughs
Of the pine-trees crusted with snow;

And have been cold a long time
To behold the junipers shagged with ice,   5
The spruces rough in the distant glitter

Of the January sun; and not to think
Of any misery in the sound of the wind,
In the sound of a few leaves,

Which is the sound of the land   10
Full of the same wind
That is blowing in the same bare place

---

3 concupiscent lustful 9 deal cheap wood 11 fantails pigeons

For the listener, who listens in the snow,
And, nothing himself, beholds
Nothing that is not there and the nothing that is.   15

—1923

Sunday Morning

I

Complacencies of the peignoir,° and late
Coffee and oranges in a sunny chair,
And the green freedom of a cockatoo
Upon a rug mingle to dissipate
The holy hush of ancient sacrifice.   5
She dreams a little, and she feels the dark
Encroachment of that old catastrophe,
As a calm darkens among water-lights.
The pungent oranges and bright, green wings
Seem things in some procession of the dead,   10
Winding across wide water, without sound.
The day is like wide water, without sound,
Stilled for the passing of her dreaming feet
Over the seas, to silent Palestine,
Dominion of the blood and sepulchre.   15

II

Why should she give her bounty to the dead?
What is divinity if it can come
Only in silent shadows and in dreams?
Shall she not find in comforts of the sun,
In pungent fruit and bright, green wings, or else   20
In any balm or beauty of the earth,
Things to be cherished like the thought of heaven?
Divinity must live within herself:
Passions of rain, or moods in falling snow;
Grievings in loneliness, or unsubdued   25
Elations when the forest blooms; gusty

1 **peignoir** woman's dressing gown

Emotions on wet roads on autumn nights;
All pleasures and all pains, remembering
The bough of summer and the winter branch.
These are the measures destined for her soul. 30

III

Jove° in the clouds had his inhuman birth.
No mother suckled him, no sweet land gave
Large-mannered motions to his mythy mind.
He moved among us, as a muttering king,
Magnificent, would move among his hinds,° 35
Until our blood, commingling, virginal,
With heaven, brought such requital to desire
The very hinds discerned it, in a star.
Shall our blood fail? Or shall it come to be
The blood of paradise? And shall the earth 40
Seem all of paradise that we shall know?
The sky will be much friendlier then than now,
A part of labor and a part of pain,
And next in glory to enduring love,
Not this dividing and indifferent blue. 45

IV

She says, "I am content when wakened birds,
Before they fly, test the reality
Of misty fields, by their sweet questionings;
But when the birds are gone, and their warm fields
Return no more, where, then, is paradise?" 50
There is not any haunt of prophecy,
Nor any old chimera° of the grave,
Neither the golden underground, nor isle
Melodious, where spirits gat them home,
Nor visionary south, nor cloudy palm 55
Remote on heaven's hill, that has endured
As April's green endures; or will endure
Like her remembrance of awakened birds,

---

31 Jove Roman name of Zeus   35 **hinds** inferiors or shepherds who saw the star of the nativity
52 **chimera** imagined monster

Or her desire for June and evening, tipped
By the consummation of the swallow's wings.   60

    V

She says, "But in contentment I still feel
The need of some imperishable bliss."
Death is the mother of beauty; hence from her,
Alone, shall come fulfilment to our dreams
And our desires. Although she strews the leaves   65
Of sure obliteration on our paths,
The path sick sorrow took, the many paths
Where triumph rang its brassy phrase, or love
Whispered a little out of tenderness,
She makes the willow shiver in the sun   70
For maidens who were wont to sit and gaze
Upon the grass, relinquished to their feet.
She causes boys to pile new plums and pears
On disregarded plate. The maidens taste
And stray impassioned in the littering leaves.   75

    VI

Is there no change of death in paradise?
Does ripe fruit never fall? Or do the boughs
Hang always heavy in that perfect sky,
Unchanging, yet so like our perishing earth,
With rivers like our own that seek for seas   80
They never find, the same receding shores
That never touch with inarticulate pang?
Why set the pear upon those river-banks
Or spice the shores with odors of the plum?
Alas, that they should wear our colors there,   85
The silken weavings of our afternoons,
And pick the strings of our insipid lutes!
Death is the mother of beauty, mystical,
Within whose burning bosom we devise
Our earthly mothers waiting, sleeplessly.   90

    VII

Supple and turbulent, a ring of men
Shall chant in orgy on a summer morn

Their boisterous devotion to the sun,
Not as a god, but as a god might be,
Naked among them, like a savage source.   95
Their chant shall be a chant of paradise,
Out of their blood, returning to the sky;
And in their chant shall enter, voice by voice,
The windy lake wherein their lord delights,
The trees, like serafin,° and echoing hills,   100
That choir among themselves long afterward.
They shall know well the heavenly fellowship
Of men that perish and of summer morn.
And whence they came and whither they shall go
The dew upon their feet shall manifest.   105

VIII

She hears, upon that water without sound,
A voice that cries, "The tomb in Palestine
Is not the porch of spirits lingering.
It is the grave of Jesus, where he lay."
We live in an old chaos of the sun,   110
Or old dependency of day and night,
Or island solitude, unsponsored, free,
Of that wide water, inescapable.
Deer walk upon our mountains, and the quail
Whistle about us their spontaneous cries;   115
Sweet berries ripen in the wilderness;
And, in the isolation of the sky,
At evening, casual flocks of pigeons make
Ambiguous undulations as they sink,
Downward to darkness, on extended wings.   120

—*1923*

---

100 serafin seraphim, a type of angel

William Carlos Williams (1883–1963)

William Carlos Williams, like his friend Wallace Stevens, followed an unconventional career for a poet, working until his death as a pediatrician in Rutherford, New Jersey. Williams is modern poetry's greatest proponent of the American idiom. His plainspoken poems have been more widely imitated than those of any other American poet of this century, perhaps because he represents a homegrown modernist alternative to the intellectualized Europeanism of Eliot and Ezra Pound (a friend of his from college days). In his later years, Williams assisted many younger poets, among them Allen Ginsberg, for whose controversial book Howl *he wrote an introduction.*

The Last Words of My English Grandmother

There were some dirty plates
and a glass of milk
beside her on a small table
near the rank, disheveled bed—

Wrinkled and nearly blind   5
she lay and snored
rousing with anger in her tones
to cry for food,

Gimme something to eat—
They're starving me—   10
I'm all right—I won't go
to the hospital. No, no, no

Give me something to eat!
Let me take you
to the hospital, I said   15
and after you are well

you can do as you please.
She smiled, Yes
you do what you please first
then I can do what I please—   20

Oh, oh, oh! she cried
as the ambulance men lifted
her to the stretcher—
Is this what you call

making me comfortable?   25
By now her mind was clear—
Oh you think you're smart
you young people,

she said, but I'll tell you
you don't know anything.   30
Then we started.
On the way

We passed a long row
of elms. She looked at them
awhile out of   35
the ambulance window and said,

What are all those
fuzzy-looking things out there?
Trees? Well, I'm tired
of them and rolled her head away.   40

—*1920*

The Red Wheelbarrow

so much depends
upon

a red wheel
barrow

glazed with rain   5
water

beside the white
chickens.

—*1923*

Spring and All

By the road to the contagious hospital°
under the surge of the blue
mottled clouds driven from the
northeast—a cold wind. Beyond, the
waste of broad, muddy fields   5
brown with dried weeds, standing and fallen

patches of standing water
the scattering of tall trees
All along the road the reddish
purplish, forked, upstanding, twiggy   10
stuff of bushes and small trees
with dead, brown leaves under them
leafless vines—

Lifeless in appearance, sluggish
dazed spring approaches—   15

They enter the new world naked,
cold, uncertain of all
save that they enter. All about them
the cold, familiar wind—

Now the grass, tomorrow   20
the stiff curl of wildcarrot leaf
One by one objects are defined—
It quickens: clarity, outline of leaf

But now the stark dignity of
entrance—Still, the profound change   25
has come upon them: rooted, they
grip down and begin to awaken

—*1923*

---

1 **contagious hospital** a hospital for quarantined patients

This Is Just to Say

I have eaten
the plums
that were in
the icebox

and which   5
you were probably
saving
for breakfast

Forgive me
they were delicious   10
so sweet
and so cold

—*1934*

Ezra Pound (1885–1972)

Ezra Pound was the greatest international proponent of modernist poetry. Born in Idaho and reared in Philadelphia, he emigrated to England in 1909, where he befriended Yeats, promoted the early work of Frost, and discovered Eliot. Pound's early promotion of the imagist movement assisted a number of important poetic principles and reputations, including those of H. D. (Hilda Doolittle) and, later, William Carlos Williams. Pound's support of Mussolini during World War II, expressed in controversial radio broadcasts, caused him to be held for over a decade after the war as a mental patient in the United States, after which he returned to Italy for the final years of his long and controversial life.

In a Station of the Metro

The apparition of these faces in the crowd;
Petals on a wet, black bough.

—*1916*

Portrait d'une Femme°

Your mind and you are our Sargasso Sea,°
London has swept about you this score years
And bright ships left you this or that in fee:
Ideas, old gossip, oddments of all things,
Strange spars of knowledge and dimmed wares of price.   5
Great minds have sought you—lacking someone else.
You have been second always. Tragical?
No. You preferred it to the usual thing:
One dull man, dulling and uxorious,°
One average mind—with one thought less, each year   10
Oh, you are patient, I have seen you sit
Hours, where something might have floated up.
And now you pay one. Yes, you richly pay.
You are a person of some interest, one comes to you
And takes strange gain away: 15
Trophies fished up; some curious suggestion;
Fact that leads nowhere; and a tale or two,
Pregnant with mandrakes,° or with something else
That might prove useful and yet never proves,
That never fits a corner or shows use,   20
Or finds its hour upon the loom of days:
The tarnished, gaudy, wonderful old work;
Idols and ambergris° and rare inlays,
These are your riches, your great store; and yet
For all this sea-hoard of deciduous things,   25
Strange woods half sodden, and new brighter stuff:
In the slow float of differing light and deep,
No! there is nothing! In the whole and all,
Nothing that's quite your own.
                    Yet this is you

                                                               —1912

Portrait d'une Femme Portrait of a Lady   **1 Sargasso Sea** area of seaweed in the mid-Atlantic where flotsam accumulates   **9 uxorious** doting and submissive   **18 mandrakes** plants with roots shaped like the lower half of the human body   **23 ambergris** intestinal secretion of the sperm whale; valuable and used in making perfumes

The River-Merchant's Wife: A Letter˘

While my hair was still cut straight across my forehead
I played about the front gate, pulling flowers.
You came by on bamboo stilts, playing horse,
You walked about my seat, playing with blue plums.
And we went on living in the village of Chokan: 5
Two small people, without dislike or suspicion.
At fourteen I married My Lord you.
I never laughed, being bashful.
Lowering my head, I looked at the wall.
Called to, a thousand times, I never looked back.   10

At fifteen I stopped scowling,
I desired my dust to be mingled with yours
Forever and forever and forever.
Why should I climb the lookout?

At sixteen you departed,   15
You went into far Ku-to-yen, by the river of swirling eddies,
And you have been gone five months.
The monkeys make sorrowful noise overhead.

You dragged your feet when you went out.
By the gate now, the moss is grown, the different mosses,   20
Too deep to clear them away!
The leaves fall early this autumn, in wind.
The paired butterflies are already yellow with August
Over the grass in the West garden;
They hurt me. I grow older.   25
If you are coming down through the narrows of the river Kiang,
Please let me know beforehand,
And I will come out to meet you
    As far as Cho-Fu-Sa.

—1915

The River-Merchant's Wife: A Letter imitation of a poem by Li-Po (AD 701–762)

Elinor Wylie (1885–1928)

Elinor Wylie, whose considerable lyrical skills found wide popularity during her relatively brief career, has recently come to the notice of the present generation. For many readers in the post-World War I era, Wylie, along with her slightly younger contemporary Edna St. Vincent Millay, helped to define the literary role of the New Woman of the 1920s. A poetic traditionalist whose lifestyle was thoroughly modern, Wylie now seems overdue for a serious reassessment of her place in the development of twentieth-century women's poetry.

Let No Charitable Hope

Now let no charitable hope
Confuse my mind with images
Of eagle and of antelope:
I am in nature none of these.

I was, being human, born alone;   5
I am, being woman, hard beset;
I live by squeezing from a stone
The little nourishment I get.

In masks outrageous and austere
The years go by in single file;   10
But none has merited my fear,
And none has quite escaped my smile.

—*1923*

Ophelia°

My locks are shorn for sorrow
Of love which may not be;
Tomorrow and tomorrow
Are plotting cruelty.

Ophelia character in Shakespeare's *Hamlet* who drowns herself after her father, Polonius, is killed by Hamlet

The winter wind tangles   5
These ringlets half-grown,
The sun sprays with spangles
And rays like his own.

Oh, quieter and colder
Is the stream; he will wait;   10
When my curls touch my shoulder
He will comb them straight.

—1921

H. D. (Hilða Doolittle) (1886–1961)

H. D. (Hilda Doolittle) was born in Bethlehem, Pennsylvania. Hilda Doolittle was a college friend of both Williams and Pound and moved to Europe permanently in 1911. With her husband Richard Aldington, H. D. was an important member of the imagist group promoted by Pound.

Pear Tree

Silver dust,
lifted from the earth,
higher than my arms reach,
you have mounted,
O, silver,   5
higher than my arms reach,
you front us with great mass;

no flower ever opened
so staunch a white leaf,
no flower ever parted silver   10
from such rare silver;

O, white pear,
your flower-tufts
thick on the branch
bring summer and ripe fruits   15
in their purple hearts.

—1916

Sea Rose

Rose, harsh rose,
marred and with stint of petals,
meager flower, thin,
sparse of leaf,

more precious   5
than a wet rose
single on a stem—
you are caught in the drift.

Stunted, with small leaf,
you are flung on the sand,   10
you are lifted
in the crisp sand
that drives in the wind.

Can the spice-rose
drip such acrid fragrance   15
hardened in a leaf?

—1916

Siegfried Sassoon (1886–1967)

Siegfried Sassoon was a decorated hero who publicly denounced World War I and became a friend and supporter of other British war poets, including Robert Graves and Wilfred Owen. His sardonic, anti-heroic war poems owe much to Thomas Hardy, whom he acknowledged as his chief poetic influence.

Dreamers

Soldiers are citizens of death's grey land,
   Drawing no dividend from time's tomorrows.
In the great hour of destiny they stand,
   Each with his feuds, and jealousies, and sorrows.

Soldiers are sworn to action; they must win   5
   Some flaming, fatal climax with their lives.

Soldiers are dreamers, when the guns begin
    They think of firelit homes, clean beds, and wives.

I see them in foul dug-outs, gnawed by rats,
    And in the ruined trenches, lashed with rain,   10
Dreaming of things they did with balls and bats,
    And mocked by hopeless longing to regain
Bank-holidays, and picture shows, and spats,
    And going to the office in the train.

—1918

Robinson Jeffers (1887–1962)

Robinson Jeffers lived with his wife and children for many years in Carmel, California, in a rock house that he built himself by the sea. Many of his ideas about man's small place in the larger world of nature have gained in relevance through the years since his death. Largely forgotten for many years, his poetry, particularly his book-length verse narratives, is once more regaining the attention of serious readers.

The Purse-Seine°

Our sardine fishermen work at night in the dark of the moon; daylight
    or moonlight
They could not tell where to spread the net, unable to see the
    phosphorescence of the shoals of fish.
They work northward from Monterey, coasting Santa Cruz; off New
    Year's Point or off Pigeon Point
The look-out man will see some lakes of milk-color light on the sea's
    night-purple; he points, and the helmsman
Turns the dark prow, the motorboat circles the gleaming shoal and
    drifts out her seine-net. They close the circle   5
and purse the bottom of the net, then with great labor haul it in.

Purse-Seine large circular fishing net; the bottom is closed (or pursed) before it is hauled in

I cannot tell you

How beautiful the scene is, and a little terrible, then, when the crowded fish

Know they are caught, and wildly beat from one wall to the other of their closing destiny the phosphorescent

Water to a pool of flame, each beautiful slender body sheeted with flame, like a live rocket   10

A comet's tail wake of clear yellow flame; while outside the narrowing

Floats and cordage of the net great sea-lions come up to watch, sighing in the dark; the vast walls of night

Stand erect to the stars.

Lately I was looking from a night mountain-top

On a wide city, the colored splendor, galaxies of light: how could I help but recall the seine-net   15

Gathering the luminous fish? I cannot tell you how beautiful the city appeared, and a little terrible.

I thought, We have geared the machines and locked all together into interdependence; we have built the great cities; now

There is no escape. We have gathered vast populations incapable of free survival, insulated

From the strong earth, each person in himself helpless, on all dependent. The circle is closed, and the net

Is being hauled in. They hardly feel the cords drawing, yet they shine already. The inevitable mass-disasters   20

Will not come in our time nor in our children's, but we and our children

Must watch the net draw narrower, government take all powers— or revolution, and the new government

Take more than all, add to kept bodies kept souls—or anarchy, the mass-disasters.

These things are Progress;

Do you marvel our verse is troubled or frowning, while it keeps its reason? Or it lets go, lets the mood flow   25

In the manner of the recent young men into mere hysteria, splintered gleams, crackled laughter. But they are quite wrong.

There is no reason for amazement: surely one always knew that cultures decay, and life's end is death.

—1937

Marianne Moore (1887–1972)

Marianne Moore called her own work poetry—unconventional and marked with the stamp of a rare personality—because, as she put it, there was no other category for it. For four years she was editor of the Dial, *one of the chief modernist periodicals. Moore's wide range of reference, which can leap from the commonplace to the wondrous within a single poem, reflects her unique set of personal interests—which range from exotic natural species to baseball.*

The Fish

wade
through black jade.
    Of the crow-blue mussel-shells, one
       keeps
       adjusting the ash-heaps;   5
    opening and shutting itself like

an
injured fan.
    The barnacles which encrust the
       side   10
       of the wave, cannot hide
    there for the submerged shafts of the

sun,
split like spun
    glass, move themselves with spotlight swift-   15
       ness
       into the crevices—
    in and out, illuminating

the
turquoise sea   20
    of bodies. The water drives a
       wedge
       of iron through the iron edge
    of the cliff; whereupon the stars,

pink   25
rice-grains, ink-
    bespattered jelly-fish, crabs like
        green
        lilies, and submarine
    toadstools, slide each on the other.   30

All
external
    marks of abuse are present on
        this
        defiant edifice—   35
    all the physical features of

ac-
cident—lack
    of cornice, dynamite grooves, burns,
        and   40
        hatchet strokes, these things stand
    out on it; the chasm-side is

dead.
Repeated
    evidence has proved that it can   45
        live
        on what can not revive
    its youth. The sea grows old in it.

                                  —*1921*

Silence

My father used to say,
"Superior people never make long visits,
have to be shown Longfellow's grave
or the glass flowers at Harvard.
Self-reliant like the cat—   5
that takes its prey to privacy,
the mouse's limp tail hanging like a shoelace from its mouth—
they sometimes enjoy solitude

and can be robbed of speech
by speech which has delighted them.   10
The deepest feeling always shows itself in silence;
not in silence, but restraint."
Nor was he insincere in saying, "Make my house your inn."
Inns are not residences.

—*1935*

T. S. Eliot (1888–1965)

T. S. Eliot was the author of The Waste Land, *one of the most famous and difficult modernist poems, and became an international figure. Born in St. Louis and educated at Harvard, he moved to London in 1914, where he remained for the rest of his life, becoming a British subject in 1927. This chief prophet of modern despair turned to the Church of England in later life, and wrote successful dramas on religious themes. As a critic and influential editor, Eliot dominated poetic taste in England and America for over twenty-five years. He was awarded the Nobel Prize in 1948.*

Journey of the Magi°

'A cold coming we had of it,
Just the worst time of the year
For a journey, and such a long journey:
The ways deep and the weather sharp,
The very dead of winter.'°   5
And the camels galled, sore-footed, refractory,
Lying down in the melting snow.
There were times we regretted
The summer palaces on slopes, the terraces,
And the silken girls bringing sherbet.   10
Then the camel men cursing and grumbling
And running away, and wanting their liquor and women,
And the night-fires going out, and the lack of shelters,
And the cities hostile and the towns unfriendly

Magi Wise Men mentioned in Matthew 2:1–2   **1–5 'A cold . . . winter'** The quotation marks indicated Eliot's source, a sermon by Lancelot Andrewes (1555–1626).

And the villages dirty and charging high prices: 15
A hard time we had of it.
At the end we preferred to travel all night,
Sleeping in snatches,
With the voices singing in our ears, saying
That this was all folly.   20

Then at dawn we came down to a temperate valley,
Wet, below the snow line, smelling of vegetation;
With a running stream and a water-mill beating the darkness,
And three trees on the low sky.
And an old white horse galloped away in the meadow.   25
Then we came to a tavern with vine-leaves over the lintel,
Six hands at an open door dicing for pieces of silver,
And feet kicking the empty wine-skins.
But there was no information, and so we continued
And arrived at evening, not a moment too soon   30
Finding the place; it was (you may say) satisfactory.

All this was a long time ago, I remember,
And I would do it again, but set down
This° set down
This: were we led all that way for   35
Birth or Death? There was a Birth, certainly,
We had evidence and no doubt. I had seen birth and death,
But had thought they were different; this Birth was
Hard and bitter agony for us, like Death, our death.
We returned to our places, these Kingdoms,   40
But no longer at ease here, in the old dispensation,°
With an alien people clutching their gods.
I should be glad of another death.

                                    —1927

33–34 set down . . . This The Magus is dictating his memoirs to a scribe   **41 old dispensation** world before the birth of Christ

The Love Song of
J. Alfred Prufrock

S'io credesse che mia risposta fosse
A persona che mai tornasse al mondo,
Questa fiamma staria senza più scosse.
Ma perciocche giammai di questo fondo
Non tornò vivo alcun, s'i'odo il vero,
Senza tema d'infamia ti rispondo.°

Let us go then, you° and I,
When the evening is spread out against the sky
Like a patient etherised upon a table;
Let us go, through certain half-deserted streets,
The muttering retreats   5
Of restless nights in one-night cheap hotels
And sawdust restaurants with oyster-shells:
Streets that follow like a tedious argument
Of insidious intent
To lead you to an overwhelming question . . .   10
Oh, do not ask, "What is it?"
Let us go and make our visit.

In the room the women come and go
Talking of Michelangelo.°

The yellow fog that rubs its back upon the window-panes,   15
The yellow smoke that rubs its muzzle on the window-panes,
Licked its tongue into the corners of the evening,
Lingered upon the pools that stand in drains,
Let fall upon its back the soot that falls from chimneys,
Slipped by the terrace, made a sudden leap,   20
And seeing that it was a soft October night,
Curled once about the house, and fell asleep.

And indeed there will be time
For the yellow smoke that slides along the street,

S'io credesse . . . rispondo From Dante's *Inferno* (Canto 27). The speaker is Guido da Montefeltro: "If I thought I spoke to someone who would return to the world, this flame would tremble no longer. But, if what I hear is true, since no one has ever returned alive from this place I can answer you without fear of infamy." **1 you** Eliot said that the auditor of the poem was a male friend of Prufrock. **14 Michelangelo** Italian painter and sculptor (1475–1564)

Rubbing its back upon the window-panes; 25
There will be time, there will be time
To prepare a face to meet the faces that you meet;
There will be time to murder and create,
And time for all the works and days of hands
That lift and drop a question on your plate: 30
Time for you and time for me,
And time yet for a hundred indecisions,
And for a hundred visions and revisions,
Before the taking of a toast and tea.

In the room the women come and go 35
Talking of Michelangelo.

And indeed there will be time
To wonder, "Do I dare?" and, "Do I dare?"—
Time to turn back and descend the stair,
With a bald spot in the middle of my hair— 40
(They will say: "How his hair is growing thin!")
My morning coat, my collar mounting firmly to the chin,
My necktie rich and modest, but asserted by a simple pin—
(They will say: "But how his arms and legs are thin!")
Do I dare 45
Disturb the universe?
In a minute there is time
For decisions and revisions which a minute will reverse.

For I have known them all already, known them all:
Have known the evenings, mornings, afternoons, 50
I have measured out my life with coffee spoons;
I know the voices dying with a dying fall
Beneath the music from a farther room.
So how should I presume?

And I have known the eyes already, known them all— 55
The eyes that fix you in a formulated phrase,
And when I am formulated, sprawling on a pin,
When I am pinned and wriggling on the wall,
Then how should I begin
To spit out all the butt-ends of my days and ways? 60
And how should I presume?

And I have known the arms already, known them all—
Arms that are braceleted and white and bare

(But in the lamplight, downed with light brown hair!)
Is it perfume from a dress   65
That makes me so digress?
Arms that lie along a table, or wrap about a shawl.
    And should I then presume?
    And how should I begin?

   . . . . .

Shall I say, I have gone at dusk through narrow streets,   70
And watched the smoke that rises from the pipes
Of lonely men in shirtsleeves, leaning out of windows? . . .

I should have been a pair of ragged claws
Scuttling across the floors of silent seas.

   . . . . .

And the afternoon, the evening, sleeps so peacefully!   75
Smoothed by long fingers,
Asleep . . . tired . . . or it malingers,
Stretched on the floor, here beside you and me.
Should I, after tea and cakes and ices,
Have the strength to force the moment to its crisis?   80
But though I have wept and fasted, wept and prayed,
Though I have seen my head (grown slightly bald) brought in
    upon a platter,
I am no prophet°—and here's no great matter;
I have seen the moment of my greatness flicker,
And I have seen the eternal Footman hold my coat, and   85
    snicker,
       And in short, I was afraid.

And would it have been worth it, after all,
After the cups, the marmalade, the tea,
Among the porcelain, among some talk of you and me,
Would it have been worth while,   90
To have bitten off the matter with a smile,
To have squeezed the universe into a ball
To roll it towards some overwhelming question,
To say: "I am Lazarus,° come from the dead,
Come back to tell you all, I shall tell you all"—   95
If one, settling a pillow by her head,

82–83 my head . . . no prophet allusion to John the Baptist   94 Lazarus raised from the dead in
John 11:1–44

Should say: "That is not what I meant at all;
That is not it, at all."

And would it have been worth it, after all,
Would it have been worth while,   100
After the sunsets and the dooryards and the sprinkled streets,
After the novels, after the teacups, after the skirts that trail
    along the floor—
And this, and so much more?—
It is impossible to say just what I mean!
But as if a magic lantern° threw the nerves in patterns on   105
    a screen:

Would it have been worth while
If one, settling a pillow or throwing off a shawl,
And turning toward the window, should say:
    "That is not it at all,
    That is not what I meant, at all."   110

    . . . . .

No! I am not Prince Hamlet, nor was meant to be;
Am an attendant lord, one that will do
To swell a progress, start a scene or two,
Advise the prince; no doubt, an easy tool,
Deferential, glad to be of use,   115
Politic, cautious, and meticulous;
Full of high sentence, but a bit obtuse;
At times, indeed, almost ridiculous—
Almost, at times, the Fool.°

I grow old . . . I grow old . . .   120
I shall wear the bottoms of my trousers rolled.

Shall I part my hair behind? Do I dare to eat a peach?
I shall wear white flannel trousers, and walk upon the beach.
I have heard the mermaids singing, each to each.

I do not think that they will sing to me.   125

I have seen them riding seaward on the waves
Combing the white hair of the waves blown back
When the wind blows the water white and black.

---

105 magic lantern old-fashioned slide projector   **111–119 not Prince Hamlet . . . the Fool** The
allusion is probably to Polonius, a character in *Hamlet.*

We have lingered in the chambers of the sea
By sea-girls wreathed with seaweed red and brown   130
Till human voices wake us, and we drown.

—1917

Preludes

I

The winter evening settles down
With smell of steaks in passageways.
Six o'clock.
The burnt-out ends of smoky days.
And now a gusty shower wraps   5
The grimy scraps
Of withered leaves about your feet
And newspapers from vacant lots;
The showers beat
On broken blinds and chimney-pots,   10
And at the corner of the street
A lonely cab-horse steams and stamps.

And then the lighting of the lamps.

II

The morning comes to consciousness
Of faint stale smells of beer   15
From the sawdust-trampled street
With all its muddy feet that press
To early coffee-stands.

With the other masquerades
That time resumes,   20
One thinks of all the hands
That are raising dingy shades
In a thousand furnished rooms.

III

You tossed a blanket from the bed,
You lay upon your back, and waited;   25
You dozed, and watched the night revealing

The thousand sordid images
Of which your soul was constituted;
They flickered against the ceiling.
And when all the world came back   30
And the light crept up between the shutters
And you heard the sparrows in the gutters,
You had such a vision of the street
As the street hardly understands;
Sitting along the bed's edge, where   35
You curled the papers from your hair,
Or clasped the yellow soles of feet
In the palms of both soiled hands.

    IV

His soul stretched tight across the skies
That fade behind a city block,   40
Or trampled by insistent feet
At four and five and six o'clock;
And short square fingers stuffing pipes,
And evening newspapers, and eyes
Assured of certain certainties,   45
The conscience of a blackened street
Impatient to assume the world.

I am moved by fancies that are curled
Around these images, and cling:
The notion of some infinitely gentle   50
Infinitely suffering thing.

Wipe your hand across your mouth, and laugh;
The worlds revolve like ancient women
Gathering fuel in vacant lots.

                                           —1917

John Crowe Ransom (1888–1974)

*John Crowe Ransom, as a professor at Vanderbilt University in Nashville,
began a little magazine called the* Fugitive, *which lent its name to a group
of young southern poets who published in it. Later he moved to Kenyon
College, where he was editor of the* Kenyon Review *for many years. Ransom was influential as both a poet and a critic.*

The Equilibrists

Full of her long white arms and milky skin
He had a thousand times remembered sin.
Alone in the press of people traveled he,
Minding her jacinth, and myrrh, and ivory.

Mouth he remembered: the quaint orifice   5
From which came heat that flamed upon the kiss,
Till cold words came down spiral from the head,
Grey doves from the officious tower illspred.

Body: it was a white field ready for love,
On her body's field, with the gaunt tower above,   10
The lilies grew, beseeching him to take,
If he would pluck and wear them, bruise and break.

Eyes talking: Never mind the cruel words,
Embrace my flowers, but not embrace the swords
But what they said, the doves came straightway flying   15
And unsaid: Honor, Honor, they came crying.

Importunate her doves. Too pure, too wise,
Clambering on his shoulder, saying, Arise,
Leave me now, and never let us meet,
Eternal distance now command thy feet.   20

Predicament indeed, which thus discovers
Honor among thieves, Honor between lovers.
O such a little word is Honor, they feel!
But the grey word is between them cold as steel.

At length I saw these lovers fully were come   25
Into their torture of equilibrium;

Dreadfully had forsworn each other, and yet
They were bound each to each, and they did not forget.

And rigid as two painful stars, and twirled
About the clustered night their prison world,   30
They burned with fierce love always to come near,
But Honor beat them back and kept them clear.

Ah, the strict lovers, they are ruined now!
I cried in anger. But with puddled brow
Devising for those gibbeted and brave   35
Came I descanting: Man, what would you have?

For spin your period out, and draw your breath,
A kinder sæculum° begins with Death.
Would you ascend to Heaven and bodiless dwell?
Or take your bodies honorless to Hell?   40

In Heaven you have heard no marriage is,
No white flesh tinder to your lecheries,
Your male and female tissue sweetly shaped
Sublimed away, and furious blood escaped.

Great lovers lie in Hell, the stubborn ones   45
Infatuate of the flesh upon the bones;
Stuprate,° they rend each other when they kiss,
The pieces kiss again, no end to this.

But still I watched them spinning, orbited nice.
Their flames were not more radiant than their ice.   50
I dug in the quiet earth and wrought the tomb
And made these lines to memorize their doom:—

    EPITAPH

Equilibrists lie here; stranger, tread light;
Close, but untouching in each other's sight;
Mouldered the lips and ashy the tall skull.   55
Let them lie perilous and beautiful.

—1927

38 sæculum era   47 stuprate infamous

Piazza° Piece

—I am a gentleman in a dustcoat° trying
To make you hear. Your ears are soft and small
And listen to an old man not at all.
They want the young men's whispering and sighing.
But see the roses on your trellis dying   5
And hear the spectral singing of the moon;
For I must have my lovely lady soon,
I am a gentleman in a dustcoat trying.

—I am a lady young in beauty waiting
Until my truelove comes, and then we kiss.   10
But what grey man among the vines is this
Whose words are dry and faint as in a dream?
Back from my trellis, Sir, before I scream!
I am a lady young in beauty waiting.

—1927

Edna St. Vincent Millay (1892–1950)

*Raised in the coastal village of Camden, Maine, Edna St. Vincent Millay
was extremely popular in the 1920s, when her sonnets seemed the ultimate
expression of the liberated sexuality of what was then called the New
Woman. Neglected for many years, her poems have recently generated renewed interest, and it seems likely that she will eventually regain her status
as one of the most important female poets of the twentieth century.*

If I Should Learn, in Some Quite Casual Way

If I should learn, in some quite casual way,
That you were gone, not to return again—
Read from the back-page of a paper, say,
Held by a neighbor in a subway train,

Piazza courtyard   **1 dustcoat** old-fashioned coat worn while driving an open car

How at the corner of this avenue 5
And such a street (so are the papers filled)
A hurrying man, who happened to be you,
At noon today had happened to be killed—
I should not cry aloud—I could not cry
Aloud, or wring my hands in such a place— 10
I should but watch the station lights rush by
With a more careful interest on my face;
Or raise my eyes and read with greater care
Where to store furs and how to treat the hair.

—1917

Oh, Oh, You Will Be Sorry for that Word

Oh, oh, you will be sorry for that word!
Give back my book and take my kiss instead.
Was it my enemy or my friend I heard,
"What a big book for such a little head!"
Come, I will show you now my newest hat, 5
And you may watch me purse my mouth and prink!°
Oh, I shall love you still, and all of that.
I never again shall tell you what I think.
I shall be sweet and crafty, soft and sly;
You will not catch me reading any more: 10
I shall be called a wife to pattern by;
And some day when you knock and push the door,
Some sane day, not too bright and not too stormy,
I shall be gone, and you may whistle for me.

—1923

6 **prink** primp

Recuerdo°

We were very tired, we were very merry—
We had gone back and forth all night on the ferry.
It was bare and bright, and smelled like a stable—
But we looked into a fire, we leaned across a table,
We lay on a hill-top underneath the moon;   5
And the whistles kept blowing, and the dawn came soon.

We were very tired, we were very merry—
We had gone back and forth all night on the ferry;
And you ate an apple, and I ate a pear,
From a dozen of each we had bought somewhere;   10
And the sky went wan, and the wind came cold,
And the sun rose dripping, a bucketful of gold.

We were very tired, we were very merry,
We had gone back and forth all night on the ferry.
We hailed, "Good morrow, mother!" to a shawl-covered head.   15
And bought a morning paper, which neither of us read;

And she wept, "God bless you!" for the apples and pears,
And we gave her all our money but our subway fares.

                                                                    —*1920*

What Lips My Lips Have Kissed, and Where, and Why

What lips my lips have kissed, and where, and why,
I have forgotten, and what arms have lain
Under my head till morning; but the rain
Is full of ghosts tonight, that tap and sigh
Upon the glass and listen for reply,   5
And in my heart there stirs a quiet pain

Recuerdo memory

For unremembered lads that not again
Will turn to me at midnight with a cry.
Thus in the winter stands the lonely tree,
Nor knows what birds have vanished one by one,   10
Yet knows its boughs more silent than before:
I cannot say what loves have come and gone,
I only know that summer sang in me
A little while, that in me sings no more.

—*1923*

Wilfred Owen (1893–1918)

Wilfred Owen was killed in the trenches only a few days before the
armistice that ended World War I. Owen showed more promise than any
other English poet of his generation. A decorated officer whose nerves
broke down after exposure to battle, he met Siegfried Sassoon at
Craiglockhart military hospital. His work was posthumously collected by
his friend. A novel by Pat Barker, Regeneration *(also made into a film),*
deals with their poetic and personal relationship.

Dulce et Decorum Est°

Bent double, like old beggars under sacks,
Knock-kneed, coughing like hags, we cursed through sludge,
Till on the haunting flares we turned our backs
And towards our distant rest began to trudge.
Men marched asleep. Many had lost their boots   5
But limped on, blood-shod. All went lame; all blind;
Drunk with fatigue; deaf even to the hoots
Of tired, outstripped Five-Nines° that dropped behind.

Gas! Gas! Quick, boys!—An ecstasy of fumbling
Fitting the clumsy helmets just in time;   10
But someone still was yelling out and stumbling
And flound'ring like a man in fire or lime . . .

Dulce et Decorum Est (pro patria mori) from the Roman poet Horace: "It is sweet and proper to die for one's country"   **8 Five-Nines** German artillery shells (59 mm)

Dim, through the misty panes and thick green light,°
As under a green sea, I saw him drowning.

In all my dreams, before my helpless sight,   15
He plunges at me, guttering, choking, drowning.
If in some smothering dreams you too could pace
Behind the wagon that we flung him in,
And watch the white eyes writhing in his face,
His hanging face, like a devil's sick of sin;   20
If you could hear, at every jolt, the blood   •
Come gargling from the froth-corrupted lungs,
Obscene as cancer, bitter as the cud
Of vile, incurable sores on innocent tongues,—
My friend,° you would not tell with such high zest   25
To children ardent for some desperate glory,
The old Lie: Dulce et decorum est
Pro patria mori.

                                                          —1920

---

e. e. cummings (1894–1962)

e. e. cummings was the son of a Harvard professor and Unitarian clergy-
man. Edward Estlin Cummings served as a volunteer ambulance driver in
France during World War I. cummings's experimentation with the typo-
graphical aspects of poetry reveals his serious interest in cubist painting,
which he studied in Paris in the 1920s. A brilliant satirist, he also excelled as
a writer of lyrical poems whose unusual appearance and idiosyncratic gram-
mar, spelling, and punctuation often overshadow their traditional themes.

in just-

in Just-
spring   when the world is mud-
luscious the little
lame balloonman
whistles   far   and wee   5

---

13 misty panes and thick green light i.e., through the gas mask   **25 My friend** The poem was
originally addressed to Jessie Pope, a writer of patriotic verse.

and eddieandbill come
running from marbles and
piracies and it's
spring

when the world is puddle-wonderful   10

the queer
old balloonman whistles
far   and   wee
and bettyandisbel come dancing

from hop-scotch and jump-rope and   15

it's
spring
and
   the

        goat-footed   20

balloonMan   whistles
far
and
wee
                                   —1920

nobody loses all the time

nobody loses all the time
i had an uncle named
Sol who was a born failure and
nearly everybody said he should have gone
into vaudeville perhaps because my Uncle Sol could
sing McCann He Was A Diver on Xmas Eve like Hell Itself which   5
may or may not account for the fact that my Uncle

Sol indulged in that possibly most inexcusable
of all to use a highfalootin phrase
luxuries that is or to
wit farming and be   10
it needlessly
added

my Uncle Sol's farm
failed because the chickens
ate the vegetables so   15
my Uncle Sol had a
chicken farm till the
skunks ate the chickens when

my Uncle Sol
had a skunk farm but   20
the skunks caught cold and
died and so
my Uncle Sol imitated the
skunks in a subtle manner

or by drowning himself in the watertank   25
but somebody who'd given my Uncle Sol a Victor
Victrola and records while he lived presented to
him upon the auspicious occasion of his decease a
scrumptious not to mention splendiferous funeral with
tall boys in black gloves and flowers and everything and   30

i remember we all cried like the Missouri
when my Uncle Sol's coffin lurched because
somebody pressed a button
(and down went
my Uncle   35
Sol

and started a worm farm)

—*1926*

pity this busy monster,manunkind

pity this busy monster,manunkind,

not. Progress is a comfortable disease:
your victim(death and life safely beyond)

plays with the bigness of his littleness
—electrons° deify one razorblade   5
into a mountainrange;lenses extend

unwish through curving wherewhen till unwish
returns on its unself.
                        A world of made
is not a world of born—pity poor flesh

and trees,poor stars and stones,but never this   10
fine specimen of hypermagical

ultraomnipotence. We doctors know

a hopeless case if—listen:there's a hell
of a good universe next door;let's go

                                        —1944

r-p-o-p-h-e-s-s-a-g-r

                        r-p-o-p-h-e-s-s-a-g-r
            who
a)s w(e loo)k
upnowgath
            PPEGORHRASS   5
                    eringint(o-
aThe):l
    eA
    !p:
S   a   10
        (r
rIvInG   .gRrEaPsPhOs)
                                    to
rea(be)rran(com)gi(e)ngly
,grasshopper;   15
                                        —1932

---

5 **electrons** in an electron microscope

Jean Toomer (1894–1967)

*Jean Toomer was born in Washington, D.C., the grandson of a black man
who served as governor of Louisiana during Reconstruction. His book
Cane (1923) is a mixed collection of prose and verse based on his observations of life in rural Georgia, where he was a schoolteacher. A complete
edition of his poetry, most of it unpublished during his life, was assembled
over twenty years after his death.*

Georgia Dusk

The sky, lazily disdaining to pursue
  The setting sun, too indolent to hold
  A lengthened tournament for flashing gold,
Passively darkens for night's barbecue,

A feast of moon and men and barking hounds,   5
  An orgy for some genius of the South
  With blood-hot eyes and cane-lipped scented mouth,
Surprised in making folk-songs from soul sounds.

The sawmill blows its whistle, buzz-saws stop,
  And silence breaks the bud of knoll and hill,   10
Soft settling pollen where plowed lands fulfill
Their early promise of a bumper crop.

Smoke from the pyramidal sawdust pile
  Curls up, blue ghosts of trees, tarrying low
  Where only chips and stumps are left to show   15
The solid proof of former domicile.

Meanwhile, the men, with vestiges of pomp,
  Race memories of king and caravan,
  High-priests, an ostrich, and a juju-man,
Go singing through the footpaths of the swamp.   20

Their voices rise . . the pine trees are guitars,
  Strumming, pine-needles fall like sheets of rain . .
  Their voices rise . . the chorus of the cane
Is caroling a vesper to the stars . .

O singers, resinous and soft your songs   25
  Above the sacred whisper of the pines,

Give virgin lips to cornfield concubines,
Bring dreams of Christ to dusky cane-lipped throngs.

—1923

Louise Bogan (1897–1970)

*Louise Bogan was for many years the poetry editor and resident critic of
the* New Yorker, *and the opinions expressed in her many book reviews
have held up well in the years since her death. In her later years Bogan suffered from severe bouts of clinical depression and wrote little poetry, but
her relatively slim output reveals a unique poetic voice.*

Women

Women have no wilderness in them,
They are provident instead,
Content in the tight hot cell of their hearts
To eat dusty bread.

They do not see cattle cropping red winter grass,   5
They do not hear
Snow water going down under culverts
Shallow and clear.

They wait, when they should turn to journeys,
They stiffen, when they should bend.   10
They use against themselves that benevolence
To which no man is friend.

They cannot think of so many crops to a field
Or of clean wood cleft by an axe.
Their love is an eager meaninglessness   15
Too tense, or too lax.

They hear in every whisper that speaks to them
A shout and a cry.
As like as not, when they take life over their door-sills
They should let it go by.   20

—1923

Hart Crane (1899–1933)

Hart Crane is one of the first modernists to make extensive poetic use of the artifacts—advertising slogans, motion picture lore, trade names—of American popular culture. Much of this material surfaces in The Bridge *(1930), his book-length attempt to write an epic sequence about modern America. Crane committed suicide by leaping from a ship returning from the Yucatán, where he spent his last year on a Guggenheim Fellowship attempting to write an epic poem about the conquest of Mexico.*

Chaplinesque°

We make our meek adjustments,
Contented with such random consolations
As the wind deposits
In slithered and too ample pockets.

For we can still love the world, who find   5
A famished kitten on the step, and know
Recesses for it from the fury of the street,
Or warm torn elbow coverts.

We will sidestep, and to the final smirk
Dally the doom of that inevitable thumb   10
That slowly chafes its puckered index toward us,
Facing the dull squint with what innocence
And what surprise!

And yet these fine collapses are not lies
More than the pirouettes of any pliant cane;   15
Our obsequies are in a way, no enterprise.
We can evade you, and all else but the heart:
What blame to us if the heart live on.

The game enforces smirks; but we have seen
The moon in lonely alleys make   20
A grail of laughter of an empty ash can,
And through all sound of gaiety and quest
Have heard a kitten in the wilderness.

—1926

Chaplinesque after Charlie Chaplin, silent-film comedian

Langston Hughes (1902–1967)

Langston Hughes was a leading figure in the Harlem Renaissance of the 1920s, and he became the most famous black writer of his day. Phrases from his poems and other writings have become deeply ingrained in the American consciousness. An important experimenter with poetic form, Hughes is credited with incorporating the rhythms of jazz into poetry.

Dream Boogie

Good morning, daddy!
Ain't you heard
The boogie-woogie rumble
Of a dream deferred?
Listen closely: 5
You'll hear their feet
Beating out and beating out a—

    You think
    It's a happy beat?

Listen to it closely: 10
Ain't you heard
something underneath
like a—

    What did I say?

Sure,   15
I'm happy!
Take it away!

    Hey, pop!
    Re-bop!
    Mop!   20
      Y-e-a-h!

—*1951*

Theme for English B

The instructor said,

> Go home and write
> a page tonight.
> And let that page come out of you—
> Then, it will be true.   5

I wonder if it's that simple?
I am twenty-two, colored, born in Winston-Salem.
I went to school there, then Durham, then here
to this college on the hill above Harlem.
I am the only colored student in my class.   10
The steps from the hill lead down into Harlem,
through a park, then I cross St. Nicholas,
Eighth Avenue, Seventh, and I come to the Y,
the Harlem Branch Y, where I take the elevator
up to my room, sit down, and write this page: 15

It's not easy to know what is true for you or me
at twenty-two, my age. But I guess I'm what
I feel and see and hear, Harlem, I hear you:
hear you, hear you—we two—you, me, talk on this page.
(I hear New York, too.) Me—who?   20
Well, I like to eat, sleep, drink, and be in love.
I like to work, read, learn, and understand life.
I like a pipe for a Christmas present,
or records—Bessie,° bop, or Bach.
I guess being colored doesn't make me *not* like   25
the same things other folks like who are other races.
So will my page be colored that I write?
Being me, it will not be white.
But it will be
a part of you, instructor.   30
You are white—
yet a part of me, as I am a part of you.
That's American.

24 **Bessie** Bessie Smith (1898–1937), blues singer

Sometimes perhaps you don't want to be a part of me.
Nor do I often want to be a part of you.   35
But we are, that's true!
I guess you learn from me—
although you're older—and white—
and somewhat more free.

This is my page for English B.   40

—*1951*

The Weary Blues

Droning a drowsy syncopated tune,
Rocking back and forth to a mellow croon,
    I heard a Negro play.
Down on Lenox Avenue the other night
By the pale dull pallor of an old gas light   5
    He did a lazy sway. . . .
    He did a lazy sway. . . .
To the tune o' those Weary Blues.
With his ebony hands on each ivory key
He made that poor piano moan with melody.   10
    O Blues!
Swaying to and fro on his rickety stool
He played that sad raggy tune like a musical fool.
    Sweet Blues!
Coming from a black man's soul.   15
    O Blues!
In a deep song voice with a melancholy tone
I heard that Negro sing, that old piano moan—
    "Ain't got nobody in all this world,
    Ain't got nobody but ma self.   20
    I's gwine to quit ma frownin'
    And put ma troubles on the shelf."

Thump, thump, thump, went his foot on the floor.
He played a few chords then he sang some more—
    "I got the Weary Blues   25

And I can't be satisfied.
Got the Weary Blues
And can't be satisfied—
I ain't happy no mo'
And I wish that I had died."   30
And far into the night he crooned that tune.
The stars went out and so did the moon.
The singer stopped playing and went to bed
While the Weary Blues echoed through his head.
He slept like a rock or a man that's dead.   35

—1926

Countee Cullen (1903–1946)

Countee Cullen, among black writers of the first half of the twentieth century, crafted poetry representing a more conservative style than that of his contemporary, Hughes. Although he wrote a number of lyrics on standard poetic themes, he is best remembered for his eloquent poems on racial subjects.

Incident

Once riding in old Baltimore,
    Heart-filled, head-filled with glee,
I saw a Baltimorean
    Keep looking straight at me.

Now I was eight and very small,   5
    And he was no whit bigger,
And so I smiled, but he poked out
    His tongue, and called me, "Nigger."

I saw the whole of Baltimore
    From May until December;   10
Of all the things that happened there
    That's all that I remember.

—1963

Yet Do I Marvel

I doubt not God is good, well-meaning, kind,
And did He stoop to quibble could tell why
The little buried mole continues blind,
Why flesh that mirrors Him must some day die,
Make plain the reason tortured Tantalus°   5
Is baited by the fickle fruit, declare
If merely brute caprice dooms Sisyphus°
To struggle up a never-ending stair.
Inscrutable His ways are, and immune
To catechism by a mind too strewn   10
With petty cares to slightly understand
What awful brain compels His awful hand.
Yet do I marvel at this curious thing:
To make a poet black and bid him sing!

—1963

A. D. Hope (1907–2000)

A. D. Hope was the first unquestionably major poet to emerge from Australia. Hope waited until he was almost fifty to publish his first collection of poetry. Even then, the sexual frankness of poems like "Imperial Adam" proved controversial in the conservative climate of mid-1950s Australia. A poet who strongly rejects most of the tendencies of modernism (most prominently free verse), Hope seems closer in spirit to eighteenth-century satirists like Swift and Pope, whom he obviously admires, and to his exact contemporary, W. H. Auden.

Imperial Adam

Imperial Adam, naked in the dew,
Felt his brown flanks and found the rib was gone.
Puzzled he turned and saw where, two and two,
The mighty spoor of Jahweh marked the lawn.

---

5 **Tantalus** mythological character tortured by unreachable fruit   7 **Sisyphus** figure in myth who endlessly rolls a boulder uphill

Then he remembered through mysterious sleep 5
The surgeon fingers probing at the bone,
The voice so far away, so rich and deep:
"It is not good for him to live alone."

Turning once more he found Man's counterpart
In tender parody breathing at his side. 10
He knew her at first sight, he knew by heart
Her allegory of sense unsatisfied.

The pawpaw drooped its golden breasts above
Less generous than the honey of her flesh;
The innocent sunlight showed the place of love; 15
The dew on its dark hairs winked crisp and fresh.

This plump gourd severed from his virile root,
She promised on the turf of Paradise
Delicious pulp of the forbidden fruit;
Sly as the snake she loosed her sinuous thighs, 20

And waking, smiled up at him from the grass;
Her breasts rose softly and he heard her sigh—
From all the beasts whose pleasant task it was
In Eden to increase and multiply

Adam had learned the jolly deed of kind: 25
He took her in his arms and there and then,
Like the clean beasts, embracing from behind,
Began in joy to found the breed of men.

Then from the spurt of seed within her broke
Her terrible and triumphant female cry, 30
Split upward by the sexual lightning stroke.
It was the beasts now who stood watching by:

The gravid elephant, the calving hind,
The breeding bitch, the she-ape big with young
Were the first gentle midwives of mankind; 35
The teeming lioness rasped her with her tongue;

The proud vicuña nuzzled her as she slept
Lax on the grass; and Adam watching too
Saw how her dumb breasts at their ripening wept,
The great pod of her belly swelled and grew, 40

And saw its water break, and saw, in fear,
Its quaking muscles in the act of birth,
Between her legs a pigmy face appear,
And the first murderer lay upon the earth.

—1955

W. H. Auden (1907–1973)

*W. H. Auden was already established as an important younger British poet
before he moved to America in 1939 (he later became a U.S. citizen). As a
transatlantic link between two literary cultures, Auden was one of the
most influential literary figures and cultural spokespersons in the English-
speaking world for almost forty years, giving a name to the postwar era
when he dubbed it "The Age of Anxiety" in a poem. In his last years he
returned briefly to Oxford, where he occupied the poetry chair.*

As I Walked Out One Evening

As I walked out one evening,
    Walking down Bristol Street,
The crowds upon the pavement
    Were fields of harvest wheat.

And down by the brimming river   5
    I heard a lover sing
Under an arch of the railway:
    "Love has no ending.

"I'll love you, dear, I'll love you
    Till China and Africa meet,   10
And the river jumps over the mountain
    And the salmon sing in the street.

"I'll love you till the ocean
    Is folded and hung up to dry,
And the seven stars go squawking   15
    Like geese about the sky.

"The years shall run like rabbits,
    For in my arms I hold
The Flower of the Ages,
    And the first love of the world."   20

But all the clocks in the city
    Began to whirr and chime:
"O let not Time deceive you,
    You cannot conquer Time.

"In the burrows of the Nightmare   25
    Where Justice naked is,
Time watches from the shadow
    And coughs when you would kiss.

"In headaches and in worry
    Vaguely life leaks away,   30
And Time will have his fancy
    Tomorrow or to-day.

"Into many a green valley
    Drifts the appalling snow;
Time breaks the threaded dances   35
    And the diver's brilliant bow.

"O plunge your hands in water,
    Plunge them in up to the wrist;
Stare, stare in the basin
    And wonder what you've missed.   40

"The glacier knocks in the cupboard,
    The desert sighs in the bed,
And the crack in the tea-cup opens
    A lane to the land of the dead.

"Where the beggars raffle the banknotes   45
    And the Giant is enchanting to Jack,
And the Lily-white Boy is a Roarer,
    And Jill goes down on her back.

"O look, look in the mirror,
    O look in your distress;   50
Life remains a blessing
    Although you cannot bless.

"O stand, stand at the window
    As the tears scald and start;
You shall love your crooked neighbor   55
    With your crooked heart."

It was late, late in the evening,
    The lovers they were gone;
The clocks had ceased their chiming,
    And the deep river ran on.   60

                                                            —1940

Musée des Beaux Arts°

About suffering they were never wrong,
The Old Masters: how well they understood
Its human position; how it takes place
While someone else is eating or opening a window or just
    walking dully along;
How, when the aged are reverently, passionately waiting   5
For the miraculous birth, there always must be
Children who did not specially want it to happen, skating
On a pond at the edge of the wood:
They never forgot
That even the dreadful martyrdom must run its course   10
Anyhow in a corner, some untidy spot
Where the dogs go on with their doggy life and the torturer's horse
Scratches its innocent behind on a tree.

In Brueghel's *Icarus*,° for instance: how everything turns away
Quite leisurely from the disaster; the ploughman may   15
Have heard the splash, the forsaken cry,
But for him it was not an important failure; the sun shone
As it had to on the white legs disappearing into the green
Water; and the expensive delicate ship that must have seen
Something amazing, a boy falling out of the sky,   20
Had somewhere to get to and sailed calmly on.

                                                            —1938

Musée des Beaux Arts Museum of Fine Arts   **14 Brueghel's** *Icarus* In this painting (c. 1550) the
famous event from Greek myth is almost inconspicuous among the other details Auden mentions.

The Unknown Citizen

To JS/07/M/378
This Marble Monument Is Erected by the State

He was found by the Bureau of Statistics to be
One against whom there was no official complaint,
And all the reports on his conduct agree
That, in the modern sense of an old-fashioned word, he was a saint,
For in everything he did he served the Greater Community.   5
Except for the War till the day he retired
He worked in a factory and never got fired,
But satisfied his employers, Fudge Motors Inc.
Yet he wasn't a scab or odd in his views,
For his Union reports that he paid his dues,   10
(Our report on his Union shows it was sound)
And our Social Psychology workers found
That he was popular with his mates and liked a drink.
The Press are convinced that he bought a paper every day
And that his reactions to advertisements were normal in every way.   15
Policies taken out in his name prove that he was fully insured,
And his Health-card shows he was once in hospital but left it cured.
Both Producers Research and High-Grade Living declare
He was fully sensible to the advantages of the Installment Plan
And had everything necessary to the Modern Man,   20
A phonograph, a radio, a car and a frigidaire.
Our researchers into Public Opinion are content
That he held the proper opinions for the time of year;
When there was peace, he was for peace; when there was war, he went.
He was married and added five children to the population,   25
Which our Eugenist says was the right number for a parent of
     his generation,
And our teachers report that he never interfered with their education.
Was he free? Was he happy? The question is absurd:
Had anything been wrong, we should certainly have heard.

—1939

Theodore Roethke (1908–1963)

Theodore Roethke was born in Michigan. Roethke was an influential teacher of poetry at the University of Washington for many years. His father was the owner of a greenhouse, and Roethke's childhood closeness to nature was an important influence on his mature poetry. His periodic nervous breakdowns, the result of bipolar manic-depression, presaged his early death.

Dolor°

I have known the inexorable sadness of pencils,
Neat in their boxes, dolor of pad and paper-weight,
All of the misery of manilla folders and mucilage,
Desolation in immaculate public places,
Lonely reception room, lavatory, switchboard,   5
The unalterable pathos of basin and pitcher,
Ritual of multigraph, paper-clip, comma,
Endless duplication of lives and objects.
And I have seen dust from the walls of institutions,
Finer than flour, alive, more dangerous than silica,°   10
Sift, almost invisible, through long afternoons of tedium,
Dropping a fine film on nails and delicate eyebrows,
Glazing the pale hair, the duplicate grey standard faces.

—1948

My Papa's Waltz

The whiskey on your breath
Could make a small boy dizzy;
But I hung on like death:
Such waltzing was not easy.

Dolor sadness   **10 silica** rock dust, a cause of silicosis, an occupational disease of miners and quarry workers

We romped until the pans   5
Slid from the kitchen shelf;
My mother's countenance
Could not unfrown itself.

The hand that held my wrist
Was battered on one knuckle;   10
At every step you missed
My right ear scraped a buckle.

You beat time on my head
With a palm caked hard by dirt,
Then waltzed me off to bed   15
Still clinging to your shirt.

—*1948*

Root Cellar

Nothing would sleep in that cellar, dank as a ditch,
Bulbs broke out of boxes hunting for chinks in the dark,
Shoots dangled and drooped,
Lolling obscenely from mildewed crates,
Hung down long yellow evil necks, like tropical snakes.   5
And what a congress of stinks!—
Roots ripe as old bait,
Pulpy stems, rank, silo-rich,
Leaf-mold, manure, lime, piled against slippery planks.
Nothing would give up life: 10
Even the dirt kept breathing a small breath.

—*1948*

Elizabeth Bishop (1911–1979)

Elizabeth Bishop for most of her life was highly regarded as a "poet's poet," winning the Pulitzer Prize for North and South *in 1956, but in the years since her death she has gained a wider readership. She traveled widely and lived in Brazil for a number of years before returning to the United States to teach at Harvard during the last years of her life.*

The Fish

I caught a tremendous fish
and held him beside the boat
half out of water, with my hook
fast in a corner of his mouth.
He didn't fight.   5
He hadn't fought at all.
He hung a grunting weight,
battered and venerable
and homely. Here and there
his brown skin hung in strips   10
like ancient wallpaper,
and its pattern of darker brown
was like wallpaper:
shapes like full-blown roses
stained and lost through age.   15
He was speckled with barnacles,
fine rosettes of lime,
and infested
with tiny white sea-lice,
and underneath two or three   20
rags of green weed hung down.
While his gills were breathing in
the terrible oxygen
—the frightening gills,
fresh and crisp with blood,   25
that can cut so badly—
I thought of the coarse white flesh
packed in like feathers,
the big bones and the little bones,

the dramatic reds and blacks 30
of his shiny entrails,
and the pink swim-bladder
like a big peony.
I looked into his eyes
which were far larger than mine 35
but shallower, and yellowed,
the irises backed and packed
with tarnished tinfoil
seen through the lenses
of old scratched isinglass.° 40
They shifted a little, but not
to return my stare.
—It was more like the tipping
of an object toward the light.
I admired his sullen face, 45
the mechanism of his jaw,
and then I saw
that from his lower lip
—if you could call it a lip—
grim, wet, and weapon-like, 50
hung five old pieces of fish line,
or four and a wire leader
with the swivel still attached,
with all their five big hooks
grown firmly in his mouth. 55
A green line, frayed at the end
where he broke it, two heavier lines,
and a fine black thread
still crimped from the strain and snap
when it broke and he got away. 60
Like medals with their ribbons
frayed and wavering,
a five-haired beard of wisdom
trailing from his aching jaw.
I stared and stared 65
and victory filled up
the little rented boat,
from the pool of bilge

40 **isinglass** semitransparent material made from fish bladders

where oil had spread a rainbow
around the rusted engine 70
to the bailer° rusted orange,
the sun-cracked thwarts,
the oarlocks on their strings,
the gunnels°—until everything
was rainbow, rainbow, rainbow! 75
And I let the fish go.

—*1946*

Sestina

September rain falls on the house.
In the failing light, the old grandmother
sits in the kitchen with the child
beside the Little Marvel Stove,
reading the jokes from the almanac, 5
laughing and talking to hide her tears.

She thinks that her equinoctial tears
and the rain that beats on the roof of the house
were both foretold by the almanac,
but only known to a grandmother.
The iron kettle sings on the stove. 10
She cuts some bread and says to the child,

It's time for tea now; but the child
is watching the teakettle's small hard tears
dance like mad on the hot black stove,
the way the rain must dance on the house. 15
Tidying up, the old grandmother
hangs up the clever almanac

on its string. Birdlike, the almanac
hovers half open above the child,
hovers above the old grandmother 20
and her teacup full of dark brown tears.
She shivers and says she thinks the house
feels chilly, and puts more wood in the stove.

71 **bailer** bucket   74 **gunnels** gunwales

It was to be, says the Marvel Stove. 25
I know what I know, says the almanac.
With crayons the child draws a rigid house
and a winding pathway. Then the child
puts in a man with buttons like tears
and shows it proudly to the grandmother. 30

But secretly, while the grandmother
busies herself about the stove,
the little moons fall down like tears
from between the pages of the almanac
into the flower bed the child 35
has carefully placed in the front of the house.

Time to plant tears, says the almanac.
The grandmother sings to the marvellous stove
and the child draws another inscrutable house.

—1965

One Art

The art of losing isn't hard to master;
so many things seem filled with the intent
to be lost that their loss is no disaster.

Lose something every day. Accept the fluster
of lost door keys, the hour badly spent. 5
The art of losing isn't hard to master.

Then practice losing farther, losing faster:
places, and names, and where it was you meant
to travel. None of these will bring disaster.

I lost my mother's watch. And look! my last, or 10
next-to-last, of three loved houses went.
The art of losing isn't hard to master.

I lost two cities, lovely ones. And, vaster,
some realms I owned, two rivers, a continent.
I miss them, but it wasn't a disaster. 15

—Even losing you (the joking voice, a gesture
I love) I shan't have lied. It's evident

the art of losing's not too hard to master
though it may look like *(Write* it!) like disaster.

—*1976*

Robert Hayden (1913–1980)

*Robert Hayden named Countee Cullen as one of the chief early influences
on his poetry. A native of Michigan, he taught for many years at Fisk University in Nashville and at the University of Michigan. Although many of
Hayden's poems are on African-American subjects, he wished to be considered a poet with strong links to the mainstream English-language tradition.*

Those Winter Sundays

Sundays too my father got up early
and put his clothes on in the blueblack cold,
then with cracked hands that ached
from labor in the weekday weather made
banked fires blaze. No one ever thanked him.   5

I'd wake and hear the cold splintering, breaking.
When the rooms were warm, he'd call,
and slowly I would rise and dress,
fearing the chronic angers of that house,

Speaking indifferently to him,   10
who had driven out the cold
and polished my good shoes as well.
What did I know, what did I know
of love's austere and lonely offices?°

—*1962*

14 **offices** daily religious ceremonies

Dudley Randall (1914–2000)

Dudley Randall was the founder of Broadside Press, a black-owned publishing firm that eventually attracted important writers like Gwendolyn Brooks and Don L. Lee. For most of his life a resident of Detroit, Randall spent many years working in that city's library system before taking a similar position at the University of Detroit.

Ballad of Birmingham

*(On the Bombing of a Church in
Birmingham, Alabama, 1963)°*

"Mother dear, may I go downtown
Instead of out to play,
And march the streets of Birmingham
In a Freedom March today?"

"No, baby, no, you may not go,   5
For the dogs are fierce and wild,
And clubs and hoses, guns and jail
Aren't good for a little child."

"But, mother, I won't be alone.
Other children will go with me,   10
And march the streets of Birmingham
To make our country free."

"No, baby, no, you may not go,
For I fear those guns will fire.
But you may go to church instead   15
And sing in the children's choir."

She has combed and brushed her night-dark hair,
And bathed rose petal sweet,
And drawn white gloves on her small brown hands,
And white shoes on her feet.   20

The mother smiled to know her child
Was in the sacred place,

Birmingham, Alabama, 1963 during the height of the civil rights movement

But that smile was the last smile
To come upon her face.

For when she heard the explosion,   25
Her eyes grew wet and wild.
She raced through the streets of Birmingham
Calling for her child.

She clawed through bits of glass and brick,
Then lifted out a shoe.   30
"O, here's the shoe my baby wore,
But, baby, where are you?"

                                                              —1969

William Stafford (1914–1993)

*William Stafford was one of the most prolific poets of the postwar era.
Stafford published in virtually every magazine in the United States. Raised
in Kansas as a member of the pacifist Church of the Brethren, Stafford
served in a camp for conscientious objectors during World War II. His first
book did not appear until he was in his forties, but he published over
thirty collections before his death at age seventy-nine.*

Traveling Through the Dark

Traveling through the dark I found a deer
dead on the edge of the Wilson River road.
It is usually best to roll them into the canyon:
that road is narrow; to swerve might make more dead.

By glow of the tail-light I stumbled back of the car   5
and stood by the heap, a doe, a recent killing;
she had stiffened already, almost cold.
I dragged her off; she was large in the belly.

My fingers touching her side brought me the reason—
her side was warm; her fawn lay there waiting,   10
alive, still, never to be born.
Beside that mountain road I hesitated.

The car aimed ahead its lowered parking lights;
under the hood purred the steady engine.
I stood in the glare of the warm exhaust turning red;   15
around our group I could hear the wilderness listen.

I thought hard for us all—my only swerving—
then pushed her over the edge into the river.

—*1960*

Dylan Thomas (1914–1953)

Dylan Thomas was a legendary performer of his and others' poetry. His popularity in the United States led to several collegiate reading tours, punctuated with outrageous behavior and self-destructive drinking that led to his early death in New York City, the victim of what the autopsy report labeled "insult to the brain." The Wales of his childhood remained a constant source of inspiration for his poetry and for radio dramas like Under Milk Wood, *which was turned into a film by fellow Welshman Richard Burton and his then-wife, Elizabeth Taylor.*

Do Not Go Gentle into That Good Night

Do not go gentle into that good night,
Old age should burn and rave at close of day;
Rage, rage against the dying of the light.

Though wise men at their end know dark is right,
Because their words had forked no lightning they   5
Do not go gentle into that good night.

Good men, the last wave by, crying how bright
Their frail deeds might have danced in a green bay,
Rage, rage against the dying of the light.

Wild men who caught and sang the sun in flight,   10
And learn, too late, they grieved it on its way,
Do not go gentle into that good night.

Grave men, near death, who see with blinding sight
Blind eyes could blaze like meteors and be gay,
Rage, rage against the dying of the light.   15

And you, my father, there on the sad height,
Curse, bless, me now with your fierce tears, I pray,
Do not go gentle into that good night.
Rage, rage against the dying of the light.

—1952

Fern Hill

Now as I was young and easy under the apple boughs
About the lilting house and happy as the grass was green,
    The night above the dingle starry,
      Time let me hail and climb
    Golden in the heydays of his eyes,   5
And honored among wagons I was prince of the apple towns
And once below a time I lordly had the trees and leaves
    Trail with daisies and barley
    Down the rivers of the windfall light.

And as I was green and carefree, famous among the barns   10
About the happy yard and singing as the farm was home,
    In the sun that is young once only,
      Time let me play and be
    Golden in the mercy of his means,
And green and golden I was huntsman and herdsman, the calves   15
Sang to my horn, the foxes on the hills barked clear and cold,
    And the sabbath rang slowly
    In the pebbles of the holy streams.

All the sun long it was running, it was lovely, the hay
Fields high as the house, the tunes from the chimneys, it was air   20
   And playing, lovely and watery
      And fire green as grass.
   And nightly under the simple stars
As I rode to sleep the owls were bearing the farm away,
All the moon long I heard, blessed among stables, the night-jars   25
   Flying with the ricks, and the horses
      Flashing into the dark.

And then to awake, and the farm, like a wanderer white
With the dew, come back, the cock on his shoulder: it was all
   Shining, it was Adam and maiden,   30
      The sky gathered again
   And the sun grew round that very day.
So it must have been after the birth of the simple light
In the first, spinning place, the spellbound horses walking warm
   Out of the whinnying green stable   35
      On to the fields of praise.

And honored among foxes and pheasants by the gay house
Under the new made clouds and happy as the heart was long,
   In the sun born over and over,
      I ran my heedless ways,   40
   My wishes raced through the house high hay
And nothing I cared, at my sky blue trades, that time allows
In all his tuneful turning so few and such morning songs
   Before the children green and golden
      Follow him out of grace,   45

Nothing I cared, in the lamb white days, that time would take me
Up to the swallow thronged loft by the shadow of my hand,
   In the moon that is always rising,
      Nor that riding to sleep
   I should hear him fly with the high fields   50
And wake to the farm forever fled from the childless land.
Oh as I was young and easy in the mercy of his means,
      Time held me green and dying
   Though I sang in my chains like the sea.

              —*1946*

Weldon Kees (1914–1955)

*Weldon Kees was a multitalented poet, painter, jazz musician, and film-
maker who went from the University of Nebraska to New York to California. His reputation, aided by posthumous publication of his stories, criticism, letters, and novels, has grown steadily since his apparent suicide by
leaping from the Golden Gate Bridge.*

For My Daughter

Looking into my daughter's eyes I read
Beneath the innocence of morning flesh
Concealed, hintings of death she does not heed.
Coldest of winds have blown this hair, and mesh
Of seaweed snarled these miniatures of hands;   5
The night's slow poison, tolerant and bland,
Has moved her blood. Parched years that I have seen
That may be hers appear; foul, lingering
Death in certain war, the slim legs green.
Or, fed on hate, she relishes the sting   10
Of others' agony; perhaps the cruel
Bride of a syphilitic or a fool.
These speculations sour in the sun.
I have no daughter. I desire none.

—1943

Randall Jarrell (1914–1965)

Randall Jarrell excelled as both a poet and a (sometimes brutally honest) reviewer of poetry. Ironically, the author of what is perhaps the best-known poem to have emerged from World War II did not see combat during the war: he served as a control tower officer in stateside bases. A native of Nashville, Kentucky, Jarrell studied at Vanderbilt University and followed his mentor, John Crowe Ransom, to Kenyon College in 1937, where he befriended another student, Robert Lowell.

90 North°

At home, in my flannel gown, like a bear to its floe,
I clambered to bed; up the globe's impossible sides
I sailed all night—till at last, with my black beard,
My furs and my dogs, I stood at the northern pole.

There in the childish night my companions lay frozen,   5
The stiff furs knocked at my starveling throat,
And I gave my great sigh: the flakes came huddling,
Were they really my end? In the darkness I turned to my rest.

—Here, the flag snaps in the glare and silence
Of the unbroken ice. I stand here,   10
The dogs bark, my beard is black, and I stare
At the North Pole . . .
                    And now what? Why, go back.

Turn as I please, my step is to the south.
The world—my world spins on this final point
Of cold and wretchedness: all lines, all winds   15
End in this whirlpool I at last discover.

And it is meaningless. In the child's bed
After the night's voyage, in that warm world
Where people work and suffer for the end
That crowns the pain—in that Cloud-Cuckoo-Land   20

I reached my North and it had meaning.
Here at the actual pole of my existence,

90 North the North Pole

Where all that I have done is meaningless,
Where I die or live by accident alone—

Where, living or dying I am still alone;   25
Here where North, the night, the berg of death
Crowd me out of the ignorant darkness,
I see at last that all the knowledge

I wrung from the darkness—that the darkness flung me—
Is worthless as ignorance: nothing comes from nothing,   30
The darkness from the darkness. Pain comes from the darkness
And we call it wisdom. It is pain.

                                                        —1942

The Death of the Ball
Turret° Gunner

From my mother's sleep I fell into the State,
And I hunched in its belly till my wet fur froze.
Six miles from earth, loosed from its dream of life,
I woke to black flak and the nightmare fighters.
When I died they washed me out of the turret with a hose.   5

                                                        —1945

Ball Turret A Plexiglas sphere set into the belly of a heavy bomber; Jarrell noted the similarity
between the gunner and a fetus in the womb.

Margaret Walker (1915–1998)

Margaret Walker, as a female African-American poet, was perhaps over-shadowed by Gwendolyn Brooks, even though Walker's receipt of the Yale Younger Poets Award in 1942 for For My People *came some years before Brooks's own recognition. A longtime teacher at Jackson State University, she influenced several generations of young writers.*

For Malcolm X

All you violated ones with gentle hearts;
You violent dreamers whose cries shout heartbreak;
Whose voices echo clamors of our cool capers,
And whose black faces have hollowed pits for eyes.
All you gambling sons and hooked children and bowery bums   5
Hating white devils and black bourgeoisie,
Thumbing your noses at your burning red suns,
Gather round this coffin and mourn your dying swan.

Snow white moslem head-dress around a dead black face!
Beautiful were your sand-papering words against our skins!   10
Our blood and water pour from your flowing wounds.
You have cut open our breasts and dug scalpels in our brains.
When and Where will another come to take your holy place?
Old man mumbling in his dotage, or crying child, unborn?

—*1970*

Gwendolyn Brooks (1917–2000)

Gwendolyn Brooks was the first African American to win a Pulitzer Prize for poetry. Brooks reflected many changes in black culture during her long career, and she wrote about the stages of her own life candidly in In the Mecca *(1968), her literary autobiography. Brooks was the last poetry consultant of the Library of Congress before that position became poet laureate of the United States. At the end of her life Brooks was one of the most honored and beloved of American poets.*

the ballad of chocolate Mabbie

It was Mabbie without° the grammar school gates.
And Mabbie was all of seven.
And Mabbie was cut from a chocolate bar.
And Mabbie thought life was heaven.

The grammar school gates were the pearly gates,   5
For Willie Boone went to school.
When she sat by him in history class
Was only her eyes were cool.

It was Mabbie without the grammar school gates
Waiting for Willie Boone.   10
Half hour after the closing bell!
He would surely be coming soon.

Oh, warm is the waiting for joys, my dears!
And it cannot be too long.
Oh, pity the little poor chocolate lips   15
That carry the bubble of song!

Out came the saucily bold Willie Boone.
It was woe for our Mabbie now.
He wore like a jewel a lemon-hued lynx
With sand-waves loving her brow.   20

1 without outside

It was Mabbie alone by the grammar school gates.
Yet chocolate companions had she:
Mabbie on Mabbie with hush in the heart.
Mabbie on Mabbie to be.

—1945

the mother

Abortions will not let you forget.
You remember the children you got that you did not get,
The damp small pulps with a little or with no hair,
The singers and workers that never handled the air.
You will never neglect or beat   5
them, or silence or buy with a sweet.
You will never wind up the sucking-thumb
Or scuttle off ghosts that come.
You will never leave them, controlling your luscious sigh,
Return for a snack of them, with gobbling mother-eye.   10

I have heard in the voices of the wind the voices of my dim killed
     children.
I have contracted. I have eased
My dim dears at the breasts they could never suck.
I have said, Sweets, if I sinned, if I seized
Your luck   15
And your lives from your unfinished reach,
If I stole your births and your names,
Your straight baby tears and your games,
Your stilted or lovely loves, your tumults, your marriages, aches, and
     your deaths,
If I poisoned the beginnings of your breaths,   20
Believe that even in my deliberateness I was not deliberate.
Though why should I whine,
Whine that the crime was other than mine?—
Since anyhow you are dead.
Or rather, or instead,   25
You were never made.
But that too, I am afraid,
Is faulty: oh, what shall I say, how is the truth to be said?
You were born, you had body, you died.

It is just that you never giggled or planned or cried.   30
Believe me, I loved you all.
Believe me, I knew you, though faintly, and I loved, I loved you
All.

—1945

We Real Cool

    The Pool Players.
    Seven at the Golden Shovel.

We real cool. We
Left school. We

Lurk late. We
Strike straight. We

Sing sin. We   5
Thin gin. We

Jazz June. We
Die soon.

—1960

Robert Lowell (1917–1977)

Robert Lowell is noted as one of the chief confessional poets because of the immense influence of his nakedly autobiographical collection of 1959, Life Studies. His literary career covered many bases—complex, formal early work; poetic dramas and translations; public figure—and he had, as the scion of one of Boston's oldest families, a ready-made stature that made him a public figure for most of his adult life.

For the Union Dead

"Relinquunt Omnia Servare Rem Publicam"°

The old South Boston Aquarium stands
in a Sahara of snow now. Its broken windows are boarded.
The bronze weathervane cod has lost half its scales.
The airy tanks are dry.

Once my nose crawled like a snail on the glass;   5
my hand tingled
to burst the bubbles
drifting from the noses of the cowed, compliant fish.

My hand draws back. I often sigh still
for the dark downward and vegetating kingdom   10
of the fish and reptile. One morning last March,
I pressed against the new barbed and galvanized

fence on the Boston Common. Behind their cage,
yellow dinosaur steamshovels were grunting
as they cropped up tons of mush and grass   15
to gouge their underworld garage.

Parking spaces luxuriate like civic
sandpiles in the heart of Boston.
A girdle of orange, Puritan-pumpkin colored girders
braces the tingling Statehouse,   20

Relinquunt . . . Publicam "They sacrificed everything to serve the state"

shaking over the excavations, as it faces Colonel Shaw°
and his bell-cheeked Negro infantry
on St. Gaudens'° shaking Civil War relief,
propped by a plank splint against the garage's earthquake.

Two months after marching through Boston, 25
half the regiment was dead;
at the dedication,
William James° could almost hear the bronze Negroes breathe.

Their monument sticks like a fishbone
in the city's throat. 30
Its Colonel is as lean
as a compass-needle.

He has an angry wrenlike vigilance,
a greyhound's gentle tautness;
he seems to wince at pleasure, 35
and suffocate for privacy.

He is out of bounds now. He rejoices in man's lovely,
peculiar power to choose life and die—
when he leads his black soldiers to death,
he cannot bend his back. 40

On a thousand small town New England greens,
the old white churches hold their air
of sparse, sincere rebellion; frayed flags
quilt the graveyards of the Grand Army of the Republic.

The stone statues of the abstract Union Soldier 45
grow slimmer and younger each year—
wasp-waisted, they doze over muskets
and muse through their sideburns . . .

Shaw's father wanted no monument
except the ditch, 50
where his son's body was thrown
and lost with his "niggers."

The ditch is nearer.
There are no statues for the last war here;

---

21 **Colonel Shaw** Robert Gould Shaw (1837–1863) led the black troops of the Massachusetts 54th regiment and died with many of them during the attack on Fort Wagner, S.C. The 1989 film *Glory* was based on these events.   23 **St. Gaudens** American sculptor (1848–1907)   28 **William James** American philosopher (1842–1910) who gave a dedication speech for the monument

on Boylston Street, a commercial photograph   55
shows Hiroshima boiling

over a Mosler Safe, the "Rock of Ages"
that survived the blast. Space is nearer.
When I crouch to my television set,
the drained faces of Negro school-children° rise like balloons.   60

Colonel Shaw
is riding on his bubble,
he waits
for the blessèd break.

The Aquarium is gone. Everywhere,   65
giant finned cars nose forward like fish;
a savage servility
slides by on grease.

—*1959*

Lawrence Ferlinghetti (b. 1919)

Lawrence Ferlinghetti, first owner of a literary landmark, San Francisco's City Lights Bookstore, has promoted and published the voice of the American avant-garde since the early 1950s. His own output has been relatively small, but Ferlinghetti's A Coney Island of the Mind *remains one of the quintessential documents of the Beat Generation.*

A Coney Island of the Mind, #15

Constantly risking absurdity
                    and death
        whenever he performs

---

60 **Negro school-children** refers to children harassed by protesters during the early days of the civil rights movement

above the heads
of his audience   5
the poet like an acrobat
climbs on rime
to a high wire of his own making
and balancing on eyebeams
above a sea of faces   10
paces his way
to the other side of day
performing entrechats
and sleight-of-foot tricks
and other high theatrics   15
and all without mistaking
any thing
for what it may not be
For he's the super realist
who must perforce perceive   20
taut truth
before the taking of each stance or step
in his supposed advance
toward that still higher perch
where Beauty stands and waits   25
with gravity
to start her death-defying leap
And he
a little charleychaplin man
who may or may not catch   30
her fair eternal form
spreadeagled in the empty air
of existence

—1958

May Swenson (b. 1919–1989)

May Swenson displayed an inventiveness in poetry that ranges from traditional formalism to many spatial or concrete poems. A careful observer of the natural world, Swenson often attempts to mimic directly the rhythms of the physical universe in her self-labeled "iconographs."

How Everything Happens

(Based on a Study of the Wave)

```
                                        happen.
                                    to
                               up
                          stacking
                        is
                   something
When nothing is happening
When it happens
              something
                      pulls
                          back
                             not
                                to
                                  happen.
When                          has happened.
     pulling back      stacking up
               happens
       has happened                      stacks up.
When it          something        nothing
                     pulls back while
Then nothing is happening
                            happens.
                          and
                     forward
                  pushes
               up
           stacks
      something
Then
```

                                                          —1967

Howard Nemerov (1920–1991)

*Howard Nemerov served as poet laureate of the United States during 1988
and 1989. A poet of brilliant formal inventiveness, he was also a skilled
satirist and observer of the American scene. His sister, Diane Arbus, was a
famous photographer. His* Collected Poems *won the Pulitzer Prize in 1978.*

A Primer of the Daily Round

A peels an apple, while B kneels to God,
C telephones to D, who has a hand
On E's knee, F coughs, G turns up the sod
For H's grave, I do not understand
But J is bringing one clay pigeon down   5
While K brings down a nightstick on L's head,
And M takes mustard, N drives into town,
O goes to bed with P, and Q drops dead,
R lies to S, but happens to be heard
By T, who tells U not to fire V   10
For having to give W the word
That X is now deceiving Y with Z,
    Who happens just now to remember A
    Peeling an apple somewhere far away.

—1958

Richard Wilbur (b. 1921)

Richard Wilbur will be remembered by posterity as perhaps the most skill-ful metricist and exponent of wit that American poetry has produced. His highly polished poetry—against the grain of much contemporary writing—is a monument to his craftsmanship and intelligence. Perhaps the most honored of all living American poets, Wilbur served as poet laureate of the United States in 1987. His translations of the verse dramas of Molière and Racine are regularly performed throughout the world.

Junk

Huru Welandes
wore ne geswices
monna a'nigum
σara σe Mimming can
heardne gehealdan.

—*Waldere°*

An axe angles
        from my neighbor's ashcan;
It is hell's handiwork,
        the wood not hickory,
The flow of the grain
        not faithfully followed.
The shivered shaft
        rises from a shellheap
Of plastic playthings,
        paper plates,   5
And the sheer shards
        of shattered tumblers
That were not annealed
        for the time needful.
At the same curbside,
        a cast-off cabinet
Of wavily-warped

The epigraph, taken from a fragmentary Anglo-Saxon poem, concerns the legendary smith Wayland, and may roughly be translated: "Truly, Wayland's handiwork—the sword Mimming which he made—will never fail any man who knows how to use it bravely." [Wilbur's note]

                        unseasoned wood
Waits to be trundled
                        in the trash-man's truck.   10
Haul them off! Hide them!
                        The heart winces
For junk and gimcrack,
                        for jerrybuilt things
And the men who make them
                        for a little money,
Bartering pride
              like the bought boxer
Who pulls his punches,
                        or the paid-off jockey   15
Who in the home stretch
                        holds in his horse.
Yet the things themselves
                        in thoughtless honor
Have kept composure,
                        like captives who would not
Talk under torture.
                        Tossed from a tailgate
Where the dump displays
                        its random dolmens,   20
Its black barrows
                        and blazing valleys,
They shall waste in the weather
                        toward what they were.
The sun shall glory
                        in the glitter of glass-chips,
Foreseeing the salvage
                        of the prisoned sand,
And the blistering paint
                        peel off in patches,   25
That the good grain
                        be discovered again.
Then burnt, bulldozed,
                        they shall all be buried
To the depth of diamonds,
                        in the making dark
Where halt Hephaestus

keeps his hammer
And Wayland's work
is worn away.   30

—*1961*

Playboy

High on his stockroom ladder like a dunce
The stock-boy sits, and studies like a sage
The subject matter of one glossy page,
As lost in curves as Archimedes° once.

Sometimes, without a glance, he feeds himself.   5
The left hand, like a mother-bird in flight,
Brings him a sandwich for a sidelong bite,
And then returns it to a dusty shelf.

What so engrosses him? The wild décor
Of this pink-papered alcove into which   10
A naked girl has stumbled, with its rich
Welter of pelts and pillows on the floor,

Amidst which, kneeling in a supple pose,
She lifts a goblet in her farther hand,
As if about to toast a flower-stand   15
Above which hovers an exploding rose

Fired from a long-necked crystal vase that rests
Upon a tasseled and vermillion cloth
One taste of which would shrivel up a moth?
Or is he pondering her perfect breasts?   20

Nothing escapes him of her body's grace
Or of her floodlit skin, so sleek and warm
And yet so strangely like a uniform,
But what now grips his fancy is her face.

4 **Archimedes** Greek mathematician (287–212 BC)

And how the cunning picture holds her still   25
At just that smiling instant when her soul,
Grown sweetly faint, and swept beyond control,
Consents to his inexorable will.

—1969

The Writer

In her room at the prow of the house
Where light breaks, and the windows are tossed with linden,
My daughter is writing a story.

I pause in the stairwell, hearing
From her shut door a commotion of typewriter-keys   5
Like a chain hauled over a gunwale.

Young as she is, the stuff
Of her life is a great cargo, and some of it heavy:
I wish her a lucky passage.

But now it is she who pauses,   10
As if to reject my thought and its easy figure.
A stillness greatens, in which

The whole house seems to be thinking,
And then she is at it again with a bunched clamor
Of strokes, and again is silent.   15

I remember the dazed starling
Which was trapped in that very room, two years ago;
How we stole in, lifted a sash

And retreated, not to affright it;
And how for a helpless hour, through the crack of the door,   20
We watched the sleek, wild, dark

And iridescent creature
Batter against the brilliance, drop like a glove
To the hard floor, or the desk-top.

And wait then, humped and bloody,   25
For the wits to try it again; and how our spirits
Rose when, suddenly sure,

It lifted off from a chair-back,
Beating a smooth course for the right window
And clearing the sill of the world.   30

It is always a matter, my darling,
Of life or death, as I had forgotten. I wish
What I wished you before, but harder.

                                                —1976

Year's End

Now winter downs the dying of the year,
And night is all a settlement of snow;
From the soft street the rooms of houses show
A gathered light, a shapen atmosphere,
Like frozen-over lakes whose ice is thin   5
And still allows some stirring down within.

I've known the wind by water banks to shake
The late leaves down, which frozen where they fell
And held in ice as dancers in a spell
Fluttered all winter long into a lake;   10
Graved on the dark in gestures of descent,
They seemed their own most perfect monument.

There was perfection in the death of ferns
Which laid their fragile cheeks against the stone
A million years. Great mammoths overthrown   15
Composedly have made their long sojourns,
Like palaces of patience, in the gray
And changeless lands of ice. And at Pompeii°

The little dog lay curled and did not rise
But slept the deeper as the ashes rose   20
And found the people incomplete, and froze
The random hands, the loose unready eyes
Of men expecting yet another sun
To do the shapely thing they had not done.

18 **Pompeii** Roman city destroyed by volcanic eruption in AD 79.

These sudden ends of time must give us pause.   25
We fray into the future, rarely wrought
Save in the tapestries of afterthought.
More time, more time. Barrages of applause
Come muffled from a buried radio.
The New-year bells are wrangling with the snow.   30

—*1950*

Philip Larkin (1922–1985)

*Philip Larkin was perhaps the latest British poet to establish a significant
body of readers in the United States. The general pessimism of his work is
mitigated by a wry sense of irony and brilliant formal control. For many
years he was a librarian at the University of Hull, and he was also a dedicated fan and critic of jazz.*

Next, Please

Always too eager for the future, we
Pick up bad habits of expectancy.
Something is always approaching; every day
Till then we say,

Watching from a bluff the tiny, clear,   5
Sparkling armada of promises draw near.
How slow they are! And how much time they waste,
Refusing to make haste!

Yet still they leave us holding wretched stalks
Of disappointment, for, though nothing balks   10
Each big approach, leaning with brasswork prinked,
Each rope distinct,

Flagged, and the figurehead with golden tits
Arching our way, it never anchors; it's
No sooner present than it turns to past.   15
Right to the last

We think each one will heave to and unload
All good into our lives, all we are owed

For waiting so devoutly and so long.
But we are wrong: 20

Only one ship is seeking us, a black-
Sailed unfamiliar, towing at her back
A huge and birdless silence. In her wake
No waters breed or break.

—1951

Aubade

I work all day, and get half drunk at night.
Waking at four to soundless dark, I stare.
In time the curtain-edges will grow light.
Till then I see what's really always there:
Unresting death, a whole day nearer now,   5
Making all thought impossible but how
And where and when I shall myself die.
Arid interrogation: yet the dread
Of dying, and being dead,
Flashes afresh to hold and horrify.   10

The mind blanks at the glare. Not in remorse
—The good not done, the love not given, time
Torn off unused—nor wretchedly because
An only life can take so long to climb
Clear of its wrong beginnings, and may never;   15
But at the total emptiness for ever,
The sure extinction that we travel to
And shall be lost in always. Not to be here,
Not to be anywhere,
And soon; nothing more terrible, nothing more true.   20

This is a special way of being afraid
No trick dispels. Religion used to try,
That vast moth-eaten musical brocade
Created to pretend we never die,
And specious stuff that says *No rational being*   25
Can fear a thing it will not feel, not seeing
That this is what we fear—no sight, no sound,
No touch or taste or smell, nothing to think with,

Nothing to love or link with,
The anaesthetic from which none come round.   30

And so it stays just on the edge of vision,
A small unfocused blur, a standing chill
That slows each impulse down to indecision.
Most things may never happen: this one will,
And realization of it rages out   35
In furnace-fear when we are caught without
People or drink. Courage is no good:
It means not scaring others. Being brave
Lets no one off the grave.
Death is no different whined at than withstood.   40

Slowly light strengthens, and the room takes shape.
It stands plain as a wardrobe, what we know,
Have always known, know that we can't escape,
Yet can't accept. One side will have to go.
Meanwhile telephones crouch, getting ready to ring   45
In locked-up offices, and all the uncaring
Intricate rented world begins to rouse.
The sky is white as clay, with no sun.
Work has to be done.
Postmen like doctors go from house to house.   50

—*1977*

This Be The Verse

They fuck you up, your mum and dad.
    They may not mean to, but they do.
They fill you with the faults they had
    And add some extra, just for you.

But they were fucked up in their turn   5
    By fools in old-style hats and coats,
Who half the time were soppy-stern
    And half at one another's throats.

Man hands on misery to man.
    It deepens like a coastal shelf.   10
Get out as early as you can,
    And don't have any kids yourself.

—*1971*

James Dickey (1923–1997)

*James Dickey became a national celebrity with the success of his novel
Deliverance (1970) and the celebrated film version. There was a long background to Dickey's success, with years spent in the advertising business
before he devoted himself fully to writing. Born in Atlanta and educated
at Clemson, Vanderbilt, and Rice Universities, Dickey rarely strayed long
from the South and taught at the University of South Carolina for over
two decades.*

The Heaven of Animals

Here they are. The soft eyes open
If they have lived in a wood
It is a wood.
If they have lived on plains
It is grass rolling
Under their feet forever.   5

Having no souls, they have come,
Anyway, beyond their knowing.
Their instincts wholly bloom
And they rise.
The soft eyes open.   10

To match them, the landscape flowers,
Outdoing, desperately
Outdoing what is required:
The richest wood,
The deepest field.   15

For some of these,
It could not be the place
It is, without blood.
These hunt, as they have done,
But with claws and teeth grown perfect,   20

More deadly than they can believe.
They stalk more silently,
And crouch on the limbs of trees,
And their descent
Upon the bright backs of their prey   25

May take years
In a sovereign floating of joy.
And those that are hunted
Know this as their life,
Their reward: to walk   30

Under such trees in full knowledge
Of what is in glory above them,
And to feel no fear,
But acceptance, compliance.
Fulfilling themselves without pain   35

At the cycle's center,
They tremble, they walk
Under the tree,
They fall, they are torn,
They rise, they walk again.   40

—1962

Alan Dugan (1923–2003)

Alan Dugan received the 1961 Yale Younger Poets Award, leading to the publication of his first collection as he neared forty. His plainspoken poetic voice, often with sardonic overtones, is appropriate for the anti-romantic stance of his most characteristic poems. For many years Dugan was associated with the Fine Arts Work Center in Provincetown, Massachusetts, on Cape Cod.

Love Song: I and Thou

Nothing is plumb, level or square:
      the studs are bowed, the joists
are shaky by nature, no piece fits
      any other piece without a gap
or pinch, and bent nails   5
      dance all over the surfacing
like maggots. By Christ
      I am no carpenter. I built

the roof for myself, the walls
    for myself, the floors   10
for myself, and got
    hung up in it myself. I
danced with a purple thumb
    at this house-warming, drunk
with my prime whiskey: rage.   15
    Oh I spat rage's nails
into the frame-up of my work:
    it held. It settled plumb,
level, solid, square and true
    for that great moment. Then   20
it screamed and went on through,
    skewing as wrong the other way.
God damned it. This is hell,
    but I planned it, I sawed it,
I nailed it, and I   25
    will live in it until it kills me.
I can nail my left palm
    to the left-hand cross-piece but
I can't do everything myself.
    I need a hand to nail the right,   30
a help, a love, a you, a wife.

                              —1961

Anthony Hecht (b. 1923)

Anthony Hecht is most often linked with Richard Wilbur as one of the American poets of the postwar era who have most effectively utilized traditional poetic forms. The brilliance of Hecht's technique, however, must be set beside the powerful moral intelligence that informs his poetry. The Hard Hours, his second collection, won the Pulitzer Prize in 1968.

The Book of Yolek

Wir haben ein Gesetz,
Und nach dem Gesetz soll er sterben.°

The dowsed coals fume and hiss after your meal
Of grilled brook trout, and you saunter off for a walk
Down the fern trail, it doesn't matter where to,
Just so you're weeks and worlds away from home,
And among midsummer hills have set up camp   5
In the deep bronze glories of declining day.

You remember, peacefully, an earlier day
In childhood, remember a quite specific meal:
A corn roast and bonfire in summer camp.
That summer you got lost on a Nature Walk;   10
More than you dared admit, you thought of home;
No one else knows where the mind wanders to.

The fifth of August, 1942.
It was morning and very hot. It was the day
They came at dawn with rifles to The Home   15
For Jewish Children, cutting short the meal
Of bread and soup, lining them up to walk
In close formation off to a special camp.

How often you have thought about that camp,
As though in some strange way you were driven to,   20
And about the children, and how they were made to walk,
Yolek who had bad lungs, who wasn't a day
Over five years old, commanded to leave his meal
And shamble between armed guards to his long home.

Wir haben . . . sterben John 19.7: We have a law, and by our law he ought to die.

We're approaching August again. It will drive home   25
The regulation torments of that camp
Yolek was sent to his small, unfinished meal,
The electric fences, the numeral tattoo,
The quite extraordinary heat of the day
They all were forced to take that terrible walk.   30

Whether on a silent, solitary walk
Or among crowds, far off or safe at home,
You will remember, helplessly, that day,
And the smell of smoke, and the loudspeakers of the camp.
Wherever you are, Yolek will be there, too.   35
His unuttered name will interrupt your meal.

Prepare to receive him in your home some day.
Though they killed him in the camp they sent him to,
He will walk in as you're sitting down to a meal.

—1990

Third Avenue in Sunlight

Third Avenue in sunlight. Nature's error.
Already the bars are filled and John is there.
Beneath a plentiful lady over the mirror°
He tilts his glass in the mild mahogany air.

I think of him when he first got out of college,   5
Serious, thin, unlikely to succeed;
For several months he hung around the Village,
Boldly T-shirted, unfettered but unfreed.

Now he confides to a stranger, "I was first scout,
And kept my glimmers peeled till after dark.   10
Our outfit had as its sign a bloody knout,
We met behind the museum in Central Park.

Of course, we were kids." But still those savages,
War-painted, a flap of leather at the loins,

3 lady over the mirror a painting

File silently against him. Hostages   15
Are never taken. One summer, in Des Moines,

They entered his hotel room, tomahawks
Flashing like barracuda. He tried to pray.
Three years of treatment. Occasionally he talks
About how he almost didn't get away.   20

Daily the prowling sunlight whets its knife
Along the sidewalk. We almost never meet.
In the Rembrandt dark he lifts his amber life.
My bar is somewhat further down the street.

—1967

Daniel Hoffman (b. 1923)

Daniel Hoffman has published ten books of poetry including Beyond Silence: Selected Shorter Poems 1948–2003 *(2003). He also has published a memoir and seven volumes of criticism. W. H. Auden chose Hoffman's first poetry collection,* An Armada of Thirty Whales *(1954), for the Yale Series of Younger Poets. Hoffman served as Consultant in Poetry to the Library of Congress from 1973 to 1974, and as Poet in Residence of New York's Cathedral of St. John the Divine, overseeing the American Poet's Corner there from 1988 to 1999. He is the Felix E. Schelling Professor of English Emeritus at the University of Pennsylvania, and lives in Swarthmore, Pennsylvania, and Harborside, Maine.*

As I Was Going to Saint-Ives

As I was going to Saint-Ives
In stormy, windy, sunny weather
I met a man with seven wives
(The herons stand in the swift water).

One drinks her beer out of his can   5
In stormy, windy, and bright weather,

And who laughs more, she or her man?
(The herons stand still on the water.)

One knows the room his candle lit
In stormy, lightning, cloudburst weather,   10
That glows again at the thought of it
(Two herons still the swift water).

His jealous, wild-tongued, Wednesday's wife—
In dreepy, wintry, wind-lashed weather
—What's better than that ranting strife?   15
(Two herons still the roaring water.)

There's one whose mind's so like his mind
In streaming wind or balmy weather
All joy, all wisdom seem one kind
(The herons stand in the swift water).   20

And one whose secret mazes he
In moon-swept, in torrential weather
Ransacks, and cannot find the key
(Two herons stand in the white water).

He'll think of none save one's slim thighs   25
In heat and sleet and windy weather
Till death has plucked his dreaming eyes
(Two herons guard the streaming water).

And the one whose love moves all he's done,
In windy, warm, and wintry weather,   30
—What can he leave but speaks thereon?
(Two herons still the swift water.)

—*1963*

Denise Levertov (1923–1997)

Denise Levertov was an outspoken opponent of U.S. involvement in the Vietnam War, an activity that has tended to overshadow her accomplishments as a lyric poet. Born of Jewish and Welsh parents in England, she emigrated to the United States during World War II.

The Ache of Marriage

The ache of marriage:

thigh and tongue, beloved,
are heavy with it,
it throbs in the teeth

We look for communion   5
and are turned away, beloved,
each and each

It is leviathan° and we
in its belly
looking for joy, some joy   10
not to be known outside it

two by two in the ark of
the ache of it.

—*1964*

---

8 leviathan great sea-creature mentioned in book of Job

Louis Simpson (b. 1923)

Louis Simpson was born in Jamaica to a colonial lawyer father and an American mother. Simpson came to the United States in his teens and served in the U.S. Army in World War II. He won the Pulitzer Prize in 1964 for At the End of the Open Road, *a volume that attempts to reexamine Walt Whitman's nineteenth-century definitions of the American experience. Subsequent collections have continued to demonstrate Simpson's unsentimental view of American suburban life.*

American Classic

It's a classic American scene—
a car stopped off the road
and a man trying to repair it.

The woman who stays in the car
in the classic American scene   5
stares back at the freeway traffic.

They look surprised, and ashamed
to be so helpless . . .
let down in the middle of the road!

To think that their car would do this!   10
They look like mountain people
whose son has gone against the law.

But every night they set out food
and the robber goes skulking back to the trees.
That's how it is with the car . . .   15

it's theirs, they're stuck with it.
Now they know what it's like to sit
and see the world go whizzing by.

In the fume of carbon monoxide and dust
they are not such good Americans   20
as they thought they were.

The feeling of being left out
through no fault of your own, is common.
That's why I say, an American classic.

—1980

My Father in the Night Commanding No

My father in the night commanding No
Has work to do. Smoke issues from his lips;
      He reads in silence.
The frogs are croaking and the street lamps glow.

And then my mother winds the gramophone:
The Bride of Lammermoor° begins to shriek—   5
      Or reads a story
About a prince, a castle, and a dragon.

The moon is glittering above the hill.
I stand before the gateposts of the King—
      So runs the story—   10
Of Thule, at midnight when the mice are still.

And I have been in Thule! It has come true—
The journey and the danger of the world,
      All that there is   15
To bear and to enjoy, endure and do.

Landscapes, seascapes . . . Where have I been led?
The names of cities—Paris, Venice, Rome—
      Held out their arms.
A feathered god, seductive, went ahead.   20

Here is my house. Under a red rose tree
A child is swinging; another gravely plays.
      They are not surprised
That I am here; they were expecting me.

6 Bride of Lammermoor *Lucia di Lammermoor*, opera by Donizetti

And yet my father sits and reads in silence,   25
My mother sheds a tear, the moon is still,
  And the dark wind
Is murmuring that nothing ever happens.

Beyond his jurisdiction as I move,
Do I not prove him wrong? And yet, it's true   30
  They will not change
There, on the stage of terror and of love.

The actors in that playhouse always sit
In fixed positions—father, mother, child
  With painted eyes.   35
How sad it is to be a little puppet!

Their heads are wooden. And you once pretended
To understand them! Shake them as you will,
  They cannot speak.
Do what you will, the comedy is ended.   40

Father, why did you work? Why did you weep,
Mother? Was the story so important?
  "Listen!" the wind
Said to the children, and they fell asleep.

        —1963

Vassar Miller (1924–1997)

Vassar Miller was a lifelong resident of Houston, born with cerebral palsy. Miller published both traditional devotional verse and a large body of autobiographical poetry in open forms. If I Had Wheels or Love, her collected poems, appeared in 1990.

Subterfuge

I remember my father, slight,
staggering in with his Underwood,°
bearing it in his arms like an awkward bouquet

for his spastic child who sits down
on the floor, one knee on the frame   5
of the typewriter, and holding her left wrist

with her right hand, in that precision known
to the crippled, pecks at the keys
with a sparrow's preoccupation.

Falling by chance on rhyme, novel and curious bubble   10
blown with a magic pipe, she tries them over and over,
spellbound by life's clashing in accord or against itself,

pretending pretense and playing at playing,
she does her childhood backward as children do,
her fun a delaying action against what she knows.   15

My father must lose her, his runaway on her treadmill,
will lose the terrible favor that life has done him
as she toils at tomorrow, tensed at her makeshift toy.

—1981

---

2 **Underwood** popular brand of manual typewriter

Donald Justice (b. 1925)

Donald Justice has published more selectively than most of his contempo-
raries. His Pulitzer Prize–winning volume of selected poems displays con-
siderable literary sophistication and reveals the poet's familiarity with the
traditions of contemporary European and Latin American poetry. As an
editor, he is responsible for rescuing the important work of Weldon Kees
from obscurity.

Counting the Mad

This one was put in a jacket,
This one was sent home,
This one was given bread and meat
But would eat none,
And this one cried No No No No   5
All day long.

This one looked at the window
As though it were a wall,
This one saw things that were not there,
This one things that were,   10
And this one cried No No No No
All day long.

This one thought himself a bird,
This one a dog,
And this one thought himself a man,   15
An ordinary man,
And this one cried No No No No
All day long.

—1960

Carolyn Kizer (b. 1925)

Carolyn Kizer has led a fascinating career that includes a year's study in Taiwan and another year in Pakistan, where she worked for the U.S. State Department. Her first collection, The Ungrateful Garden *(1961), demonstrates an equal facility with formal and free verse, but her subsequent books (including the Pulitzer Prize–winning* Yin *of 1985) have tended more toward the latter. A committed feminist, Kizer anticipated many of today's women's issues as early as the mid-1950s, just as the poem "The Ungrateful Garden" was published a decade before "ecology" became a household word.*

The Ungrateful Garden

Midas watched the golden crust
That formed over his streaming sores,
Hugged his agues, loved his lust,
But damned to hell the out-of-doors

Where blazing motes of sun impaled   5
The serried° roses, metal-bright.
"Those famous flowers," Midas wailed,
"Have scorched my retina with light."

This gift, he'd thought, would gild his joys,
Silt up the waters of his grief;   10
His lawns a wilderness of noise,
The heavy clang of leaf on leaf.

Within, the golden cup is good
To heft, to sip the yellow mead.
Outside, in summer's rage, the rude   15
Gold thorn has made his fingers bleed.

"I strolled my halls in golden shift,
As ruddy as a lion's meat.
Then I rushed out to share my gift,
And golden stubble cut my feet."   20

6 **serried** crowded in rows

Dazzled with wounds, he limped away
To climb into his golden bed.
Roses, roses can betray.
"Nature is evil," Midas said.

—1961

from "Pro Femina" Three

I will speak about women of letters, for I'm in the racket.
Our biggest successes to date? Old maids to a woman.
And our saddest conspicuous failures? The married spinsters
On loan to the husbands they treated like surrogate fathers.
Think of that crew of self-pitiers, not-very-distant,   5
Who carried the torch for themselves and got first-degree burns.
Or the sad sonneteers, toast-and-teasdales we loved at thirteen;
Middle-aged virgins seducing the puerile anthologists
Through lust-of-the-mind; barbiturate-drenched Camilles
With continuous periods, murmuring softly on sofas   10
When poetry wasn't a craft but a sickly effluvium.
The air thick with incense, musk, and emotional blackmail.

I suppose they reacted from an earlier womanly modesty
When too many girls were scabs to their stricken sisterhood.
Impugning our sex to stay in good with the men,   15
Commencing their insecure bluster. How they must have swaggered
When women themselves endorsed their own inferiority!
Vestals, vassals, and vessels, rolled into several,
They took notes in rolling syllabics, in careful journals,
Aiming to please a posterity that despises them.   20
But we'll always have traitors who swear that a woman surrenders
Her Supreme Function, by equating Art with aggression
And failure with Femininity. Still, it's just as unfair
To equate Art with Femininity, like a prettily packaged commodity
When we are the custodians of the world's best-kept secret: 25
Merely the private lives of one-half of humanity.

But even with masculine dominance, we mares and mistresses
Produced some sleek saboteuses, making their cracks

Which the porridge-brained males of the day were too thick to
    perceive,
Mistaking young hornets for perfectly harmless bumblebees.   30
Being thought innocuous rouses some women to frenzy;
They try to be ugly by aping the ways of men
And succeed. Swearing, sucking cigars and scorching the bedspread,

Slopping straight shots, eyes blotted, vanity-blown
In the expectation of glory: *she writes like a man!*   35
This drives other women mad in a mist of chiffon.
(One poetess draped her gauze over red flannels, a practical feminist.)

But we're emerging from all that, more or less,
Except for some ladylike laggards and Quarterly priestesses
Who flog men for fun, and kick women to maim competition.   40
Now, if we struggle abnormally, we may almost seem normal;
If we submerge our self-pity in disciplined industry;
If we stand up and be hated, and swear not to sleep with editors;
If we regard ourselves formally, respecting our true limitations
Without making an unseemly show of trying to unfreeze our assets; 45
Keeping our heads and our pride while remaining unmarried;
And if wedded, kill guilt in its tracks when we stack up the dishes
And defect to the typewriter. And if mothers, believe in the luck of
    our children,
Whom we forbid to devour us, whom we shall not devour,
And the luck of our husbands and lovers, who keep free women.   50

—1984

Maxine Kumin (b. 1925)

Maxine Kumin was born in Philadelphia and educated at Radcliffe. Kumin was an early literary ally and friend of Anne Sexton, with whom she co-authored several children's books. The winner of the 1973 Pulitzer Prize, Kumin has preferred a rural life raising horses for some years. Her increased interest in the natural world has paralleled the environmental awareness of many of her readers.

Noted in the *New York Times*

Lake Buena Vista, Florida, June 16, 1987

Death claimed the last pure dusky seaside sparrow
today, whose coastal range was narrow,
as narrow as its two-part buzzy song.
From hummocks lost to Cape Canaveral
this mouselike skulker in the matted grass,   5
a six-inch bird, plain brown, once thousands strong,
sang *toodle-raeee azhee,* ending on a trill
before the air gave way to rocket blasts.

It laid its dull white eggs (brown specked) in small
neat cups of grass on plots of pickleweed,   10
bulrushes, or salt hay. It dined
on caterpillars, beetles, ticks, the seeds
of sedges. Unremarkable
the life it led with others of its kind.
Tomorrow we can put it on a stamp,   15
a first-day cover with Key Largo rat,
Schaus swallowtail, Florida swamp
crocodile, and fading cotton mouse.
How simply symbols replace habitat!
The tower frames of Aerospace   20

quiver in the flush of another shot
where, once indigenous, the dusky sparrow
soared trilling twenty feet above its burrow.

—1989

Allen Ginsberg (1926–1997)

*Allen Ginsberg became the chief poetic spokesman of the Beat Generation.
He was a force—as poet and celebrity—who continued to outrage and delight four decades after the appearance of* Howl, *the monumental poem
describing how Ginsberg saw: "the best minds of my generation destroyed
by madness." Ginsberg's poems are cultural documents that provide a key
to understanding the radical changes in American life, particularly among
youth, that began in the mid-1950s.*

A Supermarket in California

What thoughts I have of you tonight, Walt Whitman, for I walked
down the sidestreets under the trees with a headache self-conscious
looking at the full moon.

In my hungry fatigue, and shopping for images, I went into the
neon fruit supermarket, dreaming of your enumerations!

What peaches and what penumbras?° Whole families shopping at
night! Aisles full of husbands! Wives in the avocados, babies in the
tomatoes!—and you, García Lorca,° what were you doing down by
the watermelons?

I saw you, Walt Whitman, childless, lonely old grubber, poking
among the meats in the refrigerator and eyeing the grocery boys.

I heard you asking questions of each: Who killed the pork chops?
What price bananas? Are you my Angel?   5

I wandered in and out of the brilliant stacks of cans following you,
and followed in my imagination by the store detective.

---

3 **penumbras** shadows   3 **García Lorca** Federico García Lorca, Spanish poet (1899–1936)

We strode down the open corridors together in our solitary fancy
tasting artichokes, possessing every frozen delicacy, and never passing
the cashier.

Where are we going, Walt Whitman? The doors close in an hour.
Which way does your beard point tonight?
(I touch your book and dream of our odyssey in the super-market
and feel absurd.)
Will we walk all night through solitary streets? The trees add shade
to shade, lights out in the houses, we'll both be lonely.   10
Will we stroll dreaming of the lost America of love past blue
automobiles in driveways, home to our silent cottage?
Ah, dear father, graybeard, lonely old courage-teacher, what
America did you have when Charon° quit poling his ferry and you got
out on a smoking bank and stood watching the boat disappear on the
black waters of Lethe?°

—1956

James Merrill (1926–1995)

*James Merrill wrote "The Changing Light at Sandover," a long poem that
resulted from many years of sessions with a Ouija board. The book became his major work and, among many other things, a remarkable memoir of a long-term gay relationship. Merrill's shorter poems, collected in
2001, reveal meticulous craftsmanship and a play of wit unequaled among
contemporary American poets.*

Casual Wear

Your average tourist: Fifty. 2.3
Times married. Dressed, this year, in Ferdi Plinthbower°
Originals. Odds 1 to 9^{10}°
Against her strolling past the Embassy

Today at noon. Your average terrorist: 5
Twenty-five. Celibate. No use for trends,

---

12 **Charon** ferryman of Hades   **Lethe** river in Hades, means forgetfulness
2 **Ferdi Plinthbower** a fictional designer   3 **1 to 9^{10}** pronounced "one to nine to the tenth power"

At least in clothing. Mark, though, where it ends.
People have come forth made of colored mist

Unsmiling on one hundred million screens
To tell of his prompt phone call to the station,   10
"Claiming responsibility"—devastation
Signed with a flourish, like the dead wife's jeans.

—1984

Charles on Fire

Another evening we sprawled about discussing
Appearances. And it was the consensus
That while uncommon physical good looks
Continued to launch one, as before, in life
(Among its vaporous eddies and false calms),   5
Still, as one of us said into his beard,
"Without your intellectual and spiritual
Values, man, you are sunk." No one but squared
The shoulders of his own unloveliness.
Long-suffering Charles, having cooked and served the meal,   10
Now brought out little tumblers finely etched
He filled with amber liquor and then passed.
"Say," said the same young man, "in Paris, France,
They do it this way"—bounding to his feet
And touching a lit match to our host's full glass.   15
A blue flame, gentle, beautiful, came, went
Above the surface. In a hush that fell
We heard the vessel crack. The contents drained
As who should step down from a crystal coach.
Steward of spirits, Charles's glistening hand   20
All at once gloved itself in eeriness.
The moment passed. He made two quick sweeps and
Was flesh again. "It couldn't matter less,"
He said, but with a shocked, unconscious glance
Into the mirror. Finding nothing changed,   25
He filled a fresh glass and sank down among us.

—1966

W. D. Snodgrass (b. 1926)

W. D. Snodgrass won the Pulitzer Prize for his first collection, Heart's
Needle *(1959), and is generally considered one of the first important confessional poets. However, in his later career he has turned away from autobiographical subjects, writing, among other poems, a long sequence of
dramatic monologues spoken by leading Nazis during the final days of the
Hitler regime.*

Mementos, I

Sorting out letters and piles of my old
    Canceled checks, old clippings, and yellow note cards
That meant something once, I happened to find
    Your picture. *That* picture. I stopped there cold,
Like a man raking piles of dead leaves in his yard   5
        Who has turned up a severed hand.

Still, that first second, I was glad: you stand
    Just as you stood—shy, delicate, slender,
In that long gown of green lace netting and daisies
    That you wore to our first dance. The sight of you stunned   10
Us all. Well, our needs were different, then,
        And our ideals came easy.

Then through the war and those two long years
    Overseas, the Japanese dead in their shacks
Among dishes, dolls, and lost shoes; I carried   15
    This glimpse of you, there, to choke down my fear,
Prove it had been, that it might come back.
        That was before we got married.

—Before we drained out one another's force
    With lies, self-denial, unspoken regret   20
And the sick eyes that blame; before the divorce
    And the treachery. Say it: before we met. Still,
I put back your picture. Someday, in due course,
        I will find that it's still there.

        —1968

Frank O'Hara (1926–1966)

Frank O'Hara suffered an untimely death in a dune buggy accident on Fire Island that robbed American poetry of one its most refreshing talents. An authority on modern art, O'Hara incorporates many of the spontaneous techniques of abstract painting in his own poetry, which was often written as an immediate reaction to the events of his daily life.

The Day Lady° Died

It is 12:20 in New York a Friday
three days after Bastille day,° yes
it is 1959 and I go get a shoeshine
because I will get off the 4:19 in Easthampton
at 7:15 and then go straight to dinner   5
and I don't know the people who will feed me

I walk up the muggy street beginning to sun
and have a hamburger and a malted and buy
an ugly NEW WORLD WRITING to see what the poets
in Ghana are doing these days   10
                         I go on to the bank
and Miss Stillwagon (first name Linda I once heard)
doesn't even look up my balance for once in her life
and in the GOLDEN GRIFFIN I get a little Verlaine
for Patsy with drawings by Bonnard although I do   15
think of Hesiod, trans. Richard Lattimore or
Brendan Behan's new play or *Le Balcon* or *Les Nègres*
of Genet, but I don't, I stick with Verlaine
after practically going to sleep with quandariness

and for Mike I just stroll into the PARK LANE   20
Liquor Store and ask for a bottle of Strega and
then I go back where I came from to 6th Avenue
and the tobacconist in the Ziegfeld Theatre and
casually ask for a carton of Gauloises and a carton
of Picayunes, and a NEW YORK POST with her face on it   25

Lady Billie Holiday (1915–1959), blues singer   **2 Bastille day** July 14

and I am sweating a lot by now and thinking of
leaning on the john door in the 5 SPOT
while she whispered a song along the keyboard
to Mal Waldron° and everyone and I stopped breathing.

—*1964*

John Ashbery (b. 1927)

John Ashbery was born in upstate New York and educated at Harvard University. His first full-length book, Some Trees, *was chosen by W. H. Auden as winner of the Yale Younger Poets Award in 1956. His enigmatic poems have intrigued readers for so long that much contemporary literary theory seems to have been created expressly for explicating his poems. Impossible to dismiss, Ashbery is now seen as the chief inheritor of the symbolist tradition brought to American locales by Wallace Stevens.*

Farm Implements and Rutabagas in a Landscape

The first of the undecoded messages read: "Popeye sits in thunder,
Unthought of. From that shoebox of an apartment,
From livid curtain's hue, a tangram emerges: a country."
Meanwhile the Sea Hag was relaxing on a green couch: "How
    pleasant
To spend one's vacation *en la casa de Popeye*," she scratched   5
Her cleft chin's solitary hair. She remembered spinach

And was going to ask Wimpy if he had bought any spinach.
"M'love," he intercepted, "the plains are decked out in thunder
Today, and it shall be as you wish." He scratched
The part of his head under his hat. The apartment   10
Seemed to grow smaller. "But what if no pleasant
Inspiration plunge us now to the stars? *For this is my country.*"

---

29 **Mal Waldron** Holiday's accompanist.

Suddenly they remembered how it was cheaper in the country.
Wimpy was thoughtfully cutting open a number 2 can of
    spinach
When the door opened and Swee'pea crept in. "How
    pleasant!"   15
But Swee'pea looked morose. A note was pinned to his bib.
    "Thunder
And tears are unavailing," it read. "Henceforth shall Popeye's
    apartment
Be but remembered space, toxic or salubrious, whole or scratched."
Olive came hurtling through the window; its geraniums scratched
Her long thigh. "I have news!" she gasped. "Popeye, forced as you
    know to flee the country   20
One musty gusty evening, by the schemes of his wizened, duplicate
    father, jealous of the apartment
And all that it contains, myself and spinach
In particular, heaves bolts of loving thunder
At his own astonished becoming, rupturing the pleasant

Arpeggio of our years. No more shall pleasant   25
Rays of the sun refresh your sense of growing old, nor the scratched
Tree-trunks and mossy foliage, only immaculate darkness and
    thunder."
She grabbed Swee'pea. "I'm taking the brat to the country."
"But you can't do that—he hasn't even finished his spinach,"
Urged the Sea Hag, looking fearfully around at the apartment.   30

But Olive was already out of earshot. Now the apartment
Succumbed to a strange new hush. "Actually it's quite pleasant
Here," thought the Sea Hag. "If this is all we need fear from spinach
Then I don't mind so much. Perhaps we could invite Alice the Goon
    over"—she scratched
One dug pensively—"but Wimpy is such a country   35
Bumpkin, always burping like that." Minute at first, the thunder

Soon filled the apartment. It was domestic thunder,
The color of spinach. Popeye chuckled and scratched
His balls: it sure was pleasant to spend a day in the country.

—1966

Paradoxes and Oxymorons

The poem is concerned with language on a very plain level.
Look at it talking to you. You look out a window
Or pretend to fidget. You have it but you don't have it.
You miss it, it misses you. You miss each other.

The poem is sad because it wants to be yours, and cannot.   5
What's a plain level? It is that and other things,
Bringing a system of them into play. Play?
Well, actually, yes, but I consider play to be

A deeper outside thing, a dreamed role-pattern,
As in the division of grace these long August days   10
Without proof. Open-ended. And before you know
It gets lost in the steam and chatter of typewriters.

It has been played once more. I think you exist only
To tease me into doing it, on your level, and then you aren't there
Or have adopted a different attitude. And the poem   15
Has set me softly down beside you. The poem is you.

                                                  —*1981*

W. S. Merwin (b. 1927)

W. S. Merwin often displays environmental concerns that have motivated much poetry in recent years. Even in earlier work his fears of the results of uncontrolled destruction of the environment are presented allegorically. Born in New York City, he currently resides in Hawaii.

For the Anniversary of My Death

Every year without knowing it I have passed the day
When the last fires will wave to me
And the silence will set out
Tireless traveller
Like the beam of a lightless star   5

Then I will no longer
Find myself in life as in a strange garment
Surprised at the earth
And the love of one woman
And the shamelessness of men   10
As today writing after three days of rain
Hearing the wren sing and the falling cease
And bowing not knowing to what

—1969

The Last One

Well they'd made up their minds to be everywhere because why not.
Everywhere was theirs because they thought so.
They with two leaves they whom the birds despise.
In the middle of stones they made up their minds.
They started to cut.   5

Well they cut everything because why not.
Everything was theirs because they thought so.
It fell into its shadows and they took both away.
Some to have some for burning.

Well cutting everything they came to the water. 10
They came to the end of the day there was one left standing.
They would cut it tomorrow they went away.
The night gathered in the last branches.
The shadow of the night gathered in the shadow on the water.
The night and the shadow put on the same head. 15
And it said Now.

Well in the morning they cut the last one.
Like the others the last one fell into its shadow.
It fell into its shadow on the water.
They took it away its shadow stayed on the water. 20

Well they shrugged they started trying to get the shadow away.
They cut right to the ground the shadow stayed whole.
They laid boards on it the shadow came out on top.
They shone lights on it the shadow got blacker and clearer.
They exploded the water the shadow rocked. 25
They built a huge fire on the roots.
They sent up black smoke between the shadow and the sun.
The new shadow flowed without changing the old one.
They shrugged they went away to get stones.

They came back the shadow was growing. 30
They started setting up stones it was growing.
They looked the other way it went on growing.
They decided they would make a stone out of it.
They took stones to the water they poured them into the shadow.
They poured them in they poured them in the stones vanished. 35
The shadow was not filled it went on growing.
That was one day.

The next day was just the same it went on growing.
They did all the same things it was just the same.
They decided to take its water from under it. 40
They took away water they took it away the water went down.
The shadow stayed where it was before.
It went on growing it grew onto the land.
They started to scrape the shadow with machines.
When it touched the machines it stayed on them. 45
They started to beat the shadow with sticks.
Where it touched the sticks it stayed on them.
They started to beat the shadow with hands.

Where it touched the hands it stayed on them.
That was another day.   50

Well the next day started about the same it went on growing.
They pushed lights into the shadow.
Where the shadow got onto them they went out.
They began to stomp on the edge it got their feet.
And when it got their feet they fell down.   55
It got into eyes the eyes went blind.
The ones that fell down it grew over and they vanished.
The ones that went blind and walked into it vanished.
The ones that could see and stood still
It swallowed their shadows.   60
Then it swallowed them too and they vanished.
Well the others ran.

The ones that were left went away to live if it would let them.
They went as far as they could.
The lucky ones with their shadows.   65

—*1969*

James Wright (1927–1980)

James Wright showed compassion for losers and underdogs of all types, an attitude evident everywhere in his poetry. A native of Martins Ferry, Ohio, he often described lives of quiet desperation in the blue-collar towns of his youth. Like many poets of his generation, Wright wrote formal verse in his early career and shifted to open forms during the 1960s.

A Blessing

Just off the highway to Rochester, Minnesota,
Twilight bounds softly forth on the grass.
And the eyes of those two Indian ponies
Darken with kindness.
They have come gladly out of the willows   5
To welcome my friend and me.
We step over the barbed wire into the pasture

Where they have been grazing all day, alone.
They ripple tensely, they can hardly contain their happiness
That we have come.   10
They bow shyly as wet swans. They love each other.
There is no loneliness like theirs.
At home once more,
They begin munching the young tufts of spring in the darkness.
I would like to hold the slenderer one in my arms,   15
For she has walked over to me
And nuzzled my left hand.
She is black and white,
Her mane falls wild on her forehead,
And the light breeze moves me to caress her long ear   20
That is delicate as the skin over a girl's wrist.
Suddenly I realize
That if I stepped out of my body I would break
Into blossom.

—1963

Saint Judas

When I went out to kill myself, I caught
A pack of hoodlums beating up a man.
Running to spare his suffering, I forgot
My name, my number, how my day began,
How soldiers milled around the garden stone   5
And sang amusing songs; how all that day
Their javelins measured crowds; how I alone
Bargained the proper coins, and slipped away.

Banished from heaven, I found this victim beaten,
Stripped, kneed, and left to cry. Dropping my rope   10
Aside, I ran, ignored the uniforms:
Then I remembered bread my flesh had eaten,
The kiss that ate my flesh. Flayed without hope,
I held the man for nothing in my arms.

—1959

Philip Levine (b. 1928)

Philip Levine was born in Detroit, Michigan. He is one of many contemporary poets to hold a degree from the University of Iowa Writers' Workshop. The gritty urban landscapes and characters trapped in dead-end industrial jobs that provide Levine subjects for many poems match exactly with his unadorned, informal idiom. As teacher and mentor, Levine has influenced many younger poets.

Animals Are Passing from Our Lives

It's wonderful how I jog
on four honed-down ivory toes
my massive buttocks slipping
like oiled parts with each light step.

I'm to market. I can smell   5
the sour, grooved block, I can smell
the blade that opens the hole
and the pudgy white fingers

that shake out the intestines
like a hankie. In my dreams   10
the snouts drool on the marble,
suffering children, suffering flies,

suffering the consumers
who won't meet their steady eyes
for fear they could see. The boy   15
who drives me along believes

that any moment I'll fall
on my side and drum my toes
like a typewriter or squeal
and shit like a new housewife   20

discovering television,
or that I'll turn like a beast

cleverly to hook his teeth
with my teeth. No. Not this pig.

—*1968*

You Can Have It

My brother comes home from work
and climbs the stairs to our room.
I can hear the bed groan and his shoes drop
one by one. You can have it, he says.

The moonlight streams in the window   5
and his unshaven face is whitened
like the face of the moon. He will sleep
long after noon and waken to find me gone.

Thirty years will pass before I remember
that moment when suddenly I knew each man   10
has one brother who dies when he sleeps
and sleeps when he rises to face this life,

and that together they are only one man
sharing a heart that always labors, hands
yellowed and cracked, a mouth that gasps   15
for breath and asks, Am I gonna make it?

All night at the ice plant he had fed
the chute its silvery blocks, and then I
stacked cases of orange soda for the children
of Kentucky, one gray box-car at a time   20

with always two more waiting. We were twenty
for such a short time and always in
the wrong clothes, crusted with dirt
and sweat. I think now we were never twenty.

In 1948 in the city of Detroit, founded   25
by de la Mothe Cadillac for the distant purposes
of Henry Ford, no one wakened or died,
no one walked the streets or stoked a furnace,

for there was no such year, and now
that year has fallen off all the old newspapers,　　　　　　30
calendars, doctors' appointments, bonds,
wedding certificates, drivers licenses.

The city slept. The snow turned to ice.
The ice to standing pools or rivers
racing in the gutters. Then bright grass rose　　　　　　35
between the thousands of cracked squares,

and that grass died. I give you back 1948.
I give you all the years from then
to the coming one. Give me back the moon
with its frail light falling across a face.　　　　　　40

Give me back my young brother, hard
and furious, with wide shoulders and a curse
for God and burning eyes that look upon
all creation and say, You can have it.

　　　　　　　　　　　　　　　　　　—1979

Anne Sexton　(1928–1974)

Anne Sexton lived a tortured life of mental illness and family troubles, becoming the model of the confessional poet. A housewife with two small daughters, she began writing poetry as the result of a program on public television, later taking a workshop from Robert Lowell in which Sylvia Plath was a fellow student. For fifteen years until her suicide, she was a vibrant, exciting presence in American poetry. A controversial biography of Sexton by Diane Wood Middlebrook appeared in 1991.

Cinderella

You always read about it:
the plumber with twelve children
who wins the Irish Sweepstakes.
From toilets to riches.
That story.　　　　　　　　　　　　　　　5

Or the nursemaid,
some luscious sweet from Denmark

who captures the oldest son's heart.
From diapers to Dior.
That story.   10

Or a milkman who serves the wealthy,
eggs, cream, butter, yogurt, milk,
the white truck like an ambulance
who goes into real estate
and makes a pile.   15
From homogenized to martinis at lunch.

Or the charwoman
who is on the bus when it cracks up
and collects enough from the insurance.
From mops to Bonwit Teller.°   20
That story.

Once
the wife of a rich man was on her deathbed
and she said to her daughter Cinderella:
Be devout. Be good. Then I will smile   25
down from heaven in the seam of a cloud.
The man took another wife who had
two daughters, pretty enough
but with hearts like blackjacks.
Cinderella was their maid.   30
She slept on the sooty hearth each night
and walked around looking like Al Jolson.°
Her father brought presents home from town,
jewels and gowns for the other women
but the twig of a tree for Cinderella.   35
She planted that twig on her mother's grave
and it grew to a tree where a white dove sat.
Whenever she wished for anything the dove
would drop it like an egg upon the ground.
The bird is important, my dears, so heed him.   40

Next came the ball, as you all know.
It was a marriage market.
The prince was looking for a wife.

---

20 Bonwit Teller an upscale department store   **32 Al Jolson** (1885–1950) American singer and
entertainer who performed in blackface

All but Cinderella were preparing
and gussying up for the big event.   45
Cinderella begged to go too.
Her stepmother threw a dish of lentils
into the cinders and said: Pick them
up in an hour and you shall go.
The white dove brought all his friends;   50
all the warm wings of the fatherland came,
and picked up the lentils in a jiffy.
No, Cinderella, said the stepmother,
you have no clothes and cannot dance.
That's the way with stepmothers.   55

Cinderella went to the tree at the grave
and cried forth like a gospel singer:
Mama! Mama! My turtledove,
send me to the prince's ball!
The bird dropped down a golden dress   60
and delicate little gold slippers.
Rather a large package for a simple bird.
So she went. Which is no surprise.
Her stepmother and sisters didn't
recognize her without her cinder face   65
and the prince took her hand on the spot
and danced with no other the whole day.

As nightfall came she thought she'd
better get home. The prince walked her home
and she disappeared into the pigeon house   70
and although the prince took an axe and broke
it open she was gone. Back to her cinders.
These events repeated themselves for three days.
However on the third day the prince
covered the palace steps with cobbler's wax   75
And Cinderella's gold shoe stuck upon it.
Now he would find whom the shoe fit
and find his strange dancing girl for keeps.
He went to their house and the two sisters
were delighted because they had lovely feet.   80
The eldest went into a room to try the slipper on
but her big toe got in the way so she simply
sliced it off and put on the slipper.

The prince rode away with her until the white dove
told him to look at the blood pouring forth.   85
That is the way with amputations.
They don't just heal up like a wish.
The other sister cut off her heel
but the blood told as blood will.
The prince was getting tired.   90
He began to feel like a shoe salesman.
But he gave it one last try.
This time Cinderella fit into the shoe
like a love letter into its envelope.

At the wedding ceremony   95
the two sisters came to curry favor
and the white dove pecked their eyes out.
Two hollow spots were left
like soup spoons.

Cinderella and the prince   100
lived, they say, happily ever after,
like two dolls in a museum case
never bothered by diapers or dust,
never arguing over the timing of an egg,
never telling the same story twice,   105
never getting a middle-aged spread,
their darling smiles pasted on for eternity
Regular Bobbsey Twins.°
That story.

—*1970*

The Truth the Dead Know

For my mother, born March 1902, died March 1959,
and my father, born February 1900, died June 1959

Gone, I say and walk from church,
refusing the stiff procession to the grave,
letting the dead ride alone in the hearse.
It is June. I am tired of being brave.

108 Bobbsey Twins characters in a series of popular juvenile novels by Laura Lee Hope

We drive to the Cape. I cultivate   5
myself where the sun gutters from the sky,
where the sea swings in like an iron gate
and we touch. In another country people die.

My darling, the wind falls in like stones
from the whitehearted water and when we touch   10
we enter touch entirely. No one's alone.
Men kill for this, or for as much

And what of the dead? They lie without shoes
in their stone boats. They are more like stone
than the sea would be if it stopped. They refuse   15
to be blessed, throat, eye and knucklebone.

                                                    —*1962*

Thom Gunn (1929–2004)

Thom Gunn was a British expatriate who lived in San Francisco for over four decades. Gunn managed to retain his ties to the traditions of British literature while writing about motorcycle gangs, surfers, gay bars, and drug experiences. The Man with Night Sweats, his 1992 collection, contains a number of forthright poems on AIDS, of which "Terminal" is one.

From the Wave

It mounts at sea, a concave wall
    Down-ribbed with shine,
And pushes forward, building tall
    Its steep incline.

Then from their hiding rise to sight   5
    Black shapes on boards
Bearing before the fringe of white
    It mottles towards.

Their pale feet curl, they poise their weight
    With a learn'd skill.   10
It is the wave they imitate
    Keeps them so still.

The marbling bodies have become
  Half wave, half men,
Grafted it seems by feet of foam   15
  Some seconds, then,

Late as they can, they slice the face
  In timed procession:
Balance is triumph in this place,
  Triumph possession.   20

The mindless heave of which they rode
  A fluid shelf
Breaks as they leave it, falls and, slowed,
  Loses itself.

Clear, the sheathed bodies slick as seals 25
  Loosen and tingle;
And by the board the bare foot feels
  The suck of shingle.

They paddle in the shallows still;
  Two splash each other;   30
Then all swim out to wait until
  The right waves gather.

                                    —1971

Terminal

The eight years difference in age seems now
Disparity so wide between the two
That when I see the man who armoured stood
Resistant to all help however good
Now helped through day itself, eased into chairs,   5
Or else led step by step down the long stairs
With firm and gentle guidance by his friend,
Who loves him, through each effort to descend,
Each wavering, each attempt made to complete
An arc of movement and bring down the feet   10
As if with that spare strength he used to enjoy,
I think of Oedipus, old, led by a boy.

                                    —1992

X. J. Kennedy (b. 1929)

X. J. Kennedy is one the few contemporary American poets who has not been attracted to free verse, preferring to remain what he calls a "dinosaur," one of those poets who continue to write in meter. He is also rare among his contemporaries in his commitment to writing poems with strong ties to song. Kennedy is also the author of Literature: An Introduction to Fiction, Poetry, and Drama, *perhaps the most widely used college literature text ever written.*

In a Prominent Bar in Secaucus One Day

To the tune of "The Old Orange Flute" or the tune of "Sweet Betsy from Pike"

In a prominent bar in Secaucus one day
Rose a lady in skunk with a topheavy sway,
Raised a knobby red finger—all turned from their beer—
While with eyes bright as snowcrust she sang high and clear:

"Now who of you'd think from an eyeload of me   5
That I once was a lady as proud as could be?
Oh I'd never sit down by a tumbledown drunk
If it wasn't, my dears, for the high cost of junk.

"All the gents used to swear that the white of my calf
Beat the down of the swan by a length and a half.   10
In the kerchief of linen I caught to my nose
Ah, there never fell snot, but a little gold rose.

"I had seven gold teeth and a toothpick of gold,
My Virginia cheroot° was a leaf of it rolled
And I'd light it each time with a thousand in cash—   15
Why the bums used to fight if I flicked them an ash.

"Once the toast of the Biltmore, the belle of the Taft,
I would drink bottle beer at the Drake,° never draft,

---

14 cheroot a thin cigar   **17–18 Biltmore, Taft, Drake** famous hotels

And dine at the Astor on Salisbury steak
With a clean tablecloth for each bite I did take.   20

"In a car like the Roxy I'd roll to the track,
A steel-guitar trio, a bar in the back,
And the wheels made no noise, they turned over so fast,
Still it took you ten minutes to see me go past.

"When the horses bowed down to me that I might choose,   25
I bet on them all, for I hated to lose.
Now I'm saddled each night for my butter and eggs
And the broken threads race down the backs of my legs.

"Let you hold in mind, girls, that your beauty must pass
Like a lovely white clover that rusts with its grass.   30
Keep your bottoms off barstools and marry you young
Or be left—an old barrel with many a bung.

"For when time takes you out for a spin in his car
You'll be hard-pressed to stop him from going too far
And be left by the roadside, for all your good deeds,   35
Two toadstools for tits and a face full of weeds."

All the house raised a cheer, but the man at the bar
Made a phonecall and up pulled a red patrol car
And she blew us a kiss as they copped her away
From that prominent bar in Secaucus, N.J.   40

                                                          —1961

September Twelfth, 2001

Two caught on film who hurtle
from the eighty-second floor,
choosing between a fireball
and to jump holding hands,

Aren't us. I wake beside you,   5
stretch, scratch, taste the air,
the incredible joy of coffee
and the morning light.

Alive, we open eyelids
on our pitiful share of time,   10

we bubbles rising and bursting
in a boiling pot.

—2002

Adrienne Rich (b. 1929)

Adrienne Rich's most recent books of poetry are Midnight Salvage:
Poems 1995–1998 *and* Fox: Poems 1998–2000. *A new selection of her
essays,* Arts of the Possible: Essays and Conversations, *was published in
2001. She has recently been the recipient of the Dorothea Tanning Prize
of the Academy of American Poets "for mastery in the art of poetry,"
and the Lannan Foundation Lifetime Achievement Award. She lives in
California.*

Aunt Jennifer's Tigers

Aunt Jennifer's tigers prance across a screen,
Bright topaz denizens of a world of green.
They do not fear the men beneath the tree;
They pace in sleek chivalric certainty.

Aunt Jennifer's fingers fluttering through her wool   5
Find even the ivory needle hard to pull.
The massive weight of Uncle's wedding band
Sits heavily upon Aunt Jennifer's hand.

When Aunt is dead, her terrified hands will lie
Still ringed with ordeals she was mastered by.   10
The tigers in the panel that she made
Will go on prancing, proud and unafraid.

—1950

Diving into the Wreck

First having read the book of myths,
and loaded the camera,
and checked the edge of the knife-blade,
I put on

the body-armor of black rubber 5
the absurd flippers
the grave and awkward mask.
I am having to do this
not like Cousteau° with his
assiduous team 10
aboard the sun-flooded schooner
but here alone.

There is a ladder.
The ladder is always there
hanging innocently 15
close to the side of the schooner.
We know what it is for,
we who have used it.
Otherwise
it is a piece of maritime floss 20
some sundry equipment.

I go down.
Rung after rung and still
the oxygen immerses me
the blue light 25
the clear atoms
of our human air.
I go down.
My flippers cripple me,
I crawl like an insect down the ladder 30
and there is no one
to tell me when the ocean
will begin.

First the air is blue and then
it is bluer and then green and then 35
black I am blacking out and yet
my mask is powerful
it pumps my blood with power
the sea is another story
the sea is not a question of power 40
I have to learn alone

9 Cousteau Jacques-Yves Cousteau (1910–1997), underwater explorer and inventor of the scuba tank

to turn my body without force
in the deep element.

And now: it is easy to forget
what I came for   45
among so many who have always
lived here
swaying their crenellated fans
between the reefs
and besides   50
you breathe differently down here.

I came to explore the wreck.
The words are purposes.
The words are maps.
I came to see the damage that was done   55
and the treasures that prevail.
I stroke the beam of my lamp
slowly along the flank
of something more permanent
than fish or weed   60

the thing I came for:
the wreck and not the story of the wreck
the thing itself and not the myth
the drowned face always staring
toward the sun   65
the evidence of damage
worn by salt and sway into this threadbare beauty
the ribs of the disaster
curving their assertion
among the tentative haunters.   70

This is the place.
And I am here, the mermaid whose dark hair
streams black, the merman in his armored body.
We circle silently
about the wreck   75
we dive into the hold.
I am she: I am he

whose drowned face sleeps with open eyes
whose breasts still bear the stress
whose silver, copper, vermeil cargo lies   80

obscurely inside barrels
half-wedged and left to rot
we are the half-destroyed instruments
that once held to a course
the water-eaten log°   85
the fouled compass

We are, I am, you are
by cowardice or courage
the one who find our way
back to this scene   90
carrying a knife, a camera
a book of myths
in which
our names do not appear.

                                                    —*1972*

Rape

There is a cop who is both prowler and father:
he comes from your block, grew up with your brothers,
had certain ideals.
You hardly know him in his boots and silver badge,
on horseback, one hand touching his gun.   5

You hardly know him but you have to get to know him:
he has access to machinery that could kill you.
He and his stallion clop like warlords among the trash,
his ideals stand in the air, a frozen cloud
from between his unsmiling lips.   10

And so, when the time comes, you have to turn to him,
the maniac's sperm still greasing your thighs,
your mind whirling like crazy. You have to confess
to him, you are guilty of the crime
of having been forced.   15

And you see his blue eyes, the blue eyes of all the family
whom you used to know, grow narrow and glisten,

85 **log** log book

his hand types out the details
and he wants them all
but the hysteria in your voice pleases him best.   20

You hardly know him but now he thinks he knows you:
he has taken down your worst moment
on a machine and filed it in a file.
He knows, or thinks he knows, how much you imagined;
he knows, or thinks he knows, what you secretly wanted.   25

He has access to machinery that could get you put away;
and if, in the sickening light of the precinct,
and if, in the sickening light of the precinct,
your details sound like a portrait of your confessor,
will you swallow, will you deny them, will you lie your way home?   30

—1972

Ted Hughes (1930–1998)

*Ted Hughes was a native of Yorkshire, England. Hughes never ventured
far from the natural world of his childhood for his subject matter. Hughes
was married to Sylvia Plath until her death in 1963;* Birthday Letters, *a
book of poems about their troubled relationship, appeared in 1998. At the
time of his death, Hughes was the British poet laureate.*

Pike

Pike, three inches long, perfect
Pike in all parts, green tigering the gold.
Killers from the egg: the malevolent aged grin.
They dance on the surface among the flies.

Or move, stunned by their own grandeur,   5
Over a bed of emerald, silhouette
Of submarine delicacy and horror.
A hundred feet long in their world.

In ponds, under the heat-struck lily pads—
Gloom of their stillness: 10

Logged on last year's black leaves, watching upwards.
Or hung in an amber cavern of weeds

The jaw's hooked clamp and fangs
Not to be changed at this date;
A life subdued to its instrument;   15
The gills kneading quietly, and the pectorals.

Three we kept behind glass,
Jungled in weed: three inches, four,
And four and a half. fed fry to them—
Suddenly there were two. Finally one   20

With a sag belly and the grin it was born with.
And indeed they spare nobody.
Two, six pounds each, over two feet long,
High and dry and dead in the willow-herb—

One jammed past its gills down the other's gullet: 25
The outside eye stared: as a vice locks—
The same iron in this eye
Though its film shrank in death.

A pond I fished, fifty yards across,
Whose lilies and muscular tench°   30
Had outlasted every visible stone
Of the monastery that planted them—

Stilled legendary depth:
It was as deep as England. It held
Pike too immense to stir, so immense and old   35
That past nightfall I dared not cast

But silently cast and fished
With the hair frozen on my head
For what might move, for what eye might move.
The still splashes on the dark pond,   40

Owls hushing the floating woods
Frail on my ear against the dream
Darkness beneath night's darkness had freed,
That rose slowly towards me, watching.

—1960

30 **tench** European freshwater fish

Gary Snyder (b. 1930)

Gary Snyder was deeply involved in poetic activity in his hometown, San Francisco, when that city became the locus of the Beat Generation in the mid-1950s. Yet Snyder, whose studies in Zen Buddhism and Oriental cultures preceded his acquaintance with Allen Ginsberg and Jack Kerouac, has always exhibited a seriousness of purpose that sets him apart from his peers. His long familiarity with the mountains of the Pacific Northwest dates from his jobs with logging crews during his college days.

A Walk

Sunday the only day we don't work:
Mules farting around the meadow,
    Murphy fishing,
The tent flaps in the warm
Early sun: I've eaten breakfast and I'll   5
      take a walk
To Benson Lake. Packed a lunch,
Goodbye. Hopping on creekbed boulders
Up the rock throat three miles
    Piute Creek—   10
In steep gorge glacier-slick rattlesnake country
Jump, land by a pool, trout skitter,
The clear sky. Deer tracks.
Bad place by a falls, boulders big as houses,
Lunch tied to belt,   15
I stemmed up a crack and almost fell
But rolled out safe on a ledge
    and ambled on.
Quail chicks freeze underfoot, color of stone
Then run cheep! away, hen quail fussing.   20
Craggy west end of Benson Lake—after edging
Past dark creek pools on a long white slope—
Lookt down in the ice-black lake
    lined with cliff
From far above: deep shimmering trout.   25
A lone duck in a gunsightpass
    steep side hill
Through slide-aspen and talus, to the east end

Down to grass, wading a wide smooth stream
Into camp. At last.   30
   By the rusty three-year-
Ago left-behind cookstove
Of the old trail crew,
Stoppt and swam and ate my lunch.

—1968

Derek Walcott (b. 1930)

*Derek Walcott is a native of the tiny Caribbean island of St. Lucia in the
West Indies. Walcott combines a love of the tradition of English poetry
with the exotic surfaces of tropical life. In many ways, his life and career
have constituted a study in divided loyalties, which are displayed in his
ambivalent poems about life in the United States, where he has lived and
taught for many years. Walcott was awarded the Nobel Prize in 1992.*

Central America

Helicopters are cutlassing the wild bananas.
Between a nicotine thumb and forefinger
brittle faces crumble like tobacco leaves.
Children waddle in vests, their legs bowed,
little shrimps curled under their navels.   5
The old men's teeth are stumps in a charred forest.
Their skins grate like the iguana's.
Their gaze like slate stones.
Women squat by the river's consolations
where children wade up to their knees,   10
and a stick stirs up a twinkling of butterflies.
Up there, in the blue acres
of forest, flies circle their fathers.
In spring, in the upper provinces
of the Empire, yellow tanagers   15
float up through the bare branches.
There is no distinction in these distances.

—1987

Miller Williams (b. 1930)

Miller Williams won the Poets' Prize in 1990 for Living on the Surface, *a volume of selected poems. A skillful translator of both Giuseppe Belli, a Roman poet of the early nineteenth century, and of Nicanor Parra, a contemporary Chilean, Williams has written many poems about his travels throughout the world yet has retained the relaxed idiom of his native Arkansas. He read a poem at the 1997 presidential inauguration.*

The Book

I held it in my hands while he told the story.

He had found it in a fallen bunker,
a book for notes with all the pages blank.
He took it to keep for a sketchbook and diary.

He learned years later, when he showed the book   5
to an old bookbinder, who paled, and stepped back
a long step and told him what he held,
what he had laid the days of his life in.
It's bound, the binder said, in human skin.

I stood turning it over in my hands,   10
turning it in my head. Human skin.

What child did this skin fit? What man, what woman?
Dragged still full of its flesh from what dream?

Who took it off the meat? Some other one
who stayed alive by knowing how to do this?   15

I stared at the changing book and a horror grew,
I stared and a horror grew, which was, which is,
how beautiful it was until I knew.

—1989

Linda Pastan (b. 1932)

Linda Pastan served as poet laureate of Maryland, where she has lived and taught for many years. Her first book, A Perfect Circle of Sun, *appeared in 1971, and a dozen more collections have been published since.*

1932–

I saw my name in print the other day
with 1932 and then a blank
and knew that even now some grassy bank
just waited for my grave. And somewhere a grey

slab of marble existed already   5
on which the final number would be carved—
as if the stone itself were somehow starved
for definition. When I went steady

in high school years ago, my boyfriend's name
was what I tried out, hearing how it fit   10
with mine; then names of film stars in some hit.
My husband was anonymous as rain.

There is a number out there, odd or even
that will become familiar to my sons
and daughter. (They are the living ones   15
I think of now; Peter, Rachel, Stephen.)

I picture it, four integers in a row
5 or 7, 6 or 2 or 9:
a period; silence; an end-stopped line;
a hammer poised . . . delivering its blow.   20

—*1998*

Sylvia Plath (1932–1963)

Sylvia Plath, whose troubled personal life is often difficult to separate from her poetry, is almost always read as an autobiographical and confessional poet. Brilliant and precocious, she served a long apprenticeship to the tradition of modern poetry before attaining her mature style in the final two years of her life. Only one collection, The Colossus *(1960), appeared in her lifetime, and her fame has mainly rested on her posthumous books of poetry and the success of her lone novel,* The Bell Jar *(1963). She committed suicide in 1963. Plath has been the subject of a half-dozen biographical studies and a feature film,* Sylvia *(2003), reflecting the intense interest that readers have in her life and work.*

Daddy

You do not do, you do not do
Any more, black shoe
In which I have lived like a foot
For thirty years, poor and white,
Barely daring to breathe or Achoo.   5

Daddy, I have had to kill you.
You died before I had time—
Marble-heavy, a bag full of God,
Ghastly statue with one gray toe
Big as a Frisco seal   10

And a head in the freakish Atlantic
Where it pours bean green over blue
In the waters off beautiful Nauset.
I used to pray to recover you.
Ach, du.°   15

In the German tongue, in the Polish town
Scraped flat by the roller
Of wars, wars, wars.
But the name of the town is common.
My Polack friend   20

15 **Ach, du** "Oh, you"

Says there are a dozen or two.
So I never could tell where you
Put your foot, your root,
I never could talk to you.
The tongue stuck in my jaw.   25

It stuck in a barb wire snare.
Ich, ich, ich, ich,°
I could hardly speak.
I thought every German was you.
And the language obscene   30

An engine, an engine
Chuffing me off like a Jew.
A Jew to Dachau, Auschwitz, Belsen.°
I began to talk like a Jew.
I think I may well be a Jew.   35

The snows of the Tyrol, the clear beer of Vienna
Are not very pure or true.
With my gypsy ancestress and my weird luck
And my Taroc pack and my Taroc pack
I may be a bit of a Jew.   40

I have always been scared of *you*,
With your Luftwaffe,° your gobbledygoo.
And your neat mustache
And your Aryan eye, bright blue.
Panzer-man, panzer-man, O You—   45

Not God but a swastika
So black no sky could squeak through.
Every woman adores a Fascist,
The boot in the face, the brute
Brute heart of a brute like you.   50

You stand at the blackboard, daddy,
In the picture I have of you,
A cleft in your chin instead of your foot

---

27 Ich, ich, ich, ich "I, I, I, I"   **33 Dachau, Auschwitz, Belsen** German concentration camps
42 Luftwaffe German Air Force

But no less a devil for that, no not
Any less the black man who   55

Bit my pretty red heart in two.
I was ten when they buried you.
At twenty I tried to die
And get back, back, back to you.
I thought even the bones would do.   60

But they pulled me out of the sack,
And they stuck me together with glue.
And then I knew what to do.
I made a model of you,
A man in black with a Meinkampf° look   65

And a love of the rack and the screw.
And I said I do, I do.
So daddy, I'm finally through.
The black telephone's off at the root,
The voices just can't worm through.   70

If I've killed one man, I've killed two—
The vampire who said he was you
And drank my blood for a year,
Seven years, if you want to know.
Daddy, you can lie back now.   75

There's a stake in your fat black heart
And the villagers never liked you.
They are dancing and stamping on you.
They always *knew* it was you.
Daddy, daddy, you bastard, I'm through.   80

                                              —*1966*

65 **Meinkampf** title of Hitler's autobiography ("My Struggle")

Edge

The woman is perfected.
Her dead

Body wears the smile of accomplishment,
The illusion of a Greek necessity

Flows in the scrolls of her toga,   5
Her bare

Feet seem to be saying:
We have come so far, it is over.

Each dead child coiled, a white serpent,
One at each little   10

Pitcher of milk, now empty.
She has folded

Them back into her body as petals
Of a rose close when the garden

Stiffens and odors bleed   15
From the sweet, deep throats of the night flower.

The moon has nothing to be sad about,
Staring from her hood of bone.

She is used to this sort of thing.
Her blacks crackle and drag.   20

—1965

Metaphors

I'm a riddle in nine syllables,
An elephant, a ponderous house,
A melon strolling on two tendrils.
O red fruit, ivory, fine timbers!

This loaf's big with its yeasty rising.   5
Money's new-minted in this fat purse.
I'm a means, a stage, a cow in calf.
I've eaten a bag of green apples,
Boarded the train there's no getting off.

—*1960*

Gerald Barrax   (b. 1933)

Gerald Barrax served as the editor of Obsidian II: Black Literature in Review, *one of the most influential journals of African-American writing. The author of five collections of poetry, he taught at North Carolina State University.*

Strangers Like Us: Pittsburgh, Raleigh, 1945–1985

The sounds our parents heard echoing over
housetops while listening to evening radios
were the uninterrupted cries running and cycling
we sent through the streets and yards, where spring summer
fall we were entrusted to the night, boys   5
and girls together, to send us home for bath
and bed after the dark had drifted down and eased
contests between pitcher and batter, hider and seeker.

Our own children live imprisoned in light.
They are cycloned into our yards and hearts,   10
whose gates flutter shut on unfamiliar smiles.
At the rumor of a moon, we call them in
before the monsters who hunt, who hurt, who haunt
us, rise up from our own dim streets.

—*1992*

Mark Strand (b. 1934)

Mark Strand displays a simplicity in his best poems that reveals the influence of Spanish-language poets like Nicanor Parra, the father of "anti-poetry," and Rafael Alberti, whom Strand has translated. Strand was named U.S. poet laureate in 1990.

The Tunnel

A man has been standing
in front of my house
for days. I peek at him
from the living room
window and at night,   5
unable to sleep,
I shine my flashlight
down on the lawn.
He is always there.

After a while   10
I open the front door
just a crack and order
him out of my yard.
He narrows his eyes
and moans. I slam   15
the door and dash back
to the kitchen, then up
to the bedroom, then down.

I weep like a schoolgirl
and make obscene gestures   20
through the window. I
write large suicide notes
and place them so he
can read them easily.
I destroy the living   25
room furniture to prove
I own nothing of value.

When he seems unmoved
I decide to dig a tunnel

to a neighboring yard.   30
I seal the basement off
from the upstairs with
a brick wall. I dig hard
and in no time the tunnel
is done. Leaving my pick   35
and shovel below,

I come out in front of a house
and stand there too tired to
move or even speak, hoping
someone will help me.   40
I feel I'm being watched
and sometimes I hear
a man's voice,
but nothing is done
and I have been waiting for days.   45

                                                  —*1968*

Russell Edson (b. 1935)

*Russell Edson is the son of a cartoonist, and his surrealistic poems (often
illustrated by himself) perhaps owe as much to the whimsical drawings
and essays of New Yorker writer James Thurber than to the direct influence of any modern poet. Edson has been called "the godfather of the
prose poem in America," and the sheer originality of his imagination and
his defiance of poetic "rules" set him apart from other poets and ally
him with such contemporary masters of cartooning as R. Crumb and
Harvey Pekar.*

Ape

You haven't finished your ape, said mother to father, who had
monkey hair and blood on his whiskers.

I've had enough monkey, cried father.

You didn't eat the hands, and I went to all the trouble to make
onion rings for its fingers, said mother.   5

I'll just nibble on its forehead, and then I've had enough, said father.

I stuffed its nose with garlic, just like you like it, said mother.

Why don't you have the butcher cut these apes up? You lay the whole thing on the table every night; the same fractured skull, the same singed fur; like someone who died horribly. These aren't dinners, these are postmortem dissections. 10

Try a piece of its gum, I've stuffed its mouth with bread, said mother.

Ugh, it looks like a mouth full of vomit. How can I bite into its cheek with bread spilling out of its mouth? cried father.

Break one of the ears off, they're so crispy, said mother. 15

I wish to hell you'd put underpants on these apes; even a jockstrap, screamed father.

Father, how dare you insinuate that I see the ape as anything more than simple meat, screamed mother.

Well, what's with this ribbon tied in a bow on its privates? screamed father. 20

Are you saying that I am in love with this vicious creature? That I would submit my female opening to this brute? That after we had love on the kitchen floor I would put him in the oven, after breaking his head with a frying pan; and then serve him to my husband, that my husband might eat the evidence of my infidelity . . . ?

I'm just saying that I'm damn sick of ape every night, cried father.

—*1994*

Mary Oliver (b. 1935)

Mary Oliver was born in Cleveland, Ohio, and educated at Ohio State University and Vassar College. She has served as a visiting professor at a number of universities and at the Fine Arts Work Center in Provincetown, Massachusetts. She has won both the Pulitzer Prize and the National Book Award for her work, which first appeared in No Voyage and Other Poems *in 1965.*

The Black Walnut Tree

My mother and I debate:
we could sell
the black walnut tree
to the lumberman,
and pay off the mortgage.   5
Likely some storm anyway
will churn down its dark boughs,
smashing the house. We talk
slowly, two women trying
in a difficult time to be wise.   10
Roots in the cellar drains,
I say, and she replies
that the leaves are getting heavier
every year, and the fruit
harder to gather away.   15
But something brighter than money
moves in our blood—an edge
sharp and quick as a trowel
that wants us to dig and sow.
So we talk, but we don't do   20
anything. That night I dream
of my fathers out of Bohemia
filling the blue fields
of fresh and generous Ohio
with leaves and vines and orchards.   25
What my mother and I both know
is that we'd crawl with shame

in the emptiness we'd made
in our own and our fathers' backyard.
So the black walnut tree   30
swings through another year
of sun and leaping winds,
of leaves and bounding fruit,
and, month after month, the whip-
crack of the mortgage.   35

—1979

Fred Chappell (b. 1936)

Fred Chappell wrote the epic-length poem Midquest *(1981), and his achievement was recognized when he was awarded the Bollingen Prize in 1985. A four-part poem written over a decade,* Midquest *uses the occasion of the poet's thirty-fifth birthday as a departure for a complex sequence of autobiographical poems that are heavily indebted to Dante for their formal structure. A versatile writer of both poetry and prose, Chappell displays his classical learning brilliantly and in unusual contexts.*

Narcissus and Echo°

Shall the water not remember   *Ember*
my hand's slow gesture, tracing above   *of*
its mirror my half-imaginary   *airy*
portrait? My only belonging   *longing*
is my beauty, which I take   *ache*   5
away and then return as love   *of*
teasing playfully the one being   *unbeing.*

whose gratitude I treasure   *Is your*
moves me. I live apart   *heart*
from myself, yet cannot   *not*   10
live apart. In the water's tone,   *stone?*
that brilliant silence, a flower   *Hour,*

Narcissus and Echo In the myth, the vain Narcissus drowned attempting to embrace his own reflection in the water. Echo, a nymph who loved him, pined away until only her voice remained.

whispers my name with such slight *light,*
moment, it seems filament of air, *fare*
the world become cloudswell. *well.*   15

—*1985*

Lucille Clifton (b. 1936)

*Lucille Clifton, a native of Depew, New York, was educated at SUNY–
Fredonia and Howard University, and has taught at several colleges, including American University in Washington, D.C. About her own work,
she has commented succinctly, "I am a Black woman poet, and I sound
like one." Clifton won a National Book Award in 2000.*

homage to my hips

these hips are big hips
they need space to
move around in.
they don't fit into little
petty places. these hips   5
are free hips.
they don't like to be held back.
these hips have never been enslaved,
they go where they want to go
they do what they want to do.   10
these hips are mighty hips.
these hips are magic hips.
i have known them
to put a spell on a man and
spin him like a top!   15

—*1980*

wishes for sons

i wish them cramps.
i wish them a strange town

and the last tampon.
I wish them no 7-11.

i wish them one week early   5
and wearing a white skirt.
i wish them one week late.

later i wish them hot flashes
and clots like you
wouldn't believe. let the   10
flashes come when they
meet someone special.
let the clots come
when they want to.

let them think they have accepted   15
arrogance in the universe,
then bring them to gynecologists
not unlike themselves.

—1991

Marge Piercy (b. 1936)

Marge Piercy was a political radical during her student days at the University of Michigan. Piercy has continued to be outspoken on political, cultural, and sexual issues. Her phrase "to be of use" has become a key measure by which feminist writers and critics have gauged the meaning of their own life experiences.

What's That Smell in the Kitchen?

All over America women are burning dinners.
It's lambchops in Peoria; it's haddock
in Providence; it's steak in Chicago;
tofu delight in Big Sur; red
rice and beans in Dallas.   5
All over America women are burning

food they're supposed to bring with calico
smile on platters glittering like wax.
Anger sputters in her brainpan, confined
but spewing out missiles of hot fat.   10
Carbonized despair presses like a clinker
from a barbecue against the back of her eyes.
If she wants to grill anything, it's
her husband spitted over a slow fire.
If she wants to serve him anything   15
it's a dead rat with a bomb in its belly
ticking like the heart of an insomniac.
Her life is cooked and digested,
nothing but leftovers in Tupperware.
Look, she says, once I was roast duck   20
on your platter with parsley but now I am Spam.
Burning dinner is not incompetence but war.

—1982

Betty Adcock (b. 1938)

*Betty Adcock was born in San Augustine, Texas. Adcock has lived for many
years in Raleigh, North Carolina, where she is poet-in-residence at Meredith
College. Her volume of selected poems,* Intervale, *appeared in 2001.*

Digression on the Nuclear Age

In some difficult part of Africa, a termite tribe
builds elaborate tenements that might be called
cathedrals, were they for anything so terminal
as Milton's God. Who was it said
the perfect arch will always separate   5
the civilized from the not? Never mind.

These creatures are quite blind and soft
and hard at labor chemically induced.
Beginning with a dish-like hollow, groups
of workers pile up earthen pellets.   10

A few such piles will reach a certain height;
fewer still, a just proximity.
That's when direction changes, or a change
directs: the correct two bands of laborers
will make their towers bow toward each other.   15
Like saved and savior, they will meet in air.
It is unambiguously an arch and it will serve,
among the others rising and the waste,
an arch's purposes. Experts are sure
a specific moment comes when the very structure   20
triggers the response that will perfect it.

I've got this far and don't know what
termites can be made to mean. Or this poem:
a joke, a play on arrogance, nothing
but language? Untranslated, the world gets on   25
with dark, flawless constructions rising,
rising even where we think we are. And think
how we must hope convergences will fail this time,
that whatever it is we're working on won't work.

                                                          —1988

Gary Gildner (b. 1938)

*Gary Gildner was born in West Branch, Michigan, and attended Michigan
State University. He lives on a ranch in the Clearwater Mountains of
Idaho. "First Practice" is the title poem of his first collection, published in
1969, and a volume of Gildner's selected poems appeared in 1984.*

First Practice

After the doctor checked to see
we weren't ruptured,
the man with the short cigar took us
under the grade school,
where we went in case of attack   5
or storm, and said
he was Clifford Hill, he was
a man who believed dogs

ate dogs, he had once killed
for his country, and if   10
there were any girls present
for them to leave now.
         No one
left. OK, he said, he said I take
that to mean you are hungry   15
men who hate to lose as much
as I do. OK. Then
he made two lines of us
facing each other,
and across the way, he said,   20
is the man you hate most
in the world,
and if we are to win
that title I want to see how.
But I don't want to see   25
any marks when you're dressed,
he said. He said, *Now*.

           —*1969*

Robert Phillips (b. 1938)

Robert Phillips labored for over thirty years as a New York advertising executive, a remarkable fact when one considers his many books of poetry, fiction, and criticism and the numerous books he has edited. He currently lives in Houston, where he teaches in the creative writing program at the University of Houston.

Compartments

Which shall be final?
      Pine box in a concrete vault,
urn on a mantel?

Last breath a rattle,
      stuffed in a black body bag,   5
he's zipped head to toe.

At the nursing home,
 side drawn to prevent a fall—
in a crib again.

His dead wife's false teeth   10
 underfoot in their bedroom.
Feel the piercing chill.

Pink flamingo lawn,
 a Florida trailer park:
one space he'll avoid.   15

The box they gave him
 on retirement held a watch
that measures decades.

The new bifocals
 rest in their satin-lined case,   20
his body coffined.

Move to the suburbs.
 Crowded train at seven-oh-two,
empty head at night.

New playpen, new crib,   25
 can't compete with the newness
of the newborn child.

Oak four-poster bed
 inherited from family—
Jack Frost defrosted.   30

Once he was pink-slipped.
 Dad helped out: "A son's a son,
Son, from womb to tomb."

Fourteen-foot ceilings,
 parquet floors, marble fireplace,   35
proud first apartment.

The Jack Frost Motel,
 its very name a portent
for their honeymoon.

Backseat of a car,   40
 cursing the inventor of
nylon pantyhose.

First-job cubicle.
    Just how many years before
a window office?   45

College quad at noon,
    chapel bells, frat men, coeds,
no pocket money.

his grandfather's barn.
    After it burned to the ground,   50
the moon filled its space.

His favorite tree—
    the leaves return to branches?
No, butterflies light.

Closet where he hid   55
    to play with himself. None knew?
Mothball orgasms.

Chimney that he scaled
    naked to sweep for his Dad:
Blake's soot-black urchin.   60

The town's swimming pool
    instructor, throwing him in
again and again . . .

Kindergarten play
    ground: swings, slides, rings, jungle gym.   65
Scraped knees, molester.

Red, blue and green birds
    mobilize over his crib,
its sides a tall fence.

Two months premature,   70
    he incubates by light bulbs,
like a baby chick.

He is impatient,
    curled in foetal position,
floating in darkness.   75

—*2000*

Dabney Stuart (b. 1938)

Dabney Stuart has written many poems populated by the supporting cast of the American family romance—parents, wives and ex-wives, and children. A Virginian who taught for many years at Washington and Lee University, Stuart published Light Years, *a volume of selected poems, in 1995.*

Discovering My Daughter

Most of your life we have kept our separate places:
After I left your mother you knew an island,
Rented rooms, a slow coastal slide northward
To Boston, and, in summer, another island
Hung at the country's tip. Would you have kept going   5
All the way off the map, an absolute alien?

Sometimes I shiver, being almost forgetful enough
To have let that happen. We've come the longer way
Under such pressure, from one person to
Another. Our trip proves again the world is   10
Round, a singular island where people may come
Together, as we have, making a singular place.

—1987

Margaret Atwood (b. 1939)

Margaret Atwood is the leading woman writer of Canada, and she excels at both poetry and prose fiction. Among her many novels, The Hand-maid's Tale *is perhaps the best known, becoming a bestseller in the United States and the subject of a motion picture. Atwood's* Selected Poems *appeared in 1976.*

Siren° Song

This is the one song everyone
would like to learn: the song
that is irresistible:

the song that forces men
to leap overboard in squadrons   5
even though they see the beached skulls

the song nobody knows
because anyone who has heard it
is dead, and the others can't remember.

Shall I tell you the secret   10
and if I do, will you get me
out of this bird suit?

I don't enjoy it here
squatting on this island
looking picturesque and mythical   15

with these two feathery maniacs,
I don't enjoy singing
this trio, fatal and valuable.

I will tell the secret to you,
to you, only to you.   20
Come closer. This song

is a cry for help: Help me!
Only you, only you can,
you are unique

Siren in Greek myth, one of the women whose irresistible song lured sailors onto the rocks

at last. Alas
it is a boring song
but it works every time.

—1974

Stephen Dunn   (b. 1939)

*Stephen Dunn is a graduate of the creative writing program at Syracuse
University. Dunn teaches at The Richard Stockton College of New Jersey
in Pomona, New Jersey. His attempt to blend ordinary experience with
larger significance is illustrated in the duality of his book titles like* Full of
Lust and Good Usage, Work and Love, *and* Between Angels. *Dunn was
awarded the Pulitzer Prize in 2001.*

The Sacred

After the teacher asked if anyone had
    a sacred place
and the students fidgeted and shrank

in their chairs, the most serious of them all
    said it was his car,   5
being in it alone, his tape deck playing

things he'd chosen, and others knew the truth
    had been spoken
and began speaking about their rooms,

their hiding places, but the car kept coming up,   10
    the car in motion,
music filling it, and sometimes one other person

who understood the bright altar of the dashboard
    and how far away
a car could take him from the need   15

to speak, or to answer, the key
    in having a key
and putting it in, and going.

—1989

ney (b. 1939)

as born in the troubled country of Northern Ireland.
y avoided the type of political divisions that have divided
tead, he has chosen to focus on the landscape of the
rural Ireland he knew while growing up as a farmer's son. Since 1982,
Heaney has taught part of the year at Harvard University. He was
awarded the Nobel Prize for Literature in 1995.

Digging

Between my finger and my thumb
The squat pen rests; snug as a gun.

Under my window, a clean rasping sound
When the spade sinks into gravelly ground:
My father, digging. I look down   5

Till his straining rump among the flowerbeds
Bends low, comes up twenty years away
Stooping in rhythm through potato drills°
Where he was digging.

The coarse boot nestled on the lug, the shaft   10
Against the inside knee was levered firmly.
He rooted out tall tops, buried the bright edge deep
To scatter new potatoes that we picked
Loving their cool hardness in our hands.

By God, the old man could handle a spade.   15
Just like his old man.

My grandfather cut more turf in a day
Than any other man on Toner's bog.
Once I carried him milk in a bottle
Corked sloppily with paper. He straightened up   20
To drink it, then fell to right away

8 **drills** furrows

Nicking and slicing neatly, heaving sods
Over his shoulder, going down and down
For the good turf. Digging.

The cold smell of potato mould, the squelch and slap 25
Of soggy peat, the curt cuts of an edge
Through living roots awaken in my head.
But I've no spade to follow men like them.

Between my finger and my thumb
The squat pen rests. 30
I'll dig with it.

—1980

Punishment

I can feel the tug
of the halter at the nape
of her neck, the wind
on her naked front.

It blows her nipples 5
to amber beads,
it shakes the frail rigging
of her ribs.

I can see her drowned
body in the bog, 10
the weighing stone,
the floating rods and boughs.

Under which at first
she was a barked sapling
that is dug up 15
oak-bone, brain-firkin:°

16 firkin a small barrel

her shaved head
like a stubble of black corn,
her blindfold a soiled bandage,
her noose a ring   20

to store
the memories of love.
Little adulteress,
before they punished you

you were flaxen-haired,   25
undernourished, and your
tar-black face was beautiful.
My poor scapegoat,

I almost love you
but would have cast, I know,   30
the stones of silence.
I am the artful voyeur

of your brain's exposed
and darkened combs,
your muscles' webbing   35
and all your numbered bones:

I who have stood dumb
when your betraying sisters,
cauled in tar,
wept by the railings,   40

who would connive
in civilized outrage
yet understand the exact
and tribal, intimate revenge.

—1975

Al Young (b. 1939)

Al Young was born on the Mississippi Gulf Coast and educated at the University of Michigan and the University of California, Berkeley. A multitalented artist (he was a musician and disk jockey in his youth), Young has written fiction, screenplays, and autobiographies in addition to ten collections of poetry. He has also edited anthologies of African-American literature and California literature and has taught and lectured at many universities in the United States and abroad.

Sundays in Democracies

for Peter Zimmels

Republicans: You're poor because
you're ignorant of all the laws
our Congress passed to cut the costs
of schooling children who get tossed,
nay, dumped upon society.   5
While we do view with piety
the right to life, we draw the line.
Clean up your act. To wine or dine
the loser class does not make sense.
Let's get this straight. We never winced   10
at taking public time to quarrel
with victims, thugs, the huge immoral
segment of the population
in our great, God-blessed, rich, free nation.

The Democrats: There was a time   15
the GOP and all its crime
got barely covered by the news,
which only aired our sins and blues.
What have they done for you, my friends?
Does making do or making ends   20
meet any measure of success?
We back the same Big Business mess
they do, but when we tighten your belt
we dig up Franklin Roosevelt.

We've given you prosperity   25
without their stark severity.
The only thing we have to fear? —
REPUBLICANS. Now, is that clear?

A Citizen: More parties, please,
more Sundays in democracies!   30
Each party dances, each side sings;
one great Big Bird with two right wings.
They'll boogie with you in the streets,
then drag you down to dark defeats.
Democracy? Look at our heroes: 35
CEO's billions, labor's zeroes —
pure DNA, unspliced and spliced.
If you think oil is over-priced,
consider what we're going to pay
for giving frequencies away—   40
the broadcast band. I say let's vote.
Let's kick some butt, let's rock some boat.

Tom Disch (b. 1940)

*Tom Disch is a science-fiction writer, author of interactive computer fiction,
resident critic for magazines as diverse as* Playboy *and* The Nation, *and
poet. Disch is possibly the most brilliant satirist in contemporary American
poetry.* Yes, Let's, *a collection of his selected poems, appeared in 1989.*

Ballade of the New God

I have decided I'm divine.
Caligula and Nero knew
A godliness akin to mine,
But they are strictly hitherto.
They're dead, and what can dead gods do?   5
I'm here and now. I'm dynamite.
I'd worship me if I were you.
A new religion starts tonight!

No booze, no pot, no sex, no swine:
I have decreed them all taboo.   10
My words will be your only wine,
The thought of me your honeydew.
All other thoughts you will eschew
And call yourself a Thomasite
And hymn my praise with loud yahoo.   15
A new religion starts tonight.

But (you might think) that's asinine!
I'm just as much a god as you.
You may have built yourself a shrine
But I won't bend my knee. Who   20
Asked you to be my god? I do,
Who am, as god, divinely right.
Now you must join my retinue:
A new religion starts tonight.

All that I have said is true.   25
I'm god and you're my acolyte.
Surrender's bliss: I envy you
A new religion starts tonight

—1995

Florence Cassen Mayers (b. 1940)

Florence Cassen Mayers is a widely published poet and children's author. Her "ABC" books include children's guides to baseball and to the National Basketball Association.

All-American Sestina

One nation, indivisible
two-car garage
three strikes you're out
four-minute mile
five-cent cigar   5
six-string guitar

six-pack Bud
one-day sale
five-year warranty
two-way street   10
fourscore and seven years ago
three cheers

three-star restaurant
sixty-
four-dollar question   15
one-night stand
two-pound lobster
five-star general

five-course meal
three sheets to the wind   20
two bits
six-shooter
one-armed bandit
four-poster

four-wheel drive   25
five-and-dime
hole in one
three-alarm fire
sweet sixteen
two-wheeler   30

two-tone Chevy
four rms, hi flr, w/vu
six-footer
high five
three-ring circus   35
one-room schoolhouse

two thumbs up, five-karat diamond
Fourth of July, three-piece suit
six feet under, one-horse town

—1996

Pattiann Rogers (b. 1940)

Pattiann Rogers is the foremost naturalist among contemporary American poets. Her poems resound with the rich names of unfamiliar species of plants and animals, most of which she seems to know on intimate terms. Song of the World Becoming: New and Collected Poems 1981–2001 *was published in 2001.*

Foreplay

When it first begins, as you might expect,
the lips and thin folds are closed, the pouting
layers pressed, lapped lightly,
almost languidly, against one another
in a sealed bud.   5

However, with certain prolonged
and random strokings of care
along each binding line, with soft
intrusions traced beneath each pursed
gathering and edge, with inquiring   10
intensities of gesture—as the sun
swinging slowly from winter back
to spring, touches briefly,
between moments of moon and masking
clouds, certain stunning points   15
and inner nubs of earth—so
with such ministrations, a slight
swelling, a quiver of reaching,
a tendency toward space,
might be noticed to commence.   20

Then with dampness from the dark,
with moisture from the falling
night of morning, from hidden places
within the hills, each seal begins
to loosen, each recalcitrant clasp   25
sinks away into itself, and every tucked
grasp, every silk tack willingly relents,

releases, gives way, proclaims a turning,
declares a revolution, assumes,
in plain sight, a surging position   30
that offers, an audacious offering
that beseeches, every petal parted wide.

Remember the spiraling, blue
valerian, remember the violet, sucking
larkspur, the laurel and rosebay   35
and pea cockle flung backwards, remember
the fragrant, funnelling lily, the lifted
honeysuckle, the sweet, open pucker
of the ground ivy blossom?

Now even the darkest crease possessed,   40
the most guarded, pulsing, least drop
of pearl bead, moon grain trembling
deep within is fully revealed, fully exposed
to any penetrating wind or shaking fur
or mad hunger or searing, plunging surprise   45
the wild descending sky in delirium
has to offer.

—1994

Billy Collins (b. 1941)

Billy Collins was born in New York City and continues to teach there. One of the few contemporary poets to reach a wide popular audience, Collins has been an enthusiastic performer, commentator on National Public Radio, and advocate for poetry. Beginning in 2001, he served two years as U.S. poet laureate, establishing the on-line anthology "Poetry 180," a website that presents a poem for every day in the school year. Sailing Alone Around the Room: New and Selected Poems *was published in 2001.*

Paradelle° for Susan

I remember the quick, nervous bird of your love.
I remember the quick, nervous bird of your love.
Always perched on the thinnest, highest branch.
Always perched on the thinnest, highest branch.
Thinnest love, remember the quick branch.   5
Always nervous, I perched on your highest bird the.

It is time for me to cross the mountain.
It is time for me to cross the mountain.
And find another shore to darken with my pain.
And find another shore to darken with my pain.   10
Another pain for me to darken the mountain.
And find the time, cross my shore, to with it is to.

The weather warm, the handwriting familiar.
The weather warm, the handwriting familiar.
Your letter flies from my hand into the waters below.   15
Your letter flies from my hand into the waters below.
The familiar waters below my warm hand.
Into handwriting your weather flies you letter the from the.

The paradelle is one of the more demanding French fixed forms, first appearing in the *langue d'oc* love poetry of the eleventh century. It is a poem of four six-line stanzas in which the first and second lines, as well as the third and fourth lines of the first three stanzas, must be identical. The fifth and sixth lines, which traditionally resolve these stanzas, must use *all* the words from the preceding lines and *only* those words. Similarly, the final stanza must use *every* word from *all* the preceding stanzas and *only* those words.
[Collins's note]

I always cross the highest letter, the thinnest bird.
Below the waters of my warm familiar pain,   20
Another hand to remember your handwriting.
The weather perched for me on the shore.
Quick, your nervous branch flew from love.
Darken the mountain, time and find was my into it was with to to.

—1998

Schoolsville

Glancing over my shoulder at the past
I realize the number of students I have taught
is enough to populate a small town

I can see it nestled in a paper landscape,
chalk dust flurring down in winter,   5
nights dark as a blackboard.

The population ages but never graduates.
On hot afternoons they sweat this final in the park
and when it's cold they shiver around stoves
reading disorganized essays out loud.   10
A bell rings on the hour and everybody zigzags
into the streets with their books.

I forgot all their last names first and their
first names last in alphabetical order.
But the boy who always had his hand up   15
is an alderman and owns the haberdashery.
The girl who signed her papers in lipstick
leans against the drugstore, smoking,
brushing like a machine.

Their grades are sewn into their clothes   20
like references to Hawthorne.
The A's stroll along with other A's.
The D's honk whenever they pass another D.

All the creative writing students recline
on the courthouse lawn and play the lute.   25
Wherever they go, they form a big circle.

Needless to say, I am the mayor.
I live in the white colonial at Maple and Main.
I rarely leave the house. The car deflates
in the driveway. Vines twirl around the porch swing.   30

Once in a while a student knocks on the door
with a term paper fifteen years late
or a question about Yeats or double-spacing.
And sometimes one will appear in a windowpane
to watch me lecturing the wallpaper,   35
quizzing the chandelier, reprimanding the air.

—*1988*

Robert Hass (b. 1941)

*Robert Hass was born and reared in San Francisco, and teaches at U. C.
Berkeley. His first book,* Field Guide, *was chosen for the Yale Series of
Younger Poets in 1973. Recently he has collaborated with Nobel
Prize–winner Czeslaw Milosz on English translations of the latter's poetry.
He was appointed U.S. poet laureate in 1995.*

Picking Blackberries with a Friend Who Has Been Reading Jacques Lacan°

August dust is here. Drought
stuns the road,
but juice gathers in the berries.

We pick them in the hot
slow-motion of midmorning.   5
Charlie is exclaiming:

for him it is twenty years ago
and raspberries and Vermont.
We have stopped talking

Jacques Lacan French psychoanalyst and literary theorist

about *L'Histoire de la vérité,*° 10
about subject and object
and the mediation of desire.

Our ears are stoppered
in the bee-hum. And Charlie,
laughing wonderfully, 15

beard stained purple
by the word *juice,*
goes to get a bigger pot.

—*1979*

Simon J. Ortiz (b. 1941)

Simon J. Ortiz was born in the Pueblo of Acoma, near Albuquerque, New Mexico. Ortiz has explained why he writes: "Because Indians always tell a story. The only way to continue is to tell a story." The author of collections of poetry and prose and of several children's books, Ortiz has taught creative writing and Native American literature at many universities.

The Serenity in Stones

I am holding this turquoise
in my hands.
My hands hold the sky
wrought in this little stone.
There is a cloud 5
at the furthest boundary.
The world is somewhere underneath.

I turn the stone, and there is more sky.
This is the serenity possible in stones,
the place of a feeling to which one belongs. 10
I am happy as I hold this sky
in my hands, in my eyes, and in myself.

—*1975*

10 *L'Histoire de la vérité The History of Truth,* by Lacan

James Reiss (b. 1941)

James Reiss was born in New York City and educated at the University of Chicago. One of his early publications (Self-Interviews, 1970) was an edited collection of prose and reminiscences by poet James Dickey. Reiss's first book of poetry, The Breathers, *appeared in 1974, and he has recently published* Riff on Six, *a volume of selected poems. A professor for many years at Miami University in Oxford, Ohio, he also heads Miami University Press.*

Arigato Means Thank You

This morning I woke with the word
arigato on my lips.
     Was it Japanese?
I lay by you in a sauna
bath of sun and wondered why *arigato*   5
instead of *breasts* or *silence.*
I had never loved language
more than the night I learned your breasts
were vessels of silence.
     Still,   10
I would never dream of saying things
like *Will you have saki, darling?*
I had certainly never taken a course
in foreign correspondences or the exotic
marriage of orange and gold possible   15
through sunny curtains.
     Yet here I lay
on a brightening plain, saying
arigato over and over
     until you   20
slid out of your pale kimono
of sleep and spoke to me in many tongues.

                  —1983

Gibbons Ruark (b. 1941)

Gibbons Ruark is a native of North Carolina. Ruark is the author of five collections of poetry. Passing Through Customs, *a volume of new and selected poems, appeared in 1999. He teaches at the University of Delaware.*

The Visitor

Holding the arm of his helper, the blind
Piano tuner comes to our piano.
He hesitates at first, but once he finds
The keyboard, his hands glide over the slow
Keys, ringing changes finer than the eye   5
Can see. The dusty wires he touches, row
On row, quiver like bowstrings as he
Twists them one notch tighter. He runs his
Finger along a wire, touches the dry
Rust to his tongue, breaks into a pure bliss   10
And tells us, "One year more of damp weather
Would have done you in, but I've saved it this
Time. Would one of you play now, please? I hear
It better at a distance." My wife plays
Stardust. The blind man stands and smiles in her   15
Direction, then disappears into the blaze
Of new October. Now the afternoon,
The long afternoon that blurs in a haze
Of music . . . Chopin nocturnes, *Clair de Lune,*
All the old familiar, unfamiliar   20
Music-lesson pieces, *Papa Haydn's*
Dead and gone, gently down the stream . . . Hours later,
After the latest car has doused its beams,
Has cooled down and stopped its ticking, I hear
Our cat, with the grace of animals free   25
To move in darkness, strike one key only,
And a single lucid drop of water stars my dream.

—1971

Gladys Cardiff (b. 1942)

Gladys Cardiff is a member of the Cherokee nation. "Combing" is taken from her first collection, To Frighten a Storm, *which was originally published in 1976.*

Combing

Bending, I bow my head
And lay my hand upon
Her hair, combing, and think
How women do this for
Each other. My daughter's hair   5
Curls against the comb,
Wet and fragrant—orange
Parings. Her face, downcast,
Is quiet for one so young.

I take her place. Beneath   10
My mother's hands I feel
The braids drawn up tight
As a piano wire and singing,
Vinegar-rinsed. Sitting
Before the oven I hear   15
The orange coils tick
The early hour before school.

She combed her grandmother
Mathilda's hair using
A comb made out of bone.   20
Mathilda rocked her oak wood
Chair, her face downcast,
Intent on tearing rags
In strips to braid a cotton
Rug from bits of orange   25
and brown. A simple act,

Preparing hair. Something
Women do for each other,
Plaiting the generations.

—*1976*

B. H. Fairchild (b. 1942)

B. H. Fairchild grew up in Liberal, Kansas, and his father's machine shop
provides the title and the setting for his prize-winning collection, The Art
of the Lathe. *Fairchild teaches at the California State University, San*
Bernardino. His most recent collection, Early Occult Memory Systems of
the Lower Midwest *(2002), won the National Book Critics Circle Award.*

Body and Soul

Half-numb, guzzling bourbon and Coke from coffee mugs,
our fathers fall in love with their own stories, nuzzling
the facts but mauling the truth, and my friend's father begins
to lay out with the slow ease of a blues ballad a story
about sandlot baseball in Commerce, Oklahoma decades ago.   5
These were men's teams, grown men, some in their thirties
and forties who worked together in zinc mines or on oil rigs,
sweat and khaki and long beers after work, steel guitar music
whanging in their ears, little white rent houses to return to
where their wives complained about money and broken
    Kenmores°   10
and then said the hell with it and sang *Body and Soul*
in the bathtub and later that evening with the kids asleep
lay in bed stroking their husband's wrist tattoo and smoking
Chesterfields from a fresh pack until everything was O.K.
Well, you get the idea. Life goes on, the next day is Sunday,   15
another ball game, and the other team shows up one man short.

They say, we're one man short, but can we use this boy,
he's only fifteen years old, and at least he'll make a game.
They take a look at the kid, muscular and kind of knowing
the way he holds his glove, with the shoulders loose,   20
the thick neck, but then with that boy's face under
a clump of angelic blonde hair, and say, oh, hell, sure,
let's play ball. So it all begins, the men loosening up,

10 **Kenmores** a brand of appliance

joking about the fat catcher's sex life, it's so bad
last night he had to hump his wife, that sort of thing,   25
pairing off into little games of catch that heat up into
throwing matches, the smack of the fungo bat, lazy jogging
into right field, big smiles and arcs of tobacco juice,
and the talk that gives a cool, easy feeling to the air,
talk among men normally silent, normally brittle and a little   30
angry with the empty promise of their lives. But they chatter
and say rock and fire, babe, easy out, and go right ahead
and pitch to the boy, but nothing fancy, just hard fastballs
right around the belt, and the kid takes the first two
but on the third pops the bat around so quick and sure   35
that they pause a moment before turning around to watch
the ball still rising and finally dropping far beyond
the abandoned tractor that marks left field. Holy shit.
They're pretty quiet watching him round the bases,
but then, what the hell, the kid knows how to hit a ball,   40
so what, let's play some goddamned baseball here.
And so it goes. The next time up, the boy gets a look
at a very nifty low curve, then a slider, and the next one
is the curve again, and he sends it over the Allis Chalmers,°
high and big and sweet. The left fielder just stands there,
    frozen.   45
As if this isn't enough, the next time up he bats left-handed.
They can't believe it, and the pitcher, a tall, mean-faced
man from Okarche who just doesn't give a shit anyway
because his wife ran off two years ago leaving him with
three little ones and a rusted-out Dodge with a cracked block,   50
leans in hard, looking at the fat catcher like he was the
    sonofabitch
who ran off with his wife, leans in and throws something
out of the dark, green hell of forbidden fastballs, something
that comes in at the knees and then leaps viciously towards
the kid's elbow. He swings exactly the way he did
    right-handed,   55
and they all turn like a chorus line toward deep right field
where the ball loses itself in sagebrush and the sad burnt
dust of dustbowl Oklahoma. It is something to see.

44 **Allis Chalmers** manufacturer of tractors and agricultural equipment

But why make a long story long: runs pile up on both sides,
the boy comes around five times, and five times the pitcher   60
is cursing both God and His mother as his chew of tobacco
    sours
into something resembling horse piss, and a ragged and bruised
Spalding baseball disappears into the far horizon. Goodnight,
Irene. They have lost the game and some painful side bets
and they have been suckered. And it means nothing to them   65
though it should to you when they are told the boy's name is
Mickey Mantle.° And that's the story and those are the facts.
But the facts are not the truth. I think, though, as I scan
the faces of these old men now lost in the innings of their
    youth,
I think I know what the truth of this story is, and I imagine   70
it lying there in the weeds behind that Allis Chalmers
just waiting for the obvious question to be asked: why, oh
why in hell didn't they just throw around the kid, walk him,
after he hit the third homer? Anybody would have,
especially nine men with disappointed wives and dirty socks   75
and diminishing expectations for whom winning at anything
meant everything. Men who know how to play the game,
who had talent when the other team had nothing except this
    ringer
who without a pitch to hit was meaningless, and they could go
    home
with their little two-dollar side bets and stride into the house   80
singing *If You've Got the Money, Honey, I've Got the Time*
with a bottle of Southern Comfort under their arms and grab
Dixie or May Ella up and dance across the gray linoleum
as if it were V-Day° all over again. But they did not.
And they did not because they were men, and this was a boy.   85
And they did not because sometimes after making love,
after smoking their Chesterfields in the cool silence and
listening to the big bands on the radio that sounded so glamorous,
so distant, they glanced over at their wives and noticed the lines
growing heavier around the eyes and mouth, felt what their
    wives   90

---

67 Mickey Mantle (1931–1995) Oklahoma-born baseball star   **84 V-Day** V-E Day (May 8, 1945)
marked the end of World War II in Europe; V-J Day (August 15, 1945) marked the end of the war in
the Pacific

felt: that Les Brown and Glenn Miller and all those dancing
    couples
and in fact all possibility of human gaiety and light-heartedness
were as far away and unreachable as Times Square or the Avalon
ballroom. They did not because of the gray linoleum lying there
in the half-dark, the free calendar from the local mortuary   95
that said one day was pretty much like another, the work gloves
looped over the doorknob like dead squirrels. And they did not
because they had gone through a depression and a war that had left
them with the idea that being a man in the eyes of their fathers
and everyone else had cost them just too goddamned much to
    lay it   100
at the feet of a fifteen year-old boy. And so they did not walk
    him,
and lost, but at least had some ragged remnant of themselves
to take back home. But there is one thing more, though it is not
a fact. When I see my friend's father staring hard into the bottomless
well of home plate as Mantle's fifth homer heads toward
    Arkansas,   105
I know that this man with the half-orphaned children and
worthless Dodge has also encountered for his first and possibly
only time that vast gap between talent and genius, has seen
as few have in the harsh light of an Oklahoma Sunday, the blonde
and blue-eyed bringer of truth, who will not easily be
    forgiven.   110

                —*1998*

Charles Martin (b. 1942)

Charles Martin is a lifelong resident of New York City. Martin has taught English as a second language for many years at Queensborough College. "E.S.L." appeared as a prefatory poem to Martin's sequence "Passages from Friday," an ironic retelling of the Robinson Crusoe story from his servant's point of view.

E.S.L.°

My frowning students carve
Me monsters out of prose:
This one—a gargoyle—thumbs its contemptuous nose
At how, in English, subject must agree
With verb—for any such agreement shows   5
    Too great a willingness to serve,
        A docility

    Which wiry Miss Choi
    Finds un-American.
She steals a hard look at me. I wink. Her grin   10
Is my reward. *In his will, our peace, our Pass:*
Gargoyle erased, subject and verb now in
    Agreement, reach object, enjoy
        Temporary truce.

    Tonight my students must   15
    Agree or disagree:
America is still a land of opportunity.
The answer is always, uniformly, *Yes*—even though
"It has no doubt that here were to much free,"
    As Miss Torrico will insist.   20
        She and I both know

    That Language binds us fast,
    And those of us without
Are bound and gagged by those within. Each fledgling
Polyglot must shake old habits: tapping her sneakered feet,   25

E.S.L. English as a Second Language

Miss Choi exorcises incensed ancestors, flout-
   ing the ghosts of her Chinese past.
       Writhing in the seat

   Next to Miss Choi, Mister
   Fedakis, in anguish   30
Labors to express himself in a tongue which
Proves *Linear B* to me, when I attempt to read it
Later. They're here for English as a Second Language,
   Which I'm teaching this semester.
       God knows they need it,   35

   And so, thank God, do they.
   The night's made easier
By our agreement: I am here to help deliver
Them into the good life they write me papers about.
English is pre-requisite for that endeavor,   40
   Explored in their nightly essays
       Boldly setting out

   To reconnoiter the fair
   New World they would enter:
Suburban Paradise, the endless shopping center   45
Where one may browse for hours before one chooses
Some new necessity—gold-flecked magenta
   Wallpaper to re-do the spare
       Bath no one uses,

   Or a machine which can,   50
   In seven seconds, crush
A newborn calf into such seamless mush
As a *mousse* might be made of—or our true sublime:
The gleaming counters where frosted cosmeticians brush
   Decades from the allotted span,   55
       Abrogating Time

   As the spring tide brushes
   A single sinister
Footprint from the otherwise unwrinkled shore
Of America the Blank. In absolute confusion   60
Poor Mister Fedakis rumbles with despair
   And puts the finishing smutches
       To his conclusion

While Miss Choi erases:
One more gargoyle routed.   65
Their pure, erroneous lines yield an illuminated
Map of the new found land. We will never arrive there,
Since it exists only in what we say about it,
As all the rest of my class is
Bound to discover.   70

—1987

Sharon Olds (b. 1942)

Sharon Olds displays a candor in dealing with the intimacies of family ro-
mance covering three generations that has made her one of the chief con-
temporary heirs to the confessional tradition. A powerful and dramatic
reader, she is much in demand on the lecture circuit. Born in San Fran-
cisco, she currently resides in New York City.

The One Girl at
the Boys Party

When I take my girl to the swimming party
I set her down among the boys. They tower and
bristle, she stands there smooth and sleek,
her math scores unfolding in the air around her.
They will strip to their suits, her body hard and   5
indivisible as a prime number,
they'll plunge into the deep end, she'll subtract
her height from ten feet, divide it into
hundreds of gallons of water, the numbers
bouncing in her mind like molecules of chlorine   10
in the bright blue pool. When they climb out,
her ponytail will hang its pencil lead
down her back, her narrow silk suit
with hamburgers and french fries printed on it
will glisten in the brilliant air, and they will   15
see her sweet face, solemn and

sealed, a factor of one, and she will
see their eyes, two each,
their legs, two each, and the curves of their sexes,
one each, and in her head she'll be doing her
wild multiplying, as the drops
sparkle and fall to the power of a thousand from her body.

Henry Taylor (b. 1942)

Henry Taylor is best known for The Flying Change, *which won the Pulitzer Prize in 1985, and* Understanding Fiction: Poems 1986–1996. *A noted horseman as well as poet, Taylor retired from teaching at American University in 2003.* Brief Candles, *the 2001 book from which the following three selections are taken, is a collection of clerihews, a light-verse form.*

from *Brief Candles*

Alexander Graham Bell
has shuffled off this mobile cell.
He's not talking any more,
but he has a lot to answer for.

*

Friedrich Nietzsche
strove vainly to reach a
steadfast decision
between Apollonian and Dionysian.

*

Judas Iscariot
missed the sweet chariot
but swung pretty low
in his wasteland of woe

—2001

from Brief Candles • 393

1983

20

l English teacher who now works
v Jersey State Council on the Arts
. She has received numerous
ed in many literary journals, but
Dress, *did not appear until 2003.*
'n read by Garrison Keillor sev-
e Writer's Almanac.

Discovers Poetry

Because my husband would not read my poems,
I wrote one about how I did not love him.
In lines of strict iambic pentameter,
I detailed his coldness, his lack of humor.
It felt good to do this.   5

Stanza by stanza, I grew bolder and bolder.
Towards the end, struck by inspiration,
I wrote about my old boyfriend,
a boy I had not loved enough to marry
but who could make me laugh and laugh.   10
I wrote about a night years after we parted
when my husband's coldness drove me from the house
and back to my old boyfriend.
I even included the name of a seedy motel
well-known for hosting quickies.   15
I have a talent for verisimilitude.

In sensuous images, I described
how my boyfriend and I stripped off our clothes,
got into bed, and kissed and kissed,
then spent half the night telling jokes,   20
many of them about my husband.
I left the ending deliberately ambiguous,
then hid the poem away
in an old trunk in the basement.

You know how this story ends,
how my husband one day loses something,
goes into the basement,
and rummages through the old trunk,
how he uncovers the hidden poem
and sits down to read it.   30

But do you hear the strange sounds
that floated up the stairs that day,
the sounds of an animal, its paw caught
in one of those traps with teeth of steel?
Do you see the wounded creature   35
at the bottom of the stairs,
his shoulders hunched over and shaking,
fist in his mouth and choking back sobs?
It was my husband paying tribute to my art.

—2003

Ellen Bryant Voigt (b. 1943)

*Ellen Bryant Voigt is a native of Virginia. Voigt was trained as a concert
pianist before earning her creative writing degree from the University of
Iowa. She has taught poetry at a number of colleges in New England and
the South.*

Daughter

There is one grief worse than any other.

When your small feverish throat clogged, and quit,
I knelt beside the chair on the green rug
and shook you and shook you,
but the only sound was mine shouting you back,   5
the delicate curls at your temples,
the blue wool blanket,
your face blue,
your jaw clamped against remedy—

how could I put a knife to that white neck?   10
With you in my lap,

hands fluttering like flags,
bend instead over your dead weight
to administer a kiss so urgent, so ruthless,
pumping breath into your stilled body,   15
counting out the rhythm for how long until
the second birth, the second cry
oh Jesus that sudden noisy musical inhalation
that leaves me stunned
by your survival.   20

—1983

Robert Morgan (b. 1944)

*Robert Morgan is a native of the mountains of North Carolina, and has
retained a large measure of regional ties in his poetry. One of his collections,* Sigodlin, *takes its title from an Appalachian word for things that are
built slightly out of square.* Gap Creek: The Story of a Marriage, *a novel
of turn-of-the-century mountain life, was a bestseller in 2000.*

Mountain Bride

They say Revis found a flatrock
on the ridge just
perfect for a natural hearth,
and built his cabin with a stick

and clay chimney right over it.   5
On their wedding night he lit
the fireplace to dry away the mountain
chill of late spring, and flung on

applewood to dye
the room with molten color while   10
he and Martha that was a Parrish
warmed the sheets between the tick

stuffed with leaves and its feather
cover. Under that wide hearth
a nest of rattlers,   15
they'll knot a hundred together,

had wintered and were coming awake.
The warming rock
flushed them out early.
It was she   20

who wakened to their singing near
the embers and roused him to go look.
Before he reached the fire
more than a dozen struck

and he died yelling her to stay   25
on the big four-poster.
Her uncle coming up the hollow
with a gift bearham two days later

found her shivering there
marooned above a pool   30
of hungry snakes,
and the body beginning to swell.

—1979

Craig Raine (b. 1944)

*Craig Raine early in his career displayed a comic surrealism that was re-
sponsible for so many imitations that critic James Fenton dubbed him the
founder of the "Martian School" of contemporary poetry. Born in Bishop
Auckland, England, and educated at Oxford, Raine is publisher of the literary magazine* Arete.

A Martian Sends a Postcard Home

Caxtons° are mechanical birds with many wings
and some are treasured for their markings—

they cause the eyes to melt
or the body to shriek without pain.

---

1 **Caxtons** i.e., books after William Caxton (1422–1491), first English printer

I have never seen one fly, but   5
sometimes they perch on the hand.

Mist is when the sky is tired of flight
and rests its soft machine on ground:

then the world is dim and bookish
like engravings under tissue paper.   10

Rain is when the earth is television.
It has the property of making colours darker.

Model T is a room with the lock inside—
a key is turned to free the world

for movement, so quick there is a film   15
to watch for anything missed.

But time is tied to the wrist
or kept in a box, ticking with impatience.

In homes, a haunted apparatus sleeps,
that snores when you pick it up.   20

If the ghost cries, they carry it
to their lips and soothe it to sleep

with sounds. And yet, they wake it up
deliberately, by tickling with a finger.

Only the young are allowed to suffer   25
openly. Adults go to a punishment room

with water but nothing to eat.
They lock the door and suffer the noises

alone. No one is exempt
and everyone's pain has a different smell.   30

At night, when all the colours die,
they hide in pairs

and read about themselves—
in colour, with their eyelids shut.

—1978

Enid Shomer (b. 1944)

Enid Shomer grew up in Washington, D.C., and lived for a number of years in Florida. Her first collection, Stalking the Florida Panther *(1987), explored both the Jewish traditions of her childhood and her adult attachment to her adopted state. In recent years she has published* Imaginary Men, *a collection of short stories, and* Black Drum, *a collection of poetry.*

Women Bathing at Bergen-Belsen°

April 24, 1945

Twelve hours after the Allies arrive
there is hot water, soap. Two women bathe
in a makeshift, open-air shower while nearby
fifteen thousand are flung naked into mass graves
by captured SS guards. Clearly legs and arms   5
are the natural handles of a corpse. The bathers,
taken late in the war, still have flesh
on their bones, still have breasts. Though nudity was
a death sentence here, they have undressed,
oblivious to the soldiers and the cameras.   10
The corpses push through the limed earth like upended
headstones. The bathers scrub their feet, bending
in beautiful curves, mapping the contours
of the body, that kingdom to which they've returned.

—*1987*

Bergen-Belsen German concentration camp in WWII

Wendy Cope (b. 1945)

Wendy Cope says, "I hardly ever tire of love or rhyme. / That's why I'm poor and have a rotten time." Her first collection, Making Cocoa for Kingsley Amis *(1986), was a bestseller in England. Whether reducing T. S. Eliot's modernist classic "The Waste Land" to a set of five limericks or chronicling the life and loves of Jason Strugnell, her feckless poetic alterego, Cope remains one of the wisest and wittiest poets writing today. "I dislike the term 'light verse' because it is used as a way of dismissing poets who allow humor into their work. I believe that a humorous poem can also be 'serious'; deeply felt and saying something that matters." She lives in Winchester, England.*

Rondeau Redoublé

There are so many kinds of awful men—
One can't avoid them all. She often said
She'd never make the same mistake again:
She always made a new mistake instead.

The chinless type who made her feel ill-bred;   5
The practised charmer, less than charming when
He talked about the wife and kids and fled—
There are so many kinds of awful men.

The half-crazed hippy, deeply into Zen,
Whose cryptic homilies she came to dread;   10
The fervent youth who worshipped Tony Benn°—
'One can't avoid them all,' she often said.

The ageing banker, rich and overfed,
who held forth on the dollar and the yen—
Though there were many more mistakes ahead,   15
She'd never make the same mistake again.

The budding poet, scribbling in his den
Odes not to her but to his pussy, Fred;
The drunk who fell asleep at nine or ten—
She always made a new mistake instead.   20

11 **Tony Benn** British politician of the 1960s

And so the gambler was at least unwed
And didn't preach or sneer or wield a pen
Or hoard his wealth or take the Scotch to bed.
She'd lived and learned and lived and learned but then
There are so many kinds.   25

—1986

Triolet

I used to think all poets were Byronic—
Mad, bad and dangerous to know.
And then I met a few. Yes it's ironic—
I used to think all poets were Byronic.
They're mostly wicked as a ginless tonic   5
And wild as pension plans. Not long ago
I used to think all poets were Byronic—
Mad, bad and dangerous to know.

—1986

Dick Davis (b. 1945)

Dick Davis was born in Portsmouth, England, and, following graduation from Cambridge and the University of Manchester, taught for many years in England and in Iran. A scholar and translator as well as a poet, he came to the United States in the 1980s and is currently a professor of Persian at Ohio State University.

A Monorhyme for the Shower

Lifting her arms to soap her hair
Her pretty breasts respond—and there
The movement of that buoyant pair
Is like a spell to make me swear

Twenty-odd years have turned to air;   5
Now she's the girl I didn't dare
Approach, ask out, much less declare
My love to, mired in young despair.

Childbearing, rows, domestic care—
All the prosaic wear and tear   10
That constitute the life we share—
Slip from her beautiful and bare
Bright body as, made half aware
Of my quick surreptitious stare,
She wrings the water from her hair   15
And turning smiles to see me there.

                                                                —*2002*

Kay Ryan   (b. 1945)

*Kay Ryan has taught for many years in California. She published her first
collection at the age of thirty-eight in 1983, and her poems have appeared
in four subsequent books and numerous appearances in* Poetry *and the*
New Yorker. *Ryan has often been compared to Emily Dickinson and Marianne Moore for her attention to details from the natural world and for
her gentle, often witty moralizing.*

Bestiary

A bestiary catalogs
bests. The mediocres
both higher and lower
are suppressed in favor
of the singularly savage   5
or clever, the spectacularly
pincered, the archest
of the arch deceivers
who press their advantage
without quarter even after   10
they've won as of course they would.
Best is not to be confused with *good*—
a different creature altogether,

and treated of in the goodiary—
a text alas lost now for centuries.   15

—1996

Leon Stokesbury   (b. 1945)

Leon Stokesbury, as an undergraduate at Lamar State College of Technology (now Lamar University), was acquainted with the legendary singer Janis Joplin, the subject of "Evening's End 1943–1970." The author of three collections of poetry, including Autumn Rhythm: New and Selected Poems, *Stokesbury has also edited anthologies of contemporary Southern poetry and the poetry of World War II.*

Evening's End 1943–1970

For the first time in what must be
the better part of two years now
I happened to hear Janis
in her glory—
all that tinctured syrup   5
dripping off
a razorblade—
on the radio today singing "Summertime."

And it took me back to this girl I knew,
a woman really, my first year   10
writing undergraduate poetry
at the Mirabeau B. Lamar
State College of Technology
in Beaumont, Texas,
back in 1966.   15

This woman was the latest in a line,
the latest steady
of my friend John Coyle that spring—
and I remember she was plain:
she was short: and plain   20
and wore her brown hair up

in a sort of bun in back
that made her plainer still.

I don't know where John met her,
but word went round   25
she had moved back in with Mom and Dad
down in Port Arthur
to get her head straight,
to attend Lamar,
to study History,   30
after several years in San Francisco
where she had drifted
into a "bad scene"
taking heroin.

I was twenty,   35
still lived with Mom and Dad myself,
and so knew nothing
about "bad scenes,"
but I do remember once or twice
each month that spring   40
John would give a party
with this woman always there.
And always as the evening's end came on
this woman, silent for hours,
would reveal, from thin air,   45
her guitar,
settle in a chair,
release her long hair
from the bun it was in,
and begin.   50

Her hair flowed over her shoulders,
and the ends of the strands of hair
like tarnished brass in lamplight
would brush and drag across
the sides of the guitar   55
as this woman bent
over it.

How low and guttural, how
slow and torchlit, how

amber her song, how absolutely   60
unlike the tiny nondescript
a few minutes before.

And I remember also,
from later on that spring,
from May of that year,   65
two nights in particular.

The first night was a party
this woman gave
at her parents' home.
Her parents' home   70
was beige:
the bricks the parents' home
was built with
were beige.
The entire house was carpeted   75
in beige.

John's girl greeted everyone at the door,
a martini in one hand
and a lit cigarette
in an Oriental   80
ivory cigarette holder in the other,
laughing
for once, and tossing back
her long brown hair.

All the women wore   85
black full-length party dresses—
and I remember the young woman's father,
how odd he seemed
in his charcoal suit and tie,
his gray hair—   90
how unamused.

Then John Coyle was drunk.
He spilled his beer
across the beige frontroom carpet:
that darker dampness sinking in,   95
the father vanished
from the scene.

The next week we double-dated.
I convinced John and his girl
to see a double feature,
Irma La Douce and *Tom Jones*,   100
at the Pines Theatre.

And I can recall John's girl
saying just one thing that night.

After the films, John was quizzical,   105
contentious, full of ridicule
for movies I had guaranteed he would enjoy.
He turned and asked her
what she thought—
and in the softest   110
of tones, a vague rumor
of honeysuckle in the air,
she almost whispered,
"I thought they were beautiful."

That was the last time I saw her,   115
the last thing that I heard her say.

A few weeks later,
she drove over to John's house
in the middle of the afternoon,
and caught him in bed   120
with Suzanne Morain,
a graduate assistant
from the English Department at Lamar.

John told me later
that when she saw them in the bedroom   125
she ran into the kitchen,
picked up a broom,
and began to sweep the floor—
weeping.

When John sauntered in   130
she threw the broom at him,
ran out the door,
got in her car and drove away.
And from that day on,
no one ever saw that woman   135
in Beaumont again.

The next day she moved to Austin.
And later on, I heard,
back to San Francisco.
And I remember when John told me this,   140
with a semi-shocked expression
on his face, he turned
and looked up, and said, "You know,
I guess she must have really *loved* me."

I was twenty years old.   145
What did I know?
What could I say?

I could not think
of anything to say,
except, "Yes,   150
I guess so."

It was summertime.

Thus runs the world away.

—*1996*

Marilyn Nelson (b. 1946)

Marilyn Nelson is the author of The Homeplace, *a sequence of poems on family history. The* Homeplace *is remarkable for its sensitive exploration of the mixed white and black bloodlines in the poet's family history.* Carver: A Life in Poems, *a poetic biography of George Washington Carver, appeared in 2001 and won a National Book Award.*

The Ballad of Aunt Geneva

Geneva was the wild one.
Geneva was a tart.
Geneva met a blue-eyed boy
and gave away her heart.

Geneva ran a roadhouse.   5
Geneva wasn't sent
to college like the others:
Pomp's pride her punishment.

She cooked out on the river,
watching the shore slide by,   10
her lips pursed into hardness,
her deep-set brown eyes dry.

They say she killed a woman
over a good black man
by braining the jealous heifer   15
with an iron frying pan.

They say, when she was eighty,
she got up late at night
and sneaked her old, white lover in
to make love, and to fight.   20

First, they heard the tell-tale
singing of the springs,
then Geneva's voice rang out:
I need to buy some things,

So next time, bring more money.   25
And bring more moxie, too.
I ain't got no time to waste
on limp white mens like you.

Oh yeah? Well, Mister White Man,
it sure might be stone-white,   30
but my thing's white as it is.
And you know damn well I'm right.

Now listen: take your heart pills
and pay the doctor mind.
If you up and die on me,   35
I'll whip your white behind.

They tiptoed through the parlor
on heavy, time-slowed feet.
She watched him, from her front door,
walk down the dawnlit street.   40

Geneva was the wild one.
Geneva was a tart.
Geneva met a blue-eyed boy
and gave away her heart.

—1990

Ai (b. 1947)

*Ai has written a number of realistic dramatic monologues that often reveal
the agonies of characters trapped in unfulfilling or even dangerous lives.
With her gallery of social misfits, she is the contemporary heir to the tradition begun by Robert Browning.*

Child Beater

Outside, the rain, pinafore of gray water, dresses the town
and I stroke the leather belt,
as she sits in the rocking chair,
holding a crushed paper cup to her lips.
I yell at her, but she keeps rocking;   5
back, her eyes open, forward, they close.
Her body, somehow fat, though I feed her only once a day,
reminds me of my own just after she was born.
It's been seven years, but I still can't forget how I felt.
How heavy it feels to look at her.   10

I lay the belt on a chair
and get her dinner bowl.
I hit the spoon against it, set it down
and watch her crawl to it,
pausing after each forward thrust of her legs   15
and when she takes her first bite,
I grab the belt and beat her across the back
until her tears, beads of salt-filled glass, falling,
shatter on the floor.

I move off. I let her eat,   20
while I get my dog's chain leash from the closet.

I whirl it around my head.
O daughter, so far, you've only had a taste of icing,
are you ready now for some cake?

—1973

Jim Hall (b. 1947)

*Jim Hall is one of the most brilliantly inventive comic poets in recent
years. He has also written a successful series of crime novels set in his native south Florida, beginning with* Under Cover of Daylight *in 1987.*

Maybe Dats Your Pwoblem Too

All my pwoblems,
who knows, maybe evwybody's pwoblems
is due to da fact, due to da awful twuth
dat I am SPIDERMAN.

I know, I know. All da dumb jokes: 5
No flies on you, ha ha,
and da ones about what do I do wit all
doze extwa legs in bed. Well, dat's funny yeah.
But you twy being
SPIDERMAN for a month or two. Go ahead.   10

You get doze cwazy calls fwom da
Gubbener askin you to twap some booglar who's
only twying to wip off color T.V. sets.
Now, what do I cawre about T.V. sets?
But I pull on da suit, da stinkin suit,   15
wit da sucker cups on da fingers,
and get my wopes and wittle bundle of
equipment and den I go flying like cwazy
acwoss da town fwom woof top to woof top.

Till der he is. Some poor dumb color T.V. slob   20
and I fall on him and we westle a widdle
until I get him all woped. So big deal.

You tink when you SPIDERMAN
der's sometin big going to happen to you.
Well, I tell you what. It don't happen dat way.   25
Nuttin happens. Gubbener calls, I go.
Bwing him to powice, Gubbener calls again,
like dat ovei and over.
I tink I twy sometin diffunt. I tink I twy
sometin excitin like wacing cawrs. Sometin to make   30
my heart beat at a difwent wate.
But den you just can't quit being sometin like
SPIDERMAN.
You SPIDERMAN for life. Fowever. I can't even
buin my suit. It won't buin. It's fwame wesistent.   35
So maybe dat's youwr pwoblem too, who knows.
Maybe dat's da whole pwoblem wif evwytin.
Nobody can buin der suits, dey all fwame wesistent.
Who knows?

—1980

Yusef Komunyakaa (b. 1947)

*Yusef Komunyakaa is a native of Bogulusa, Louisiana. Komunyakaa has
written memorably on a wide range of subjects, including jazz and his service during the Vietnam War.* Neon Vernacular: New and Selected Poems
(1993) won the Pulitzer Prize in 1994, and Pleasure Dome: New and Collected Poems *appeared in 2001.*

Facing It

My black face fades,
hiding inside the black granite.
I said I wouldn't,
dammit: No tears.
I'm stone. I'm flesh.   5
My clouded reflection eyes me
like a bird of prey, the profile of night
slanted against morning. I turn
this way—the stone lets me go.

I turn this way—I'm inside   10
the Vietnam Veterans Memorial
again, depending on the light
to make a difference.
I go down the 58,022 names,
half-expecting to find   15
my own in letters like smoke.
I touch the name Andrew Johnson;
I see the booby trap's white flash.
Names shimmer on a woman's blouse
but when she walks away   20
the names stay on the wall.
Brushstrokes flash, a red bird's
wings cutting across my stare.
The sky. A plane in the sky.
A white vet's image floats   25
closer to me, then his pale eyes
look through mine. I'm a window.
He's lost his right arm
inside the stone. In the black mirror
a woman's trying to erase names: 30
No, she's brushing a boy's hair.

—1988

R. S. Gwynn (b. 1948)

R. S. Gwynn is the editor of this volume and (with Dana Gioia) of The Longman Anthology of Short Fiction. *He teaches at Lamar University.* No Word of Farewell: Selected Poems 1970–2000 *appeared in 2001.*

Approaching a Significant Birthday, He Peruses an Anthology of Poetry

All human things are subject to decay.
Beauty is momentary in the mind.
The curfew tolls the knell of parting day.
If Winter comes, can Spring be far behind?

Forlorn! the very word is like a bell   5
And somewhat of a sad perplexity.
Here, take my picture, though I bid farewell;
In a dark time the eye begins to see

The woods decay, the woods decay and fall—
Bare ruined choirs where late the sweet birds sing.   10
What but design of darkness to appall?
An aged man is but a paltry thing.

If I should die, think only this of me:
Crass casualty obstructs the sun and rain
When I have fears that I may cease to be,   15
To cease upon the midnight with no pain

And hear the spectral singing of the moon
And strictly meditate the thankless muse.
The world is too much with us, late and soon.
It gathers to a greatness, like the ooze.   20

Do not go gentle into the good night.
Fame is no plant that grows on mortal soil.
Again he raised the jug up to the light:
Old age hath yet his honor and his toil.

Downward to darkness on extended wings, 25
Break, break, break, on thy cold gray stones, O Sea,
and tell sad stories of the death of kings.
I do not think that they will sing to me.

—*1990*

Timothy Steele (b. 1948)

*Timothy Steele has written a successful scholarly study of the rise of free
verse,* Missing Measures, *and is perhaps the most skillful craftsman of the
contemporary New Formalist poets. Born in Vermont, he has lived for a
number of years in Los Angeles, where he teaches at California State University, Los Angeles.*

Sapphics° Against Anger

Angered, may I be near a glass of water;
May my first impulse be to think of Silence,
Its deities (who are they? do, in fact, they
        Exist? etc.).

May I recall what Aristotle says of   5
The subject: to give vent to rage is not to
Release it but to be increasingly prone
        To its incursions.

May I imagine being in the Inferno,
Hearing it asked: "Virgilio mio,° who's   10
That sulking with Achilles there?" and hearing
        Virgil say: "Dante,

That fellow, at the slightest provocation,
Slammed phone receivers down, and waved his arms like
A madman. What Attila did to Europe,   15
        What Genghis Khan did

To Asia, that poor dope did to his marriage."
May I, that is, put learning to good purpose,

Sapphics stanza form named after Sappho (c. 650 BC)   10 Virgilio mio Dante is addressing Virgil, his guide through hell.

Mindful that melancholy is a sin, though
    Stylish at present.   20

Better than rage is the post-dinner quiet,
The sink's warm turbulence, the streaming platters,
The suds rehearsing down the drain in spirals
    In the last rinsing.

For what is, after all, the good life save that   25
Conducted thoughtfully, and what is passion
If not the holiest of powers, sustaining
    Only if mastered.

                                     —1986

James Fenton   (b. 1949)

James Fenton was born in Lincoln, England, and educated at Oxford. Fenton has worked extensively as a book and drama critic. A brilliant satirical poet, he has also written lyrics for Les Misérables, *the musical version of Victor Hugo's novel, and has served as a journalist in Asia.*

God, a Poem

A nasty surprise in a sandwich,
A drawing-pin caught in your sock,
The limpest of shakes from a hand which
You'd thought would be firm as a rock,

A serious mistake in a nightie,   5
A grave disappointment all around
Is all that you'll get from th'Almighty.
Is all that you'll get underground.

Oh, he *said:* 'If you lay off the crumpet°
I'll see you alright in the end.   10

---

9 crumpet vulgar British slang for women

Just hang on until the last trumpet.
Have faith in me, chum—I'm your friend.'

But if you remind him, he'll tell you:
'I'm sorry, I must have been pissed—°
Though your name rings a sort of a bell. You   15
Should have guessed that I do not exist.

'I didn't exist at Creation,
I didn't exist at the Flood.
And I won't be around for Salvation
To sort out the sheep from the cud—   20

'Or whatever the phrase is. The fact is
In soteriological° terms
I'm a crude existential malpractice
And you are a diet of worms.

'You're a nasty surprise in a sandwich.   25
You're a drawing-pin caught in my sock.
You're the limpest of shakes from a hand which
I'd have thought would be firm as a rock,

'You're a serious mistake in a nightie,
You're a grave disappointment all round—   30
That's all that you are,' says th'Almighty,
'And that's all that you'll be underground.'

                                                        —*1983*

14 pissed drunk   **22 soteriological** relation to salvation

Sarah Cortez (b. 1950)

Sarah Cortez grew up in Houston, Texas, and holds degrees in psychology and religion, classical studies, and accounting. She also serves as Visiting Scholar at the University of Houston's Center for Mexican-American Studies. She is a deputy constable in Harris County, Texas.

Tu Negrito

She's got to bail me out,
he says into the phone outside the holding cell.
She's going there tomorrow anyway for Mikey.
Tell her she's got to do this for me.

He says into the phone outside the holding cell,   5
Make sure she listens. Make her feel guilty, man.
Tell her she's got to do this for me.
She can have all my money, man.

Make sure she listens. Make her feel guilty, man.
Tell her she didn't bail me out the other times.   10
She can have all my money, man.
She always bails out Mikey.

Tell her she didn't bail me out the other times.
I don't got no one else to call, cousin.
She always bails out Mikey.   15
Make sure you write all this down, cousin.

I don't got no one else to call, cousin.
I really need her now.
Make sure you write this all down, cousin.
Page her. Put in code 333. That's me.   20

I really need her now.
Write down "Mommie." Change it from "Mom."
Page her. Put in code 333. That's me.
Write down *"Tu Negrito."* Tell her I love her.

Write down "Mommie." Change it from "Mom."   25
I'm her littlest. Remind her.

Write down *"Tu Negrito."*
Tell her I love her. She's got to bail me out.

—*2000*

Carolyn Forché (b. 1950)

Carolyn Forché won the Yale Younger Poets Award for her first collection, Gathering the Tribes *(1975).* The Country Between Us, *Forché's second collection, contains poems based on the poet's experiences in the war-torn country of El Salvador in the early 1980s.*

The Colonel

What you have heard is true. I was in his house.° His wife carried a tray of coffee and sugar. His daughter filed her nails, his son went out for the night. There were daily papers, pet dogs, a pistol on the cushion beside him. The moon swung bare on its black cord over the house. On the television was a cop show. It was in English. Broken bottles were embedded in the walls around the house to scoop the kneecaps from a man's legs or cut his hands to lace. On the windows there were gratings like those in liquor stores. We had dinner, rack of lamb, good wine, a gold bell was on the table for calling the maid. The maid brought green mangoes, salt, a type of bread. I was asked how I enjoyed the country. There was a brief commercial in Spanish. His wife took everything away. There was some talk then of how difficult it had become to govern. The parrot said hello on the terrace. The colonel told it to shut up, and pushed himself from the table. My friend said to me with his eyes: say nothing. The colonel returned with a sack used to bring groceries home. He spilled many human ears on the table. They were like dried peach halves. There is no other way to say this. He took one of them in his hands, shook it in our faces, dropped it into a water glass. It came alive there. I am tired of fooling around he said. As for the rights of anyone, tell your people they can go fuck themselves. He swept the ears to the floor with his arm and held the last of his wine in the air. Something for your poetry, no? he

1 **his house** in El Salvador

said. Some of the ears on the floor caught this scrap of his voice. Some of the cars on the floor were pressed to the ground.

—1978

Dana Gioia (b. 1950)

Dana Gioia grew up in the suburbs of Los Angeles. He took a graduate degree in English from Harvard but made a successful career in business before devoting his full time to writing. The editor of several textbooks and anthologies, he is also an influential critic whose essay "Can Poetry Matter?" stimulated much discussion when it appeared in The Atlantic. In-*terrogations at Noon,* his third collection of poetry, appeared in 2001. *Gioia became chairman of the National Endowment for the Arts in 2002.*

Planting a Sequoia

All afternoon my brothers and I have worked in the orchard,
Digging this hole, laying you into it, carefully packing the soil.
Rain blackened the horizon, but cold winds kept it over the Pacific,
And the sky above us stayed the dull gray
Of an old year coming to an end.   5

In Sicily a father plants a tree to celebrate his first son's birth—
An olive or a fig tree—a sign that the earth has one more life to bear.
I would have done the same, proudly laying new stock into my father's
     orchard,
A green sapling rising among the twisted apple boughs,
A promise of new fruit in other autumns.   10

But today we kneel in the cold planting you, our native giant,
Defying the practical custom of our fathers,
Wrapping in your roots a lock of hair, a piece of an infant's birth cord,
All that remains above earth of a first-born son,
A few stray atoms brought back to the elements.   15

We will give you what we can—our labor and our soil,
Water drawn from the earth when the skies fail,
Nights scented with the ocean fog, days softened by the circuit of bees.
We plant you in the corner of the grove, bathed in western light,
A slender shoot against the sunset.   20

And when our family is no more, all of his unborn brothers dead,
Every niece and nephew scattered, the house torn down,
His mother's beauty ashes in the air,
I want you to stand among strangers, all young and ephemeral to you,
Silently keeping the secret of your birth.   25

                                                            —*1991*

Rodney Jones (b. 1950)

*Rodney Jones was born in Alabama and received important national atten-
tion when* Transparent Gestures *won the Poets' Prize in 1990. Like many
younger southern poets, he often deals with the difficult legacy of racism
and the adjustments that a new era have forced on both whites and blacks.*

Winter Retreat: Homage to Martin Luther King, Jr.

There is a hotel in Baltimore where we came together,
we black and white educated and educators,
for a week of conferences, for important counsel
sanctioned by the DOE° and the Carter administration,
to make certain difficult inquiries, to collate notes   5
on the instruction of the disabled, the deprived,
the poor, who do not score well on entrance tests,
who, failing school, must go with mop and pail
skittering across the slick floors of cafeterias,
or climb dewy girders to balance high above cities,   10
or, jobless, line up in the bone cold. We felt
substantive burdens lighter if we stated it right.
Very delicately, we spoke in turn. We walked
together beside the still waters of behaviorism.
Armed with graphs and charts, with new strategies   15
to devise objectives and determine accountability,
we empathetic black and white shone in seminar rooms.
We enunciated every word clearly and without accent.

4 DOE Department of Education

We moved very carefully in the valley of the shadow
of the darkest agreement error. We did not digress.   20
We ascended the trunk of that loftiest cypress
of Latin grammar the priests could never
successfully graft onto the rough green chestnut
of the English language. We extended ourselves
with that sinuous motion of the tongue that is half   25
pain and almost eloquence. We black and white
politely reprioritized the parameters of our agenda
to impact equitably on the Seminole and the Eskimo.
We praised diversity and involvement, the sacrifices
of fathers and mothers. We praised the next white   30
Gwendolyn Brooks° and the next black Robert Burns.°
We deep made friends. In that hotel we glistened
over the *pommes au gratin*° and the *poitrine de veau.*°
The morsels of lamb flamed near where we talked.
The waiters bowed and disappeared among the ferns.   35
And there is a bar there, there is a large pool.
Beyond the tables of the drinkers and raconteurs,
beyond the hot tub brimming with Lebanese tourists
and the women in expensive bathing suits doing laps,
if you dive down four feet, swim out far enough,   40
and emerge on the other side, it is sixteen degrees.
It is sudden and very beautiful and colder
than thought, though the air frightens you at first,
not because it is cold, but because it is visible,
almost palpable, in the fog that rises from difference.   45
While I stood there in the cheek-numbing snow,
all Baltimore was turning blue. And what I remember
of that week of talks is nothing the record shows,
but the revelation outside, which was the city
many came to out of the fields, then the thought   50
that we had wanted to make the world kinder,
but, in speaking proudly, we had failed a vision.

—1989

---

31 **Gwendolyn Brooks** African-American poet (1917–2000)   **Robert Burns** Scottish poet (1759–
1796)   33 *pommes au gratin* potatoes baked with cheese   *poitrine de veau* brisket of veal

Timothy Murphy (b. 1951)

Timothy Murphy, a former student of Robert Penn Warren at Yale, returned to his native North Dakota to make a career as a venture capitalist in the agricultural field. Unpublished until his mid-forties, Murphy has brought four collections to print during the last decade.

Case Notes

for Dr. Richard Kolotkin

MARCH 7, 2002

Raped at an early age
by older altar boy.
"Damned by the Church to Hell,
never to sire a son,
perhaps man's greatest joy,"   5
said father in a rage.
Patient was twenty-one.
Handled it pretty well.

MARCH 14, 2002

Curiously, have learned
patient was Eagle Scout.   10
Outraged that Scouts have spurned
each camper who is "out."
Questioned if taunts endured
are buried? "No, immured."

MARCH 21, 2002

Immersed in verse and drink   15
when he was just sixteen,
turned to drugs at Yale.
Patient began to sink,
to fear he was a "queen,"
a "queer" condemned to fail   20
or detox in a jail.

APRIL 1, 2002

Into a straight town
he brought a sober lover.
"Worked smarter, drank harder
to stock an empty larder,"   25
wrote poetry, the cover
for grief he cannot drown.

APRIL 9, 2002

Uneasy with late father,
feared for by his mother,
lover, and younger brother.   30
Various neuroses,
but no severe psychosis.
Precarious prognosis.

—2004

Joy Harjo (b. 1951)

Joy Harjo, a member of the Creek tribe, is one of the leading voices of contemporary Native American poetry. She is a powerful performer and was one of the poets featured on Bill Moyers's television series, The Power of the Word.

She Had Some Horses

She had some horses.
She had horses who were bodies of sand.
She had horses who were maps drawn of blood.
She had horses who were skins of ocean water.
She had horses who were the blue air of sky.   5
She had horses who were fur and teeth.
She had horses who were clay and would break.
She had horses who were splintered red cliff.

She had some horses.

She had horses with eyes of trains.   10
She had horses with full brown thighs.

She had horses who laughed too much.
She had horses who threw rocks at glass houses.
She had horses who licked razor blades.

She had some horses.   15

She had horses who danced in their mother's arms.
She had horses who thought they were the sun and
their bodies shone and burned like stars.
She had horses who waltzed nightly on the moon.
She had horses who were much too shy, and kept quiet   20
in stalls of their own making.

She had some horses.

She had horses who liked Creek Stomp Dance songs.
She had horses who cried in their beer.
She had horses who spit at male queens who made   25
them afraid of themselves.
She had horses who said they weren't afraid.
She had horses who lied.
She had horses who told the truth, who were stripped
bare of their tongues.   30

She had some horses.

She had horses who called themselves "horse."
She had horses who called themselves "spirit,"
and kept their voices secret and to themselves.
She had horses who had no names.   35
She had horses who had books of names.

She had some horses.

She had horses who whispered in the dark, who were afraid to speak.
She had horses who screamed out of fear of the silence,
who carried knives to protect themselves from ghosts.   40
She had horses who waited for destruction.
She had horses who waited for resurrection.

She had some horses.

She had horses who got down on their knees for any savior.
She had horses who thought their high price had saved them. 45
She had horses who tried to save her,
who climbed in her bed at night and prayed as they raped her.

She had some horses.

She had some horses she loved.
She had some horses she hated.   50

They were the same horses.

—1983

Andrew Hudgins (b. 1951)

*Andrew Hudgins, reared in Montgomery, Alabama, has demonstrated his
poetic skills in a wide variety of poems, including a book-length sequence
of dramatic monologues,* After the Lost War, *in the voice of Sidney Lanier,
the greatest Southern poet of the late nineteenth century.*

Air View of an
Industrial Scene

There is a train at the ramp, unloading people
who stumble from the cars and toward the gate.
The building's shadows tilt across the ground
and from each shadow juts a longer one
and from that shadow crawls a shadow of smoke   5
black as just-plowed earth. Inside the gate
is a small garden and someone on his knees.
Perhaps he's fingering the yellow blooms
to see which ones have set and will soon wither,
clinging to a green tomato as it swells.   10
The people hold back, but are forced to the open gate,
and when they enter they will see the garden
and some, gardeners themselves, will yearn
to fall to their knees there, untangling vines,
plucking at weeds, cooling their hands in damp earth.   15
They're going to die soon, a matter of minutes.
Even from our height, we see in the photograph
the shadow of the plane stamped dark and large
on Birkenau,° one black wing shading the garden.

---

19 **Birkenau** German concentration camp in World War II

We can't tell which are guards, which prisoners.   20
We're watchers. But if we had bombs we'd drop them.

—*1985*

Judith Ortiz Cofer (b. 1952)

*Judith Ortiz Cofer was born in Puerto Rico, the daughter of a member of
the United States Navy, and came to the United States at the age of four,
when her father was posted to the Brooklyn Naval Yard. After college, she
studied at Oxford and began her teaching career in the United States. A
skilled writer of fiction and autobiography, she published* The Year of Our
Revolution: New and Selected Stories and Poems *in 1998.*

The Latin Deli:
An Ars Poetica

Presiding over a formica counter,
plastic Mother and Child magnetized
to the top of an ancient register,
the heady mix of smells from the open bins
of dried codfish, the green plantains   5
hanging in stalks like votive offerings,
she is the Patroness of Exiles,
a woman of no-age who was never pretty,
who spends her days selling canned memories
while listening to the Puerto Ricans complain   10
that it would be cheaper to fly to San Juan
than to buy a pound of Bustelo coffee here,
and to Cubans perfecting their speech
of a "glorious return" to Havana—where no one
has been allowed to die and nothing to change until then,   15
to Mexicans who pass through, talking lyrically
of *dólares* to be made in El Norte—
                              all wanting the comfort
of spoken Spanish, to gaze upon the family portrait
of her plain wide face, her ample bosom   20
resting on her plump arms, her look of maternal interest

as they speak to her and each other
of their dreams and their disillusions—
how she smiles understanding,
when they walk down the narrow aisles of her store   25
reading the labels of packages aloud, as if
they were the names of lost lovers: *Suspiros,*
Merengues, the stale candy of everyone's childhood.
                                                    She spends her days
slicing *jamón y queso* and wrapping it in wax paper   30
tied with string: plain ham and cheese
that would cost less at the A&P, but it would not satisfy
the hunger of the fragile old man lost in the folds
of his winter coat, who brings her lists of items
that he reads to her like poetry, or the others,   35
whose needs she must divine, conjuring up products
from places that now exist only in their hearts—
closed ports she must trade with.

                                                    —*1995*

Rita Dove (b. 1952)

Rita Dove won the Pulitzer Prize in 1987 for Thomas and Beulah, a se-
quence of poems about her grandparents' lives in Ohio. She is one of the
most important voices of contemporary African-American poetry and
served as poet laureate of the United States from 1993 to 1995.

Adolescence—III

With Dad gone, Mom and I worked
The dusky rows of tomatoes.
As they glowed orange in sunlight
And rotted in shadow, I too
Grew orange and softer, swelling out   5
Starched cotton slips.

The texture of twilight made me think of
Lengths of Dotted Swiss.° In my room

8 **Dotted Swiss** type of sheer fabric

I wrapped scarred knees in dresses
That once went to big-band dances;   10
I baptized my earlobes with rosewater.
Along the window-sill, the lipstick stubs
Glittered in their steel shells.

Looking out at the rows of clay
And chicken manure, I dreamed how it would happen: 15
He would meet me by the blue spruce,
A carnation over his heart, saying,
"I have come for you, Madam;
I have loved you in my dreams."
At his touch, the scabs would fall away.   20
Over his shoulder, I see my father coming toward us:
He carries his tears in a bowl,
And blood hangs in the pine-soaked air.

—1980

Mark Jarman (b. 1952)

Mark Jarman was born in Kentucky and has lived in California and Tennessee, where he currently teaches at Vanderbilt University. With Robert McDowell, he edited The Reaper, *a magazine specializing in narrative poetry. His most recent collection is* Unholy Sonnets, *released in 2000.*

After Disappointment

To lie in your child's bed when she is gone
Is calming as anything I know. To fall
Asleep, her books arranged above your head,
Is to admit that you have never been
So tired, so enchanted by the spell   5
Of your grown body. To feel small instead
Of blocking out the light, to feel alone,
Not knowing what you should or shouldn't feel,
Is to find out, no matter what you've said
About the cramped escapes and obstacles   10

You plan and face and have to call the world,
That there remain these places, occupied
By children, yours if lucky, like the girl
Who finds you here and lies down by your side.

—*1997*

Naomi Shihab Nye (b. 1952)

Naomi Shihab Nye, a dedicated world traveler and humanitarian, has read her poetry in Bangladesh and the Middle East. Many of her poems are informed by her Palestinian ancestry, and she has translated contemporary Arabic poetry.

The Traveling Onion

> It is believed that the onion originally came from India. In Egypt it
> was an object of worship—why I haven't been able to find out.
> From Egypt the onion entered Greece and on to Italy, thence into
> all of Europe.
>
> —*Better Living Cookbook*

When I think how far the onion has traveled
just to enter my stew today, I could kneel and praise
all small forgotten miracles,
crackly paper peeling on the drainboard,
pearly layers in smooth agreement,   5
the way knife enters onion, straight
and onion falls apart on the chopping block,
a history revealed.

And I would never scold the onion
for causing tears.   10
It is right that tears fall
for something small and forgotten.
How at meal, we sit to eat,
commenting on texture of meat or herbal aroma
but never on the translucence of onion,   15
now limp, now divided,

or its traditionally honorable career:
For the sake of others,
disappear.

—*1986*

Alberto Ríos (b. 1952)

Alberto Ríos was born in Nogales, Arizona, the son of a Mexican-American father and an English-born mother. He won the Walt Whitman Award of the Academy of American Poets for his first book, Whispering to Fool the Wind *(1982). He has also written a collection of short stories,* The Iguana Killer: Twelve Stories of the Heart, *which won the Western States Book Award in 1984.*

The Purpose of Altar Boys

Tonio told me at catechism
the big part of the eye
admits good, and the little
black part is for seeing
evil—his mother told him   5
who was a widow and so
an authority on such things.
That's why at night
the black part gets bigger.
That's why kids can't go out   10
at night, and at night
girls take off their clothes
and walk around their
bedrooms or jump on their
beds or wear only sandals   15
and stand in their windows.
I was the altar boy
who knew about these things,
whose mission on some Sundays
was to remind people of   20
the night before as they
knelt for Holy Communion.
To keep Christ from falling

I held the metal plate under chins,
while on the thick   25
red carpet of the altar
I dragged my feet
and waited for the precise
moment: plate to chin
I delivered without expression   30
the Holy Electric Shock,
the kind that produces
a really large swallowing
and makes people think.
I thought of it as justice.   35
But on other Sundays the fire
in my eyes was different,
my mission somehow changed.
I would hold the metal plate
a little too hard   40
against those certain same
nervous chins, and I
I would look
with authority down
the tops of white dresses.   45
                                                        —*1982*

Julia Alvarez (b. 1953)

Julia Alvarez published her first collection, Homecoming, *in 1984. It contained both free verse and "33," a sequence of 33 sonnets on the occasion
of the poet's thirty-third birthday. She has gained acclaim for* In the Time
of the Butterflies, *a work of fiction, and* The Other Side/El Otro Lado, *a
collection of poems.*

Bilingual Sestina

Some things I have to say aren't getting said
in this snowy, blond, blue-eyed, gum-chewing English:
dawn's early light sifting through *persianas*° closed
the night before by dark-skinned girls whose words

3 **persianas** venetian blinds

evoke *cama,°   aposento,°   sueños°* in *nombres°*   5
from that first world I can't translate from Spanish.

Gladys, Rosario, Altagracia—the sounds of Spanish
wash over me like warm island waters as I say
your soothing names: a child again learning the *nombres*
of things you point to in the world before English   10
turned *sol,°   sierra,°   cielo,°   luna°* to vocabulary words—
sun, earth, sky, moon. Language closed

like the touch-sensitive *morivivi°* whose leaves closed
when we kids poked them, astonished. Even Spanish
failed us back then when we saw how frail a word is   15
when faced with the thing it names. How saying
its name won't always summon up in Spanish or English
the full blown genie from the bottled *nombre.*

Gladys, I summon you back by saying your *nombre.*
Open up again the house of slatted windows closed   20
since childhood, where *palabras°* left behind for English
stand dusty and awkward in neglected Spanish.
Rosario, muse of *el patio,°* sing in me and through me say
that world again, begin first with those first words

you put in my mouth as you pointed to the world—   25
not Adam, not God, but a country girl numbering
the stars, the blades of grass, warming the sun by saying,
¡Qué calor!° as you opened up the morning closed
inside the night until you sang in Spanish,
Estas son las mañanitas,° and listening in bed, no English   30

yet in my head to confuse me with translations, no English
doubling the world with synonyms, no dizzying array of words
—the world was simple and intact in Spanish—
luna, sol, casa,°   luz, flor,° as if the *nombres*
were the outer skin of things, as if words were so close   35
one left a mist of breath on things by saying

---

5 **cama** bed   **aposento** apartment   **sueños** dreams   **nombres** names   **11 sol** sun   **sierra** mountain
cielo sky   **luna** moon   **13 morivivi** a type of Caribbean bush   **21 palabras** words   **23 el patio**
outdoor terrace   **28 Qué calor** What heat!   **30 Estas son las mañanitas** These are birthday songs
34 casa house   **flor** flower

their names, an intimacy I now yearn for in English—
words so close to what I mean that I almost hear my Spanish
heart beating, beating inside what I say *en inglés.*°

—*1995*

Harryette Mullen (b. 1953)

Harryette Mullen says, "I intend the poem to be meaningful: to allow, or suggest, to open up, or insinuate possible meanings, even in those places where the poem drifts between intentional utterance and improvisational wordplay." Born in Florence, Alabama, Mullen grew up in Fort Worth, Texas, and holds degrees from the University of Texas and the University of California, Santa Cruz. She currently teaches African-American literature and creative writing at the University of California, Los Angeles.

Dim Lady°

My honeybunch's peepers are nothing like neon. Today's special at Red Lobster is redder than her kisser. If Liquid Paper is white, her racks are institutional beige. If her mop were Slinkys, dishwater Slinkys would grow on her noggin. I have seen tablecloths in Shakey's Pizza Parlors, red and white, but no such picnic colors do I see in her mug. And in some minty-fresh mouthwashes there is more sweetness than in the garlic breeze my main squeeze wheezes. I love to hear her rap, yet I'm aware that Muzak has a hipper beat. I don't know any Marilyn Monroes. My ball and chain is plain from head to toe. And yet, by gosh, my scrumptious Twinkie has as much sex appeal for me as any lanky model or platinum movie idol who's hyped beyond belief.

—*2003*

39 **en inglés** in English
Dim Lady See Shakespeare's *Sonnet 130*

Michael Donaghy (b. 1954)

Michael Donaghy was born in the Bronx, New York, but has lived in London since 1985. Donaghy studied at Fordham University and the University of Chicago, where he served as poetry editor of the Chicago Review. *The author of four collections, Donaghy is a past winner of the Whitbread Prize. He teaches at City University and Birkbeck College and is a fellow of the Royal Society of Literature.*

The River in Spate

sweeps us both down its cold grey current.
Grey now as your father was when I met you,
I wake even now on that shore where once,
sweat slick and still, we breathed together—
in—soft rain gentling the level of the lake,   5
out—bright mist rising from the lake at dawn.
How long before we gave each other to sleep,
to air—drawing the mist up, exhaling the rain?
Though we fight now for breath and weaken
in the torrent's surge to the dark of its mouth,   10
you are still asleep in my arms by its source,
small waves lapping the gravel shore,
and I am still awake and watching you,
in wonder, without sadness, like a child.

—2000

Kim Addonizio (b. 1954)

Kim Addonizio is the author of four books of poetry and a book of short stories. Born in Washington, D.C., Addonizio earned a B.A. and an M.A. from San Francisco State University and has worked as a waitress, tennis instructor, Kelly Girl, attendant for the disabled, and auto parts store bookkeeper. She currently teaches private writing workshops in the San Francisco Bay area.

Sonnenizio° on a Line from Drayton°

Since there's no help, come let us kiss and part;
or kiss anyway, let's start with that, with the kissing part,
because it's better than the parting part, isn't it—
we're good at kissing, we like how that part goes:
we part our lips, our mouths get near and nearer,   5
then we're close, my breasts, your chest, our bodies partway
to making love, so we might as well, part of me thinks—
the wrong part, I know, the bad part, but still
let's pretend we're at that party where we met
and scandalized everyone, remember that part? Hold me   10
like that again, unbutton my shirt, part of you
wants to I can tell, I'm touching that part and it says
yes, the ardent partisan, let it win you over,
it's hopeless, come, we'll kiss and part forever.

—2004

Sonnenizio The sonnenizio was originated in Florence in the thirteenth century by Vanni Fucci as an irreverent form whose subject was usually the impossibility of everlasting love. Dante retaliated by putting Fucci into the seventh chasm of the *Inferno* as a thief. Originally composed in hendeca-syllabics, the sonnenizio gradually moved away from metrical constraints and began to tackle a wider variety of subject matter. The sonnenizio is 14 lines long. It opens with a line from someone else's sonnet, repeats a word from that line in each succeeding line of the poem, and closes with a rhymed couplet. [Addonizio's note]   **Drayton** Michael Drayton (1563–1631) see *Idea: Sonnet 61*

David Mason (b. 1954)

David Mason is best known for the title poem of The Country I Remember, *a long narrative about the life of a Civil War veteran and his daughter. The poem has been performed in a theatrical version. Mason edited, with Mark Jarman,* Rebel Angels, *an anthology of recent poetry written in traditional forms.*

Song of the Powers

Mine, said the stone,
mine is the hour.
I crush the scissors,
such is my power.
Stronger than wishes,   5
my power, alone.

Mine, said the paper,
mine are the words
that smother the stone
with imagined birds,   10
reams of them, flown
from the mind of the shaper.

Mine, said the scissors,
mine all the knives
gashing through paper's   15
ethereal lives;
nothing's so proper
as tattering wishes.

As stone crushes scissors,
as paper snuffs stone   20
and scissors cut paper,
all end alone.
So heap up your paper
and scissor your wishes
and uproot the stone   25
from the top of the hill.
They all end alone
as you will, you will.

—1996

Mary Jo Salter (b. 1954)

Mary Jo Salter has traveled widely with her husband, poet and novelist Brad Leithauser, and has lived in Japan, Italy, and Iceland. A student of Elizabeth Bishop at Harvard, Salter brings to her art a devotion to the poet's craft that mirrors that of her mentor. She has published five collections of poetry and The Moon Comes Home, *a children's book.*

Welcome to Hiroshima

is what you first see, stepping off the train:
a billboard brought to you in living English
by Toshiba Electric. While a channel
silent in the TV of the brain

projects those flickering re-runs of a cloud   5
that brims its risen columnful like beer
and, spilling over, hangs its foamy head,
you feel a thirst for history: what year

it started to be safe to breathe the air,
and when to drink the blood and scum afloat   10
on the Ohta River. But no, the water's clear,
they pour it for your morning cup of tea

in one of the countless sunny coffee shops
whose plastic dioramas advertise
mutations of cuisine behind the glass: 15
a pancake sandwich; a pizza someone tops

with a maraschino cherry. Passing by
the Peace Park's floral hypocenter (where
how bravely, or with what mistaken cheer,
humanity erased its own erasure),   20

you enter the memorial museum
and through more glass are served, as on a dish
of blistered grass, three mannequins. Like gloves
a mother clips to coatsleeves, strings of flesh

hang from their fingertips; or as if tied   25
to recall a duty for us, *Reverence*

the dead whose mourners too shall soon be dead,
but all commemoration's swallowed up

in questions of bad taste, how re-created
horror mocks the grim original,   30
and thinking at last *They should have left it all*
you stop. This is the wristwatch of a child.

Jammed on the moment's impact, resolute
to communicate some message, although mute,
it gestures with its hands at eight-fifteen   35
and eight-fifteen and eight-fifteen again

while tables of statistics on the wall
update the news by calling on a roll
of tape, death gummed on death, and in the case
adjacent, an exhibit under glass   40

is glass itself: a shard the bomb slammed in
a woman's arm at eight-fifteen, but some
three decades on—as if to make it plain
hope's only as renewable as pain,

and as if all the unsung   45
debasements of the past may one day come
rising to the surface once again—
worked its filthy way out like a tongue.

—*1985*

Cathy Song (b. 1955)

Cathy Song was born in Honolulu, Hawaii, and holds degrees from Wellesley College and Boston University. Her first book, Picture Bride, *won the Yale Series of Younger Poets Award in 1983.* The Land of Bliss, *her fourth collection, appeared in 2001.*

Stamp Collecting

The poorest countries
have the prettiest stamps
as if impracticality were a major export
shipped with the bananas, t-shirts, and coconuts.

Take Tonga, where the tourists,   5
expecting a dramatic waterfall replete with birdcalls
are taken to see the island's peculiar mystery:
hanging bats with collapsible wings
like black umbrellas swing upside down from fruit trees.
The Tongan stamp is a fruit.   10
The banana stamp is scalloped like a butter-varnished seashell.
The pineapple resembles a volcano, a spout of green on top,
and the papaya, a tarnished goat skull.

They look impressive,
these stamps of countries without a thing to sell   15
except for what is scraped, uprooted and hulled
from their mule-scratched hills.
They believe in postcards,
in portraits of progress: the new dam;
a team of young native doctors   20
wearing stethoscopes like exotic ornaments;
the recently constructed "Facultad de Medicina,"°
a building as lack-lustre as an American motel.

The stamps of others are predictable.
Lucky is the country that possesses indigenous beauty.   25
Say a tiger or a queen.
The Japanese can display to the world
their blossoms: a spray of pink on green.
Like pollen, they drift, airborne.
But pity the country that is bleak and stark.   30

Beauty and whimsey are discouraged as indiscreet.
Unbreakable as their climate, a monument of ice,
they issue serious statements, commemorating
factories, tramways and aeroplanes;
athletes marbled into statues.   35
They turn their noses upon the world, these countries,
and offer this: an unrelenting procession
of a grim, historic profile.

                                                                    —1988

22 **Facultad de Medicina** Medical Faculty (building)

Ginger Andrews (b. 1956)

Ginger Andrews won the 1999 Nicholas Roerich Poetry Prize for her first book, An Honest Answer, *which explores the difficulties of working-class life in a Northwestern lumber town. Born in North Bend, Oregon, she cleans houses for a living, and is a janitor and Sunday school teacher. Her poems have been featured many times on National Public Radio's "The Writer's Almanac."*

Primping in the Rearview Mirror

after a solid ten-minute bout of tears,
hoping that the Safeway man who stocks the shelves
and talked to you once for thirty minutes about specialty jams,
won't ask if you're all right, or tell you you look like shit
and then have to apologize as he remembers that you don't   5
like cuss words and you don't date ex-prison guards
because you're married. The truth is you're afraid
this blue-eyed charismatic sexist hunk of a reject just might
trigger another round of tears, that you'll lean into him
right in front of the eggs and milk, crying like a baby,   10
your face buried in his chest just below the two opened
buttons of his tight white knit shirt, his big cold hands
pressed to the small of your back, pulling you closer
to whisper that everything will be all right.

—*2002*

Annie Finch (b. 1956)

Annie Finch is the daughter of a professor of philosophy and a doll artist who also wrote poetry. Having published her first poem at the age of nine, Finch continued her studies at Yale, the University of Houston, and Stanford. The author of an acclaimed critical work, The Ghost of Meter *(1993), on the effects of meter on free-verse poets (most of them women), she has published three full-length collections of poems and has edited anthologies of criticism and poetry. She teaches at Miami University.*

Coy Mistress

Sir, I am not a bird of prey:
a Lady does not seize the day.
I trust that brief Time will unfold
our youth, before he makes us old.
How could we two write lines of rhyme   5
were we not fond of numbered Time
and grateful to the vast and sweet
trials his days will make us meet?
The Grave's not just the body's curse;
no skeleton can pen a verse!   10
So while this numbered World we see,
let's sweeten Time with poetry,
and Time, in turn, may sweeten Love
and give us time our love to prove.
You've praised my eyes, forehead, breast: 15
you've all our lives to praise the rest.

—*1997*

April Lindner (b. 1962)

April Lindner teaches at St. Joseph's University. Her first collection of po-etry, Skin, *appeared in 2002, and she has also written studies of the work of Dana Gioia and other contemporary poets of the American West. She is the co-editor of* Contemporary American Poetry: A Pocket Anthology *(2004).*

First Kiss

This collision of teeth, of tongues and lips,
is like feeling for the door
in a strange room, blindfolded.
He imagines he knows her
after four dates, both of them taking pains   5
to laugh correctly, to make eye contact.
She thinks at least this long first kiss
postpones the moment she'll have to face
four white walls, the kitchen table,
its bowl of dried petals and nutmeg husks,   10
the jaunty yellow vase with one jaunty bloom,
the answering machine's one bloodshot eye.

—2002

Catherine Tufariello (b. 1963)

Catherine Tufariello grew up in upstate New York and holds a Ph.D. from Cornell University. Her first full-length collection, Keeping My Name, *appeared in 2004. A translator of the sonnets of Petrarch, she has taught at the University of Miami.*

Useful Advice

You're 37? Don't you think that maybe
It's time you settled down and had a baby?

No wine? You're pregnant, aren't you? I knew it!

Hey, are you sure you two know how to do it?

All Dennis has to do is look at me   5
And I'm knocked up.
                    Some things aren't meant to be.
It's sad, but try to see this as God's will.

I've heard that sometimes when you take the Pill . . .

Does he wear boxers? Briefs are bad for sperm.

A former partner at my husband's firm   10
Who tried for years got pregnant when she stopped
Working so hard.
                    Why don't you two adopt?
You'll have one of your own then, like my niece.

At work I heard about this herb from Greece—

My sister swears by dong quai. Want to try it?   15

Forget the high-tech stuff. Just change your diet.

Yoga is good for that. My cousin Carol—

It's true! Too much caffeine can make you sterile.

They have these ceremonies in Peru—

You mind my asking, is it him or you?   20

Have you tried acupuncture? Meditation?

It's in your head. Relax! Take a vacation
And have some fun. You think too much. Stop trying.

Did I say something wrong? Why are you crying?

—2004

Sherman Alexie (b. 1966)

Sherman Alexie is a Spokane/Coeur d'Alene Indian and grew up on a reservation in Wellpinit, Washington. While attending Washington State University as a premed major, Alexie attended a poetry workshop and soon began to publish his work. A prolific author of novels, poems, and short stories, Alexie has also performed professionally as a stand-up comedian.

The Exaggeration of Despair

I open the door

(this Indian girl writes that her brother tried to hang himself
with a belt just two weeks after her other brother did hang himself

and this Indian man tells us that back in boarding school,
five priests took him into a back room and raped him repeatedly   5

and this homeless Indian woman begs for quarters, and when I ask
her about her tribe, she says she's horny and bends over in front of me

and this homeless Indian man is the uncle of an Indian man
who writes for a large metropolitan newspaper, and so now I know
     them both

and this Indian child cries when he sits to eat at our table   10
because he had never known his own family to sit at the same table

and this Indian woman was born to an Indian woman
who sold her for a six-pack and a carton of cigarettes

and this Indian poet shivers beneath the freeway
and begs for enough quarters to buy pencil and paper   15

and this fancydancer passes out at the powwow
and wakes up naked, with no memory of the evening, all of his
    regalia gone

and this is my sister, who waits years for an eagle, receives it
and stores it with our cousins, who then tell her it has disappeared

and this is my father, whose own father died on Okinawa, shot   20
by a Japanese soldier who must have looked so much like him

and this is my father, whose mother died of tuberculosis
not long after he was born, and so my father must hear coughing ghosts

and this is my grandmother who saw, before the white men came,
three ravens with white necks, and knew our God was going to
    change)   25

and invite the wind inside.

                                                            —1996

Suji Kwock Kim (b. 1968)

Suji Kwock Kim received the 2002 Walt Whitman Award for Notes from
the Divided Country, *a book exploring the Japanese occupation of Korea
and the Korean War. Kim's family emigrated to Poughkeepsie, New York,
in the 1970s. She studied at Yale, the Iowa Writers' Workshop, Seoul National University, where she was a Fulbright Scholar, and Stanford University. She lives in New York and San Francisco.*

Occupation

The soldiers
are hard at work
building a house.
They hammer
bodies into the earth   5
like nails,
they paint the walls
with blood.
Inside the doors
stay shut, locked   10

as eyes of stone.
Inside the stairs
feel slippery,
all flights go down.
There is no floor: 15
only a roof,
where ash is falling—
dark snow,
human snow,
thickly, mutely   20
falling.
Come, they say.
This house will
last forever.
You must occupy it.   25
And you, and you—
And you, and you—
Come, they say.
There is room
for everyone.   30

—2003

Morri Creech (b. 1970)

Morri Creech published his first collection in 2001. Paper Cathedrals *contains both dramatic monologues and personal lyrics. A native of rural South Carolina, Creech studied at Winthrop University and at McNeese State University in Louisiana, where he currently teaches.*

Broken Glass

In 1970 my father returned
to the sweetness of desolation,
wandering past rows of mobile homes,
past the hulls of cars
splayed in the wheatgrass   5
that whiskered their silent engines,
past the skeletons of stripped machines,

dismantled harrows,
to the pine grove where shattered glass
gleamed beneath a bed of straw needles.   10
I had never been there before,
never seen the blazing fragments,
small as I was,
with a handful of rocks in my pocket
for the moment when my father   15
lined the bottles like years
against a rotten stump
and reared back to hurl the first stone.
I had never seen him raise his hand
against the world.   20
But the emptied bottles
of bourbon and scuppernong wine
flashed beneath the trees,
and he burned to splinter them all
to a heap of slivers.   25
He pitched the curve,
the fastball, the slider, the knuckle.
He left nothing intact, that man whose life
was an arrangement of tools
hung in a garage   30
for repairing bush hogs and cultivators;
his mind whirled
beyond the gears of perfect machinery,
and he reveled in the dust
and gravity of human error,   35
shouting as he threw each stone
with all the rage he could muster.
Feet planted firm,
he ground the pitcher's mound dirt into his palms,
rubbed them together,   40
then wound up the sidewind
and fractured the barrier
between him and the weeds
springing up around the dead-rooted pine,
chanting the names of his heroes,   45
those faded figures
from the box of trading cards in his closet,
chanting them in the language

of failure, oblivious to me
standing next to him, silent and afraid—   50
until at last he grew tired,
hefted me onto his shoulders,
and headed back
toward the O-rings and gaskets
that required his attention,   55
back toward his ordered life,
leaving the wreckage behind him,
scattered and shining.

                                                    —*2001*

Beth Ann Fennelly (b. 1971)

Beth Ann Fennelly wrote Open House, *which received the 2001 Kenyon*
Review Prize. Raised in a suburb north of Chicago, she studied at the Uni-
versity of Notre Dame and the University of Arksansas. She has taught at
Knox College in Galesburg, Illinois, and the University of Mississippi, and
is married to the fiction writer Tom Franklin.

Asked for a Happy Memory of Her Father, She Recalls Wrigley Field

His drinking was different in sunshine,
as if it couldn't be bad. Sudden, manic,
he swung into a laugh, bought me
two ice creams, said *One for each hand.*

Half the hot inning I licked Good Humor   5
running down wrists. My bird-mother
earlier, packing my pockets with sun block,
has hopped her warning: *Be careful.*

So, pinned between his knees, I held
his Old Style in both hands   10

while he streaked the lotion on my cheeks
and slurred *My little Indian princess.*

Home run: the hairy necks of men in front
jumped up, thighs torn from gummy green bleachers
to join the violent scramble. Father   15
held me close and said *Be careful,*

be careful. But why should I be full of care
with his thick arm circling my shoulders,
with a high smiling sun, like a home run,
in the upper right-hand corner of the sky?   20

—*2002*

Appendix 1

Poems Grouped by Genre, Technique, or Subject

Because it is possible to classify the poems in the anthology in many different ways, the following appendix is not exhaustive, and some poems appear under several headings. The appendix should, however, provide suggestions for reading and writing about works that share thematic similarities.

Poems in each genre are listed in chronological order. Consult the *Index of Authors, Titles, and First Lines of Poems* for their page numbers in the text.

Aging (See also Carpe Diem)

Shakespeare, "Sonnet 73"
Milton, "How Soon Hath Time"
Tennyson, "Ulysses
Eliot, "The Love Song of J. Alfred Prufrock"
Millay, "What Lips My Lips Have Kissed"
Kennedy, "In a Prominent Bar in Secaucus One Day"
Phillips, "Compartments"

Allegorical and Symbolic Poetry

Southwell, "The Burning Babe"
Herbert, "Redemption"
Burns, "John Barleycorn"
Poe, "The Haunted Palace"
Dickinson, "Because I Could Not Stop for Death"
Rossetti, "Uphill"
Stevens, "Anecdote of the Jar"

Stevens, "The Emperor of Ice-Cream"
Stevens, "The Snow Man"
Eliot, "Journey of the Magi"
cummings, "in Just-"
Larkin, "Next, Please"
Kizer, "The Ungrateful Garden"
Merwin, "The Last One"
Rich, "Diving into the Wreck"

Animals

Smart, "Jubilate Agno (selection)"
Blake, "The Tyger"
Tennyson, "The Eagle"
Dickinson, "A Narrow Fellow in the Grass"
Moore, "The Fish"
cummings, "r-p-o-p-h-e-s-s-a-g-r"
Bishop, "The Fish"
Stafford, "Traveling Through the Dark"
Dickey, "The Heaven of Animals"
Wright, "A Blessing"
Hughes, "Pike"
Harjo, "She Had Some Horses"

Art

Spenser, "Amoretti: Sonnet 75"
Shakespeare, "Sonnet 18"
Shelley, "Ozymandias"
Keats, "Ode on a Grecian Urn"
Yeats, "Sailing to Byzantium"
Stevens, "Anecdote of the Jar"
Auden, "Musée des Beaux Arts"

Ballads and Narratives

Anonymous, "Bonny Barbara Allen"
Anonymous, "Sir Patrick Spens"
Burns, "John Barleycorn"
Keats, "La Belle Dame Sans Merci"
Randall, "Ballad of Birmingham"
Fairchild, "Body and Soul"
Stokesbury, "Evening's End"
Nelson, "The Ballad of Aunt
    Geneva"

Carpe Diem Poetry

Herrick, "To the Virgins, to Make
    Much of Time"
Waller, "Song"
Marvell, "To His Coy Mistress"
Housman, "Loveliest of Trees, the
    Cherry Now"
Ransom, "Piazza Piece"

Childhood and Adolescence

Blake, "The Chimney Sweeper"
Blake, "The Little Black Boy"
Wordsworth, "Ode: Intimations of
    Immortality"
cummings, "in Just-"
Dunn, "The Sacred"
Olds, "One Girl at the Boys Party"
Dove, "Adolescence — III"
Soto, "The Purpose of Altar Boys"
Lindner, "First Kiss"

Conceit and Extended Metaphor

Donne, "A Valediction: Forbidding
    Mourning"
Donne, "Holy Sonnet 14"
Herbert, "Easter Wings"
Herbert, "The Pulley"
Bradstreet, "The Author to Her Book"
Taylor, "Huswifery"
Poe, "The Haunted Palace"
Longfellow, "The Arsenal at Spring-
    field"
Dugan, "Love Song: I and Thou"
Plath, "Metaphors"
Chappell, "Narcissus and Echo"
Adcock, "Digression on the Nuclear
    Age"

Conceit: Petrarchan

Shakespeare, "Sonnet 130"
Campion, "There Is a Garden in Her
    Face"
Mullen, "Dim Lady"

Death (See also Elegy)

Donne, "Holy Sonnet 10"
Keats, "When I Have Fears"
Dickinson, "Because I Could Not
    Stop for Death"
Dickinson, "I Died for Beauty — But
    Was Scarce"
Dickinson, "I Heard a Fly Buzz —
    When I Died"
Hardy, "Ah, Are You Digging on My
    Grave?"
Housman, "Eight O'Clock"
Frost, "Home Burial"
Williams, "Last Word of My English
    Grandmother"
Thomas, "Do Not Go Gentle into
    That Good Night"

Jarrell, "The Death of the Ball Turret Gunner"
Brooks, "We Real Cool"
Larkin, "Next, Please"
Merwin, "For the Anniversary of My Death"
Gunn, "Terminal"
Phillips, "Compartments"

Dramatic Dialogues

Hardy, "Ah, Are You Digging on My Grave"
Hardy, "The Ruined Maid"
Frost, "Home Burial"
Ransom, "Piazza Piece"
Randall, "Ballad of Birmingham"
Chappell, "Narcissus and Echo"

Dramatic Monologues

Blake, "The Chimney Sweeper"
Blake, "The Little Black Boy"
Blake, "A Poison Tree"
Tennyson, "Ulysses"
Browning, "My Last Duchess"
Browning, "Porphyria's Lover"
Pound, "The River-Merchant's Wife: A Letter"
Eliot, "Journey of the Magi"
Eliot, "The Love Song of J. Alfred Prufrock"
Jarrell, "The Death of the Ball Turret Gunner"
Brooks, "the mother"
Brooks, "We Real Cool"
Wright, "Saint Judas"
Kennedy, "In a Prominent Bar in Secaucus One Day"
Atwood, "Siren Song"
Hall, "Maybe Dats Your Pwoblem Too"
Cortez, "*Tu Negrito*"

Duty

Anonymous, "Sir Patrick Spens"
Lovelace, "To Lucasta, Going to the Wars"
Lowell, "For the Union Dead"

Elegy

Jonson, "On My First Son"
Dryden, "To the Memory of Mr. Oldham"
Gray, "Elegy Written in a Country Churchyard"
Longfellow, "The Cross of Snow"
Ransom, "Bells for John Whiteside's Daughter"
Millay, "If I Should Learn, in Some Quite Casual Way"
O'Hara, "The Day Lady Died"
Sexton, "The Truth the Dead Know"
Gunn, "Terminal"
Gioia, "Planting a Sequoia"

Fate

Randall, "Ballad of Birmingham"
Frost, "Design"
Yeats, "Leda and the Swan"
Frost, "The Road Not Taken"
Auden, "The Unknown Citizen"

History

Milton, "On the Late Massacre in Piedmont"
Gray, "Elegy Written in a Country Churchyard"
Shelley, "Ozymandias"
Yeats, "The Second Coming"
Jeffers, "The Purse-Seine"
Lowell, "For the Union Dead"
Wilbur, "Year's End"
Merrill, "Casual Wear"
Walcott, "Central America"

Hoffman, "As I Was Going to Saint-Ives"
Dugan, "Love Song: I and Thou"
Levertov, "The Ache of Marriage"
Rich, "Aunt Jennifer's Tigers"
Piercy, "What's That Smell in the Kitchen!"
Lockward, "My Husband Discovers Poetry"
Morgan, "Mountain Bride"

Myth

Poe, "To Helen"
Yeats, "Leda and the Swan"
Eliot, "The Love Song of J. Alfred Prufrock"
Hope, "Imperial Adam"
Auden, "Musée des Beaux Arts"
Merwin, "The Last One"
Plath, "Edge"
Chappell, "Narcissus and Echo"
Atwood, "Siren Song"

Nature and God

Wordsworth, "It Is a Beauteous Evening"
Wordsworth, "Ode: Intimations of Immortality"
Whitman, "A Noiseless Patient Spider"
Whitman, "Song of Myself, 6"
Whitman, "When I Heard the Learn'd Astronomer"
Hopkins, "God's Grandeur"
Frost, "Design"
Stevens, "The Snow Man"
Stevens, "Sunday Morning"

Nature: Descriptive Poetry

Swift, "Description of a City Shower"
Wordsworth, "I Wandered Lonely As a Cloud"

Bryant, "To the Fringed Gentian"
Hopkins, "Pied Beauty"
Frost, "The Need of Being Versed in Country Things"
Frost, "Stopping by Woods on a Snowy Evening"
H. D., "Pear Tree"
H. D., "Sea Rose"
Eliot, "Preludes"
Roethke, "Root Cellar"
Thomas, "Fern Hill"
Swenson, "How Everything Happens"
Snyder, "A Walk"

Nature: The Environment

Hopkins, "God's Grandeur"
Jeffers, "The Purse-Seine"
cummings, "pity this busy monster"
Bishop, "The Fish"
Stafford, "Traveling Through the Dark"
Kizer, "The Ungrateful Garden"
Kumin, "Noted in The New York Times"
Merwin, "The Last One"
Oliver, "The Black Walnut Tree"

Nature: Seasons of the Year

Shakespeare, "When Daisies Pied (Spring and Winter)"
Shelley, "Ode to the West Wind"
Bryant, "To the Fringed Gentian"
Williams, "Spring and All"
Eliot, "Preludes"
cummings, "in Just-"
Wilbur, "Year's End"

Parents and Children

Coleridge, "Frost at Midnight"
Moore, "Silence"

Roethke, "My Papa's Waltz"
Hayden, "Those Winter Sundays"
Thomas, "Do Not Go Gentle into
    That Good Night"
Kees, "For My Daughter"
Brooks, "the mother"
Wilbur, "The Writer"
Larkin, "This Be the Verse"
Simpson, "My Father in the Night
    Commanding No"
Sexton, "The Truth the Dead Know"
Plath, "Daddy"
Heaney, "Digging"
Voight, "Daughter"
Cortez, "*Tu Negrito*"
Fennelly, "Asked for a Happy
    Memory of Her Father, She
    Recalls Wrigley Field"

Physical Disabilities and Mental Problems

Milton, "When I Consider How My
    Light Is Spent"
Dickinson, "Much Madness is
    Divinest Sense"
Hecht, "Third Avenue in Sunlight"
Miller, "Subterfuge"
Plath, "Edge"
Ruark, "The Visitor"
Murphy, "Case Notes"

Poetry

Bradstreet, "The Author to Her
    Book"
Pope, "Essay on Criticism (selec-
    tion)"
Wordsworth, "Nuns Fret Not at
    Their Convent's Narrow Room"
Keats, "On First Looking into Chap-
    man's Homer"
Housman, "'Terence, This Is Stupid
    Stuff'"

Kizer, "From *Pro Femina*: Three"
Ashbery, "Paradoxes and Oxy-
    morons"
Heaney, "Digging"
Lockward, "My Husband Discovers
    Poetry"
Cope, "Triolet"

Poetry: Inspiration

Sidney, "Astrophel and Stella:
    Sonnet 1"
Coleridge, "Kubla Khan"
Keats, "Ode to a Nightingale"
Whitman, "Out of the Cradle End-
    lessly Rocking"
Wilbur, "The Writer"

Political and Social Themes

Milton, "On the Late Massacre in
    Piedmont"
Blake, "The Chimney Sweeper"
Housman, "Eight O'Clock"
Robinson, "The Mill"
Auden, "The Unknown Citizen"
Roethke, "Dolor"
Brooks, "the mother"
Simpson, "American Classic"
Merrill, "Casual Wear"
Walcott, "Central America"
Young, "Sundays in Democracies"
Ai, "Child Beater"
Cortez, "*Tu Negrito*"
Forché, "The General"
Song, "Stamp Collecting"

Racial Identity and Racism

Blake, "The Little Black Boy"
Dunbar, "We Wear the Mask"
Hughes, "Dream Boogie"
Hughes, "Theme for English B"

Cullen, "Incident"
Cullen, "Yet Do I Marvel"
Randall, "Ballad of Birmingham"
Walker, "For Malcolm X"
Lowell, "For the Union Dead"
Nelson, "Ballad of Aunt Geneva"
Jones, "Winter Retreat: Homage to Martin Luther King, Jr."
Alexie, "The Exaggeration of Despair"

Religious Themes

Southwell, "The Burning Babe"
Donne, "The Canonization"
Donne, "Holy Sonnet 10"
Donne, "Holy Sonnet 14"
Herbert, "Easter Wings"
Herbert, "Love (III)"
Herbert, "The Pulley"
Herbert, "Redemption"
Milton, "On the Late Massacre in Piedmont"
Milton, "When I Consider How My Light Is Spent"
Taylor, "Huswifery"
Whitman, "Song of Myself, 6"
Dickinson, "Some Keep the Sabbath Going to Church"
Hopkins, "God's Grandeur"
Hopkins, "Pied Beauty"
Hopkins, "The Windhover"
Yeats, "The Second Coming"
Stevens, "Sunday Morning"
Eliot, "The Journey of the Magi"
Hope, "Imperial Adam"
Hayden, "Those Winter Sundays"
Dickey, "The Heaven of Animals"
Wright, "Saint Judas"
Disch, "Ballade of the New God"
Fenton, "God, a Poem"
Murphy, "Case Notes"
Ríos, "The Purpose of Altar Boys"

Satire and Humor

Swift, "Description of a City Shower"
Byron, "Stanzas"
Hardy, "The Ruined Maid"
Stevens, "Disillusionment of Ten O'Clock"
Auden, "The Unknown Citizen"
Wilbur, "Playboy"
Martin, "E.S.L."
Cope, "Rondeau Redouble"
Cope, "Triolet"
Fenton, "God, a Poem"
Hall, "Maybe Dats Your Pwoblem Too"

Sexual Themes (See also Carpe Diem)

Shakespeare, "Sonnet 20 "
Shakespeare, "Sonnet 129"
Donne, "The Flea"
Marvell, "To His Coy Mistress"
Hardy, "The Ruined Maid"
Eliot, "The Love Song of J. Alfred Prufrock"
cummings, "in Just-"
Wilbur, "Playboy"
Rich, "Rape"
Rogers, "Foreplay"
Ríos, "The Purpose of Altar Boys"
Addonizio, "Sonnenizio on a Line from Drayton"
Lindner, "First Kiss"

Solitude

Pope, "Ode on Solitude"
Dickinson, "The Soul Selects Her Own Society"
Yeats, "The Lake Isle of Innisfree"
Thomas, "Acquainted with the Night"
Frost, "Home Burial"

Sports and Games

Gunn, "From the Wave"
Gildner, "First Practice"
Fairchild, "Body and Soul"
Creech, "Broken Glass"
Fennelly, "Asked for a Happy Memory of Her Father, She Recalls Wrigley Field"

Suicide

Anonymous, "Bonny Barbara Allen"
Robinson, "The Mill"
Robinson, "Richard Cory"
Parker, "Résumé"
Wright, "Saint Judas"
Plath, "Edge"

War

Longfellow, "The Arsenal at Springfield"
Whitman, "A Sight in Camp in the Daybreak Gray and Dim"
Crane, "War Is Kind"
Sassoon, "Dreamers"
Owen, "Dulce et Decorum Est"
Jarrell, "Death of the Ball Turret Gunner"
Snodgrass, "Mementos, I"
Adcock, "Digression on the Nuclear Age"

Komunyakaa, "Facing It"
Salter, "Welcome to Hiroshima"

Women's Issues

Pound, "Portrait d'une Femme"
Millay, "Oh, Oh, You Will Be Sorry for That Word"
Parker, "One Perfect Rose"
Bogan, "Women"
Wilbur, "Playboy"
Kizer, "From *Pro Femina*: Three"
Sexton, "Cinderella"
Rich, "Aunt Jennifer's Tigers"
Rich, "Rape"
Plath, "Daddy"
Plath, "Metaphors"
Clifton, "homage to my hips"
Clifton, "wishes for sons"
Piercy, "What's That Smell in the Kitchen!"
Atwood, "Siren Song"
Cardiff, "Combing"
Olds, "The One Girl at the Boys Party"
Lockward, "My Husband Discovers Poetry"
Cope, "Rondeau Redoublé"
Finch, "Coy Mistress"
Tufariello, "Useful Advice"

Appendix 2

Traditional Stanza, Fixed, and Nonce Forms

Acrostic Verse

Stuart, Dabney: "Discovering My Daughter"

Accentual Meter

Bishop, Elizabeth: "The Fish"
Brooks, Gwendolyn: "We Real Cool"
Cardiff, Gladys: "Combing"
Hardy, Thomas: "The Convergence of the Twain"
Wilbur, Richard: "Junk"
Wilbur, Richard: "The Writer"

Ballad Stanza (and Variants)

Anonymous: "Bonny Barbara Allan"
Anonymous: "Sir Patrick Spens"
Auden, W.H.: "As I Walked Out One Evening"
Brooks, Gwendolyn: "Ballad of Chocolate Mabbie"
Burns, Robert: "John Barleycorn"
Fenton, James: "God, a Poem"
Keats, John: "La Belle Dame sans Merci"

Plath, Sylvia: "Daddy"
Poe, Edgar Allan: "The Haunted Palace"
Roethke, Theodore: "My Papa's Waltz"
Rossetti, Christina: "Up-Hill"
Tennyson, Alfred, Lord: "The Lady of Shallot"
Waniek, Marilyn Nelson: "The Ballad of Aunt Geneva"
Whitman, Walt: "O Captain! My Captain!"
Wylie, Elinor: "Ophelia"

Ballade

Disch, Tom: "Ballade of the New God"

Blank Verse

Coleridge, Samuel Taylor: "Frost at Midnight"
Frost, Robert: "Home Burial"
Hudgins, Andrew: "Air View of an Industrial Scene"
Merrill, James: "Charles on Fire"
Stafford, William: "Traveling Through the Dark"

Stevens, Wallace: "Sunday Morning"
Tennyson, Alfred, Lord: "Ulysses"
Yeats, William Butler: "The Second
   Coming"

Cento

Gwynn, R. S.: "Approaching a
   Significant Birthday, He Peruses
   an Anthology of Poetry"

Cinquain

Crapsey, Adelaide: "Amaze"
Crapsey, Adelaide: "Languor after
   Pain"
Crapsey, Adelaide: "Trapped"

Clerihew

Taylor, Henry: "From *Brief Candles*"

Common Meter

Anonymous: "Western Wind"
Burns, Robert: "Red, Red Rose, A"
Cullen, Countee: "Incident"
Dickinson, Emily: "After Great Pain,
   a Formal Feeling Comes"
Dickinson, Emily: "Because I Could
   Not Stop for Death"
Dickinson, Emily: "I Died for Beauty
   — But Was Scarce"
Dickinson, Emily: "I Felt a Funeral in
   My Brain"
Dickinson, Emily: "Much Madness is
   Divinest Sense"
Dickinson, Emily: "Narrow Fellow in
   the Grass, A"
Dickinson, Emily: "Some Keep the
   Sabbath Going to Church"
Dickinson, Emily: "There's a Certain
   Slant of Light"
Herrick, Robert: "To the Virgins, to
   Make Much of Time"

Lovelace, Richard: "To Lucasta, Going to the Wars"

Concrete Poetry

cummings, e.e.: "r-p-o-p-h-e-s-sa-g-r"
Herbert, George: "Easter Wings"
Swenson, May: "How Everything
   Happens"

Couplets, Short

Blake, William: "Poison Tree, A"
Blake, William: "The Tyger"
Bryant, William Cullen: "To the
   Fringed Gentian"
Finch, Annie: "Coy Mistress"
Housman, A.E.: "Loveliest of Trees,
   the Cherry Now"
Housman, A.E.: "'Terence, This Is
   Stupid Stuff . . .'"
Marvell, Andrew: "To His Coy Mis-
   tress"
Young, Al: "Sundays in Democra-
   cies"

Couplets, Heroic

Bradstreet, Anne: "The Author to
   Her Book"
Browning, Robert: "My Last
   Duchess"
Dryden, John: "Epigram on Milton"
Jonson, Ben: "On My First Son"
Pope, Alexander: "Essay on Criti-
   cism, An (selection)"
Ransome, John Crowe: "The Equilib-
   rists"
Rich, Adrienne: "Aunt Jennifer's
   Tigers"
Swift, Jonathan: "A Description of a
   City Shower"
Tufariello, Catherine: "Useful Ad-
   vice"

Fourteeners

Southwell, Robert: "The Burning Babe"

Haiku

Phillips, Robert: "Compartments"

Long Meter

Donne, John: "A Valediction Forbidding Mourning"
Frost, Robert: "The Need of Being Versed in Country Things"
Larkin, Philip: "This Be the Verse"

Ode, Irregular

Arnold, Matthew: "Dover Beach"
Coleridge, Samuel Taylor: "Kubla Khan"
Frost, Robert: "After Apple-Picking"
Owen, Wilfred: "Dulce Et Decorum Est"
Wordsworth, William: "Ode: Intimations of Immortality"

Ode, Regular

Keats, John: "Ode on a Grecian Urn"
Keats, John: "Ode to a Nightingale"

Ottava Rima

Yeats, William Butler: "Sailing to Byzantium"

Pantoum

Cortez, Sarah: "*Tu Negrito*"

Paradelle

Collins, Billy: "Paradelle for Susan"

Prose Poem

Edson, Russell: "Ape"
Forché, Carolyn: "The Colonel"
Mullen, Harryette: "Dim Lady"

Quatrain, English

Blake, William: "The Little Black Boy"
Gray, Thomas: "Elegy Written in a Country Churchyard"
Gwynn, R. S.: "Approaching a Significant Birthday, He Peruses an Anthology of Poetry"
Hecht, Anthony: "Third Avenue in Sunlight"
Hope, A. D.: "Imperial Adam"
Longfellow, Henry Wadsworth: "The Arsenal at Springfield"
Robinson, Edwin Arlington: "Richard Cory"

Quatrain, Italian

Merrill, James: "Casual Wear"
Toomer, Jean: "Georgia Dusk"
Wilbur, Richard: "Playboy"

Rime Royal

Wyatt, Sir Thomas: "They Flee from Me"

Rondeau

Dunbar, Paul Laurence: "We Wear the Mask"

Rondeau Redoublé

Cope, Wendy: "Rondeau Reboublé"

Rubaiyat Stanza

Frost, Robert: "Stopping by Woods on a Snowy Evening"

Sapphic Stanzas

Steele, Timothy: "Sapphics Against Anger"

Sestet

Frost, Robert: "The Road Not Taken"

Sestina

Alvarez, Julia: "Bilingual Sestina"
Ashbery, John: "Farm Implements and Rutabagas in a Landscape"
Bishop, Elizabeth: "Sestina"
Hecht, Anthony: "The Book of Yolek"
Mayers, Florence Cassen: "All-American Sestina"

Sonnenizio

Addonizio, Kim: "Sonnenizio on a Line from Drayton"

Sonnet, Curtal

Hopkins, Gerard Manley: "Pied Beauty"

Sonnet, English

Drayton, Michael: "Idea: Sonnet 61"
Keats, John: "When I Have Fears"
Millay, Edna St. Vincent: "If I Should Learn, in Some Quite Casual Way"
Millay, Edna St. Vincent: "Oh, Oh, You Will Be Sorry for that Word"
Nemerov, Howard: "Primer of the Daily Round, A"
Shakespeare, William: "Sonnet 18"
Shakespeare, William: "Sonnet 29"
Shakespeare, William: "Sonnet 20"
Shakespeare, William: "Sonnet 30"
Shakespeare, William: "Sonnet 73"
Shakespeare, William: "Sonnet 116"
Shakespeare, William: "Sonnet 129"
Shakespeare, William: "Sonnet 130"

Sonnet, Italian

Browning, Elizabeth Barrett: "Sonnets from the Portuguese, 18"
Browning, Elizabeth Barrett: "Sonnets from the Portuguese, 43"
Donne, John: "Holy Sonnet 10"
Donne, John: "Holy Sonnet 14"
Frost, Robert: "Design"
Hopkins, Gerard Manley: "God's Grandeur"
Keats, John: "On First Looking into Chapman's Homer"
Lazarus, Emma: "The New Colossus"
Longfellow, Henry Wadsworth: "The Cross of Snow"
Millay, Edna St. Vincent: "What Lips My Lips Have Kissed, and Where, and Why"
Milton, John: "How Soon Hath Time"
Milton, John: "On the Late Massacre in Piedmont"
Milton, John: "When I Consider How My Light Is Spent"
Robinson, Edwin Arlington: "Firelight"
Wordsworth, William: "It Is a Beauteous Evening"
Wordsworth, William: "Nuns Fret Not at Their Narrow Convent Cell"
Wyatt, Thomas: "Whoso List to Hunt"

Sonnet, Nonce

Barrax, Gerald: "Strangers like Us: Pittsburgh, Raleigh, 1945-1985"
Coleridge, Samuel Taylor: "Work Without Hope"

Cullen, Countee: "Yet Do I Marvel"
Cummings, E.E.: "pity this busy
  monster"
Herbert, George: "Redemption"
Jarman, Mark: "Disappointment"
Kees, Weldon: "For My Daughter"
Ransom, John Crowe: "Piazza Piece"
Shelley, Percy Bysshe: "Ozymandias"
Shomer, Enid: "Women Bathing at
  Bergen-Belsen"
Sidney, Sir Philip: "Astrophel and
  Stella: Sonnet 1"
Wright, James: "Saint Judas"
Wroth, Mary: "In This Strange
  Labyrinth How Shall I Turn"
Yeats, William Butler: "Leda and the
  Swan"

Sonnet, Spenserian

Spenser, Edmund: "Amoretti: Sonnet
  75"

Syllabics

Moore, Marianne: "The Fish"
Plath, Sylvia: "Metaphors"
Thomas, Dylan: "Fern Hill"

Terza Rima

Frost, Robert: "Acquainted with the
  Night"
Ruark, Gibbons: "The Visitor"
Shelley, Percy Bysshe: "Ode to the
  West Wind"

Triplets

Hardy, Thomas: "The Convergence
  of the Twain"
Tennyson, Alfred, Lord: "The Eagle"

Villanelle

Bishop, Elizabeth: "One Art"
Thomas, Dylan: "Do Not Go Gentle
  into That Good Night"

Acknowledgments

Betty Adcock, "Digression on the Nuclear Age" Reprinted by permission of Louisiana State University Press from *Beholdings* by Betty Adcock. Copyright © 1988 by Betty Adcock.

Kim Addonizio, "Sonnenizio on a Line from Drayton" from *What is This Thing Called Love: Poems* by Kim Addonizio. Copyright 2004 by Kim Addonizio. Used by permission of W. W. Norton and Company, Inc.

Ai, "Child Beater" from *Cruelty* published by Houghton Mifflin Company. Reprinted by permission of the author.

Sherman Alexie, "The Exaggeration of Despair" Reprinted from *The Summer of Black Widows* © 1996 by Sherman Alexie, by permission of Hanging Loose Press.

Julia Alvarez, "Bilingual Sestina" from *The Other Side/El Otro Lado*, copyright © 1995 by Julia Alvarez. Published by Plume/Penguin, a division of Penguin Group (USA). Reprinted by permission of Susan Bergholz Literary Services, New York. Dutton, 1995

Ginger Andrews, "Primping in the Rearview Mirror" from *Hudson Review*, Spring 2003 Reprinted by permission from *The Hudson Review*, Vol. LV, No. 2 (2002). Copyright © 2002 Ginger Andrews.

John Ashbery, "Farm Implements and Rutabagas in a Landscape" from *The Double Dream of Spring* by John Ashbery. Copyright © 1970, 1969, 1968, 1967, 1966 by John Ashbery. Reprinted by permission of Georges Borchardt, Inc., for the author. "Paradoxes and Oxymorons" from *Shadow Train* by John Ashbery. Copyright © 1980, 1981 by John Ashbery. Reprinted by permission of Georges Borchardt, Inc., for the author.

Margaret Atwood, "Siren Song" from *You Are Happy, Selected Poems 1965–1975* Copyright © 1975 by Margaret Atwood. Reprinted by permission of Houghton Mifflin Company. All Rights reserved. "Siren Song" from *Selected Poems 1966–1984* Copyright © Margaret Atwood 1990. Reprinted by permission of Oxford University Press Canada.

W.H. Auden, "As I Walked Out One Evening," "Musee des Beaux Arts" and "The Unknown Citizen" from *W. H. Auden, Collected Poems* by W. H. Auden. Reprinted by permission of Random House, Inc.

Gerald Barrax, "Strangers Like Us" Reprinted by permission of Louisiana State University Press from *From a Person Sitting in the Darkness* by Gerald Barrax. Copyright © 1998 by Gerald Barrax.

Elizabeth Bishop, "The Fish" and "One Art" from *The Complete Poems 1927–1979* by Elizabeth Bishop. Copyright © 1979, 1983 by Alice Helen Methfessel. Reprinted by permission of Farrar, Straus, and Giroux, LLC.

Louise Bogan, "Women" from *The Blue Estuaries* by Louise Bogan. Copyright

E. E. Cummings, edited by George J. Firmage. Used by permission of Liveright Publishing Corporation. "r-p-o-p-h-e-s-s-a-g-r" Copyright 1935 © 1963, 1991 by the Trustees for the E. E. Cummings Trust. Copyright © 1978 by George James Firmage, from *Complete Poems: 1904–1962*, by E. E. Cummings, edited by George J. Firmage. Used by permission of Liveright Publishing Corporation.

Dick Davis, "A Monorhyme for the Shower" from *Belonging* (Swallow Press/Ohio University, 2003). Reprinted with permission.

Emily Dickinson, "After Great Pain, a Formal Feeling Comes" "I Felt a Funeral, in My Brain" "Much Madness Is Divinest Sense" "Some Keep the Sabbath Going to Church" "There's a Certain Slant of Light" and "Wild Nights—Wild Nights!" edited by Thomas H. Johnson, 1955 Reprinted by permission of the publishers and the Trustees of Amherst College from *The Poems of Emily Dickinson*, Thomas H. Johnson, ed., Cambridge, Mass: The Belknap Press of Harvard University Press, Copyright © 1951, 1955, 1979 by the President and Fellows of Harvard College. "Because I Could Not Stop for Death" "A Narrow Fellow in the Grass" "The Soul Selects Her Own Society" edited by Thomas H. Johnson Reprinted by permission of the publishers and the Trustees of Amherst College from *The Poems of Emily Dickinson*, Thomas H. Johnson, ed., Cambridge, Mass: The Belknap Press of Harvard University Press, Copyright © 1951, 1955, 1979 by the President and Fellows of Harvard College.

Thomas Disch, "Ballade of the New God" from *The Dark Horse*. Copyright © 1966 Thom Disch. Reprinted by permission of the author.

Michael Donaghy, "The River in Spate" from *Conjure* by Michael Donaghy, copyright 2000. Reprinted by permission of Macmillan London, UK

H.D. Doolittle, "Pear Tree" and "Sea Rose" from *Collected Poems 1912–1944* copyright © 1982 by The Estate of Hilda Doolittle. Reprinted by permission of New Directions Publishing Corp.

Rita Dove, "Adolescence–III" from *The Yellow House on theCorner*, Carnegie-Mellon University Press, © 1980 by Rita Dove. Reprinted by permission of the author

Alan Dugan, "Love Song: I and Thou" from *New and Collected Poems*. Reprinted by permission of The Ecco Press.

Stephen Dunn, "The Sacred" from *Between Angels*, by Stephen Dunn Copyright © 1989 by Stephen Dunn. Used by permission of W. W. Norton & Company, Inc.

Russell Edson, "Ape" from *The Tunnel. Selected Poems*, FIELD Poetry Series V. 3, Copyright 1994 by Russell Edson. Reprinted by permission of Oberlin College Press.

T.S. Eliot, "Journey of the Magi" from *Collected Poems 1909–1962* by T.S. Eliot, copyright 1936 by Harcourt, Inc., copyright © 1964, 1963 by T.S. Eliot, reprinted by permission of Harcourt, Inc. and Faber and Faber, Ltd. "The Love Song of J. Alfred Prufrock" from *Collected Poems 1909 1962* by T. S. Eliot, Copyright © 1964, 1963 by T. S. Eliot, reprinted by permission of Faber and Faber, Ltd. "Preludes" from *Prufrock and Other Observations*, by T. S. Eliot

B.H. Fairchild, "Body and Soul" from *The Art of the Lathe*

Beth Ann Fennelly, "Asked for a Happy Memory of her Father, She Recalls Wrigley Field" from *Open House*, 2001© Beth Ann Fennelly, published by Zoo Press, zoopress.org, all rights reserved.

James Fenton, "God: a Poem" from *Children in Exile* by James Fenton. Copyright © 1972 1978, 1980, 1982, 1983 by James Fenton. Reprinted by permission of Random House, Inc.

Lawrence Ferlinghetti, "Constantly Risking Absurdity" by Lawrence Ferlinghetti, from *A Coney Island of the Mind*, copyright © 1958 by Lawrence Ferlinghetti.

Reprinted by permission of New Directions Publishing Corp.

Annie Finch, "Coy Mistress" from *Eve*, 1997 Reprinted with permission of the author and Story Line Press (http://www.storylinepress.com).

Carolyn Forche, "The Colonel" All lines from "The Colonel" by Carolyn Forche. Copyright © 1981 by Carolyn Forche. Originally appeared in *Women's International Resource Exchange*. Reprinted by permission of HarperCollins Publishers, Inc.

Robert Frost, "Acquainted with the Night," "Design," "Stopping by Woods on a Snowy Evening," and "The Need of Being Versed in Country Things" from *The Poetry of Robert Frost* edited by Edward Connery Lathem. Copyright 1923, 1928, © 1969 by Henry Holt and Company, copyright 1936, 1951, 1956 by Robert Frost, © 1964 by Lesley Frost Ballantine. Reprinted by permission of Henry Holt and Company, LLC. "The Road Not Taken" from *The Poetry of Robert Frost*, edited by Edward Connery Lathem Copyright 1916, 1969 by Henry Holt and Company. Copyright 1944 by Robert Frost. Reprinted by permission of Henry Holt and Company, LLC.

Gary Gildner, "First Practice" is reprinted from *First Practice* by Gary Gildner, © 1969. Reprinted by permission of the University of Pittsburgh Press.

Allen Ginsberg, "A Supermarket in California" All lines from "A Supermarket in California" from *Collected Poems 1947–1980* by Allen Ginsberg. Copyright © 1955 by Allen Ginsberg. Reprinted by permission of HarperCollins Publishers, Inc.

Dana Gioia, "Planting a Sequoia" copyright 1991 by Dana Gioia. Reprinted from *The Gods of Winter* with the permission of Graywolf Press, Saint Paul, Minnesota.

Thom Gunn, "From the Wave" and "Terminal" from *Collected Poems* by Thom Gunn. Reprinted by permission of Farrar, Straus and Giroux, LLC, and Faber and Faber Ltd

Jim Hall, "Maybe Dats Your Pwoblem Too" from *The Mating Reflex*. By permission of Carnegie Mellon University Press, © 1980 by Jim Hall

Joy Harjo, "She Had Some Horses" from the book *She Had Some Horses* by Joy Harjo. Copyright © 1983, 1997 Thunder's Mouth Press. Appears by permission of the publisher, Thunder's Mouth Press, a division of Avalon Publishing Group.

Robert Hass, "Picking Blackberries With a Friend Who Has Been Reading Jacques Lacan" from *Praise* by Robert Hass. Copyright © 1979 by Robert Hass. Reprinted by permission of HarperCollins Publishers Inc.

Robert Hayden, "Those Winter Sundays". Copyright © 1966 by Robert Hayden from *Collected Poems of Robert Hayden* by Robert Hayden, edited by Frederick Glaysher. Used by permission of Liveright Publishing Corporation.

Seamus Heaney, "Digging" and "Punishment" from *Selected Poems 1966–1987 by Seamus Heaney Copyright © 1980 by Seamus Heaney. Reprinted by permission of* Farrar, Straus and Giroux, LLC and Faber and Faber, Ltd.

Anthony Hecht, "The Book of Yolek" from *The Transparent Man* by Anthony Hecht, copyright © 1990 by Anthony E. Hecht. Used by permission of Alfred A. Knopf, a division of Random House, Inc. "Third Avenue in Sunlight" from *Collected Earlier Poems* by Anthony Hecht, copyright © 1990 by Anthony E. Hecht. Used by permission of Alfred A. Knopf, a division of Random House, Inc.

Daniel Hoffman, "As I Was Going to Saint-Ives" from *Hang-gliding from Helicon*, 1988 Reprinted by permission of Louisiana State University Press from *Hang-gliding from Helicon* by Daniel

Hoffman. Copyright © 1988 by Daniel Hoffman.

A.D. Hope, "Imperial Adam" from *Collected Poems* by A. D. Hope. Copyright © 1968 A. D. Hope. Reprinted by permission of Collins/Angus & Robertson Publishers.

A. E. Housman, "Eight O'Clock" and "Stars, I have seen them Fall" from *The Collected Poems of A. E. Housman*. Copyright 1922, 1936, 1950 by Barclays Bank Ltd., © 1964 by Robert E. Symons, © 1965 by Henry Holt and Company. Reprinted by permission of Henry Holt and Company, LLC.

Andrew Hudgins, "Air View of an Industrial Scene" from *Saints and Strangers* by Andrew Hudgins. Copyright © 1985 by Andrew Hudgins. Reprinted by permission of Houghton Mifflin Company. All rights reserved.

Langston Hughes, "Dream Boogie" and "Theme for English B" from *The Collected Poems of Langston Hughes* by Langston Hughes, copyright © 1994 by the Estate of Langston Hughes. Used by permission of Alfred A. Knopf, Inc. a division of Random House, Inc. "The Weary Blues" from *The Collected Poems of Langston Hughes* by Langston Hughes, copyright © 1994 by The Estate of Langston Hughes. Used by permission of Alfred A. Knopf, a division of Random House, Inc.

Ted Hughes, "Pike" from Selected Poems 1957–1981 by Ted Hughes. Reprinted by permission of Faber and Faber, Ltd.

Mark Jarman, "After Disappointment" from *Questions for Ecclesiastes* Reprinted with permission of the author and Story Line Press (http://www.storylinepress.com).

Randall Jarrell, "The Death of the Ball Turret Gunner" and "90 North" from *The Complete Poems* by Randall Jarrell. Copyright © 1969, renewed 1997 by Mary von S. Jarrell. Reprinted by permission of Farrar, Straus and Giroux, LLC

Robinson Jeffers, "The Purse-Seine" copyright 1938 and renewed 1966 by Donnan & Garth Jeffers, from *The Selected Poems of Robinson Jeffers* by Robinson Jeffers. Used by permission of Random House, Inc.

Rodney Jones, "Winter Retreat: Homage to Martin Luther King, Jr." from *Transparent Gestures* by Rodney Jones. Copyright © 1989 by Rodney Jones. Reprinted by permission of Houghton Mifflin Company. All rights reserved.

Donald Justice, "Counting the Mad" from *New and Selected Poems* by Donald Justice, copyright © 1995 by Donald Justice. Used by permission of Alfred A. Knopf, a division of Random House, Inc.

Weldon Kees, "For My Daughter" Reprinted from *The Collected Poems of Weldon Kees* edited by Donald Justice by permission of the University of Nebraska Press. Copyright 1975 by the University of Nebraska Press. © renewed 2003 by the University of Nebraska Press.

X.J. Kennedy, "In a Prominent Bar in Secaucus One Day" Copyright © 1961 by X. J. Kennedy. Reprinted by permission of Curtis Brown, Ltd. "September 12, 2001" from *The Lords of Misrule: Poems 1992–2001*, pp. 88, © 2002. Reprinted with permission of The Johns Hopkins University Press.

Suji Kwock Kim, "Occupation" Reprinted by permission of Louisiana State University Press from *Notes from a Divided Country: Poems* by Suji Kwock Kim. Copyright © 2003 by Suji Kwock Kim.

Carolyn Kizer, "Pro Femina" (Part Three) from *Cool, Calm and Collected: Poems 1960–2000*. Copyright © 2001 by Carolyn Kizer. Reprinted with the permission of Copper Canyon Press, P.O. Box 271, Port Townsend, WA 98368–0271. "The Ungrateful Garden" from *Midnight Was My Cry: New and Se-*

lected Poems Copyright © 1961. Reprinted by the permission of the author.

Yusef Komunyakaa, "Facing It" from *Dien Cai Dau* by Yusef Komunyakaa © 1988 by Yusef Komunyakaa. Reprinted by permission of Wesleyan University Press.

Maxine Kumin, "Noted in the New York Times" from *Nurture* by Maxine Kumin. Copyright © 1989 by Maxine Kumin. Used by permission of Viking Penguin, a division of Penguin Books USA Inc.

Philip Larkin, "Aubade" and "This Be The Verse" from *Collected Poems* by Philip Larkin. Copyright © 1988, 1989 by the Estate of Philip Larkin. Reprinted by permission of Farrar, Straus and Giroux, LLC and Faber and Faber Ltd. "Next Please" by Philip Larkin is reprinted from *The Less Deceived* by permission of The Marvell Press, England and Australia.

Philip Levine, "Animals Are Passing from Our Lives" from *Not This Pig*, copyright © 1968 by Philip Levine. "You Can Have It" from *New Selected Poems* by Philip Levine, copyright © 1991 by Philip Levine. Used by permission of Alfred A. Knopf, a division of Random House, Inc.

April Lindner, "First Kiss" from *Skin*, 2002 Reprinted by permission of the author.

Diane Lockward, "My Husband Discovers Poetry" from *Eve's Red Dress*, 2003. Reprinted by permission of Wind Publications.

Robert Lowell, "For the Union Dead" from *Life Studies* by Robert Lowell. Copyright © 1959 by Robert Lowell. Copyright renewed 1987 by Harriet Lowell, Sheridan Lowell, and Caroline Lowell. Reprinted by permission of Farrar, Straus and Giroux, LLC

Charles Martin, "E.S.L." from *Steal the Bacon* by Charles Martin, pp. 21–23, © 1987. Reprinted by permission of the author.

David Mason, "Song of the Powers" from *The Country I Remember* Reprinted with permission of the author and Story Line Press (http://www.storylinepress .com).

Florence Cassen Mayers, "All American Sestina" © 1996 Florence Cassen Mayers, as first published in the *Atlantic Monthly*, Reprinted by permission of the author.

James Merrill, "Casual Wear" and "Charles on Fire" from *Selected Poems 1946–1985* by James Merrill, copyright © 1992 by James Merrill. Used by permission of Alfred A. Knopf, Inc., a division of Random House, Inc.

W.S. Merwin, "For the Anniversary of My Death" and "The Last One" from *The Lice* Copyright © 1967 by W.S. Merwin, reprinted with the permission of The Wylie Agency, Inc.

Edna St. Vincent Millay, "If I should learn, in some quite casual way," "Oh, Oh, you will be sorry for that word!," and "What lips my lips have kissed," and "Recuerdo" by Edna St. Vincent Millay. From *Collected Poems*, HarperCollins. Copyright © 1917, 1922, 1923, 1945, 1950, 1951 by Edna St. Vincent Millay and Norma Millay Ellis. All rights reserved. Reprinted by permission of Elizabeth Barnett, Literary Executor

Vassar Miller, the text of "Subterfuge" (copyright © 1981 by Vassar Miller) from *If I Had Wheels or Love: Collected Poems of Vassar Miller* is reprinted with the permission of Southern Methodist University Press.

Marianne Moore, "Silence" reprinted with the permission of Scribner, an imprint of Simon & Schuster, Adult Publishing Group, from *The Collected Poems of Marianne Moore*. Copyright © 1935 by Marianne Moore; copyright renewed © 1963 by Marianne Moore and T. S. Eliot.

Robert Morgan, "Mountain Bride" from *Groundwork*, Cnomon Press, Copyright © 1979. Reprinted by permission of the author.

Harryette Mullen, "Dim Lady" from *Sleeping with the Dictionary*, by Harryette Mullen. Copyright © 2002 The Regents of the University of California. Reprinted by permission.

Timothy Murphy, "Case Notes" from *Hudson Review*, forthcoming 2004 Reprinted by permission from *The Hudson Review*, Vol. LVI, No. 4 (2004). Copyright © 2004 Timothy Murphy.

Marilyn Nelson, "The Ballad of Aunt Geneva" Reprinted by permission of Louisiana State University Press from *The Home Place: Poem* by Marilyn Nelson Waniek Copyright © 1990 by Marilyn Nelson Waniek.

Howard Nemerov, "A Primer of the Daily Round" from *New and Selected Poems* by Howard Nemerov, copyright © 1960 by Howard Nemerov (University of Chicago Press) Reprinted by permission of Margaret Nemerov.

Naomi Shihab Nye, "The Traveling Onion" Reprinted by permission of Naomi Shihab Nye from *Yellow Glove*, Breitenbush Books, Portland, OR. Copyright © 1986 by Naomi Shihab Nye.

Frank O'Hara, "The Day the Lady Died" from *Lunch Poems* © 1964 by Frank O'Hara. Reprinted by permission of City Lights Books.

Sharon Olds, "The One Girl at the Boys Party" from *The Dead and the Living* by Sharon Olds, copyright © 1987 by Sharon Olds. Used by permission of Alfred A. Knopf, a division of Random House, Inc.

Mary Oliver, "The Black Walnut Tree" from *Twelve Moons* by Mary Oliver. Copyright © 1972, 1973, 1974, 1976, 1977, 1978, 1979 by Mary Oliver. By permission of Little, Brown and Company.

Simon J. Ortiz, "The Serenity in Stones" Permission to reprint given by author Simon J. Ortiz, Copyright 1975.

Linda Pastan, "Crocuses" Copyright © 1989 by Linda Pastan, and "1932–" from *Heroes in Disguise* by Linda Pastan.

Copyright © 1991 by Linda Pastan. Used by permission of W. W. Norton & Company, Inc.

Robert Phillips, "Compartments" from *Spinach Days* pp. 91–93, © 2000. Reprinted with permission of The Johns Hopkins University Press.

Marge Piercy, "Barbie Doll" and "What's That Smell in the Kitchen?" from *Circles on the Water* by Marge Piercy © 1982 by Marge Piercy. Used by permission of Alfred A. Knopf, a division of Random House, Inc.

Sylvia Plath, "Daddy" and "Edge" all lines from "Daddy" and "Edge" from from *Aerial* by Sylvia Plath. Copyright © 1963 by Ted Hughes. Reprinted by permission of HarperCollins Publishers and Faber and Faber Ltd. All lines from "Metaphors" from *Crossing the Water* by Sylvia Plath. Copyright © 1960 by Ted Hughes. Reprinted by permission of HarperCollins Publishers, Inc. and Faber and Faber Ltd.

Craig Raine, "A Martian Sends a Postcard Home" from *A Martian Sends a Postcard Home* Reprinted with kind permission of the author, Craig Raine.

Dudley Randall, "Ballad of Birmingham" from *Cities Burning* By permission of Broadside Press.

John Crowe Ransom, "The Equilibrists" from Selected Poems, 3rd Edition, Revised and Enlarged by John Crowe Ransom, copyright 1924 by Alfred A. Knopf, a division of Random House, Inc. "Piazza Piece" Copyright 1927 by Alfred A. Knopf, Inc and renewed 1955 by John Crowe Ransom. From *Selected Poems* by John Crowe Ransom. Reprinted by permission of the publisher.

James Reiss, "*Arigato* Means Thank You" from *Express* by James Reiss. © 1983. Reprinted by permission of the University of Pittsburgh Press

Adrienne Rich, "Aunt Jennifer's Tigers," Copyright © 2002, 1951 by Adrienne Rich, from *The Fact of a Doorframe: Se-*

lected Poems 1950–2001 by Adrienne Rich. Used by permission of the author and W. W. Norton & Company Inc. "Diving in to the Wreck" Copyright © 2002, by Adrienne Rich, Copyright 1973 by W. W. Norton & Company, Inc. from *The Fact of a Doorframe: Selected Poems 1950–2001* by Adrienne Rich. Used by permission of the author and W. W. Norton & Company, Inc. "Rape" Copyright © 2002 by Adrienne Rich, Copyright © 1973 by W. W. Norton & Company, Inc. from *The Fact of a Doorframe: Selected Poems 1950–2001* by Adrienne Rich. Used by permission of the author and W. W. Norton & Company

Alberto Rios, "The Purpose of Alter Boys" from *Whispering to Fool the Wind* (Sheep Meadow Press). Copyright © 1982 by Alberto Rios. Reprinted by permission of the author.

Theodore Roethke, "My Papa's Waltz" copyright 1942 by Hearst Magazines, Inc. "Root Cellar" copyright 1943 by Modern Poetry Association from *The Collected Poems of Theodore Roethke* by Theodore Roethke. Used by permission of Doubleday, a division of Random House, Inc.

Pattiann Rogers, "Foreplay" from Firekeeper: New and Selected Poems by Pattiann Rogers (Milkweed Editions, 1994). Copyright © 1994 by Pattiann Rogers Reprinted by permission of Milkweed Editions and Pattiann Rogers.

Gibbons Ruark, "The Visitor" is reprinted by permission of Louisiana State University Press from *Passing Through Customs: New and Selected Poems*, by Gibbons Ruark. Copyright © 1999 by Gibbons Ruark.

Kay Ryan, "Bestiary" from *Elephant Rocks* by Kay Ryan. Copyright © 1996 by Kay Ryan. Used by permission of Grove/Atlantic, Inc.

Mary Jo Salter, "Welcome to Hiroshima" from *Henry Purcell In Japan* by Mary Jo Salter, copyright © 1984 by Mary Jo Salter. Used by permission of Alfred A. Knopf, a division of Random House, Inc.

Siegfried Sassoon, "Dreamers" from *Collected Poems of Sigfried Sassoon*, copyright 1918, 1920 by E.P. Dutton. Copyright 1936,1946,1947,1948 by Siegfried Sassoon. Used by permission of Viking Penguin, a division of Penguin Group (USA) Inc.

Anne Sexton, "Cinderella" from *Transformations* by Anne Sexton. Copyright © 1971 by Anne Sexton. Reprinted by permission of Houghton Mifflin Company. All rights reserved. "The Truth the Dead Know" from *All My Pretty Ones* by Anne Sexton. Copyright © 1962 by Anne Sexton, renewed 1990 by Linda G. Sexton. Reprinted by permission of Houghton Mifflin Company. All rights reserved.

Enid Shomer, "Women Bathing at Bergen-Belson" winner of Negative Capability's Eve of St. Agnes Award. Reprinted from *Stalking the Florida Panther*, published by The Word Works. Copyright © 1987 by Enid Shomer. Reprinted by permission of the author.

Louis Simpson, "My Father in the Night Commanding No" from *At the End of the Open Road* by Louis Simpson, copyright 1963 by Louis Simpson, Wesleyan University Press. Reprinted by permission of University Press of New England.

W.D. Snodgrass, "Momentos, I" reprinted by permission of Soho Press Inc. from W. D. Snodgrass *Selected Poems 1957–1987* © 1968, 1978 by W. D. Snodgrass

Gary Snyder, "A Walk" by Gary Snyder from *The Back Country*, copyright © 1968 by Gary Snyder. Reprinted by permission of New Directions Publishing Corp.

Cathy Song, "Stamp Collecting" from *Frameless Windows, Squares of Light: Poems* by Cathy Song. Copyright © 1988 by Cathy Song. Used by permission of W. W. Norton & Company, Inc.

William Stafford, "Traveling through the Dark" copyright 1962, 1998 by the Estate of William Stafford. Reprinted from *The Way It Is: New and Selected Poems* with the permission of Graywolf Press, Saint Paul, Minnesota.

Timothy Steele, "Sapphics Against Anger" by Timothy Steele from *Sapphics and Uncertainties: Poems 1970–1986*. Reprinted by permission of the University of Arkansas Press.

Wallace Stevens, "Anecdote of the Jar," "Disillusionment of Ten O'Clock," "Sunday Morning," and "The Snow Man" from *The Collected Poems of Wallace Stevens* by Wallace Stevens, Copyright 1954 by Wallace Stevens. Used by permission of Alfred A. Knopf, Inc., a division of Random House, Inc. "The Emperor of Ice-Cream" (originally published 1922) from *The Collected Poems of Wallace Stevens* by Wallace Stevens, copyright 1954 by Wallace Stevens and renewed 1982 by Holly Stevens. Used by permission of Alfred A. Knopf, a division of Random House, Inc.

Leon Stokesbury, "Evening's End" from *Autumn Rhythm: New and Selected Poems by Leon Stokesbury* Copyright © 1996. Reprinted by permission of the University of Arkansas Press, Inc.

Strand, Mark. "The Tunnel" from *Selected Poems* by Mark Strand, copyright © 1979, 1980 by Mark Strand. Used by permission of Alfred A. Knopf, Inc., a division of Random House.

Dabney Stuart, "Discovering My Daughter" from *Light Years* Reprinted by permission of Louisiana State University Press from *Light Years: New and Selected Poems* by Dabney Stuart. Copyright © 1994 by Dabney Stuart.

May Swenson, "How Everything Happens (Based on a Study of the Wave)" from *The Complete Poems to Solve*. Used with permission of The Literary Estate of May Swenson.

Henry Taylor, excerpt from *Brief Candles*, 2000 Reprinted by permission of Louisiana State University Press from Brief Candles: 101 Clarihews by Henry Taylor. Copyright © 2000 by Henry Taylor

Dylan Thomas, "Do Not Go Gentle Into That Good Night" by Dylan Thomas, from *The Poems of Dylan Thomas*, copyright © 1952 by Dylan Thomas. Reprinted by permission of New Directions Publishing Corp. and David Higham Associates Limited. "Fern Hill" by Dylan Thomas, from *The Poems of Dylan Thomas*, copyright © 1945 by The Trustees for the Copyrights of Dylan Thomas. Reprinted by permission of New Directions Publishing Corp. and David Higham Associates Limited

Jean Toomer, "Georgia Dusk" from *Cane* by Jean Toomer. Copyright 1923 by Boni & Liveright, renewed 1951 by Jean Toomer. Used by permission of Liveright Publishing Corporation

Ellen Bryant Voight, "Daughter" from *The Forces of Plenty* by Ellen Bryant Voigt. Copyright © 1983 by Ellen Bryant Voight. Used by permission of W. W. Norton and Company, Inc.

Derek Walcott, "Central America" from *The Arkansas Testament*. Copyright © 1987 by Derek Walcott. Reprinted by permission of Farrar, Straus, and Giroux, LLC.

Margaret Walker, "For Malcolm X" from *This is My Century: New and Collected Poems* by Margaret Walker. Reprinted by permission of the University of Georgia Press. "

Richard Wilbur, "Junk" from *Advice to a Prophet and Other Poems*, copyright © 1961 and renewed 1989 by Richard Wilbur, reprinted by permission of Harcourt, Inc. "Playboy" from *Walking to Sleep: New Poems and Translations*, copyright © 1968 and renewed 1996 by Richard Wilbur, reprinted by permission of Harcourt, Inc. "The Writer" from *The Mind-Reader*, copyright © 1971 by

Richard Wilbur, reprinted by permission of Harcourt, Inc." "Years-End" from *Ceremony and Other Poems*, copyright 1949 and renewed 1977 by Richard Wilbur, reprinted by permission of Harcourt, Inc.

Miller Williams, "The Book" Reprinted by permission of Louisiana State University Press from *Living On the Surface: New and Selected Poems* by Miller Williams. Copyright © 1989 by Miller Williams.

William Carlos Williams, "Spring and All, Section I," "Spring and All, Section I," "The Last Words of My English Grandmother," "The Red Wheelbarrow," and "This Is Just to Say" by William Carlos Williams, from *Collected Poems: 1909–1939, Volume I*, copyright © 1938 by New Directions Publishing Corp. Reprinted by permission of New Directions Publishing Corp.

James Wright, "A Blessing" from *The Branch Will Not Break* by James Wright. © 1959 by James Wright. Reprinted by permission of Wesleyan University Press. "Saint Judas" from *Saint Judas* by James Wright. © 1959 by James Wright. Reprinted by permission of Wesleyan University Press.

Yeats, W.B. "The Lake Isle of Innisfree" and "The Song of Wandering Aengus" reprinted with the permission of Scribner, an imprint of Simon & Schuster Adult Publishing Group, from *The Collected Works of W. B. Yeats, Volume I: The Poems, Revised*, edited by Richard J. Finneran. (New York: Scribner, 1997). "The Second Coming" reprinted with the permission of Scribner, an imprint of Simon & Schuster Adult Publishing Group, from, *The Collected Works of W. B. Yeats, Volume I: The Poems, Revised*, edited by Richard J. Finneran. Copyright © 1924 by The Macmillan Company; copyright renewed © 1952 by Bertha Georgie Yeats. "Leda and the Swan" and "Sailing to Byzantium" reprinted with the permission of Scribner, an imprint of Simon & Schuster Adult Publishing Group and A.P. Watt Ltd., from *The Collected Works of W. B. Yeats, Volume I: The Poems, Revised*, edited by Richard J. Finneran. Copyright © 1928 by The Macmillan Company, copyright renewed © 1956 by Georgie Yeats.

Al Young, "Sundays in Democracies" from *The Sound of Dreams Remembered: Poems 1990–2000* © 2001 by Al Young, reprinted by permission of the author.

Index of Critical Terms

Index of Authors, Titles, and First Lines of Poems

Note: Authors' names appear in boldface type. Titles of poems appear in double quotation marks.

Additional Titles of Interest

Note to Instructors: Any of these Penguin-Putnam, Inc., titles can be packaged with this book at a special discount. Contact your local Allyn & Bacon/Longman sales representative for details on how to create a Penguin-Putnam, Inc., Value Package.

Albee, *The Three Tall Women*
Allison, *Bastard Out of Carolina*
Alvarez, *How the García Girls Lost Their Accents*
Austen, *Persuasion*
Austen, *Pride & Prejudice*
Bellow, *The Adventures of Augie March*
Boyle, *Tortilla Curtain*
Cather, *My Antonia*
Cather, *O Pioneers!*
Cervantes, *Don Quixote*
Chopin, *The Awakening*
Conrad, *Nostromo*
DeLillo, *White Noise*
Desai, *Journey to Ithaca*
Douglass, *Narrative of the Life of Frederick Douglass*
Golding, *Lord of the Flies*
Hawthorne, *The Scarlet Letter*
Homer, *Iliad*
Homer, *Odyssey*
Huang, *Madame Butterfly*
Hulme, *Bone People*
Jen, *Typical American*
Karr, *The Liar's Club*
Kerouac, *On The Road*
Kesey, *One Flew Over the Cuckoo's Nest*
King, *Misery*
Larson, *Passing*
Lavin, *In a Cafe*
Marquez, *Love in the Time of Cholera*
McBride, *The Color of Water*
Miller, *Death of a Salesman*
Molière, *Tartuffe and Other Plays*

Morrison, *Beloved*
Morrison, *The Bluest Eye*
Morrison, *Sula*
Naylor, *Women of Brewster Place*
Orwell, *1984*
Postman, *Amusing Ourselves to Death*
Rayben, *My First White Friend*
Rose, *Lives on the Boundary*
Rose, *Possible Lives: The Promise of Public*
Rushdie, *Midnight's Children*
Shakespeare, *Four Great Comedies*
Shakespeare, *Four Great Tragedies*
Shakespeare, *Four Histories*
Shakespeare, *Hamlet*
Shakespeare, *King Lear*
Shakespeare, *Macbeth*
Shakespeare, *Othello*
Shakespeare, *Twelfth Night*
Shelley, *Frankenstein*
Silko, *Ceremony*
Solzhenitsyn, *One Day in the Life of Ivan Denisovich*
Sophocles, *The Three Theban Plays*
Spence, *The Death of Woman Wang*
Steinbeck, *Grapes of Wrath*
Steinbeck, *The Pearl*
Stevenson, *Dr. Jekyll & Mr. Hyde*
Swift, *Gulliver's Travels*
Twain, *Adventures of Huckleberry Finn*
Wilde, *The Importance of Being Earnest*
Wilson, *Joe Turner's Come and Gone*
Wilson, *Fences*
Woolf, *Jacob's Room*